Wild Geese

Wild Geese

Buddhism in Canada

Edited by

JOHN S. HARDING

VICTOR SŌGEN HORI

and

ALEXANDER SOUCY

McGILL-QUEEN'S UNIVERSITY PRESS

Montreal & Kingston • London • Ithaca

ISBN 978-0-7735-3666-1 (cloth)
ISBN 978-0-7735-3667-8 (paper)

Legal deposit second quarter 2010
Bibliothèque nationale du Québec

Printed in Canada on acid-free paper that is 100% ancient forest free
(100% post-consumer recycled), processed chlorine free.

This book has been published with the help of a grant from the Canadian Federation for the
Humanities and Social Sciences, through the Aid to Scholarly Publications Programme, using
funds provided by the Social Sciences and Humanities Research Council of Canada.

McGill-Queen's University Press acknowledges the support of the Canada Council for the
Arts for our publishing program. We also acknowledge the financial support of the Government
of Canada through the Book Publishing Industry Development Program (BPIDP) for our
publishing activities.

Library and Archives Canada Cataloguing in Publication

Wild geese : Buddhism in Canada / edited by John S. Harding, Victor Sōgen Hori
and Alexander Soucy.

Includes bibliographical references and index.
ISBN 978-0-7735-3666-1 bnd
ISBN 978-0-7735-3667-8 pbk

1. Buddhism–Canada–History. I. Harding, John S., 1971– II. Hori, Victor Sōgen
III. Soucy, Alexander Duncan, 1968–

BQ742.B832 2010   294.3'0971   C2009-906386-7

This book was designed and typeset by studio oneonone in Minion 10.5/14

We gratefully acknowledge the support of the Montreal branch of the
Buddhist Compassion Relief Tzu Chi Foundation.
We gratefully acknowledge the support of the Bukkyo Dendo Kyokai Canada
(Society for the Promotion of Buddhism).

Contents

Illustrations

Tables

Conventions

The editors found it impossible to impose a consistent form of romanization on Chinese terms and names. For a very long time in Western scholarship, the standard for romanization was the Wade-Giles system and much scholarship was written with this system. In recent decades, scholars have switched to the Pinyin system. Numerous inconsistencies in romanization can thus occur. For example, an author who uses Pinyin may quote a passage from an older text which uses Wade-Giles. Or, an author wishing to use Pinyin, names Chinese organizations or persons that use Wade-Giles to romanize their own names. In such situations, both Pinyin and Wade-Giles forms of romanization may occur on the same page. Throughout this book, we have tried to follow a policy of being faithful to the source. Quotations from other sources follow the system of romanization used in that original source. Similarly, we have followed the romanization used by Chinese people and organizations for their own names. In the remaining situations, we use Pinyin.

USE OF DIACRITICAL MARKS

For similar reasons, the editors found it impossible to maintain a consistent policy on the use of diacritical marks for Buddhist terms taken from the many Buddhist languages. Academic scholars normally apply diacritical marks to Buddhist names and technical vocabulary, such as Śākyamuni, *pratītyasam-utpāda*, *śūnyatā*, *vipassanā*, etc. We follow this convention with this one exception: when Buddhist terms have been accepted into the English language, as judged by the Concise Oxford English Dictionary (eleventh edition), we have omitted diacritical marks. These terms include, for example, nirvana, samsara, Mahayana, Theravada, Vajrayana, vipassana, prajna, sangha, dharma, sunyata, roshi, samadhi, Pali, and sutra.

The Buddhist organizations that we are studying in this book use the same Buddhist vocabulary as do academic scholars but without diacritical marks. Scholars write "*vipassanā*" but the Vipassana BC meditation group does not; neither do any of the other groups that teach *vipassana* meditation across Canada. Scholars write "Theravāda" but the Theravada Buddhist Community of Vancouver does not; neither do any of the other groups across Canada that affiliate themselves with Theravada. Scholars of Zen Buddhism write "*kenshō, kōan,* and *rōshi*" but Zen master Albert Low writes "*kensho, koan,* and *roshi*." Scholars of Japanese Pure Land Buddhism write "Jōdo Shinshū"; practitioners of Japanese Pure Land Buddhism in Canada write "Jodo Shinshu." In this book, words in quoted passages appear exactly as they appear in the original text, even when they lack diacritical marks. This means that it is quite possible for the same word to appear on the same page with and without diacritical marks.

NAMES

Names of well-known places are written without diacritical marks; thus, Kyoto not Kyōto, Tokyo not Tōkyō.

Names of persons are written as the person himself or herself normally writes it or as normally appears on the person's publications. Usually diacritical marks are omitted. Thus, we write Thich Nhat Hanh not Thích Nhất Hạnh; Orai Fujikawa not Ōrai Fujikawa; Hsuan Hua not Hsüan Hua or Xuan Hua; Hsing Yun not Xingyun; Cheng Yen not Zhengyan. An exception is Chögyam Trungpa, since this is the way his name appears on most of his publications.

Japanese names are a particular problem. Our rule is that when the person in question is based in Japan, then his or her name is presented in Japanese order (surname first) with diacritical marks. Thus we write Ōtani Kōshin, Shaku Sōen. But if the person in question has immigrated to Canada, then the name is presented in Western order (surname last) and without diacritical marks. Thus we write Kyojo Ikuta, Genjiro Mori, Orai Fujikawa. For both immigrants and those based in Japan, we use diacritics for Japanese titles such as sōchō (bishop).

We follow an organization's own format for writing and transcription of its own name in its English language publications or website. Thus, we write Tzu Chi not Ciji; Soka Gakkai not Sōka Gakkai; Nichiren Shoshu not Nichiren Shōshū. The Buddhist Churches of Canada uses Jodo Shinshu not Jōdo Shinshū; Higashi Hongwanji Temple uses Hongwanji, not Honganji.

Acknowledgments

The editors would like to acknowledge the support of Mme She Pi-chen of the Montreal Branch of the Tzu Chi Buddhist Relief and Compassion Foundation, and of Brian Nagata (US office) and Yasuo Honjo (Canada Office) of the Bukkyo Dendo Kyokai (Society for the Promotion of Buddhism), otherwise known as the Numata Foundation. Melissa Curley provided us with excellent editorial skills. Jonathan Crago of McGill-Queen's University Press was a patient mentor. Kate Merriman of MQUP whipped our manuscript into shape. Additionally, we would like to acknowledge the anonymous readers for their insightful comments which greatly improved this volume. The book is supported by the Aid to Scholarly Publications Program (ASPP) of the Social Sciences and Humanities Research Council (SSHRC) which put the book manuscript through a review and provided a publication subvention. We thank the many staff people of Buddhist organizations across the country who assisted us with this volume.

We would also like to thank our family members and colleagues who patiently tolerated our absence each time our attention was focused on this project. Inevitably in a volume like this, there are numerous factual claims to be checked, numerous references to previous scholarship that have to be verified. For any mistakes or omissions, the editors take full responsibility.

JOHN S. HARDING, University of Lethbridge
VICTOR SŌGEN HORI, McGill University
ALEXANDER SOUCY, Saint Mary's University

Wild Geese

The wild geese do not intend to leave traces,

The water has no mind to receive their image.

– Zen verse

Introduction

At the Zen Centre of Vancouver, Zen teacher Eshin Godfrey rings a bell and a roomful of Western Zen students cross their legs and settle into meditation. The centre was founded in 1970 and Eshin, who trained at the Mount Baldy Zen Center in Los Angeles, is a full-time abbot guiding a full house of students. In Raymond, Alberta on 4 July 2004, hundreds of Japanese Canadians gathered to commemorate the 75th anniversary of the Raymond Buddhist Church. Three generations of past and present members listened to each other's stories of trial and tribulation, faith and hope. At the Winnipeg Centre of Soka Gakkai International (SGI), members gather to chant *Namu Myōhō Renge Kyō,* the title of the *Lotus Sūtra*; after the chanting, one after another, they give testimony of how the daily practice of chanting transforms their lives. In Mississauga, on the western outskirts of Toronto, at the imposing Fo Guang Shan Buddhist temple, a nun in red and gold robes leads a congregation of hundreds of Chinese lay people in prostrations before the Buddha. The temple is one of a worldwide network of Fo Guang Shan temples, whose master in Taiwan, Hsing Yun, teaches a modernized "Humanistic Buddhism." North of Montreal at Monastère Tam Bảo Son in Harrington, Quebec, a Vietnamese monk guides visitors around the hall of one thousand buddhas. Arranged strategically around the several hundred acres of the monastery grounds are statues representing the major events in the life of the Buddha. At Gampo Abbey on Cape Breton Island, Nova Scotia, monastics prepare their students for the Sopa Chöling retreat. The Sopa Chöling retreat lasts three years during which retreatants withdraw from society and spend each day from 5:00 a.m. to 9:30 p.m. in Buddhist practice. Canadians are practising Buddhism from sea to sea.

The story of Buddhism in Canada is told in two parts: before and after 1967. Before 1967, the scene of Buddhism in Canada is painted chiefly with the Japanese in the foreground. It was the Japanese who built the first Buddhist temple in Vancouver in 1905, and it was also the Japanese Jodo Shinshu Buddhists who built the first Buddhist churches in the provinces east of British Columbia, in Alberta at the end of the 1920s, Toronto in the 1940s, Manitoba in the 1950s, and Quebec in the 1960s. Their story is a tale of struggle against overt and systematic discrimination marked by such incidents as the Anti-Asiatic Riot of 1907 and the forced removal of the Japanese into relocation camps during the Second World War.[1]

Two great social changes occurred in the 1960s. First, in 1967, Canada revised its immigration laws. The old laws were based on controlling the flow of undesirable races; perhaps the most dramatic examples of these laws were the Chinese Immigration Act of 1885 and the subsequent laws that imposed the Chinese head tax.[2] The new immigration laws after 1967 were race-neutral and based on points – points for the level of education, ability to speak one of the national languages, type of occupation, etc. Those with enough points, regardless of race, were allowed to immigrate. In the 1970s under the government of Pierre Elliot Trudeau, Canada adopted a policy of multiculturalism, officially welcoming people of all races and cultures. From the world's Buddhist countries – China, Vietnam, Sri Lanka, Tibet, Korea, Thailand, Laos, Cambodia, and others – the new immigrants brought their religion, Buddhism.

A second great social change began in the 1960s. In fact, the phrase "the sixties" is shorthand for a time when, all around the world, people demonstrated against the war in Vietnam, students held sit-ins against their university administrations, the Black Power and Women's Lib movements began, and many people rejected conventional religion and sought a new spirituality. During this era, people from all walks of life associated themselves with "the counter-culture" and experimented with new music, new ideas, new social relations, and new ways of life. D.T. Suzuki and Alan Watts had been writing about Zen and Buddhism for decades but in this time of cultural ferment, their writings suddenly gained a new momentum and planted the seed of Buddhism among Westerners. The San Francisco Zen Center, the first Zen centre in the West, was opened in 1962 by Shunryu Suzuki Roshi. Since then, Buddhism in many forms has grown exponentially among Westerners.

We now live in a Canada shaped by all this history. As the Buddhism in Canada website graphically shows, every form of Buddhism can be found in every province in Canada.[3] The 1971 policy of multiculturalism in Canada and the new social openness to alternative forms of spirituality have contributed to the increasing religious diversity, and hence to the surge of the Buddhist population. But one cannot escape history. In fact, it was the hostile attitude toward Japanese Canadians that first dispersed Buddhism across the continent when the Canadian government forced the Japanese to move from the west coast and relocate inland during World War II. Until 1965, the only Buddhist group in Toronto was the Japanese Toronto Buddhist Church, and as late as 1970, only two Buddhist groups were to be found in Montreal, one based in Japanese tradition and the other Chinese. Chinese immigrants represent the other force that brought Buddhism from British Columbia to eastern parts of Canada. The early Chinese immigrants, who came in the late 1880s, were chiefly miners and railway workers responsible for the construction of the Canadian Pacific Railway in British Columbia. However, after completion of the Canadian Pacific Railway, the Canadian government banned the immigration of Chinese to Canada. To escape the hostility they found in British Columbia, Chinese settlers began moving eastward and some brought their Buddhist faith with them. While Buddhism came from the East to the West, its transmission on Canadian soil actually went gradually from the west coast to the east driven by racial hostility. History is not without a sense of irony.

Today, while still relatively small, the number of Buddhists in Canada is steadily and rapidly increasing. Just as important as numerical growth among both immigrants and Westerners, Buddhism is quickly gaining acceptance in mainstream culture. The benevolent, smiling face of the Dalai Lama frequently appears in newscasts. Movie stars and rock musicians are known to be Buddhist. And everyone has a friend or relative who practises Buddhist meditation. High schools teach about Buddhism; many Canadian universities offer courses in Buddhism and a few have full-fledged doctoral programs in Buddhist studies. Scholars in the United States were the first to start studying the phenomenon of "Buddhism in America." An increasing number of Canadian scholars are now beginning to focus their research on Buddhism in Canada.

In 2006, at the annual conference for the Canadian Asian Studies Association (CASA), John Harding and Alec Soucy organized two sessions which dealt with the subject of Buddhism in Canada, with the specific intention of increasing scholarly interest in this nascent area of study and gathering together some of the people who have been thinking about particular problems, cases, and questions, as well as the overall shape of Buddhism in Canada. Among the presenters at the conference was Victor Hori, who had also long been interested in studying Buddhism in Canada and who had for years been informally collecting the names of scholars in Canada doing such research. Following the meeting, the contributors discussed the possibility of the book and Victor joined John and Alec as editors of the project and brought in additional authors beyond the original eight presenters in Montreal. Because of the scarcity of research on Buddhism in Canada, everyone recognized that the book was sorely needed.

The first book to be published on Buddhism in Canada was Janet McLellan's *Many Petals of the Lotus: Five Asian Buddhist Communities in Toronto* (1999). McLellan gave us five highly detailed ethnographic portraits of the Japanese Canadian, Tibetan, Cambodian, Vietnamese, and Chinese Buddhist communities of the city of Toronto, based on several years of participant-observer fieldwork. This excellent beginning to the study of Buddhism in Canada was not meant to cover the entire field, and so, many aspects of the study of Buddhism in Canada went untouched: Buddhism in other parts of Canada, the more than a century of history of Buddhism in Canada, the spread of Buddhism among Westerners, and the many other forms of ethnic Buddhism. Nor did it attempt to set out a technical vocabulary for analysing Buddhism or theoretical constructs for thinking about or explaining Buddhism in Canada.

The second book to be published on Buddhism in Canada was *Buddhism in Canada*, edited by Bruce Matthews (2006). Its ten essays were organized geographically and generally followed a common format. They gave some estimate of the number of Buddhists in each region, using Statistics Canada data. They then described the temples and centres in their region, usually under two categories, "Asian/ethnic" and "Western/convert" (or some similar vocabulary). Several essays further subdivided these two categories with a three-category division into Theravada, Mahayana, and Vajrayana, or with a breakdown into ethnic groups. The volume is descriptive in nature and provides an account of the status of Buddhist groups in Canada circa 2004–2005, in some cases with short histories. This book made an important contribution to our understanding of Buddhism in Canada by providing a survey of the state of Buddhism across the entire country. The essays came to no common conclusion, except to affirm that the number of Buddhist temples and meditation centres, and the size of their memberships, have grown dramatically in the last thirty to forty years. Where McLellan's book was a highly focused in-depth study of Asian immigrant communities in a single city, the Matthews book swept across the entire country, giving a wide-angle snapshot of the number and variety of Buddhist groups. Inevitably it too could not devote much concentrated attention to other aspects of the study of Buddhism in Canada.

With these two contributions in mind, the editors of the present book saw clearly that the job was to bring order to an unorganized field, to address not one but a variety of interrelated issues. We felt that the way forward would be to look more closely at the particular traditions while using such particular case studies to explore general themes, such as global interconnections, the attraction of converts to Buddhism, and the debate concerning how to describe Buddhists and Buddhism(s) in the West. In conjunction with statistical analyses, historical surveys, and biographical life stories, these studies will foster reflection on, and critical engagement with, theoretical issues that might offer guidance to this still nascent field of Buddhism in Canada.

Victor Hori's essay in chapter 1 begins by challenging the "Two Buddhisms" categories used to classify the various kinds of Buddhism now found in the West. These categories have often drawn a distinction between immigrant Buddhists from Asia who have largely sought to maintain traditional practices, and Westerners who have converted to Buddhism and have been selective about which aspects they want to maintain. Hori suggests that not only are these categories too imprecise, but they also disguise value judgments, latent in such terms as "ethnic," which base types of Buddhism on a racial divide. Soucy too challenges the notion of this divide by pointing out that many of the major transformations that have been associated with Western forms of Buddhism were developed in Asia by Asian reformers. Soucy also goes on to examine the question of whether there is a "Canadian Buddhism." The "Two Buddhisms" categories have been found to be unsatisfactory by a number of authors in this book.

In his chapter, Terry Watada shows that most of the history of Buddhism in Canada has been the history of Buddhism practised by the Japanese community in Canada since 1905 – Jodo Shinshu (Pure Land) Buddhism – rather than by the Zen and Tibetan Buddhist traditions, which have attracted the most popular attention in the West, or by the larger recent waves of Buddhist immigrants from Asia. This century of history, long invisible, needs to be presented. The more recent developments in Buddhism in Canada all build upon this history. Henry Shiu gives a broad survey of the many forms of Buddhism that have appeared in Canada since the 1970s. In addition to cataloguing the different Buddhist traditions and main immigrant groups, he also tracks the growth of academic Buddhist studies in Canadian universities. Peter Beyer provides a clear and detailed statistical analysis of the different Buddhist groups in Canada and also explains why StatsCan statistics cannot provide a precise estimate of the number of Western Buddhists in Canada.

All our authors attempt to show that the growth of Buddhism in Canada involves two processes: the transformation of Buddhist traditions to adapt to local conditions in Canada, and the transformation of local groups to adapt to Buddhist tradition. Globalization and localization are not opposing processes. Every adaptation is both an example of the global becoming local, and the local going global. Supplementing Watada's history, John Harding's study of the Pure Land Buddhist community in Raymond, Alberta tracks how the community was shaped by both global political currents and local community interests; it is particularly valuable because it provides us with the only long-term study of how a Buddhist community changes and evolves through three and four generations. The study by Marybeth White of the Lao Buddhist community explores how the community used ritual and symbol to recreate a sense of Lao Buddhist sacred space on Canadian land. The study by Patricia Campbell focuses on practitioners in a Toronto Zen Buddhist temple, asking what motivated them to approach Buddhism and how they understood the Buddhism they encountered. By contrast, the studies by Lina Verchery and Lynn Eldershaw focus more on the Buddhist organization, the Chinese Fo Guang Shan and the Tibetan Shambhala International respectively. These organizations skilfully adapt themselves to meet the special needs their practitioners may have or to meet the crises which history may throw their way.

Tannie Liu's study of Chinese Buddhism in Canada shows how the founding of local temples in Canada is linked to larger historical movements, such as the Buddhist modernization movement in early twentieth-century China. André Laliberté and Manuel Litalien's study links the Tzu Chi Buddhist Compassion and Relief Foundation in Canada to the rise of Tzu Chi in Taiwan and its spread around the globe. While setting out a history of Tibetan Buddhism in Canada, Sarah Haynes also attempts to answer the difficult question of why Westerners are so attracted to Tibetan Buddhism and how that attraction came about.

All these chapters make a similar point. Studies of Buddhism in the West until now have automatically assumed that modernization meant adapting Buddhism to Western culture; very few studies recognize that local Buddhist groups are parts of global networks and that many of these global networks long ago began the process of modernization in Asia. Buddhism is not some entity fixed within a fossilized tradition. Everywhere in Asia, Buddhism has been dynamically evolving and modernizing. Local developments in Canada naturally reflect and contribute to that global development.

Buddhism is a lived religion. To convey what it means to live a life in Buddhism, we include the biographies of two people whose lives have been devoted to the practice and teaching of Buddhism. The first is Mauro Peressini's biography of Zen Master Albert Low. Now in his eightieth year, Low granted a series of extensive interviews to Peressini, recalling the long path that he has walked in Zen. The second is Victor Hori and Janet McLellan's biography of Suwanda Sugunasiri, originally from Sri Lanka, who has spent decades tirelessly speaking for Buddhism in the media, on government committees, and in interreligious dialogue, and forging Canadian Buddhist alliances and institutions.

The list of authors in this volume includes a wide spectrum of scholars, from the well-established to the new generation, but the centre of gravity lies with younger scholars. Research in the study of Buddhism traditionally meant that the scholar studied an ancient text written in a classical language. Only recently has this paradigm started to break down. Now, new scholars are emerging whose interests, and sometimes training, encourages them to study not classical Buddhism in its Asian context but the many forms of Buddhism today in their local Asian and Western contexts. It is fitting that the new generation of scholars play an important role in shaping this new field.

For a number of reasons there are several traditions that are important in Canada, but do not appear in this book. Most notable of these is the Vipassana organization, which is a secular meditation movement based on the Burmese Theravada Buddhist tradition. There are also important Buddhist communities which are underrepresented in this book. The Vietnamese Buddhist community, for example, is very prominent in the Canadian Buddhist scene today, but is mentioned only briefly in Shiu's essay and somewhat more extensively in Soucy's discussion of Thich Nhat Hanh's community in its local and global dimensions. However, while Thich Nhat Hanh is certainly mentioned, neither he nor his groups in Canada represent the traditional form of Buddhism that engages most Vietnamese Buddhists, in Canada, Vietnam, or elsewhere. While some may take exception to these and other omissions, the reasons for them were practical; we could not locate a capable author to deal with the subject, and a single book cannot possibly cover everything. The editors do not pretend to have told the entire story of Buddhism in Canada; our task is to maintain the momentum created by McLellan and Matthews. We look forward to future studies by other scholars who will target the areas we have missed.

NOTES

1 The relocation in Canada, unlike the wartime policy of the United States toward the Japanese, in the beginning forced the male evacuees either into road camps, internment in compounds that resembled prisoner-of-war camps, or sugar beet projects across Canada; the women and children were resettled in the inland towns of British Columbia or with other family members working on sugar beet farms. It was not until 1949, well after the 1945 surrender of Japan that ended the Second World War, that the dispersed Japanese families were allowed to return to British Columbia where they originally resided. However, most Japanese chose to remain in the newly resettled areas, and brought with them their practice of Buddhism to areas outside British Columbia. In 1988, as a result of a redress movement, Prime Minister Brian Mulroney offered a formal apology to Japanese Canadians and a compensation of $21,000 each to the survivors of wartime detention.

2 The Canadian government passed The Chinese Immigration Act in 1885 to levy a head tax on the Chinese who had immigrated to Canada. The act was further revised in 1900 and 1904, each time increasing the tax exponentially, from the originally $50 per head in 1885 to $500 in 1904. The act received a further revision in 1923, when the prohibitive tax was replaced by a ban on Chinese immigrants altogether (with the exception of students and some "elite" groups such as diplomats). It was not until 2006, a result of a redress movement, that the Canadian government, represented by Prime Minister Stephen Harper, offered an official apology and $20,000 compensation to the survivors or their spouses.

3 See http://www.buddhismcanada.com.

PART ONE Openings

How Do We Study Buddhism in Canada?

VICTOR SŌGEN HORI

Members of Fo Guang Shan Buddhist temple sit for an
examination in Buddhist studies. The exam, offered in either
Chinese or English, has several categories from introductory
to advanced. Note the young people in Boy Scout uniform.
Photo courtesy of Fo Guang Shan Toronto

For several decades now, more and more Canadians have been practising Buddhism. Most are immigrants but a surprisingly large number are Canadians who have turned to Buddhism. As academics begin to study this new phenomenon, a new academic field is coming into existence, the study of Buddhism in Canada. What do we need to do to ensure that this academic field accurately describes and explains Buddhism in Canada?

Among the new scholars now focusing their research on Buddhism in Canada, Janet McLellan has led the way with her book-length study *Many Petals of the Lotus* (1999), which examines five immigrant Buddhist communities in Toronto. In her wake, young scholars across Canada have created a steady stream of research: Louis Cormier, "Tibetans in Quebec: Profile of a Buddhist Community" (MA thesis, Université du Québec à Montréal, 2001); Angie Danyluk, "Caught between Worlds: An Ethnography of Western Tibetan Buddhists in Toronto" (PHD diss., McMaster University, 2003); Tannie Liu, "Globalization and Chinese Buddhism: The Canadian Experience" (PHD diss., University of Ottawa, 2004); Patricia Campbell, "Buddhist Values and Ordinary Life among Members of the Toronto Zen Buddhist Temple" (MA thesis, Wilfrid Laurier University, 2004): Kelly Braun, "The Tzu Chi Foundation and the Buddha's Light International Association: The Impact of Ethnicity in the Transmission of Chinese Buddhism to Canada" (MA thesis, University of Alberta, 2004). In 2006, a second book was published, Bruce Matthews's edited volume *Buddhism in Canada*. The Matthews book nicely complemented McLellan's book, providing a coast to coast Canada-wide context as a background for McLellan's highly focused local ethnographic studies of Asian immigrant communities in the city of Toronto.

Suddenly, in the academy, Buddhism in Canada has become a popular topic. The Canadian Asian Studies Association Conference held in 2006 in Montreal had two panels on Buddhism in Canada, one dealing with identities and practices and one with power and politics. The Eastern International Region Conference of the American Academy of Religion held in 2007 in Waterloo began with a colloquium on "The Future of the Study of Buddhism in North America" and continued with five consecutive Buddhism panels in which about half the panellists were researching Buddhism in Canada. In 2009, the American Academy of Religion conference held in Montreal featured panels entitled "Buddhism in Quebec" and "Buddhism in the West: A Canadian Focus." The University of Waterloo and Wilfrid Laurier University recently joined forces to create a new doctoral program, Religious Diversity in North America. According to its website, three of the eighteen students in the program are researching some aspect of Buddhism in Canada.

These new developments make us reflect on what we need to do to establish this field of study, Buddhism in Canada. Of course, researchers will do the fieldwork studies of individual Buddhist temples and historical studies of particular Buddhist lineages. But for the field as a whole, what do we need to ensure that the study of Buddhism in Canada accurately and responsibly describes and explains its target? In what follows, I sketch some rough guidelines.

First, I think we need to resist the distinction between Asian/ethnic and Western/convert Buddhism, found wherever Buddhism in the West is discussed. Aside from lack of clarity about what the terms are meant to categorize, the distinction also incorporates invidious value judgments.

Second, we need two kinds of basic information for the study of Buddhism in Canada – statistical and historical. Despite the efforts of Census Canada to identify how many Canadians belong to what religion, we still do not have accurate basic statistical data about Buddhists. In particular, we do not know how many "Western Buddhists" there are. Aside from statistics, researchers need to take into account the surprisingly long history of Buddhism in Canada; the first Buddhist priest, Sasaki Senju, arrived in Canada to start a temple in 1904. Furthermore, few people understand how the revision of Canada's immigration laws in the 1960s suddenly allowed the world's Buddhisms to come to Canada.

Third, because the study of Buddhism in Canada is not merely the study of statistics and history, we need to hear the life stories of people who have lived their lives as Buddhists. One branch of the study needs to record "Buddhist Lives," to hear the voices of practitioners who have tried to lead a Buddhist life.

Fourth, we need to be aware that the study of Buddhism in Canada requires us to make scholarly decisions about theory. In what field of research and scholarship should the study of Buddhism in Canada be located? Should Buddhism in Canada be studied together with religion in Asia? Should it be studied together with religion in North America? Is it better studied as a new religious movement?

Fifth, we need to take account of globalization. When people in Toronto or Vancouver or Montreal pass the doors of a local Chinese Buddhist temple, they assume that they are seeing a quaint religion lifted from the rice paddies of Asia and dropped onto a Canadian street to serve the needs of the ethnic community. But often that temple is a branch of a large, modern, global network of temples. Several major Asian Buddhist movements have recast the Buddhist message in modern terms; they now run television studios and publishing houses to transmit that message, operate up-to-date monasteries and schools to train their monks and nuns, organize their considerable lay followers into relief teams ready to go into action at any emergency. Focused entirely on the question of how Buddhism is adapting to the West, we in the West fail to notice that the Buddhism being transmitted from Asia has already undergone a modernization. And for these new, modern, sophisticated, global Buddhist networks, the West is an undeveloped field for Buddhist missionary work.

Sixth, and finally, in order to train researchers to study Buddhism in Canada, we need a new template for academic Buddhist studies. The philological model is no longer adequate. Universities with graduate programs in Buddhist studies must also train their students in fieldwork in order to study contemporary Buddhism.

ASIAN/ETHNIC VS WESTERN/CONVERT

Although various labels are used, most authors who write on Buddhism in the West use the terminology of "Two Buddhisms," "Asian/ethnic" and "Western/convert" Buddhism (or some equivalent vocabulary). Is dividing the field into two a useful way to organize the study of Buddhism in Canada?

There are several definitional issues involved. First, what is the extension of these categories? Are the categories, Asian/ethnic and Western/convert, mutually exclusive and jointly exhaustive? Who fits under each category? Second, what is the intension of these categories? What do the categories mean to categorize? Do the categories of Asian/ethnic and Western/convert categorize groups of people or do they categorize different styles of Buddhist practice?

What is the extension of these categories? I am an example of the problem with these terms. As a third generation Japanese Canadian, I come from a cultural group which originated in Asia and then immigrated to Canada, but I was born in Canada and grew up speaking English as my first language. By racial origin, I am Asian/ethnic but by birthplace and upbringing I am a Western/convert (I did not grow up in a Buddhist family). The existence of people like me, who fall into both categories, shows that the meanings of the terms "Asian," "ethnic," "Western," and "convert" are not precise. Richard Seager, in his book *Buddhism in America*, uses a three-part distinction precisely because he thinks people like me are numerous enough to constitute a separate category. He has three categories: 1) convert Buddhists, who are native-born Americans, 2) immigrant and refugee Buddhists, who were born and raised in an Asian country with a Buddhist culture, and 3) "Asian Americans, primarily from Chinese and Japanese backgrounds, who have practised Buddhism in this country for four and five generations" (Seager 1999, 9–10).[1] Even a three-part distinction does not really provide clear definition. Suwanda Sugunasiri argues that the distinction between "Ethnic-Buddhist" and "Euro-Buddhist" (his terminology for the Two Buddhisms) is determined not by a single criterion but by a combination of criteria: geographical heritage, spiritual heritage, and cultural heritage. He concludes that the many possible combinations of geographical, spiritual, and cultural heritage produce so many different kinds of Ethnic-Buddhists and Euro-Buddhists that the terms "Ethnic-Buddhist" and "Euro-Buddhist" become meaningless; they are "descriptively inadequate" (Sugunasiri 2006a).

In an attempt to get away from the definitional problems of who is Asian/ethnic and who is Western/convert, some authors have opted to focus on whether the person has passively inherited his or her Buddhism or has actively converted to it. Thus Thomas Tweed uses the terminology "cradle" Buddhist and "convert" Buddhist (Tweed 2002, 20ff) and Sugunasiri advocates the terminology "Inherited Buddhist" and "Acquired Buddhist" (Sugunasiri 2006a). But as soon as one considers the next generation, this terminology, too, appears inadequate. Since the children of Western/convert Buddhists, sometimes called "dharma brats," will themselves inherit their parents' Buddhism, they will not count as Western/converts. Where do we classify them? Likewise, the children of immigrant Buddhists are not themselves immigrants; they are Westerners but they have not converted to their Buddhism. They should most appropriately be classified under Seager's third category of Western-born Buddhists from an ethnic background. Not only will this third class, Western-born Buddhists who are neither Asian/ethnic nor Western/convert, continue to increase, but in the coming generations they will likely make up the category with the largest number.

When we confront the Buddhism practised by the next generation, it becomes increasingly difficult to say just what it is we are trying to distinguish. Asian/ethnic Buddhism, for some people, implies a socially oriented devotion to ancestors tinged with beliefs about karma and rebirth, while Western/convert Buddhism implies an individually oriented practice of Buddhism based on meditation aimed at clear self-understanding. With the terms "Western/convert" and "Asian/ethnic," are we trying to distinguish groups of people regardless of what kind of Buddhism they practise? Or are we trying to distinguish two styles of Buddhist practice, regardless of the ethnic and cultural origins of the people who practise them?

Other scholars have suggested other categories. Jan Nattier has noticed that the Soka Gakkai International (sgi) does not fall neatly under either Asian/ethnic or Western/convert. Soka Gakkai International originated in Japan but, with branches around the world, it is widely recognized as the only Buddhist organization to attract members from every economic class and every racial group. Its members do not join to associate with other people of the same Asian/ethnic group and most do not fit the profile of a white Western/convert. So Nattier also proposes three categories: 1) Elite Buddhists, who are distinguished by neither ethnicity nor sectarian affiliation, but by their class background which allows them to "import" their Buddhism; 2) Evangelical Buddhists, like sgi, who "export" Buddhism through their proselytization practices, and 3) Ethnic Buddhists, who immigrate to the West bringing Buddhism as part of their "cultural baggage" (Nattier 1998, 188–90). Nattier's three-part division classifies both styles of Buddhist practice and groups of people.

In his important essay "Who Is a Buddhist?" Thomas Tweed wants to capture a group of people that the usual categories do not. First, he makes the preliminary point that scholars have tended to essentialize religious identity and failed to take into account that everywhere religious traditions are "hybrid," "creole," "ambivalent" (Tweed 2002, 19). Second, he proposes a new third category. In addition to "cradle Buddhists" born into a Buddhist culture and "convert Buddhists" who explicitly choose to become Buddhist, he proposes a third category which he calls "night-stand" Buddhists, people who are not part of a formal organization but are sympathizers whose lifestyles are influenced in some way by Buddhism (Tweed 2002, 20ff). They read themselves to sleep at night with a book about Buddhism. In answer to the question "Who is a Buddhist?" Tweed adds his voice to the scholars who say we should count anyone who self-identifies as a Buddhist (Tweed 2002, 24). This is a classification intended to identify not styles of Buddhist practice but groups of people.

Because the terms "immigrant" and "convert" can only be plausibly applied to the first generation of immigrants and converts, Martin Baumann has argued that we should not be trying to identify groups of people but styles of Buddhist practice. He opts for the categories "traditionalist" and "modernist." With this distinction, he draws a sharp line cutting into two what used to be considered one. For instance, he divides the Theravada tradition into two: traditionalist temples where ordained monks from ethnic communities emphasize the performance of devotional rituals, teach the making of merit, and even incorporate folk practices such as selling protective amulets, reading palms, and telling fortunes (Baumann 2002b, 56–7) and the modernist meditation movement, led by lay Western teachers, who de-emphasize ritual and merit-making and emphasize meditation, mindfulness, and rational understanding (Baumann 2002b, 57-8). This distinction can plausibly be applied to several other forms of Buddhism: Zen Buddhist temples in Japan are traditionalist while Zen meditation centres in the West are modernist, and so on.

At first glance, the categories of Asian/ethnic and Western/convert seem to be the natural categories for classifying Buddhism in North America, but even a cursory examination shows that these categories cannot be used for rigorous research. Despite their inadequacy, many people will not want to give up this classification. The distinction between Asian/ethnic and Western/convert has, after all, a familiar political nuance.

Political Uses

The categories of Asian/ethnic and Western/convert unfortunately import value judgments into the analysis of our data. Although scholars attempt to offer objective definitions of the word, in fact "ethnic" itself is used, so to speak, ethnocentrically.

Social scientists are attempting to define "ethnic" in objective terms but subjective elements keep intruding. For example, in a recent publication, Paul

Bramadat has offered this definition of ethnicity: "An ethnic group is any significant group of people, typically related through common filiation, or blood, whose members usually feel a sense of attachment to a particular place, a history, and a culture (including a common language, food, and clothing)" (Bramadat 2005, 8). But he qualifies this definition by saying that some scholars argue that ethnicity is "constructed," that is, it is based less on connections of blood ties and more on a subjective sense of belonging to an imagined community. The "sense of belonging to an imagined community" is an important qualification because it inserts subjectivity into an otherwise objective definition, but this still omits an essential feature. François Thibeault hits that missing feature precisely: "ethnic identity is a social construction that implies self- and other-observation" (Thibeault 2006, 5). That is, ethnicity presupposes a self/other distinction. Ethnics are the others. And Thibeault also explains that in discussions about Buddhism in the West, "convert Buddhists are non-ethnic, because ethnicity is usually conceived as a specific feature of those minority groups of individuals who have migrated to Western societies" (Thibeault 2006, 3). In other words, ethnicity is the majority population's way of labelling minorities' identities. Only they are ethnic; we are not. As Bruce Matthews says, "Ethnic Buddhism ... is clearly not 'ethnic' to those who practice it" (Matthews xviii).

There is no denying that the dichotomy between Asian/ethnic and Western/convert Buddhist is very handy; I use the terms all the time since, for people in Canada, the distinction is immediately understood. I suggest, however, that the very fact that the distinction is so immediately understood is a clue to what is wrong with the distinction. Basically, the distinction between Asian/ethnic and Western/convert fundamentally divides Buddhists into "us" and "them." "Them" are the minority groups, the non-whites, the immigrants, the non-speakers of English, the outsiders. "Us" are the majority, the whites, the people who did not immigrate here, the speakers of English, the insiders. Most people in Canada know immediately which side of the us/them line they fall on. And they therefore overlook the problems of defining precisely "Western/convert" and "Asian/ethnic." They know that this is the academics' way of talking about "us" and "them."

Now see what mischief this distinction creates. In North America, Westerners do not have ethnicity; only Asian immigrants do. Westerners are the keepers of the Western tradition; Asian immigrants are outsiders seeking to gain entry into Western culture. But the subject of our research is not Western culture and how immigrants assimilate into it; we are talking about Buddhism. From the point of view of the long history of Buddhism, Asians are the keepers of the tradition and Westerners have only recently arrived at the gates seeking to gain entry. But in discussions of Buddhism in America, some people treat ethnics as both outsiders to America and outsiders to Buddhism in America. In what is now becoming a classic statement, Helen Tworkov, the editor of *Tricycle* magazine, wrote in a 1991 editorial, "The spokespeople for Buddhism in America have been, almost exclusively, educated members of the white middle class. Meanwhile, even with varying statistics, Asian-American Buddhists number at least one million, but so far have not figured prominently in the development of something called American Buddhism" (Tworkov 4). This statement, which claimed that educated members of the white middle class were almost exclusively the spokespeople for Buddhism in America and relegated Asian Americans to irrelevance, triggered a strong reaction. We do not need to investigate the details of the controversy; other scholars have done that (see, for example, Tanaka 1999, Gregory 2001). Our point is that the distinction between "Western/convert" and "Asian/ethnic" is used to divide Buddhists into "us" and "them," "inside" and "outside," and wrongly puts Asians on the outside.

One final comment is in order. The term "ethnic" has a history of incorporating discriminatory value judgments. Sugunasiri has pointed out that the 1964 edition of *Webster's New World Dictionary* defines "ethnic" as "[of nations or] groups that are neither Christian nor Jewish" (Sugunasiri 2006a, 109). The 1933 *Oxford English Dictionary* gives the same definition and, to make things explicit, gives as synonyms "Gentile, heathen, pagan." Frustrated by the imprecision of terms like "American Buddhist" or "Euro-American Buddhist" or "Western Buddhist," Rick Fields finally coined the term "white Buddhist" (Fields 1997). The term accurately captures an essential feature of most forms of Westernized Buddhism, that it is white and middle class. The term also makes explicit the underlying racial divide politely covered over by the terminology of "Asian/ethnic" and "Western/convert."

"Religion"

The word "ethnic" has a friend, equally mischievous, whose name is "religion." Just as the distinction between Asian/ethnic and Western/convert implies that only Asians have ethnicity, it also implies that only Westerners have religion.

The distinction between Asian/ethnic and Western/convert is silently mapped onto a methodological distinction. Asian/ethnic Buddhism is studied sociologically while Western/convert Buddhism is studied as religion. The Buddhist temples built by the Asian/ethnic communities are usually described as social centres; their function is, on the one hand, to maintain the language, the food, the culture of the Asian/ethnic community and, on the other hand, to help the newly arrived immigrants learn English, fill out tax returns, and in general assimilate into mainstream culture. The scholar who studies ethnic or immigrant religion focuses attention on sociological issues and not on religious issues. For example, in his study "The Life-Cycle of Ethnic Churches in Sociological Perspective," Mark Mullins quotes Joshua Fishman; "the more 'successful' religion becomes, the more de-ethnicized it becomes" (Fishman, 621; quoted in Mullins, 323). Ethnic religion "succeeds" when it helps people cross the ethnic barrier, as if its purpose is primarily to assist immigrants in assimilating into mainstream culture. Mullins has argued that in an idealized life-cycle, an ethnic church is monolingual in the first generation, speaking the ethnic language, is bilingual in the second generation with the children also speaking English, and is monolingual in the third generation, the grandchildren speaking only English. In the fourth generation, it faces a crisis. If it insists on maintaining a strong ethnic identity, it may not survive. If it opens itself to other ethnicities, it may survive but at the loss of its ethnic identity. Mullins, whose paper is based on research on the Japanese United Church of Canada and the Buddhist Churches of Canada, concludes, "If ethnic churches de-ethnicize their religious tradition and broaden their base of relevance, organizational survival is a possibility" (Mullins 327). Again, Mullins seems to imply that the primary function of an ethnic religion – and he is explicitly including Buddhism in Canada – is to help its members assimilate. Little attention is paid to the activities of the ethnic church as religious activity.

By contrast, Westerners are converts to Buddhism. In religious studies, the very word "convert" has strong nuances. Converts have made a deliberate and conscious choice to leave the religion of their parents and to accept Buddhism. In the Western conception of religion, merely following the religion of one's parents is considered pro-forma religion. Making a conscious decision to convert to a religion is the model *par excellence* of an authentic religious decision. Robert Bellah and his associates in *Habits of the Heart* write, "The self-reliant American is required not only to leave home but to 'leave church' as well" (Bellah et al., 62). That is because "The American understanding of the autonomy of the self places the burden of one's own deepest definitions on one's own individual choice" (Ibid., 65). Bellah's work should be familiar to all scholars of religion, so I will not labour this point. In a culture which reveres the autonomy of the self and individual choice, Western/convert Buddhism, just because it is the personal choice of an individual, fits the notion of real religion. By contrast, Asian/ethnic Buddhism is depicted as if it were not authentic religion; its function is not really religious but sociological, to assist its members to assimilate into mainstream culture.

These two terms, "ethnicity" and "religion," ought to be neutral but when deployed in the distinction Asian/ethnic and Western/convert they privilege the Westerner and disenfranchise the Asian. The devaluation of ethnic Buddhism as less authentically religious than convert Buddhism is ironic. When Charles Prebish first introduced the distinction between two kinds of Buddhism in 1979, he characterized one type as having "primary emphasis on sound basic doctrines, shared by all Buddhists, and on solid religious practice" (Prebish 1979, 51). He later associated this type of Buddhism with ethnic Asian American groups. The other type of Buddhism, associated with the Beat Generation and the drug culture, he characterized as based on "the personal charisma of a flamboyant leader," "flashy, opaquely exotic, 'hip'" (Prebish 1979, 51). In Prebish's original formulation of the distinction between two Buddhisms, it was Asian/ethnic Buddhism that was considered "solid religious practice" and Westerner's Buddhism that was considered less authentic. In the thirty years that have passed, the value judgments have reversed.

When Prebish first introduced the distinction of the two Buddhisms, it may have accurately characterized the data then available. Now, thirty years later, it is becoming increasingly clear that a simple distinction into "Two Buddhisms" not only is too broad and imprecise but also subtly imposes an "us" and "them" distinction on Buddhists. It is time to move on to a better classification system.

Some Recommendations

Let us stop contrasting Western and ethnic. Instead let us recognize that Western Buddhism is an ethnic Buddhism. Just as the Chinese perceived and understood Buddhism through Chinese assumptions based on the Confucian family system with its elaborate hierarchy, based on Taoist notions of freedom and spontaneity, based on folk religious ideas about death and the afterlife, so also Westerners are now attempting to perceive and understand Buddhism through Western assumptions about the primary importance of the individual. Let us resist the assumption that the cultures of Asia distorted true Buddhism and that Western culture is going to recover the true Buddhism that existed prior to cultural distortion. There is no such thing as a true Buddhism undistorted by culture; even the Buddhism taught by Śākyamuni was imbedded in Indian culture. All cultures interpret Buddhism, and Western Buddhism is just another cultural (ethnic) interpretation.

One obvious way to encourage research into the ethnic character of Western Buddhism is to conduct in-depth comparisons of similar practices and institutions found in both Asian Buddhism and Western Buddhism. Here we have a successful model in scholarship to emulate. Scholarship in business management has for several decades been making detailed comparisons of work practices in Japanese companies and Western companies; much of this research shows how different work practices result from different cultural assumptions. Such research shows clearly that the Western way of doing things is just as ethnic as the Asian way of doing things.[2]

STATISTICS

Let us assume, for the moment, that the terms "Asian/ethnic" and "Western/convert" label groups of people rather than styles of Buddhist practice. What is the size of the populations of each group? Statistics Canada data unfortunately cannot give us precise estimates. There is no question on the Canadian Census form that asks "Are you an Asian/ethnic Buddhist or a Western/convert Buddhist?" Scholars have to combine the data generated by two or more other questions on the census form to arrive at any statistical estimate.

Question 22 on the 2001 Census Long Form (Statistics Canada 2001) asks people to identify their religion, "For example, Roman Catholic, Ukrainian Catholic, United Church, Anglican, Lutheran, Baptist, Greek Orthodox, Jewish, Islam, Buddhist, Hindu, Sikh, etc." It instructs, "Specify one denomination or religion only." Here StatsCan is probably being influenced by the Western assumption that a person has exclusive affiliation to one and only one religion; this is quite inconsistent with the Asian inclusivist practice where people often engage in the activities of several religions at once. It is also inconsistent with the practice of many Westerners who practise Buddhism as a second religion alongside their first religion (Jewish Buddhists, Catholic contemplatives, etc.).

Question 9, Census Long Form, asks whether the respondent was born inside or outside Canada.

Question 11, Census Long Form, asks whether the respondent is or ever has been a landed immigrant.

Question 17 asks people to identify their ethnic or cultural group: "Canadian, French, English, Chinese, Italian, German, Scottish, Irish, Cree, Micmac, Métis, Inuit (Eskimo), East Indian, Ukrainian, Dutch, Polish, Portuguese, Filipino, Jewish, Greek, Jamaican, Vietnamese, Lebanese, Chilean, Somali, etc."

The infamous Question 19, which tries to identify race without using the word "race," asks whether the respondent is "white, Chinese, South Asian, black, Filipino, Latin American, Southeast Asian, Arab, West Asian, Japanese, Korean, other."

When scholars give estimates of the size of a Buddhist population, they are combining the statistics generated by the above questions. But such combinations do not give us precise estimates of Asian/ethnic or Western/convert Buddhists.

In the essay that Peter Beyer contributed to the book *Religion and Ethnicity in Canada*, edited by Paul Bramadat and David Seljak, he tells us that judging from StatsCan 2001 census data, the total population of Buddhists in Canada is 300,345 comprising Non-Immigrants 74,070 and Immigrants 217,780 (Beyer 2005, 237). Here Beyer must be combining the statistics from Question 22 on religion and Question 11 on immigrant status. If one associates the non-immigrants with Western/converts and the immigrants with Asian/ethnics, that would imply that about 25 per cent of the Buddhists in Canada are Western/converts – and that seems to me to be much too high. When I asked Beyer about this, he confirmed my suspicion. The non-immigrants include the Canada-born children of immigrants. The children of immigrants are Westerners born in Canada but they do not practise Western/convert style Buddhism. If one subtracts their numbers, then, first, this estimate of the size of the Western/convert population drops considerably, and second, we have no precise statistical measure of it.

In another study, Placzek and Devries state that in British Columbia in 2005, Canadian-born Buddhists numbered 13,220 while foreign-born Buddhists numbered 59,153 (Placzek and Devries, 2–3). Here Placzek and Devries must be combining the statistics from Question 22 on religion and from Question 9 on being born inside or outside Canada. If one assumes that Canadian-born Buddhists are the Western/converts and they number 13,220while the foreign-born Buddhists are the Asian/ethnics and they number 59,153, then Western/converts number about 23 per cent of the Buddhists in British Columbia. The problem is that again "Canadian-born Buddhist" also includes the children and grandchildren of Asian immigrants. These are not Western/converts.

If you subtract their numbers, the estimate for Western/converts drops dramatically, and again we have no precise statistical measure of this group.

Mathieu Boisvert, in his essay "Buddhists in Canada: Impermanence in a Land of Change," states that the Buddhist population in Canada breaks down as follows: Chinese 42 per cent, Indo-Chinese 34 per cent, Japanese 10 per cent (2005, 72). The total of these three groups is 86 per cent. Here Boisvert must be combining the statistics from Question 22 on religion and from Question 17 on ethnic or cultural group. Again, making allowance for the addition of smaller Asian Buddhist groups such as Koreans, Tibetans, Sri Lankans, one is tempted to say that Western/converts = (Total Buddhists) minus (Asian/ethnics). That seems to imply that 14 per cent of the total Buddhist population of Canada is Western/converts. But again, the children and grandchildren of Asian immigrants identify themselves not as ethnically Asian but as Canadian. Are they Western or Asian? As we all know, a very large proportion of the Canadian population identifies itself as hyphenated Canadian (Italian-Canadian, Japanese-Canadian, French-Canadian, Chinese-Canadian, etc.). As Beyer says, "It is in fact difficult to isolate the 'Western' Buddhists since no ethnic or place of birth category really captures them" (email 24 August 2006). And so long as that is true, it will be inherently difficult to get any precise statistical measure of Asian/ethnic or Western/convert Buddhists.

The moral of the statistics story is not that we should persuade Statistics Canada to put a new question on the census form: "Are you an Asian/ethnic Buddhist or a Western/convert Buddhist?" Many people would answer "Neither" or perhaps "Both." The discussion thus far shows that we are unclear about what we want to identify. Are we trying to identify groups of people, regardless of the kind of Buddhism they practise? Or are we trying to identify styles of Buddhist practice? Until the terms "Asian/ethnic Buddhist" and "Western/convert Buddhist" are given more precise meaning, they will not be useful for research despite the fact that everyone uses them.

STORY AND HISTORY

The most important publication in the new field of Buddhism in the West is the late Rick Fields's *How the Swans Came to the Lake: A Narrative History of Buddhism in America*. Fields was not a scholar and did not pretend to be a scholar. But he wrote the single most important book in this new field. The book presents the coming of Buddhism to America as a great historical saga. It begins at the beginning with Śākyamuni Buddha and as it sweeps through the centuries, it touches down to catch momentary glimpses of Alexander the Great, St Francis Xavier in Japan, William Jones discovering Sanskrit in India, Emerson and Thoreau writing in America, the Chinese emigrating to Gold Mountain, Colonel Olcott and Madame Blavatsky in Ceylon, the World Parliament of Religions in Chicago in 1893, D.T. Suzuki lecturing in America, the Beat poets in the fifties, and then the coming of Buddhist teachers in the sixties. Fields's eloquence makes all who are interested in Buddhism feel they are participating in a great epic. Buddhism comes to America with irresistible, inevitable historical force. Of course, scholars have criticized Fields's book, chiefly for focusing on the Buddhism that interests white people and neglecting the Buddhism of Asian immigrant groups. But every professional scholar interested in Buddhism in the West has read this book so that by default it constitutes the common reference ground for all academics. Though it itself is not scholarship, Fields's story of Buddhism has emotionally propelled a great deal of the scholarly research into Buddhism in the West.

For the study of Buddhism in Canada, we now need someone to write a comparable book. It would be the story about how Buddhism adapted to Canadian culture. Eventually, a history of Buddhism in Canada might also become a story of how Canadian culture adapted to Buddhism. In 1905, the Reverend Sasaki Senju, a priest of the Honganji Temple, a head temple in the Japanese True Pure Land tradition, came to Canada to establish the first Buddhist temple in Canada. The Buddhist Churches of Canada commemorated this event and celebrated its centennial in 2005. For the first sixty years, the hundred-year history of Buddhism in Canada is basically a history of Japanese Pure Land Buddhism in Canada and its long struggle to establish itself in a hostile environment. At the beginning of the twentieth century, provincial laws and Canadian federal policies were explicitly racist. The Provincial Elections Act of British Columbia of 1895 stated, "no Chinaman, Japanese or Indian shall have his name placed on the Register of Voters for any Electoral District or be entitled to vote at any election" (cited in Boisvert, 80). Official laws and unofficial discrimination prevented Asians from owning property, working in many occupations, entering into regular schools, or living in any area of town except the Asian ghettos. The Canadian government passed a series of immigration laws targeting the Chinese beginning with the Chinese Immigration Act of 1885, the law that established the Chinese head tax. The explicit purpose of this and other such laws was to keep out undesirable races. The west coast, in particular, was a hotbed of racist activity. A little after Sasaki Senju arrived, Vancouver experienced the Anti-Asiatic Riot of 1907. A mob marched through the streets of Vancouver invading both Chinatown and Little Tokyo, smashing windows and causing destruction. Mr H.H. Stevens, a Vancouver municipal councillor and a leader of the Asiatic Exclusion League, stated, "We contend that the destiny of Canada is best left in the hands of the Anglo-Saxon race, and are unalterably and irrevocably opposed to any move which threatens in the slightest degree this position."[3] I will not mention the forced relocation of the Japanese during World War II, as it is dealt with later in this volume by Watada and Harding. Canadian immigration laws continued to embody explicitly racist attitudes right into the 1960s.

Then, along with the United States, Canada overhauled its immigration laws, instituting a race-neutral, points-based system. With the explicit promotion of a policy of multiculturalism in the 1970s under Prime Minister Pierre Elliot Trudeau, Canada turned its back on official racism. Immigrants from Buddhist countries began to arrive in Canada in large numbers. Almost all the many forms of Buddhism we now find in Canada – Zen, Tibetan, Chinese, Thai, Sri Lankan, Korean, Lao, etc. – were transplanted and started to grow in Canadian soil in that period. The arrival of the immigrants coincided with the great counterculture ruptures of the sixties and seventies: widespread protests against the American war in Vietnam, campus rebellions against university authority and academic involvement in the "military-industrial complex," the women's liberation movement, the Black power revolt, and, in general, a great wave of social experimentation and openness to unorthodox ideas and styles of life.

The second great chapter in the history of Buddhism in Canada is the story of how Buddhism, outside of immigrant communities, proliferated and spread into Western culture beginning with the social and cultural upheavals of the 1960s. Before the sixties, books on Zen had been in print for decades but they were read by only a small minority. Then, during the sixties, great waves of young people seeking new religious options hungrily devoured books on Zen philosophy and Zen practice. Zen was linked to everything from archery to motorcycle maintenance. The Zen boom was not merely a social fashion. Serious practitioners of Zen meditation established monasteries. The San Francisco Zen Center opened its doors in 1962; the Zen Center of Los Angeles followed suit in 1967. In Canada, Montreal during the 60s was an interesting place for Buddhists. The Korean Zen monk Samu Sunim resided there before he moved on and subsequently opened temples in Toronto, Ann Arbor, and Chicago. Chögyam Trungpa lived there with his sixteen-year-old wife, Diana Pybus, for a short while awaiting his visa to the United States; the group of students he taught in Montreal established a centre which continues today, a centre which prides itself on being the first and oldest centre in the world-wide Shambhala network. During the sixties, Philip Kapleau came up from Rochester to teach in Montreal; his teaching legacy eventually evolved into the Montreal Zen Centre now led by Albert Low, whose story forms a separate chapter in this book.

In the years that followed, the Zen wave subsided but other forms of Buddhism swept in to take its place. In 1959, the 14th Dalai Lama fled the Chinese occupation of Tibet. Over the next several decades, numerous Tibetan lamas settled in the West and taught the dharma to Western students. Today, although no precise statistics have been compiled, it is a safe guess that more Westerners are practitioners of Tibetan Buddhism than of any other form of Buddhism. On the Buddhism in Canada website, for the British Columbia Lower Mainland area which includes Vancouver, of ninety Buddhist groups twenty-eight have some connection with Tibetan Buddhism. Close behind Tibetan Buddhism is the vipassana meditation movement represented by the school of S.N. Goenka and by the Insight Meditation movement founded by Jack Kornfield, Joseph Goldstein, and Sharon Salzberg.

In the forty years since the change in immigration laws and the spread of Buddhism among Westerners, Buddhism has come in from the fringe. Today, ordinary people do Buddhist meditation practice and are not thought to be strange. Music and movie personalities are known to be Buddhist. The Dalai Lama is widely recognized and widely admired. Buddhism is more and more being accepted into mainstream Canadian culture.

BUDDHIST LIVES

The study of Buddhism in Canada is not merely the study of statistics and history, of ethnic groups and immigrants, of Western converts. Buddhism is a living religion; it is a lived religion. The average person is less interested in scholarly analysis than in the question, what does it mean to live one's life as a Buddhist. Thus, the study of Buddhism in Canada must include the recording of Buddhist practitioners' accounts of their life journeys in Buddhism.

George Klima's Buddhism in Canada website lists several hundred Buddhist temples and meditation centres. Many of these sites are led by people whose entire adult lives have been spent in Buddhist practice and Buddhist teaching. Some are members of ethnic minorities, and because their first language is not English, their life stories are not as accessible as those who do speak English. But the scholarship on Buddhism in Canada would not be complete without their stories. Some of these teachers are Westerners who have experimented in making the message and the practice of the dharma more readily available to Westerners. For example, the late Namgyal Rinpoche (Leslie George Dawson) of the Ontario Dharma Centre, born in Canada, was an early pioneer in melding Tibetan Buddhism and vipassana meditation into a new kind of practice adapted for Westerners. The story of Buddhism in Canada is told through the life stories of such individuals.

THEORY

In what field of research and scholarship should the study of Buddhism in Canada be located? The study of Buddhism in Canada bears little resemblance to research in Buddhist studies as it is conducted at present in North American universities. Typically, a scholar in Buddhist studies reads texts written in a primary language like Sanskrit or ancient Chinese or classical Tibetan and writes a historical or philosophical commentary on those texts. While it is helpful to know something of the history and philosophy of Buddhism in Asia, clearly the study of Buddhism in Canada requires a researcher to bring other kinds of scholarship to bear. What other kinds of scholarship?

A short while ago, one of my graduate students completed a field research project on an American Zen monastery in upper New York state (Arslanian). The resulting thesis has five chapters, of which the first and last are introduction and conclusion. The second chapter considers the Zen monastery against the scholarship on religion in America, drawing especially on the work of Robert Bellah and associates. It argues that in the 1960s to practise Zen was considered "opting out" of establishment culture but by the year 2005, Zen had become so acceptable that it was considered an option within mainstream culture. The third chapter considers the Zen monastery against the scholarship in the sociology of religion, using in particular sociological research on the history of the commune movement in America. The thesis shows, for example, clear parallels between the "commitment mechanisms" made by religious communes in the past (Kanter) and the American Zen monastery today. The fourth chapter considers the American Zen monastery against the scholarship on Buddhist monasticism in Asia. The thesis shows the compromises and modifications made by the Zen monastery today concerning traditional Buddhist practices such as celibacy, vegetarianism, ordination, use of money, and so on. Three different bodies of theory were required to analyse and illuminate what is happening at an American Buddhist monastery.

There is no clearly defined body of accumulated research called Buddhism in Canada against which a particular research project can be compared. As this example shows, it is clearly necessary to situate any research project in the study of Buddhism in Canada against bodies of research drawn from other fields. Because we are at the very beginning stages of defining our field, we need to be methodologically sophisticated to make the appropriate scholarly decisions about what body of theory to apply.

GLOBALIZED BUDDHISMS

Part of our problem in understanding Buddhism in the West is that we are quick to assume that ethnic Buddhism is "traditional," a survivor from the premodern world, focused on devotionalist ancestor and memorial rituals, offering lay people only merit-making exercises, teaching only karma and rebirth. In this assumption, we are implicitly associating Asia with the traditional and the West with the modern. But if we paid more attention to the Buddhism that is being sent out of Asian countries and less to the adaptation of Buddhism in the West, we would see this stereotype for what it is. Asia can sometimes be more modern than the West.

The first encounters between Asian forms of Buddhism and Western culture did not take place in the West in the twentieth century; they took place in Asia in the nineteenth century. Perhaps the best-studied example is that of Theravada Buddhism in Ceylon (now Sri Lanka). Under pressure from a British colonial government, Christian missionaries, and a restive population, the Buddhists in Ceylon redefined Buddhism, emphasizing its rationality over ritual practices, promoting the use of texts (including a newly composed catechism), and encouraging education and social reform. The Christian missionary example exerted so strong an influence that scholars now describe aspects of modern Sri Lankan Buddhism as "Protestant Buddhism" (Gombrich 1988).[4] At the end of the 1800s, Buddhists in Japan, persecuted by their own national government which was fiercely intent on modernizing the country, attempted to create a "New Buddhism" with similar features;[5] it stressed compatibility with science, eschewed superstition, and envisaged a role for lay practice (Ketelaar 1990). These new forms of Buddhism evolved as they continued their encounter with Western culture. Both the new Theravada Buddhism and the new Japanese Zen Buddhism began to emphasize meditation, which till then had been a neglected practice, because meditation appealed to the strong Western interest in psychology and mysticism. In this way, Sharf explains the rise of the modern Westernized vipassana movement and the invention of D.T. Suzuki's version of Zen (Sharf 1993, 1995). In the West, practitioners of vipassana and Zen meditation, two of the most successful Buddhist movements in the West, believe they are following a tradition with two thousand years of history; if Sharf is correct, they are following a practice which basically got started a little more than a hundred years ago when Asian Buddhism began to modernize.

Scholars are just now catching up with a wave of more recent changes, which can justifiably be called both modernist and global. One of the first of the modern forms of lay Buddhism to attract scholarly attention was the Soka Gakkai International movement, which originated in Japan. More recently, scholars have started to study Thich Nhat Hanh's work in creating a worldwide socially engaged Buddhist movement. This movement has caught the attention of Westerners, who have become his followers both in meditation practice and social action. But Chinese Buddhism, starting in the republican period which began in 1911, has also undergone a thoroughgoing modernization, resulting in the creation of the Humanistic Buddhism movement. This has not been adequately studied in the West.

Leading the Humanistic Buddhism movement are organizations such as Buddha Light Mountain (Fo Guang Shan), the Buddhist Compassion and Relief Tzu Chi Foundation, and Dharma Drum, all based in Taiwan. Buddha Light Mountain, otherwise known as the International Buddhist Progress Society (IBPS), has a worldwide global network of temples: five temples in Taiwan, six in other countries of Asia including Japan, five in Europe, three in the Pacific including a major temple in Australia, one in South Africa, and twelve temples in the United States and Canada. Fo Guang Shan or IBPS temples are massive structures built in the Chinese red and gold palace style. In Canada, there are IBPS temples in Vancouver, Mississauga, Ottawa, and Montreal. The IBPS Hsi Lai Temple in Los Angeles is a huge complex the size of a small campus.

And speaking of campus, Fo Guang Shan also operates the University of the West in Los Angeles, an accredited Buddhist university offering both undergraduate and graduate programs in Buddhism.

From the point of view of Westerners passing by their local IBPS temple, the temple is just another ethnic enclave where Chinese gather to speak their own language, eat their own food, maintain their own traditions. The Buddhism of Chinese temples is thought to be traditional, not modern. And indeed this may be so. Though parts of Buddhism have modernized in Asia, the old Buddhism, which incorporates spirit worship, divination, and intense devotionalism, also continues, so that old and new forms of Buddhism coexist. Some of the older forms of Buddhism have been imported to the West. But it would be quite mistaken to assume that all Chinese temples harbour that kind of Buddhism. Seen from the point of view of the Taiwanese society where it originated, IBPS Buddhism is the sophisticated product of a great modernization. Humanistic Buddhism, as taught by Master Hsing Yun of Fo Guang Shan, promotes a revised version of Buddhist doctrine emphasizing human life in this world, not life in some future rebirth. It is steadfastly optimistic, countering the criticism that the Buddhist teaching of suffering is dark and pessimistic. Fo Guang Shan not only emphasizes the compatibility of Buddhism with modern education but also operates its own schools and universities. While still incorporating much ritual, it also offers its lay and ordained followers meditation and other practice techniques. It is directed at people who live in modern society and are juggling career, family, urban life, the raising of children, etc., providing them with a Buddhist outlet for their desire to do something for society. With a television station, media publications, and international outreach programs, Fo Guang Shan is clearly at home with modern technology. On the international front, it actively promotes world peace, human rights, and humanistic values. Fo Guang Shan has already evolved into the kind of organization Western Buddhist groups hope to become.

Much the same can be said for the Buddhist Relief and Compassion Tzu Chi Foundation. Under the leadership of its founder, the charismatic Buddhist nun Cheng Yen, Tzu Chi has developed a worldwide network of branches in more than thirty countries. In Canada, Tzu Chi branches can be found in Vancouver, Toronto, and Montreal. Rather than teaching dharma in the traditional way, it focuses on providing relief to people in need. When Master Cheng Yen was a young nun visiting a hospital, she found blood on the hospital floor. A young woman had had a miscarriage and been brought to the hospital but the hospital refused her medical treatment as she did not have enough money to pay. Cheng Yen vowed that that would never happen again. In Taiwan, Tzu Chi runs several state-of-the-art hospitals and medical clinics providing medical aid to everyone regardless of income. It has a comprehensive school system providing education from primary school through university. In its medical school, it infuses medical instruction with Buddhism. Around the world, its branches are organized not only to provide ongoing relief to people in need but also to respond immediately in times of emergency. Within hours after an earthquake or a flood, Tzu Chi has its teams of volunteer doctors, nurses, and other staff on the disaster sites providing medical aid, water, food, and relief supplies. For example, Tzu Chi's mobile clinic provided medical care to victims of Hurricane Katrina in Louisiana. It was one of the first organizations to offer organized relief in Indonesia after the tsunami. The Indonesia relief work is particularly interesting because, in addition to the provision of immediate relief, an entire village, including an Islamic mosque, was reconstructed so that people would have stable housing. Again, like Fo Guang Shan, Tzu Chi is quite at home in modern society and with modern technology (it has its own television station, publishing house, hospitals, schools, etc.). It too has already evolved into the kind of socially engaged organization many Western Buddhist groups hope to become.

There is a flip side to this coin. Modern Asian Buddhist organizations like Fo Guang Shan, Tzu Chi, Soka Gakkai of Japan, Won Buddhism from Korea, and others are not quaint forms of Buddhism lifted from the rice paddies of the East to serve the Asians who have come to the West. They are large, sophisticated organizations comfortably taking the globe as home base. In some ways, they resemble the Christian missions that mounted ambitious campaigns to save the souls of Asians during the colonial period. Just as those Christian missions did not wait to be invited into the countries of Asia and Africa, so also the modern Asian Buddhist organizations do not wait to be invited into the countries where they are active. They often piggyback on the local Chinese populations in the countries where they set up branches, but they make their own decisions about where there is a dharma need or dharma opportunity. Some Westerners will feel that they are the victims of a Buddhist missionary effort which they did not want and did not invite, just as Asians during the colonial period were subjected to Christian missionaries who were not invited and not wanted.

TRAINING GRADUATE STUDENTS

To this point, my focus has been on the study of Buddhism in Canada and the problems associated with it. However, I now wish to expand my focus to the study of modern Buddhism in general, regardless of whether it is Buddhism in Canada or Buddhism in Taiwan. Our Buddhist studies graduate programs are presently organized in such a way that it is difficult for a doctoral student to study Buddhism in modern Canada or Buddhism in modern Asia.

At McGill University, for more than ten years we have been receiving inquiries from graduate students who apply for admission proposing to do a thesis on some aspect of modern Buddhism, either in the West or in Asia. In the early days, my colleague Richard Hayes was unsure about how to handle these applications. Canvassing his colleagues at other universities, he found that most of them could not accommodate a thesis on Buddhism in the West within Buddhist studies programs. Such a thesis project would require field research, a kind of research quite different from text-based philology. The hold of the philological model has weakened somewhat. Today, the ability to translate alone does not suffice for a PHD. The student must also discuss the content of the primary text against theoretical issues in current scholarship, which may require expertise in philosophy, ritual studies, Orientalism, deconstruction, etc. Nevertheless, Buddhist studies as a field clings to the philological model; it has not developed an alternative research paradigm which would freely allow the study of modern Buddhist movements.

The philological model is open to several criticisms. In the Middle Ages, very few people were literate. The Buddhist texts that have come down to us were written by the elite of their day. Critics say that in contemporary Buddhist studies, the elite of today study the written works of the elite of yesterday, ignoring the daily lives of the great majority of illiterate Buddhists. Furthermore, the interests of text-based scholars are usually historical or philosophical; there is thus a scarcity of works on Buddhism written from the viewpoint of sociology, anthropology, economics, political theory, etc. Also text-based translations of monastic rulebooks give a prescriptive account of how people are supposed to behave; there is very little ethnographic research, which can provide a descriptive account of how they actually behave. Finally, philological scholarship encourages the study of the past and discourages a research focus on the present. In its favour, the philological model has the admirable feature of being rigorous. Many years of concentrated study are required before the student becomes competent in Sanskrit or classical Chinese or classical Tibetan. This great effort usually discourages the people who want to link Buddhism to new age spirituality or to astrology or flying saucers or the lost continent of Atlantis. The philological study of primary texts is an essential part of Buddhist studies but there are good reasons for wanting to find additional models for Buddhist studies research.

Two years ago at a meeting of some Buddhist studies scholars at the annual meeting of the American Academy of Religion, I asked my colleagues how they handle the growing number of applications from students proposing to do a research project on Buddhism in the West or on modern Buddhism in Asia. Some replied that their schools were not prepared to handle such requests. One scholar suggested that students who wanted to study Buddhism in the West should be directed to a specialist in the field of American religion. Although this suggestion was probably motivated by the desire to escape a problem, nevertheless it contains the insight that Buddhism in North America is no longer a wholly Asian religion; it behaves according to the rules of the American religion game.

As mentioned at the beginning of this essay, the University of Waterloo and Wilfrid Laurier University offer a joint PHD program, Religious Diversity in America. It has been designed deliberately to accommodate graduate students who want to study contemporary religion in North America. A similar PHD program at Arizona State University is called Religion in the Americas. At the time of this writing, the Waterloo-Wilfrid Laurier program had three students studying Buddhism in North America. Professor Ronald Grimes, director of the joint program, tells these students, "We're not offering a degree in Buddhism. We offer only one area of concentration, religious diversity in North America. We are making North Americanists out of you, not Buddhologists" (email correspondence, 2 October 2006).

The study of Buddhism in Canada fits somewhere in the middle of a spectrum with traditional Buddhist studies at one end and the study of North American religion at the other. Traditional Buddhist studies scholars have a training that is deep but narrow; they read ancient languages and have an intimate knowledge of Buddhist history and philosophy. But they are not well trained in the history and ethnographic study of contemporary North American religion. Those traditional Buddhist studies scholars who write on Buddhism in the West do so as amateurs. On the other hand, North Americanists have a training that is not as deep but much wider. In particular, they will have training in social science methods, statistics, ethnographic field research, disciplines which are not part of the regular curriculum of traditional Buddhist studies. Buddhist studies scholars are competent to study Buddhist philosophy and history in Asia; North Americanists are competent to study religion in North America. But no one is properly trained to do the very research that concerns us in this book: how does Buddhism change when translated from its Asian environment to a Western environment?

I recently received a proposal from a student for a PHD project which would compare transmission of the dharma in Asian countries with transmission of the dharma in the West. To do this comparative project, the student would require the language ability to do both archive research and field research in an Asian country, as well as the ability to do ethnographic field research in both Asia and America. There are two ways to go on this. The Waterloo-Wilfrid Laurier joint program could develop students who speak Asian languages and can work in Asian cultures; or Buddhist studies programs should teach the study of North American religion and train students in statistics and ethnographic fieldwork. Both alternatives should be explored.

CONCLUSION

In a new subject field, the first step in intellectual organization is the identification of types or categories. If you have good types or categories, then you can do analysis, because analysis is the sorting of data into categories. The next step in intellectual organization is to try to order the types or categories as positions along some spectrum; this provides the argument for saying you have found a variable. And the third step in intellectual organization is to show that there is a relationship between two variables, either a direct relationship or an inverse relationship; if you can do that, then you might have a theory. And if you have a theory, then you can offer explanations of why your data are the way they are. If you are so foolhardy as to stick your neck out, you can use your theory not only to explain past events but also to predict future events. If the future event is consistent with your prediction, you will look like a great scholar; if the future event is not consistent with your data, then you should suppress publication of the results until after you get tenure. When scholars argue for two or three categories (Asian/ethnic, Western/convert and/or some hybrid) or argue about what it is the categories categorize (groups of people or styles of Buddhist practice), they are engaged in the usual sort of criticisms offered when a set of categories first claims to structure the data in an unorganized field. That is where we are in the study of Buddhism in Canada, still struggling to find basic types or categories to order our data (see also Wallace 2002).

However, although we are just setting out on the organized study of Buddhism in Canada, we fortunately can draw lessons from the scholarship conducted in the United States on Buddhism in America, which is at a more advanced state. One lesson we have learned is that there is a racial distinction which is expressed politely in terminology like "Asian/ethnic" and "Western/convert" and which sometimes comes to the surface, as in the claim of Helen Tworkov that "Asian-American Buddhists ... have not figured prominently in the development of something called American Buddhism" (Tworkov 4). Scholars setting out on the study of Buddhism in Canada, now aware of this issue, can hope to advance without triggering unnecessary racial tensions. A second lesson lies in the excessively narrow focus of the American researchers, interested almost entirely in what happens within the borders of their country. Much has been written about the new Buddhism which Americans are creating, but as Soucy points out in his chapter, the characteristics of an Americanized Buddhism strongly resemble the features of modernized Buddhism wherever it occurs in Asia, whether it is "Protestant Buddhism" in Sri Lanka, "Humanistic Buddhism" in China, or Thich Nhat Hanh's Order of Interbeing. The lesson we take from this for the study of Buddhism in Canada is that the development of Buddhism in Canada can only be properly understood against development and changes to Buddhism globally.

Buddhism is an ancient religion that teaches inner peace of mind and the cessation of suffering, self-discipline, and realistic perception of the world. Canada, more than other countries of the West, through its official stance of multiculturalism, is open to the influences of other cultures and other religions. It is reasonable to expect, then, that Buddhism will continue to flourish in Canada. Undoubtedly Buddhism will change and adapt to Canadian culture, but in any Asian country where Buddhism has historically flourished, the country and culture themselves have changed to become more Buddhist. It is too early to predict whether this change will occur in Canada and what shape it will take. We cannot know if Canada, being a more open country, will become

"Buddhified" earlier than other countries in the West. But whatever the case, it is the special responsibility of academic scholars to study the great change as it takes place and to make their understanding available to the pubic at large.

NOTES

1 Paul Numrich has coined the phrase "parallel congregations" to describe another in-between category, groups of Western/convert Buddhists who practice under a Buddhist teacher in an ethnic Buddhist temple (Numrich 1996, ch. 4).

2 When Japanese companies like Toyota started outperforming Western companies in the 1980s and 1990s, Western business analysts began to study Japanese corporations, especially the organization of work at the factory level (Womack et al. 1990, Womack and Jones 1996). Differences became immediately visible but here one could not make the usual silent assumption that the Asians were still stuck in their quaint culture and needed to emulate the West and modernize.

3 http://www.harbourpublishing.com/excerpt/BecomingCanadians/267.

4 To compete with the Christian festival of Christmas, the Buddhists in Sri Lanka made a public festival out of Wesak, till then a minor event in the monastic calendar. See Turpie 2001.

5 Jørn Borup says that Shaku Sōen, one of the leaders of the New Buddhism movement in Japan, had learned of the Buddhist reform movement in Ceylon and was inspired by it to reform Japanese Buddhism (Borup 2004, 465).

Asian Reformers, Global Organizations
An Exploration of the Possibility of a "Canadian Buddhism"

ALEXANDER SOUCY

Thich Nhat Hanh delivering his first dharma talk in
Vietnam in forty years on 15 January 2005, Dình Quán
Temple near Hanoi
Photo by Joe Peters

First in India and then throughout the Asian world, Buddhism has continually adapted to the changing circumstances of time and place. Yet against the panoramic diversity of the Buddhist tradition, what may be the most sweeping change in its long history is passing unnoticed by most of the world. After fading out in the land of its birth centuries ago and teetering on the edge of twentieth-century extinction in Tibet and China, a new Buddhism is now emerging in the industrialized nations of the West.

COLEMAN, *The New Buddhism: The Western Transformation of an Ancient Tradition*

INTRODUCTION

The study of Buddhism in the West, still in a nascent stage, has so far been dominated by American scholars studying Buddhist developments in the United States. Studies of Buddhism in other countries outside Asia have been scattered.[1] As a result, "American Buddhism" has been the default term often applied to the new forms of Buddhism outside Asia. This term has been employed to designate not just Buddhism that is in America but a new Buddhism that is uniquely American, having been altered to suit Americans; a few have claimed (like Helen Tworkov 1991) that the changes have been largely made by Americans as well.

There is general agreement that Buddhism has changed in the West but the issue of who has been behind these changes is often left unstated. Frequently the language is abstract, as in "Buddhism has continually adapted to the changing circumstances of time and place" (Coleman 2001, 3), as though "Buddhism" were an independent entity that could change itself. While Asian teachers and important figures like D.T. Suzuki, Thich Nhat Hanh, and the Dalai Lama are acknowledged, it is often implied that Westerners/Americans were somehow behind the major changes that have occurred. For example, Coleman writes, "Most of the first generation of Western teachers had a firm tie to one of the three major Asian traditions, but it wasn't long before Buddhism's encounter with Western individualism led to the emergence of new approaches and new allegiances" (2001, 81), and Peter Beyer writes, "the Buddhism of Western converts has spawned new Buddhist variations in their own way just as legitimate or authentic as those of the older Buddhist regions" (2007, 451). The notorious division of Buddhists in the West into ethnic and elite, with Asians being "ethnic" and Westerners being "elite," also implies that the changes have come from Westerners/Americans. Nattier notes that the greatest accommodation to American cultural values has taken place among the "Elite Buddhists" (1998, 194) or "Import Buddhists" who are largely of European ancestry and who actively seek out Buddhism and import it (1998, 189), presumably like "Zen" decor in a Western home. Of course, there are many scholars who point out the complexity of these changes; for example, Seager acknowledges that ethnic Buddhists have also played a role in adapting Buddhism to the American setting (1999, 33–4). Nonetheless, the sense in much of the writing on Buddhism outside Asia has been that the main changes have somehow been due to Western practitioners adapting Buddhism to their cultural needs.

The study of Buddhism in Canada is very new, and so far only two book-length works have been published. Both largely avoid the question of whether there is a Canadian parallel that is distinct from "American Buddhism." The exception is Koppedrayer and Fenn's essay in *Buddhism in Canada*, in which they write, "the make-up, organisation and affiliations implicitly operating within the Buddhist groups in Ontario will work against any assertion of a Canadian Buddhism" (2006, 73).

I make the case in this chapter that it is worthwhile considering the question of whether there is something we can call "Canadian Buddhism" and do this through a critique of the notion of an American Buddhism, examining two important examples. The first is the Shambhala organization (formerly called Vajradhatu) founded by Chögyam Trungpa Rinpoche and currently led by his son Sakyong Mipham Rinpoche. The second is Thich Nhat Hanh's Order of Interbeing. Both organizations have frequently been included in volumes discussing American Buddhism and Buddhism in the West. Both also represent a marked break from the Buddhist traditions from which they emerged, having changed in ways seen as emblematic of the new forms of Buddhism attributed to Buddhism's move West. Finally, both have a strong Canadian presence, so are especially relevant to exploring the possibilities of a Canadian Buddhism.

AMERICAN BUDDHISM

Layman was the first to ask the question, "Is there a characteristically American style of Buddhism?" (1976, xiii). However, Prebish really got the discussion started with his book *American Buddhism* (1979), in which he explicitly attempted to document the transformation of Buddhism into a new form. He elaborated on Layman's question: "What she is questioning here is whether we have Asian Buddhism transplanted onto (but not necessarily into) American soil, or whether we have a new cultural amalgam that we should properly identify as 'American Buddhism'" (1979, xvii). His conclusion was that we are witnessing Buddhism in transition rather than a new, established form. Unfortunately, many scholars seized upon the compelling nature of Prebish's title – *American Buddhism* – and passed over his tempering statements.

Clearly Buddhism is practised outside Asia quite differently from the way it has traditionally been practised in Asia. Hori, in his provocative essay on whether Zen practice in America is like the celebration of Valentine's Day in Japan (i.e., changed), concludes that the very fact of relocation to America means that there is change. He notes that changes in the practices of the Rinzai Zen school in America which may appear minor in fact have a profound impact. Even such simple acts as eating and washing dishes have been changed in seemingly small, but still fundamental, ways (1998, 56–7). Nonetheless, the fact of adaptation, due in part to imperatives imposed by different cultures, norms, and institutions and in part to a more conscious attempt to make Buddhism more appealing or practicable, is not in itself sufficient grounds to proclaim a new form. Tweed may be closer in labelling the process "hybridization," pointing out that it is the norm rather than the exception in Buddhist history (2002, 19).

The debate, in fact, has never been focused on whether an American Buddhism actually exists, but rather on the contours of that Buddhism. That is, scholars have been most interested in distinguishing certain groups as contributing to an American Buddhism and others as not, or determining different subcategories of American Buddhists. The unfortunate result has often been the creation of implicitly racist distinctions, with the underlying implication that the Buddhism practised by white people is "American" and Buddhism practised by Asians is not (Tanaka 1998, 288).

In formulating these distinctions it is sometimes intimated that American Buddhism is the product of American innovation. This claim is not usually stated quite as forthrightly as in Tworkov's now famous pronouncement that "the spokespeople for Buddhism in America have been, almost exclusively, educated members of the white middle class," and that Asian Americans "so far have not figured prominently in the development of something called American Buddhism" (1991, 4). Instead, the exclusion of Asians as actors in the creation of an American Buddhism is usually implicit. For example, Jan Nattier's reinterpretation of the ethnic/elite division to include import, export, and baggage Buddhisms contains the same implication. "Elite Buddhism" (understood to be American Buddhism in that it has been changed to fit American sensitivities), is called Import Buddhism by Nattier and identified with the main groups commonly understood to be at the forefront of this cultural shift: Tibetan Buddhism, Vipassana, and Zen. Nattier is clear that "Elite Buddhism" is a product of the initiative of its participants, who have overwhelmingly been of European ancestry and economically privileged (1998, 189).

The debate on whether an American Buddhism can be said to exist at present is important in its own right but becomes more important when we turn our attention to the development of Buddhism in other countries, like Canada, and even extend our vision to the global level. I am proposing that if the existence of an American Buddhism – with its greater concentration of practitioners as well as greater number of academic studies – is not substantiated, claims of a distinctly Canadian (or Australasian, or European) Buddhism are unlikely to be convincing.

While there has been much debate about how to mark the difference between Buddhism in America and American Buddhism (in Prebish's terms, "ethnic Buddhism" and "elite Buddhism"), there has been a great deal less debate over the attributes of this American Buddhism. A prominent characteristic often cited is a decreased emphasis on monasticism and greater emphasis on lay practice.[2] A second characteristic that follows from this is a focus on the achievement of enlightenment rather than bettering this life and preparing for the next.[3] The next, which Coleman (2001, 14) asserts is the single feature that characterizes the "new Buddhism," is an accent on practice, especially meditation,[4] or as Alan Wallace puts it, "an increasing emphasis on the psychological, as opposed to the purely religious, nature of practice" (2002, 35). A number of scholars have noted that equality and democratization are more prevalent in Western Buddhism.[5] This includes Western Buddhism's stress on gender equality, as opposed to the "extreme sexism" of Asians (Coleman 2001, 15).[6] Other noted features are greater social activism or engagement,[7] and a tendency toward eclecticism.[8]

There are a number of obvious problems with the way in which the proposition of an American Buddhism has been formulated. These include the sheer variety of organizations, types of Buddhism, and culturally grounded traditions that have been grouped under the one heading; the problem of distinguishing characteristics and categories at such an early period; and the serious issues of hegemony and racism that are implicit in the identity practices of American Buddhism, which parse "ethnic" from "American" Buddhists. Other issues include criteria for identifying an American Buddhist and the blurring of categories that is already occurring as the progeny of both immigrants and converts make differentiation between "ethnic" and "elite Buddhism" more elusive. These obstacles are not insurmountable to establishing American Buddhism as a valid category. However, there are larger problems that I will approach now through two case studies which place the notion in greater jeopardy.

CASE ONE: SHAMBHALA – AN AMERICAN BUDDHISM IN CANADA

The Canadian connection with the Shambhala organization provides an interesting challenge to the notion of American Buddhism. Chögyam Trungpa Rinpoche and the organization that he founded have been central to the discussion of American Buddhism from the beginning and seem to be emblematic in some way of what is being claimed as a new tradition.[9] Layman dedicated a substantial section of a chapter on Tantrism to Chögyam Trungpa in the first book on Buddhism in America (1976, ch. 5). In his definitive work, *American Buddhism*, Prebish devoted twice as much space to Shambhala than to any other organization. In his later work, *Luminous Passage*, he continued to give a prominent place to Shambhala International in his chapter on North American Buddhist communities (1999, ch. 3). He writes, "Although the sangha of Chögyam Trungpa Rinpoche was undoubtedly the most complex and highly organized American Buddhist community of that time, a major factor in my decision to spend so many pages on the community was the huge impact that Chögyam Trungpa had made on the American Buddhist landscape" (1999, 158–9).

Shambhala Buddhism is a mainstay in the discussion of American Buddhism because it exhibits many of the features that have been used to define American Buddhism against traditional forms of Buddhism in Asia. Indeed, as Sarah Haynes points out in this volume, it was never Chögyam Trungpa's intention to replicate traditional Tibetan Buddhist forms, but to adapt them and make them meaningful to Western society. The movement is lay-based rather than monastic (Chögyam Trungpa himself felt that his monasticism was a barrier to the transmission of Buddhism to the West and so removed his robes and married). It stresses egalitarianism, gender equality, and a relatively democratic structure within the constrictions of a guru-based system. It has been innovative in finding models that would resonate with Western culture, such as the concept of warriorship and the formation of a paramilitary guard with Western-style uniforms. While personal practices are rooted in Buddhist teachings and take Asian forms, organizationally Shambhala has a very rational structure that includes a teacher training program, graduated courses, and levels with prerequisites. It is also eclectic, adopting numerous practices from Japan, especially *ikebana* (Japanese flower arrangement), calligraphy, and archery. A traditional tea house has been set up in the basement of the Shambhala Centre in Halifax to practise the Japanese tea ceremony. It has also been at the forefront in establishing businesses and institutions such as *Shambhala Sun* and *Buddhadharma* magazines, the Nalanda Translation Committee to translate Tibetan texts, a private elementary and high school in Halifax, and an accredited university in Colorado (Naropa University). Finally, as with most "American Buddhist" organizations, a central focus is meditation. Meditation instruction is the defining feature of introductory sessions and continues to be the focus at all levels. This focus emerged very early on as Chögyam Trungpa developed a form of Buddhism attractive to and suitable for his followers. This attraction was cemented by the personal charisma of Chögyam Trungpa, regarded as the embodiment of the "crazy wisdom" tradition, a style that had particular resonance with young Americans in the 1970s because of its disregard of social norms.

In short, Shambhala has gone to greater lengths than almost any other organization to invent/transform a tradition that would be appealing to and useful for Westerners.[10] However, while on the surface Shambhala Buddhism seems a perfect example of American Buddhism, there are a number of problems with this label that have yet to be articulated.

As Lynn Eldershaw explains in this volume, in the 1980s Shambhala shifted its headquarters from Colorado to Halifax, Nova Scotia, with around five hundred members of the American sangha moving to this new community.[11] The move raises an important question. Why did Chögyam Trunpa conclude that America was not the best place for the centre of his global organization? My informants, who followed Chögyam Trungpa to Canada, stress that he usually had layers of reasons and some may never be known. Nonetheless, the most prominent reason that they give echoes those found by Eldershaw: America was too violent and materialistic to develop a full Buddhist practice. An early follower who came to Halifax recalled:

Trungpa Rinpoche identified Nova Scotia as the place where our community would have its headquarters and future. We weren't exactly sure why.

He actually set up a little search committee to figure out where we should go. He felt that we would survive and be able to do more for ourselves and for others if we had a base and a centre that was in an environment that was less caught up in the extreme views that were so prevalent and emerging – and we see now even more how extreme things have become in the United States and he sensed what was going on in the United States back then in the late '70s. And as we entered the Reagan era it became even more apparent to us why this was a good idea.[12]

People I interviewed in Halifax were clear that the move was not only about escaping the United States but also about opening up new personal possibilities by coming to Canada. Another American who moved to Halifax in the 1980s and who has struggled economically to stay commented,

I think the major difference in America is a sense of speed and arrogance. The major thing that the sangha did was teach patience. Basically, you see someone who moves in, who first comes up from the States and you say, oh, he just came up from the States. After a year or two they slow down and get a little bit more humble. And therefore become a little bit more Canadian. I think it's very much a Canadian situation – maybe not in Toronto, maybe not even in Montreal, but certainly in Nova Scotia things are slower … I think there is a huge cultural difference between Canada and the United States that only an immigrant can discover. On the surface they are very similar. The arrogance [of Americans] is exemplified by the fact that Canadians didn't have a revolution and Americans had a revolution … Canada was populated by draft dodgers starting in 1776 even, and every year since. Loyalists, they called them then – people who don't want to fight, and people who aren't so arrogant that they think they are right all the time … and so there is an enormous difference. How do you get fifty Canadians out of the pool? You say, "Could you all please get out of the pool?" And you know, they just all get out of the pool! Americans would say, "What the fuck for?"[13]

Chögyam Trungpa chose a region of Canada that he felt still held traditional values and a sense of community. Nova Scotia also had a relatively small population and those coming here believed that their presence would have re-

ciprocal benefits: while they could live in an environment that was more conducive to focusing on their practice, they could also make a positive impact on
Halifax as a whole – and they have. Shambhala members have played a significant part in Symphony Nova Scotia, the Atlantic Film Festival, and the
Discovery Centre in Halifax, among other cultural initiatives (Swick 1996, 154).

It is, therefore, with some irony that we find this emblematic organization
for an "American Buddhism" headquartered in Canada rather than in the
United States. However, there is no sense that it has been made into a Canadian
Buddhism or that Shambhala Buddhism has turned out to be better suited to
Canadians. Instead, it is evident that Chögyam Trungpa felt Halifax and Nova
Scotia to be sufficiently traditional and outside the rush and materialism of
major urban centres to serve as Shambhala's capital. Colorado has remained a
major Shambhala centre as well, and Naropa University is still located there.
As one of my informants wrote to me in an email,

> There are social aspects to Shambhala Buddhism, and these differ depend-
> ing on the culture where the particular centre may be, e.g., Halifax.
> However, the meditation and contemplative practices that we are taught,
> and perform, and teach, are all the same, whether the location is L.A., NY,
> St Louis, Hamburg, London, Paris, Rome, Santiago, Washington D.C.,
> Vancouver, Toronto, Moncton, Gampo Abbey in Cape Breton, Boulder or
> Halifax, or any of the 50 or more centres around the world.
>
> Also, the meditation practices that we students of the Shambhala lineage
> perform are the same Buddhist meditation practices that are performed in
> Tibet, Sikkim, Nepal, and India in the Tibetan monasteries and practice
> centres of the Kagyu, Nyingma, Rimey and Shambhala lineages of Tibetan
> Buddhism. We found that out markedly when many of us visited the
> monasteries and found that we were doing the same things, the same way –
> just a different language.
>
> I would say emphatically that THERE IS NO AMERICAN OR CANADIAN
> BUDDHISM, at least not in the Shambhala lineage. It's all the same as Bud-
> dhism in the Tibetan Vajrayana variety. It's just that we are mostly
> American, or Canadian, or Americans moved to Canada. [emphasis his][14]

To what extent, then, can we call Shambhala Buddhism in Halifax "American Buddhism"? One problem with the label is the lack of clarity about

whether it designates a type of Buddhism particular to Americans or whether it is just an American-centric label for Buddhism in the West. This chapter questions the proposition that if there is something identifiable as "American Buddhism," which has uniquely American characteristics, then we might also legitimately look for the characteristics of a "Canadian Buddhism." The question should entice Canadians, who are generally preoccupied with national identity relative to the United States. However, the quest must, as Koppedrayer and Fenn conclude (2006, 73), be abandoned at this nascent stage due to lack of conclusive evidence.

While there have been particular historical circumstances that have shaped Buddhism in Canada, when we survey the landscape it is difficult to discern any essential difference. The overwhelming majority of non-Asian practitioners are engaged in some form of meditation-centred practice, as in the United States, Europe, and Australasia. Further, most of the organizations that are active in Canada have international affiliations that make them global rather than either American or Canadian. Shambhala was drawn to set up the headquarters of its multinational organization in Canada because Trungpa perceived qualities in Nova Scotia that he saw as conducive to establishing a society based on Buddhist values, and because he felt that the organization would thrive in a calmer location. However, the organization was maintained in the United States and most practitioners did not move to Canada. Further, the one-year anniversary celebration of Sakyong Mipham's marriage to Semo Tseyang Palmo – a marriage which had political implications of bringing together two different Tibetan noble families and strengthening ties between two associated Buddhist schools – was attended by both Shambhala Buddhists and important Tibetan monks. As I witnessed this celebration in 2007, I concluded that Shambhala was neither Tibetan Buddhism nor Western Buddhism, but something that brought together the two and transcended both.

A number of scholars have proposed laying aside the American label and instead referring to "Western Buddhism." Coleman alternates between "Western Buddhism" and "new Buddhism," both of which he distinguishes from "ethnic Buddhism of the migrant enclaves" and "traditional Asian Buddhism." Again, this solution implies that the new Buddhism is white and Western, which appears to not really be the case, as we shall see more explicitly in the second example.

CASE 2: ORDER OF INTERBEING – ETHNICS, ELITES, AND GLOBAL BUDDHISMS

The second case is the Order of Interbeing (*Tiếp Hiện*), founded by the renowned Vietnamese activist monk Thich Nhat Hanh. Likely inspired by the Chinese Buddhist reformer Taixu, Thich Nhat Hanh started to express progressive views as early as 1955 (Chapman 2007, 299–300; DeVido 2007, 257–8). He wrote about the need to unify the various Buddhist groups in Vietnam as editor of the Buddhist journal *Vietnamese Buddhism* (*Phật Giáo Việt Nam*). Encountering opposition from the Buddhist traditional establishment, Thich Nhat Hanh decided to accept a one-year fellowship at Princeton University in 1961. He then taught at Columbia University until 1963, when Buddhist unrest in central Vietnam prompted Thích Trí Quang, a leader of Vietnamese Buddhist activism, to urge his return.[15] The struggles brought about the formation of the Unified Buddhist Church of Vietnam (*Giáo Hội Phật Giáo Thống Nhất Việt Nam*) which included most Buddhist organizations in South Vietnam. However, by 1966 factions developed within the organization during a second major Buddhist uprising.[16] On one side stood Thích Trí Quang, who was a proponent of open activism, pushing for democracy and an end to American involvement. On the other stood Thích Tâm Châu, who had fled the Communists in the north in 1954 and supported both the war and American involvement (and who, incidentally, now lives in Montreal). In between stood Thich Nhat Hanh who called for a cessation to hostilities from a neutralist perspective, while working for social justice (Chapman 2007, 302; Topmiller 2002, 7–8). His lecture tour in the United States in 1966 and his book *Lotus in the Sea of Fire*, which proposed a peace plan (1967, 83–4), led to accusations that he was a Communist by the South Vietnamese Government and pro-American by the North Vietnamese Government. He concluded that it would be unsafe to return to Vietnam. Thus began his exile which finally ended in 2005 with a major homecoming accompanied by almost two hundred overseas Vietnamese and Western followers.

In 1966 Thich Nhat Hanh set up the Order of Interbeing which has developed into a global organization. It is now based at Plum Village in France but has major centres in California (Deer Park Monastery), New York State (Blue Cliff Monastery), Vermont (Green Mountain Dharma Center and Maple

Forest Monastery), the Eastern Townships of Quebec (Maple Village – Société Bouddhique les Érables). Money is being raised to build a centre in the United Kingdom. There are groups in thirty-six different countries with approximately twenty groups in Canada alone.[17] By 1998 there were five hundred monastic and lay core members, about seventy-five lay and monastic dharma teachers, and about three hundred local practice centres worldwide.

Like Chögyam Trungpa, Thich Nhat Hanh has been a prolific writer, penning more than a hundred books with at least forty in English. His central teachings revolve around the concept of mindfulness and peaceful activism which he first set out in *The Miracle of Mindfulness* and *Being Peace*, written for peace activists during the war. Their message is that one has to "be peace" in order to make peace, by practising mindfulness in the everyday activities of one's life (King 1996a, 342), a message that is reflected in his saying "I have arrived. I am home" which is used by his followers as a *gāthā* (verse) for both sitting and walking meditation.

Like Shambhala, the Order of Interbeing is a very prominent example of Western Buddhism, though it has been discussed less extensively.[18] Nevertheless, the organization and Thich Nhat Hanh's teachings exhibit a number of characteristics that would qualify it as American Buddhism according to the criteria mentioned earlier. These include a focus on meditation, secularization and ecumenism, social activism, eclecticism, empowerment of women, and an emphasis on lay practice. Most groups are lay run and the primary activities include sitting and walking meditation as well as listening to dharma talks. The stress on mindfulness as a central practice is particularly applicable for lay practitioners: the message is not to cease activity and retire but to continue being active while meditating on those actions. Thus, the practice is open to all, regardless of gender, race, or religion. Women play an active role and are prominent leaders in the organization (for example, Sister Chân Không, who has been with Thich Nhat Hanh from the beginning of the Order, and Sister Annabel Laity, who is the Abbess of the Blue Cliff Monastery in Woodstock, New York). Participation by people from other faiths is encouraged, with the understanding that mindfulness is a practice open to anyone. As Hunt-Perry and Fine put it, "Ecumenism, interfaith and 'post-denominational' connections were another hallmark of Thich Nhat Hanh's engaged Buddhism in the West in the 1980s and 1990s" (2000, 46).

Thich Nhat Hanh is often credited with introducing the term "Engaged Buddhism." With the end of the war he helped Vietnamese refugees to resettle. Since then he has been actively promoting peace, including holding retreats for Israelis and Palestinians and calling for peace in the Middle East. He held a peace walk in Los Angeles in 2005 attended by Cindy Sheehan. She had gained notoriety for setting up a peace camp outside the ranch of American president George W. Bush after her son died while fighting in Iraq.

In 2005 and again in 2007, he returned to Vietnam with the intention of healing the rift between the state-run Vietnamese Buddhist Association (*Hội Phật Giáo Việt Nam*) and the dissident Unified Buddhist Church of Vietnam (UBCV) (Chapman 2007, 306). He also intended to bring his teachings back to Vietnam. Thus, he made his return visit conditional on the Vietnamese government allowing him to bring translations of some of his books into the country (they had previously been outlawed) and to bring a sizeable group of followers from overseas. His 2007 visit focused on great chanting ceremonies for the war dead of both sides and providing support for the growing number of his followers in Vietnam.

Dorais points out that the emphasis on meditation rather than ritual has led many Vietnamese to consider Thich Nhat Hanh's organization a "watered down" version of Buddhism (2006, 128). This opinion has also been expressed to me by Vietnamese, both in Canada and in Vietnam, and runs contrary to the opinion of most Western practitioners, who feel that meditation is the central, and even essential, practice of Buddhism. Some critics have pointed out that Thich Nhat Hanh's credentials are not clear. His claim, for instance, to be part of the Trúc Lâm lineage is difficult to sustain objectively because the lineage appears to have essentially come to an end with the death of the third patriarch in 1308 CE (Nguyen 1997, 342 n49).[19]

Though Thich Nhat Hanh's organization exhibits all the hallmarks of American Buddhism, the sangha consists of both ethnic Vietnamese and Western disciples and is perhaps the best example of a Buddhist organization that straddles the ethnic-Western divide. In this regard the Order of Interbeing is a truly transnational organization that nonetheless continues to be culturally grounded in Vietnamese traditional structures and idioms (Dorais 2006, 129). Despite the inclusion of both Westerners and Vietnamese in the sangha, there remains a distance between the two communities. In many locations the Western practitioners meet separately from the Vietnamese and there is little communication between the two groups. This is the case in Ottawa, for example, and Dorais reports that in Quebec, also, most meditation retreats are held separately for Vietnamese and Westerners (2006, 129). Thus, the Order of Interbeing points to a much more international and globalized movement of Buddhism than is usually acknowledged.

GLOBALIZED BUDDHISM

The desire to be able to say that there is a form of Buddhism new (and due) to America has not adequately taken into account the process by which change has come about. In fact, most of the change attributed to Buddhism in the West first occurred in Asia, not as a way to modernize by becoming more Western, but as a way to confront the challenge of Western imperialism and Christian missionization. With Thich Nhat Hanh's Order of Interbeing, we have an organization with a global presence which fits all the criteria of an American Buddhism yet cannot credit America or Americans for its transformation. Both Shambhala and the Order of Interbeing figure prominently in the landscape of Buddhism in Canada and in America. However, while one felt compelled to relocate its "capital" to Halifax, the other has always been headquartered in France. Scholars are correct in noting that there is something new afoot, but they have been inaccurate in attributing these transformations to America. The characteristics of American Buddhism are clearly the characteristics of something much broader. Thus, it seems that the argument for a new category of American Buddhism is at the very least premature (perhaps by several hundred years), if not completely erroneous. By extension, we would be heading in the wrong direction if we looked for a Canadian Buddhism. Instead, it is more fruitful to look at how Buddhism has been spreading around the world.

The two cases we have examined challenge the notion that America and Americans are responsible for the innovation behind American/Western Buddhism. Queen has pointed out that in most cases the leaders of American Buddhism have been Asian missionaries – teachers such as D.T. Suzuki, Maezumi Roshi, Geshe Wangyal, Chögyam Trungpa, Thich Thien-an, Seung Sahn, Anagarika Dharmapala, and the Dalai Lama (1999, xv–xvi). McMahan has also noted that "The original efforts to bring Zen into a dynamic relationship with modernity and the West were undertaken not by Westerners, but by Japanese Zen Buddhists who understood the ethos of European and American intellectual and religious culture" (2002, 219). Discussions about the adaptation of Buddhism to the West have not acknowledged strongly enough that, with global organizations emanating from Asia, Westerners are recipients rather than progenitors of a new Buddhism.

The perception held by some (and reflected in the quotation at the beginning of this essay) is that the West is rescuing Buddhism from superstitious, erroneous, and misleading cultural accretions of Asian Buddhists (or, pointedly, non-Buddhist culture). That is, when discussing Buddhism with many non-Asian Buddhists, one senses that the perceived task is to scrape off the layers of culture that hide the true teachings of Siddhārtha Gautama; they see themselves at the forefront of preserving his legacy. Asian Buddhists are viewed as in dire need of a Buddhist renewal. The implication is that Westerners do *even* Asian religion better than Asians. Coleman's *The New Buddhism* is a recent and overt expression of this view: "Most importantly, like most of the new Buddhists, Shakyamuni Buddha focused unwaveringly on the struggle for liberation. In both the newest and the oldest Buddhism, the highest goal is not faith and belief, proper behavior, or ritual devotion, but the direct experience of enlightenment. Both attach great importance to the practice of meditation and both feel that liberation must spring from each individual's own life and practice, not the intercession of the supernormal beings who have assumed such great importance in some forms of Asian Buddhism" (2001, 218).

In a discussion I had in 2006 with a Canadian follower of Thich Nhat Hanh, she insisted that her Buddhism was a "practice," which she defined in opposition to "religion." Religion, she felt, was too dogmatic and hierarchical. The distinction between religion and practice is commonly drawn by Western practitioners with whom I have spoken. The ritual emphasis of most of the Buddhist traditions practised by Asian immigrants too closely resembles, it seems, the traditions that Westerners have rejected. Seen in this light, the contrast is completely understandable, though not always objectively accurate.[20] Notably, Vietnamese followers of Thich Nhat Hanh are more likely to include ritual chanting and more devotional practices into their overall Buddhist practice than are their Western counterparts.

The result of the Western transformation of Buddhism is not a culturally neutral Buddhism, but one that is in fact ethnically Western. This observation provides a very good analytical starting point. However, we can go further by putting at the forefront the fact that, in most cases, the cultural translation was done by *Asian* missionaries. The package they put together to market to the West has been successful, but does this make it a Western product?

The view that Buddhism in Asia was corrupt and in need of renewal was partly a reaction to hegemonic processes of colonialism and pressure from the West. The reaction led to Buddhist reform movements throughout Buddhist Asia in the late nineteenth and early twentieth centuries. Obeyesekere's important work illustrates how Buddhism was rationalized in Sri Lanka in response to the threat of Christian missionaries and Western colonial hegemony. A concerted effort was made at the elite level to remove "'vulgar' qualities" and make Buddhism "more 'respectable'" (Obeyesekere 1972, 62). The American Theosophist Colonel Olcott and the prominent monk Anagarika Dharmapala sought to modernize Buddhism and remove the taint of popular culture. They used such tactics as designing a Buddhist flag that could establish a sense of unitary Buddhist identity, creating a catechism that would unify (and purify) Buddhist belief, and setting up Buddhist schools modelled after missionary public schools (Obeyesekere 1972, 61). At the same time, they put forward a form of Buddhism with a distinctly Western flavour that Obeyesekere has come to call "Protestant Buddhism" (1972, 1975, 2003).

In Meiji, Japan, the reform movement was called *shin bukkyō* and was intended to be simultaneously modern, cosmopolitan, humanistic, and socially responsible, while representing the "true" or "pure" Buddhist tradition that could join the ranks of "World Religions" (Sharf 1993, 4). In China, Taixu (1889–1947) introduced the concept of *renjian fojiao*, translated as "Humanistic Buddhism," and established the foundation for later Buddhist masters such as Hsing Yun, who founded the Fo Guang Shan organization, and Cheng Yen, founder of the Tzu Chi Merit Society (Chandler 2004, 43), both of which are discussed in others chapters of this book. In Vietnam, a strong revival movement was underway by the 1920s, heavily influenced by Taixu's teachings (translated as *Nhân Gian Phật Giáo* [DeVido 2007, 252]). Components of this revival were textual orthodoxy; a rationalized, demythologized, and atheistic practice (McHale 2004, 157–64); and engagement with this world. As with other revival movements, it had a strong nationalist aspect which fused religion with the construction of national and cultural identity (McHale 2004, 157; Woodside 1976, 192). There came to be a strong stress on Zen (*Thiền* in Vietnamese), which not only fit the desire to move away from popular practices and beliefs but also more clearly emphasized orthodox ties with Chinese Ch'an lineages. The stress on Zen was bolstered by the "discovery" of historical texts which supported the claim, if read uncritically, of a Buddhist golden age of Zen in the Lý and Trần dynasties (1009–1400) (McHale 2004, 147). Cuong Tu Nguyen has persuasively argued that the Zen foundation of Vietnamese Buddhism, which some scholars put forward and which has been slavishly repeated by subsequent scholars, is a construction that does not bear out (1995, 1997). Nonetheless, Zen tradition continues to be stressed in order to claim authority both in Vietnam and within the overseas Vietnamese communities

(Soucy 2007). Thich Nhat Hanh's focus on meditative practices, egalitarianism, and social engagement – all hailed as characteristics of American/Western Buddhism – are rooted primarily in this revivalist form of Buddhism that he inherited from an elite group of monks of a generation before.[21] His bias toward Zen is characteristic of the reformist disdain of "folk" practices that resulted from Asian encounters with the West, but still should be seen as an Asian reaction rather than an American adaptation.[22]

Similarly, Robert Sharf notes that Zen in Japan was tied to the nationalist interest of *Nihonjinron* (a body of scholarship that focused on Japan's uniqueness). He points out that the Zen missionaries to the West, most famously D.T. Suzuki, were not products of traditional Zen monasteries but were lay Buddhists educated in Western secular thought and European philosophy. In response to the challenges of Western cultural dominance they asserted a spirituality that was uniquely Japanese (Sharf 1993, 34). In doing so, they accentuated the importance of Zen experience in a way that was anything but traditional (Sharf 1993, 22).

Given that the supposed characteristics of American/Western Buddhism are apparent in these earlier reform movements in Asia, dating from the nineteenth and first half of the twentieth century, it seems presumptuous to call the changes we see in Buddhism practised in the West either American or Western. Although reforms occurred partially in response to Western colonialism in Asia, they were nonetheless mostly exported to America rather than developed by Americans for Americans, as claimed by Tworkov, implied in the dichotomy of ethnic vs elite, and sometimes repeated to me by a number of my Western Buddhist informants. In Asia reformed Buddhism continues to exist alongside more traditional forms and has the very characteristics that have been used to define American Buddhism.[23]

Teachers who presented Buddhism to Americans (and Canadians) were often members of these progressive movements and were convinced that this was the true Buddhism: they were the activists and often the ones most attuned to the West. Consequently, as Sharf notes in the Zen context, the Buddhism presented to Western audiences was largely a narcissistic reflection of their own culture (1993, 39). Meanwhile, these reformers remained a small minority in their countries of origin. This is particularly true in Vietnam, where Buddhism in practice reflects more devotional forms and is often concerned with easing suffering in personal lives here and now rather than aiming toward a better rebirth or enlightenment. In Taiwan progressivist movements have been more successful, and there is some evidence that they are starting to have more of an impact in Vietnam, almost a century after the revival movement began (Soucy 2007).

Thus, it appears that not only have leaders and progenitors of so-called Western Buddhist traditions been mostly Asians, but the "American Buddhism" that they introduced to Americans is not, at least directly, grounded in American cultural idioms. Instead, it is based on Asian reforms born partially out of experiences of colonialism, Western military and hegemonic uses of power, and the threat of Christian missionaries. Americans have been mostly recipients of an Asian-born reform Buddhism rather than active contributors to a new form of Buddhism. This is not to say that the move to the West has not had attendant changes, but the most profound changes – those that have been listed as the main characteristics of American Buddhism – preceded Buddhism's move west.

Studies of Buddhism in the West appear to have generally followed a model of unidirectional East to West transmission of Buddhism to North America. As we have seen, it is problematic to presume that Western groups are specifically American and that their uniqueness is at all connected with the move to the West. There has always been an exchange which undermines the adequacy of this model. Moreover, Thich Nhat Hanh's example further problematizes this East/West model of transmission. Thich Nhat Hanh has refined his brand of Buddhism and has taken it back to Vietnam in 2005 and 2007, where it has found a mostly welcoming audience, though questions of authenticity are frequently posed. At the same time, in Vietnam today Buddhist leaders like Thích Thanh Từ are building meditation-based Buddhist practices that look back to an idealized version of a Vietnamese Zen called Trúc Lâm (Soucy 2007), also evoked by Thich Nhat Hanh (Hunt-Perry and Fine 2000, 37). Thích Thanh Từ's teachings seem to reflect the same influences as Thich Nhat Hanh, as well as the changing requirements of overseas Vietnamese, who have been exposed to Western forms of Buddhism. Thus, a model of simple transmission from East to West and subsequent Western transformation ignores the dynamic exchange that has been taking place in the last two centuries.

CONCLUSION

This essay began by testing the premise that there is a new category of Buddhism, often labelled American Buddhism, for if an American Buddhism exists, then perhaps we should start looking for a Canadian Buddhism as well.

However, the difficulties with the label render it unsatisfactory. They range from the presumptions that Americans make of their own uniqueness, the wide range of types of Buddhism, and the fact that Buddhism was changed primarily by Asians rather than Americans, often prior to being introduced to the West. Thus, the project of identifying a Canadian Buddhism dies with the devalidation of "American Buddhism."

Clearly, we have to move away from a distinction between Western Buddhists and Asian Buddhists, with the former being considered "elite" and the latter "traditional" or "ethnic." Hori (in this volume), along with Fields (1998), Lin (1999, 134–6) and Tanaka (1998, 287–9), rightly points out that there are racist overtones in this division that imply that the Buddhist practice of Asian Buddhists has been degraded by cultural modifications, and that American (or Western) Buddhists have managed to scrape off the thick cultural crust and get to the "original" Buddhism as it was intended by Siddhārtha Gautama – the historical Buddha. This view is inherited in part from Asian Buddhist reform movements that were responding to Western colonialism and the orientalist gaze. It is also a cultural product of the West which, in its religious discourses, has been particularly concerned with orthodoxy, authenticity, and textual authority.

All of this is not to say that there have been no changes with the transmission of Buddhism to the West. As Tweed puts it, "There is hybridity all the way down" (2002, 19). Change is inevitable and Buddhism has certainly changed in the West. However, the question that this essay has tried to answer is not whether change has taken place but whether the search for a Canadian Buddhism would be a worthwhile or practical endeavour in the first place.

My emphatic conclusion is that it would not. The characteristics that have been used to point to an American/Western Buddhism are much more complicated than can be explained by a simple model of East-West transmission followed by a Western transformation. Instead, all evidence seems to indicate that the most dramatic changes came about in response to Western colonialism and the challenge of missionaries, and actually occurred in Asia prior to transmission to the West. In this sense, the encounter with the West did transform Buddhism, but the transformation did not take place by virtue of or for Westerners, but occurred prior to the transmission to the West. The Buddhist missionaries who brought Buddhism to the West had been heavily impacted by Asian Buddhist revival movements. Hybridization has been an essential part of Buddhism, as with all religions, from the very beginning, and we need to resist the temptation to think that there are pure forms like "Chinese Buddhism" and "Japanese Buddhism," much less "American Buddhism." Adaptation has been continuous and borrowing has been ongoing since the beginning. Therefore, in the study of Buddhism in Canada, a greater contribution could be made by problematizing categories and definitions while shifting focus toward processes of global interactions. It is particularly fitting that Canadian scholars, with our now historical stress on multiculturalism, examine how these global transformations are taking place in a non-linear fashion through cross-cultural exchange, diasporic-homeland connections, and enormous breakthroughs in global communication.

NOTES

1 Notable works on Western, non-American Buddhism are Cristina Rocha's recent work on Buddhism in Brazil (2006), the collection edited by Bruce Matthews on Buddhism in Canada (2006), Janet McLellan's work on five Buddhist communities in Toronto (1999), David Kay's work on Zen and Tibetan Buddhism in Britain, Sally McAra's work on Buddhism in New Zealand (2007a), Robert Bluck's work on Buddhism in Britain (2006), as well as sections of Stuart Chandler's study of the Fo Guang Shan Buddhist organization (2004). There are also a scattering of shorter essays, such as Martin Baumann's on Buddhism in Europe (2002a), Michelle Spuler's on Buddhism in New Zealand and Australia (2002), Michel Clasquin's on Buddhism in South Africa, Frank Usarski's on Buddhism in Brazil (2002), and Lionel Obadia's on Buddhism in Israel (2002). In addition, a number of essays have been published in the online journal *The Journal of Global Buddhism* going back to 2000. It has featured essays on Europe in general (Koné 2001, Offermanns 2005), Britain (Bell 2000, Bluck 2004), France (Obadia 2001), Russia (Ostrovsaya 2004), Brazil (Rocha 2000, Shoji 2003), Australia (Barker 2007, Bubna-Litic and Higgins 2007, McAra 2007b, Metraux 2003), and New Zealand (Kemp 2007).

2 Coleman (1999, 92; 2001, 13); Fields (1992, 371; 1998, 201, 202); Wallace (2002, 35); Wetzel (2002).

3 Coleman (2001, 13); Fields (1998, 204); Layman (1976, 263).

4 Coleman (1999, 92; 2001, 14); Fields (1998, 200, 202); Fronsdal (2002, 285); Prebish (1979, 191; 1999, 63), and Wallace (2002, 35). Tanaka also includes chanting in the overall characteristic of "practice," particularly in reference to the Soka Gakkai (1998, 290–2). Queen has used a broader characteristic of "pragmatism," by which he means "an emphasis on *ritual practice or observance* (particularly meditation, chanting, devotional and ethical activities) and its benefit to the practitioner, with a concomitant de-emphasis of beliefs, attitudes, or states of mind" (emphasis his) (1999, xix).

5 Coleman (1999, 92); Fields (1998, 201, 202); Kornfield (1988); Tanaka (1998, 289–90); Wallace (2002, 35), Queen (1999, xviii).

6 Coleman (2001, 15); Fields (1992, 371; 1998, 202); Prebish (1999, 75–9); Seager (1999, 200); Simmer-Brown (2002, 312).

7 Fields (1998, 199, 202); Queen (2002, 324); Tanaka (1998, 292–4); Queen (1999, xix); Wallace (2002, 35).

8 Coleman (1999, 92; 2001, 16); Prebish (1979, 182–3).

9 For example, the conference proceedings *Buddhism in America: Proceedings of the First Buddhism in America Conference*, edited by Rapaport and Hotchkiss (especially Bercholz [1998] and Seonaidh [1998]); Seager's *Buddhism in America* (1999, chap. 8); Williams and Queen's collected work *American Buddhism: Methods and Findings in Recent Scholarship* (especially Goss [1999]); Coleman's *The New Buddhism: The Western Transformation of an Ancient Tradition* (2001, 73–7); and Prebish and Baumann's collected work *Westward Dharma: Buddhism beyond Asia* (especially Seager [2002, 111–12], and Matthews [2002, 126, 133]).

10 While the structure is very Western in its design, there is nonetheless a retention of the authority of the guru. The sheer charisma of Chögyam Trungpa is likely responsible for persuading his followers to submit to a religious authoritarianism that many thought they were leaving behind with the traditions of their upbringing (with many coming from Catholic and Jewish traditions.) It remains to be seen whether Sakyong Mipham Rinpoche will be as successful. My impression from conversations with long-standing Shambhalians is that they still hold Chögyam Trungpa as their guru and look at Sakyong Mipham quite differently.

11 For more on the move, see Swick (1996).

12 Interview in Halifax, December 2005.

13 Interview in Halifax, May 2006.

14 Email sent by an interviewee in August 2006.

15 Those events included the self-immolation of the monk Thích Quảng Đức and a *coup d'état* that was brought about partly due to mass Buddhist protests and resulted in the assassination of President Ngô Đình Diệm.

16 Topmiller documents the Buddhist peace movement during this period and deals to some extent with the various factions that formed (2002). In contrast to 1963, the Buddhist uprising of 1966 was unsuccessful.

17 According to http://www.iamhome.org.

18 A chapter is devoted to Thich Nhat Hanh in Queen's edited volume (Hunt-Perry and Fine 2000). Prebish mentions him in passing in his later work on American Buddhism (1999, 82, 108, 251), as do Coleman (2001, 88–90) and Fields (1992, 377–8), while Seager

has a more substantial section devoted to him (1999, 202–7). He is also mentioned throughout the essays in the collected works on American Buddhism/Buddhism in America by Prebish and Baumann (2002a), Prebish and Tanaka (1998), Williams and Queen (1999).

19 Significantly, he is not the only one to lay claim to Trúc Lâm Buddhism. Thích Thanh Tu' is making extensive use of the symbolic value of Trúc Lâm in order to create a Zen Buddhist movement in Vietnam (see Soucy 2007).

20 For example, in a celebration of the one-year anniversary of the marriage of the leader of Shambhala, Sakyong Mipham Rinpoche, high ritual rather than any search for liberation was prominent in the opening ceremony held on the front lawn of Saint Mary's University, where the multi-day events were held.

21 Thich Nhat Hanh intimates as much in *Vietnam: Lotus in a Sea of Fire* (1967, chap. 2).

22 His bias, for example, can be seen in *Lotus in a Sea of Fire*: "In the history of Vietnamese Buddhism ... [Zen] is by far the most important sect" (1967, 4). While he considers Zen important, he is forced to admit two pages later that it is not the form of Buddhism that is most widely practised in Vietnam: "The small village pagoda often does not have a well-qualified Zen Master, since most people, and in particular the villagers, cannot practise Zen as taught in the monastery" (Thich Nhat Hanh 1967, 6).

23 Modernized Chinese Buddhist movements in Taiwan, such as Fo Guang Shan, Tzu Chi, and Dharma Drum, similarly, 1) are strongly lay oriented; 2) are very "this worldly"; 3) emphasize practice (though the focus is much less on meditation and more on ritual, and Tzu Chi has no practice outside its charity work); 4) are not democratically organized, but have a strong emphasis on women's equal participation (e.g., Fo Guang Shan has an "affirmative action" program for men).

PART TWO Histories and Overviews

Looking East
Japanese Canadians and Jodo Shinshu Buddhism
1905–1970

TERRY WATADA

Sasaki Senju and his wife, Tomie, 1905.
First Buddhist priest in Canada
Photo courtesy of the Japanese Canadian
Cultural Centre Archives

The effort to establish Jodo Shinshu, "True Pure Land" Buddhism, in Canada began not so much as an expression of religious zeal but rather out of a need on the part of Japanese immigrants to preserve Japanese culture and transmit that culture to their children and their children's children. As the trials and tribulations of daily life increased, however, the Buddhist church[1] became more than a bastion for the Japanese language and Japanese traditions: it evolved into a sanctuary of comfort and reassurance. As the government moved repeatedly to restrict the rights and freedoms of Japanese Canadians, policies culminating in the evacuation and internment of the war years and attempts at expulsion and forced repatriation that followed the end of World War II,[2] Shin Buddhists adhered to their religion and practised its precepts wherever they found themselves. Out of pure determination, Jodo Shinshu devotees and their churches survived and prospered. The history of Shin Buddhism in Canada is an account of how various congregations and priests overcame adversity, racism, and isolation to carve out a place for the religion in this country.

BEGINNINGS: 1905–1925

The earliest Japanese immigrants to Canada, arriving at the end of the nineteenth century, had what Ken Adachi characterizes as "an astonishingly high rate of mobility, occupational as well as geographic, spending years without definite occupations, shifting from job to job, place to place" (1976, 28). By 1905, however, the *issei* – the first generation of Japanese in Canada – had established a foothold in British Columbia: they had entered such primary industries as lumbering, fishing, mining, and farming; they had established a

"Japan Town" in Vancouver's east end with residences, community organizations, and Japanese-owned-and-operated businesses; and they had begun to
raise families – the first *nisei* (or second-generation Japanese Canadian) had
been born in 1889. The *issei*, naturally enough, began to be concerned about
their children's upbringing.

On the one hand, some members of the community pushed for assimilation;
conversion to Christianity was presented as a means of achieving that goal. In
1896, Shinkichi Tamura,[3] a successful businessman and banker, joined with
Reverend Goro Kaburagi in establishing the Japanese Methodist Church in Vancouver; in the same year, Tamura and Kaburagi began publishing the community's first Japanese-language newsletter, the *Bankuba Shuho* (Vancouver Weekly
Report). In 1903, the *Bankuba Shuho* became a daily newspaper and was rechris-
tened the *Kanada Shinpo* (Canada Press). Kaburagi must have been bolstered
by the presence of Christian missions in Victoria and Vancouver; together,
Kaburagi and the missionaries worked to convert the Japanese, preaching from
the pulpit and in editorials that to be Christian was to be Canadian, appealing
to the understanding that Christianity represented Western civilization. The
Christian missions, which provided help to Japanese immigrants in the form of
English classes and interpreters, employment agents, and legal aid, may also
have benefited from the *issei*'s sense of obligation: "The missionary comes to the
door and in very polite Japanese invites the *Issei* mother to a tea at the church.
There she sits around and talks to some of her neighbours. As she is leaving, the
missionary politely expresses the wish to see her again. And the *Issei* mother,
having accepted his hospitality, feels obligated to attend the church" (Adachi
1976, 112). By the 1930s the United Church formed, following the amalgamation of the Methodist and Congregationalist Churches in 1925, and claimed
4,789 Japanese members, with some of the *issei* sending their children to the
Christian church to be taught moral values.

On the other hand, despite the success of this proselytization, a good 68 per
cent of the Japanese preferred to be known as Buddhist, the majority identifying themselves as Jodo Shinshu Buddhists. They saw Buddhism as a link to
Japan and an excellent tool for teaching their children obedience to the em-
peror, their teachers, their parents, and their elder brothers and sisters. Lay
Buddhists took on leadership roles in the community. Hatsutaro Nishimura,
for instance, held dharma talks every Sunday in his living room, where he had
pinned a scroll portrait of the Buddha to the wall. But with the growing interest in passing Buddhism on to the *nisei*, and the additional need for someone

trained in performing religious rites for the dead, these informal services were increasingly felt to be inadequate. On 10 October 1904, at the residence of Tadaichi Nagao, discussions began around the establishment of a Buddhist church in Canada.

The Nagao committee formed a Dobo-daikai, or Fellow Travellers Conference, resolving to build a church and to request that the Nishi Hongwanji send a priest to Canada.[4] On 12 October 1905, Reverend Sasaki Senju and his wife, Tomie, arrived in Vancouver. Reverend Sasaki was born in Fukui, not far from Kyoto. He had travelled extensively, having previously been appointed to a post in Singapore and toured India. He quickly got down to business. On 26 October, Sasaki delivered a talk on the Buddha at Vancouver City Hall. He then visited every sawmill in the Vancouver area to advertise his arrival and solicit donations. By March 1906, he and the Foundation Committee had raised $5,568, enough to purchase a house in Vancouver. This property, 32 Alexander Street, was renovated and became a centre of activity for Jodo Shinshu Buddhism. The number of active Shin Buddhists increased rapidly, and meeting places were quickly established in Sapperton, Barnet, and Port Moody. By 1907, the total number of members of the congregation reached 650. In the same year, the city was rocked by the Anti-Asiatic Riot.

The 1907 riot, instigated by the Asiatic Exclusion League, caused extensive damage to Vancouver's Chinese and Japanese neighbourhoods. Although the rioters were rebuffed and defeated by Japanese residents of the Powell Street area, the riot itself reflected growing anxiety on the part of the city's white communities over the economic success of East Asian and South Asian immigrants. The federal government, interested in pacifying white communities on the west coast, came to a "Gentleman's Agreement" with Japan, sharply curtailing the number of Japanese labourers permitted to enter Canada each year. Japanese women, however, were not similarly restricted, and so the agreement had the effect of encouraging large numbers of women to immigrate, many through the so-called picture-bride system of arranged marriage. The unintended result of the government's effort to curtail the growth of the Japanese Canadian population was thus a rapid increase in the birth rate and a dramatic expansion of the Japanese community.

On 21 April 1909, British Columbia officially recognized Jodo Shinshu as a religion. The following year, the Shin Buddhist congregation in Vancouver sold the Alexander Street property, which continued to serve as a Japanese language school, and bought a property on two adjoining lots at 1603 Franklin Street, located in the part of the city known as "Heaps," close to the Pacific National Exhibition grounds and outside the Japanese enclave. This spot was chosen in anticipation of the natural growth of the Japanese community over time. The dedication service for the new church was held on 25 September 1911.

With the opening of the church, Reverend Sasaki saw his work come to completion and decided to return to Japan. Unfortunately, subsequent events nearly undid all the work that had gone into establishing a Shin community in Canada. Reverend Sasaki was succeeded by Reverend Katō Gungai but his tenure did not last long; following complaints from members of the community over his handling of financial matters, Reverend Katō was ordered by the Nishi Hongwanji to return to Japan in 1913. He was replaced by Reverend Junichi Shigeno. To the community's shock, however, Reverend Katō defied orders, remaining in Vancouver and working to discredit Reverend Shigeno by spreading gossip about his "libertine" behaviour.[5] Reverend Katō's activities eventually led to a schism in the community: in 1921, Reverend Shigeno's detractors established a new church at 326 Jackson Street, while his supporters stayed at the Franklin Street church. The splinter church, calling itself the Canada Bukkyokai (Canada Buddhism Society), quickly gained official recognition from the Nishi Hongwanji and from the provincial government, which empowered it to officially suspend Reverend Shigeno.[6]

The split lasted more than three years, but ultimately the community could not tolerate such divided loyalties. Movements toward reconciliation were undertaken, and in February 1925, the province's three Japanese-language newspapers[7] reported that the two churches had merged.

UNCERTAIN TIMES: 1925–1941

In the late 1920s and 1930s, employment for Japanese Canadians became diversified. Although the British Columbia legislature continued to pass draconian and racist laws designed to limit opportunities for Japanese seeking employment in the province, members of the community were increasingly able to create jobs for themselves by establishing their own businesses – opening Japanese owned-and-operated lumber camps, and buying and developing farmland.

The Buddhist church also prospered during this period. In 1929 the first Shin Buddhist church outside British Columbia was established in the town of Raymond, Alberta. By the mid-1930s, British Columbia itself was home to ten Buddhist churches.

The development of Shin Buddhist institutions in Canada was checked in part by the concerns of some in the larger Japanese Canadian community. S. Yoshida, a spokesman for the Christian members of the community, recalls in Ken Adachi's *The Enemy That Never Was*, "Almost all of the Japanese immigrants who came to Steveston in the early days were Buddhists. When a large number of them … first proposed to erect a Buddhist temple … I objected … for I thought that erecting a temple and spreading out this religion in the community might create unnecessary suspicion and fear on the part of the lower classes of white Canadians … the temple was postponed until 1928 when the Japanese decided that the adoption of Buddhism should not necessarily be inharmonious to the Canadian people" (Adachi 1976, 114–15).

Shin Buddhists responded to this concern by self-consciously "Christianizing" their Buddhist practice. Temples were referred to as churches; religious leaders were referred to as priests, ministers, or reverends. In the late 1920s, Reverend Takunen Nishimoto (who had replaced Reverend Shigeno in the Vancouver church) began running a Buddhist Sunday school, and while some objected to this as smacking of Christian-style proselytization, its popularity convinced members of its value. As racial tensions mounted in the early 1940s, this "Christianization" process intensified: "The altar of the Buddhist temple with its lotus flowers, candles, and icons of the Amida Buddha came to be housed in an auditorium containing pews, hymn books and organs in the Christian manner. The kindergarten was adopted … Moreover Buddhists adopted Sunday services, Sunday schools and societies paralleling those found in Christian churches. The Buddhist children even sang hymns such as 'Buddha loves me, this I know / For the *sutra* tells me so'" (Adachi 1976, 114). These changes were seen as a way of appeasing the public at large, and of appealing to the *nisei*, who wanted to be more "Canadian."

The development of Shin Buddhism in Canada was also checked, however, by the fact that priests were a scarce commodity. The federal government imposed strict limitations on the number of priests who could enter the country, and on how long they could stay. For the few priests allowed into Canada, this meant taking on the burdensome duty of administering to all the needs of all the churches; they were in constant demand and forced to travel extensively. For the far-flung Shin Buddhist communities, this meant that individual priests came and went in rapid succession, not only because of federal immigration requirements, but also because of the high rate of burn-out. As the churches in smaller centres grew, most became independent of the Vancouver church, and began lobbying for resident priests of their own.

On 20 June 1933, the first move toward creating a Canadian Buddhist infrastructure was made with the establishment of the Buddhist Churches of Canada (BCC), a network of churches with its head offices in Vancouver. The BCC would oversee all ministry affairs and establish a supervisory office to tend to these affairs, including appointing priests for all the churches, coordinating education materials, training lay leaders and Sunday school teachers, and setting up a foundation to raise funds for the churches.

The 1930s also saw the second-generation *nisei* entering adolescence and young adulthood, and the consequent growth of the Bussei or Young Buddhists Association (YBA). By 1941, YBA membership had reached over eight hundred. The YBA was for the most part a social organization, but members did deal with religious and social concerns, especially issues related to racism. In 1941, for example, a conference was held in Victoria over the Thanksgiving weekend to discuss "the problems *nisei* face in the world." These problems included finding employment and expanding career opportunities, and reconciling the demands made by their parents seeking to preserve Japanese cultural identity with Western norms and expectations. The same year, the *nisei* acquired a new voice within the church: after three years of study and training at Ryūkoku University in Kyoto, Reverend Kenryu Tsuji, the first *nisei* priest, arrived back in Canada in October 1941. He left on what turned out to be the last boat that would sail from Japan to Canada; Japan entered World War II on 7 December 1941.

EVACUATION, INTERNMENT, AND THE AFTERMATH: 1942–1946

During World War I, Japan had been an ally of England, Canada, and the United States, although very few *issei* living in Canada had been permitted to serve in the military.[8] But with the approach of World War II, the church became more and more mindful of its increasingly complicated position. The church had celebrated the marriage of the Gomonshu[9] (Head Abbot) in Japan in 1937 and held a memorial service for Japanese soldiers who died in Manchuria in 1938. But many in the congregation, especially *nisei* and young *issei*, wanted to join the Canadian war effort[10] and affirm their Canadian citizenship; the Bussei Renmei (Buddhist Young Person's Association) had already sent a telegram to Ottawa asserting its loyalty to Canada. Unfortunately, politicians in British Columbia continued nonetheless to push the federal government to do something about the "enemy aliens" – including those "aliens" who were Canadian citizens.

The internment began with the War Measures Act, invoked in 1941, and several orders-in-council enacted in January and February 1942. First, all able-bodied men of Japanese ancestry between the ages of eighteen and forty-five were forced to move at least one hundred miles from the British Columbia coast; most were sent to work on road camps in the Rockies. This was followed by notices to the elderly, the sick, women, and children to evacuate the coast starting on 26 February 1942. At the beginning of March, the British Columbia Security Commission was established to plan, supervise, and direct the expulsion. Property belonging to these "enemy aliens" was entrusted to the Custodian of Enemy Alien Property as a "protective measure only."

The Vancouver Buddhist Church had been shut down following the service on Sunday, 7 December 1941. Although British Columbia politicians and journalists had argued, some rabidly, that Buddhism was a major obstacle to assimilation, the federal government did not focus its gaze on the Buddhist community in particular. The Security Commission did, however, initially decide to organize the evacuation and internment around religion, which seemed the easiest way to divide the detained into groups. This plan was abandoned for two reasons: first, for the detainees at a single camp to share the same religion was seen as potentially giving rise to a sense of solidarity among the interned and, consequently, as a catalyst for activism; second, the sheer number of Buddhist detainees made it impossible to intern them all in a single location.

Japanese Buddhists themselves, however, were concerned that they stay together: Terrie Komori recalls, "The Roman Catholics had picked out Greenwood and the United Church had picked out Kaslo, and I suppose some of the members were apprehensive about where they were going."[11] The first wave of Buddhists was sent to Sandon, a deserted mining town some five hundred miles from Vancouver, between the Selkirk and Purcell mountain ranges. The town was in the middle of a steep valley, with its buildings creeping up the sides of the mountains. It enjoyed only two or three hours of sunlight a day. Detainees waiting in the holding camps in Hastings Park were told that it was "a land of perpetual night, a mere ravine caught between two mountain precipices where men dared not breathe, lest their very breaths turn to ice" (Adachi 1976, 256). After Sandon was full, evacuees were interned elsewhere – in Tashme, Lemon Creek, Kaslo. By the fall of 1942, internees began to establish relatively "normal" lives in the camps. Reverend Tsuji travelled up and down the Slocan Valley, holding services and tending to the needs of the many Buddhists interned there. Toshio Mori remembers:

> There were many young Buddhist members there, both in Sandon and in the Slocan Valley. In Sandon, I remember the first Bon Odori [Obon Dance]. This was soon after we settled in that town, July of 1942 ... The men built a large platform in the centre of the town and the girls came down from the top of a hill, dancing to the music blaring from the P.A. system. They danced around the platform and soon everyone joined in the *odori*. It was a time to celebrate, and despite everything terrible happening to us, we could still follow the teachings of the Buddha.[12]

With the end of the war approaching, the British Columbia Security Commission and the federal government began the process of dispersing the internees. In 1942, Japanese Canadian-owned farms had begun to be leased and sold, without consultation with the owners. In 1943, the Custodian of Enemy Alien Property had been given permission to sell or dispose of the confiscated belongings of the internees. In 1945, the camps were closed and the internees were given an ultimatum: repatriate to Japan or resettle east of the Rockies. No-one was to return to the west coast. The Christian churches instituted resettlement and employment programs to assist internees headed to eastern Canada, and many young Buddhists sought this help. Thus, the end of World War II saw the resurgence of the Japanese Canadian community, despite biased mistreatment and reallocation of their property, and the spread of Buddhism across Canada due to discriminatory resettlement policies.

THE POSTWAR YEARS

Alberta

There had been a Japanese Canadian presence in Alberta since 1903. Most early immigrants had settled in and around Raymond, in the southern part of the province. The first Buddhist church outside British Columbia had been established in Raymond in 1929, with Reverend Shingo Nagatomi arriving in 1930. The congregation had thrived despite the hardships of the Dirty Thirties.

The small community of Japanese Canadians in Alberta was not forced into internment during the war but they were subject to RCMP investigation and harassment, and the Raymond church adopted an attitude of caution, making it a policy to keep a low profile, abolishing official meetings, and stripping the church of anything that looked Japanese. However, as a result of a British Columbia Security Commission directive to allow families to stay together if they were willing to settle in Alberta, the area was inundated with Buddhists from British Columbia, in numbers far too great to be accommodated by the existing church. Many priests had already been deported, and so the Raymond church had to petition the RCMP to allow a new priest to serve the new congregations settling in the towns outside Lethbridge. Reverend Yutetsu Kawamura and family returned to Raymond from Haney-Hammond, British Columbia, in 1942. He had first served the Raymond church from 1934 to 1940. One month after Reverend Kawamura's return, Reverend Shinjo Ikuta arrived. Both ministers initially worked as labourers on the sugar beet farms, holding services on Sunday. After several months, Reverend Kawamura moved with his family to Picture Butte, while Reverend Ikuta became the centre of the Raymond church's activities.

After the war, Raymond naturally became a magnet for the exiled Japanese Canadians who had chosen resettlement over repatriation. The congregation grew quickly because of this second influx of new arrivals. According to a 1946 RCMP report, the total number of Japanese Canadians in Alberta that year was four thousand; three thousand of that number had been displaced from the West Coast.

Several Buddhist artifacts from abandoned churches in British Columbia were brought to Raymond, and this may have caused controversy in the larger Japanese Canadian community. In 1946, some members of the Japanese Christian church began a campaign of persecution against the Buddhists, arguing that all Japanese Canadians must give up what they called "Japanese nationalistic ways," including speaking Japanese, learning martial arts, and practising Buddhism: "through the acceptance of Christianity," they insisted, "the Japanese will find themselves accepted as an integral part of Canadian society" (Ichikawa 1993, 24). Unfortunately, the federal government responded by ordering the deportation of the then-six Japanese priests living in Canada.

The Raymond Buddhists reacted quickly to the news of Reverend Ikuta's deportation order: according to an RCMP report of 21 June 1946, the order "threw the Buddhist executive of Raymond into a flurry of activity and a party under J. Sawada of Raymond went to Lethbridge on the fifth of June where they engaged the services of a lawyer ... as a result of which telegrams were sent to Ottawa to stop the deportation."[13] With the help of W. Baker, chairman of the Sugar Beet Growers Association, and Senator William A. Buchanan, the congregation managed to gain a one-year extension of the permits for both Reverend Ikuta and Reverend Kawamura, to be reviewed and renewed annually. The other four priests were in fact deported. Reverend Tsuji, the first *nisei* priest and, of course, a Canadian citizen safe from the threat of deportation, moved from Sandon, British Columbia to Toronto, where he would go on to establish that city's first Buddhist church.

During the deportation crisis, the BCC, which had been disbanded during the war, was re-established in Raymond under the name the Buddhist Foundation of Canada (BFC). The BFC's purpose, as an umbrella organization, was to raise money and oversee all the churches in Canada. With the scarcity of priests and the growing number of new churches, the BFC designated four *kyōku*, or administrative and electoral districts in Canada: Eastern Canada (Toronto, Hamilton, and Montreal), Manitoba (Winnipeg), Alberta (Raymond, Coaldale, and others), and British Columbia (Kelowna and New Denver). The BFC also set about organizing a lay priest system to alleviate the burden of travel for the few remaining ordained priests. All activities of the BFC churches were subject to the approval of the bishop of the Buddhist Churches of America.

From the 1940s on into the 1970s, Buddhism flourished in southern Alberta. Churches sprang up in Picture Butte, Taber, Rosemary, Coaldale, Calgary, and Lethbridge. While thriving, however, the community also endured a schism that the Nishi Hongwanji came to refer to as "the Alberta Problem." The situation arose from strains and personal disputes within the community including disagreements about the administration of religious leadership. It spilled over into other arenas, including the 1965 decision to build a Japanese garden in Lethbridge as a Canadian Centennial Project. The garden, called the Nikka Yuko, or Japanese Friendship Garden, was supported by Reverend Kawamura, and many objected to his involvement in the project. Reverend Kawamura himself has commented that "some people thought that I would be coming around asking for money for the Japanese garden. Emotions were so high that some people threatened to kill me."[14] Although much of the drive behind this project was motivated by the desire to attract more tourists to the city, controversy accompanied speculation about other motives for the creation of the garden.[15] As a result of various tensions and personal disputes, the Alberta churches split into factions: the Raymond, Rosemary, and Coaldale churches and the Southern Alberta Sunday School Teachers League supported Reverend Yutetsu Kawamura and his son, Reverend Leslie Kawamura, while the Lethbridge, Taber, and Picture Butte churches opposed them. Reverend Kawamura and his supporters officially broke with the organizing body for the Alberta churches, the Alberta *kyōku* (or Alberta Parish), and formed the Honpa Buddhist Church of Alberta. The Honpa churches, suffering a lack of priests, appealed to the Nishi Hongwanji, but the Hongwanji administration wanted the schism resolved, since they believed that Alberta could not support two Buddhist organizations. And they were right: many churches suffered acrimonious divisions during this period. Attendance fell immediately and rapidly in many of the churches; at one monthly meeting, the Taber Buddhist Church had only three members in its congregation. In 1969, the Coaldale church elected to return to the Alberta *kyōku*, but its congregation was split over this issue, and half of its members remained with the Honpa; lawyers were brought in to dictate the division of the congregation's holdings. In the late 1960s, with the establishment of the Lethbridge Honpa Church of Alberta, forty-five families out of 160 moved to the Lethbridge Buddhist Association. Official mediators sent from the Nishi Hongwanji tried and failed to reach a resolution. Nonetheless, while the "Alberta Problem" continued to grow, both the Alberta Buddhist Association and the Honpa Buddhist Church of Alberta survived the 1960s and 1970s, finally coming to an uneasy truce with the formation of the Buddhist Federation of Alberta in 1982.[16]

British Columbia

Although Jodo Shinshu churches had been established in British Columbia during the war and shortly thereafter in Kamloops and Sandon, none stood on the lower mainland until many years after the end of the war. Only with the formal lifting of the War Measures Act in 1949 could Japanese Canadians freely return to the west coast and re-establish their institutions. By the spring of 1951, some six hundred Japanese Canadians had come back to Vancouver. That summer, the first Obon, or commemoration of the ancestors, was held in Vancouver since before the internment; the festival was followed by a general meeting of Buddhists. The service and the meeting were sponsored by the Japanese Canadian Citizens Association and held at the old language school on Alexander Street. At that moment, Jodo Shinshu began its resurgence in British Columbia.

Throughout the 1950s, Buddhism flourished in pockets across the province. By 1966, Reverend Ikuta had taken on the responsibility for the whole region, serving not only Vancouver and Steveston, but also Kamloops, Kelowna, and Vernon. He also visited Greenwood, Midway, Slocan, and New Denver twice each year. What followed was a period of rebirth for Buddhism in British Columbia, lasting well into the 1970s. Its strong presence in that province served as an anchor for the religion as it spread across Canada.

Saskatchewan, Northern Ontario, and Manitoba

A handful of Buddhists settled in Saskatchewan after the war, most near Moose Jaw, but no formal Buddhist group formed. Instead, Reverend Kawamura travelled from Raymond to perform graveside services and the annual Obon commemoration. Another small handful of Buddhists migrated from the west coast to Fort William and Port Arthur (now Thunder Bay) during the exile of the war years. After the war, remaining church funds from the British Columbia churches were distributed to settlements of Japanese Canadian Buddhists across the country, and Fort William/Port Arthur was no exception. With the small amount of money they received, Buddhists began gathering in Fort William for services led by lay priest Shinzo Miyazaki. The first Obon was held in August 1949, with Reverend Tsuji presiding. Throughout the next twenty years, Buddhists in the Lakehead held services and enjoyed dharma talks in Jimmy Saisho's store and Chu Hayashi's country home.

In Manitoba, though, the community grew large enough to support a church of its own. In the spring of 1942, some Japanese Canadians chose to come to Manitoba for the same reason others had chosen to go to Alberta; the British Columbia Security Commission had agreed to allow families to remain intact if they chose resettlement east of the Rockies. These families were attracted to Manitoba by the promise of fair wages, free housing, public school education, and welfare and medical services. Altogether, 1053 people were allowed to settle in Manitoba; grudgingly welcomed as labourers for the province's sugar beet farms, they had to endure the humiliation of "stock-yard inspection" by local farmers looking for families with plenty of able-bodied sons. Once settled, the Japanese Canadians suffered severe living conditions.

Following the end of the war, the Buddhists living in and around Winnipeg felt secure enough to consider establishing a Buddhist church for social gatherings and spiritual solace. The first Obon in Manitoba took place in 1947. Following the service, a committee was established to organize the building of an actual church in Winnipeg. The church was completed in 1951 and opened in February. As a tribute to the tenacity of the Winnipeg congregation, and a testament to their devotion, the Gomonshu and his entourage came from Kyoto to visit the church in 1952. The Manitoba church went on to establish a Japanese language school, a Buddhist Young Women's Club which came to be known as the Maya Club, the Manitoba Young Buddhist Association, and the Chidori Kai, a performing choir. The Manitoba church thrived into the 1970s.

Quebec

Buddhists in Montreal first gathered at the Hori family home on 2 February 1947, a modest gathering of six people which led, however, to a larger general meeting a month later, at which a new Norinokai (Official Committee) was established. The Montreal Buddhists held their first service on 6 April 1947, to celebrate *Hanamatsuri* (the Buddha's Birthday Festival). Reverend Tsuji – who had moved to Toronto in 1944 – presided. On 1 February 1948, the organization became formally known as the Montreal Buddhist Church. Several highlights marked the two decades that followed in the life of the church.

In 1952, the fifth anniversary of the inception of the church was celebrated with over three hundred people in attendance. Later the same year, the Gomonshu and his wife, the Lady Ōtani, visited the church. Annual bazaars took in a substantial sum, helping to defray the costs of running the church, while groups like the Montreal Sangha Society, a club for *nisei* members, and the Montreal Dana Club, a women's group, were formed to oversee social and spiritual activities. In 1961, the congregation bought a house on St Urbain, in Montreal's Mile End neighbourhood, and in September, the bishop of the Buddhist Churches of America, Bishop Hanayama, led the dedication service for the new church, assisted by Canadians Reverend Ishiura and Reverend Yamada.

With the organization firmly established, the Montreal Buddhist Church sought incorporation from 1950 through to the early 1960s. They were not successful in gaining the charter. At that time, the Quebec Civil Code required that marriages and funerals be solemnized by a representative of the Catholic, Protestant, or Jewish faith only. Without a provincial charter, the Montreal Buddhist Church had the right of "free exercise and enjoyment of religious profession and worship"[17] but could not legally preside over marriage ceremonies or register births and deaths within the congregation. Buddhist marriages and funerals in Montreal were therefore presided over by both a Buddhist priest and a representative of one of the legally recognized religions.

Bishop Ishiura urged the Montreal church to act by challenging the Civil Code. The congregation, however, did not want to "rock the boat" and so declined any offer of help. Bishop Ishiura had no choice but to respect their wishes. The Montreal Buddhist Church carried on into the 1970s and beyond without ever becoming incorporated.

Southern Ontario

The Toronto Buddhist Church began with the arrival of Reverend Kenryu Tsuji from British Columbia in 1944. Reverend Tsuji recalls: "I knew there was going to be quite a congregation of Japanese Canadians in this area [Toronto] because it was a big city, the possibility of employment was very great. At the time [1944] however, there was a restriction on the number of Japanese who could come to the city. So I went to Port Credit. After a couple of months, I applied as a student … at the University of Toronto, and naturally as a student, I could live in Toronto. I checked to find a place where I could hold meetings … the Ukrainian Hall and various halls where ethnic groups could meet. But we weren't organised to be able to rent a hall."[18] The first gathering in Toronto was held at 52 Leonard Street, the home of Genjiro Mori, on 5 August 1945. People came together to celebrate Obon. Word spread quickly of the popular priest's presence, and many requested memorial services and the like. Unfortunately, the only place Reverend Tsuji could hold such services was his small room at 13 Division Street, which contained a double bed and a large *butsudan*, or family altar, donated by the internees from Tashme.

After the Toronto restrictions were lifted, Japanese Canadians started moving into the city from places like London and St Catharines. In response to the growing size of the community, the Buddhists had to organize and they rented a room at the Ukrainian Hall on Bathurst Street. In 1946 the church's first organization, the Toronto Young Buddhist Society (TYBS), was formed. Within a year, the one-hundred-member TYBS had organized a Dharma School, held their first social at the Jewish Synagogue on Henry Street, and put on the Nisei Variety Parade, a concert with singers, musicians, and actors. In September 1947, the TYBS incorporated, and – against opposition from the *issei* group, the Bukkyokai – decided to buy a house for Reverend Tsuji and his wife Sakaye. They placed a down payment on a house at 134 Huron Street by soliciting loans of $100 from each supporter.

The Huron Street church quickly became a focal point of Buddhist activity in eastern Canada, which in turn fostered co-operation between the TYBS and the Bukkyokai. Soon after its establishment, new groups formed, in Montreal – as discussed above – and in Hamilton. When Japanese Canadians began to arrive in Hamilton in 1946, they first gathered in private homes to practise their faith. Two years later, in 1948, Tomekichi Yoshida and Tsuneto Yamashita bought a house at 44 Strachan Street East, which became the first site of the Hamilton Buddhist Church. Reverend Tsuji extended his responsibilities from Toronto to Hamilton, and the church enjoyed many fruitful community activities through to the 1970s, including picnics, bazaars, Obon celebrations, and various fundraising events.

In Toronto, too, the church was flourishing. By the late 1940s, it was necessary to rent the Legion Hall on College Street to accommodate the expanding congregation. The church newsletter *The Guiding Light* began publication in 1947 under the editorship of Toyo Takata, one-time editor of the *New Canadian,* the English-language *nisei* paper which had been the only Japanese community paper permitted to continue publication during the war. The same year, Reverend Ikuta visited from British Columbia and urged the congregation to find a way to hire Reverend Tsuji full-time; the latter had been working at a chemical plant and performing his ministerial duties in his spare time. By 1948, the members had canvassed sufficient funds to be able to offer him a salary of $120 a month; not a princely sum, but enough for him to accept. In 1948, nineteen women from the congregation came together, at Reverend Tsuji's suggestion, to form the Fujinkai (Women's Association). A language school was set up at the house on Huron Street in 1949 and grew to the point where lessons had to be held at the Legion Hall. And in the same year, a group concerned with bridging the gap between *issei* and *nisei* in the congregation formed the Sonenkai (Prime of Life Association), which in 1950 would change its name to the Sangha; the Sangha gave rise to a women's auxiliary. Also in 1950, the Continental Family Co-operative came together with the assistance of the church to provide the community with a Japanese grocery store. The storefront operation at 618 Dundas Street West was supported financially by Eikichi Kagetsu, Shinkuro Kozai, Zentaro Shin, and Sukegoro Mori, to name a few. Eventually the store privatized, changing its name to Furuya.

With all of these developments, it soon became apparent that the Huron Street church was far too small for the needs of the congregation. A building committee, headed by Zentaro Shin, started to look for new premises. After a few missteps, the committee found a lot at 918 Bathurst Street, north of Bloor. Buying the property and building the new church would cost $63,000. The congregation formed a fundraising committee and hired architects George Yamazaki and Roy Matsui. The temple on Bathurst would include as one of its unique features an original, hand-crafted *onaijin*, or inner shrine, designed by architect Nobuo Kubota in consultation with Reverend Tsuji. The project was completed in 1955. The list of those in attendance at the dedication ceremony in March reveals the rich diversity of the community:

> The Dedication Service included ritual offerings of incense by representatives of the Japanese Canadian Citizens Association, the Japanese [Language] School, the Buddhist Churches of Canada, and the East Coast Young Buddhist League, a bilateral organisation that had held annual conferences since 1946. Individuals in attendance included Rev. Gyodo Kono of the Midwest Buddhist Church of Chicago, who gave a sermon, and the Vice-Consul of the Toronto Japanese Consulate, which had just opened in May 1954. Church groups participating included the Club Ami, a teenage club, the Toronto Young Buddhist Society, a group of young unmarried *Nisei* numbering 125 to 150, the Sangha, a group of older married *Nisei*, consisting of about 60 to 70 couples, the Fujinkai, and the Asoka Society, a philosophical group of largely white students of Buddhism. (Armstrong 1991, 106–7)

By the late 1950s, with all this growth, the church had become something of a hodgepodge of organizations. Forward movement was made difficult by the agendas specific to each group. When Reverend Tsuji retired in 1958, the church found itself at a crossroads. Fortunately, the new leaders – Reverend Newton Ishiura and his wife Mary – came with the vision, energy, and progressive attitude needed to lead the congregation into an era of great social change.

Under their leadership, the various groups excelled in their creativity. The Fujinkai began the Obon Odori, the first taking place during the TYBS picnics at the Greenwood Conservation Park. In 1961, Chiyo Seko instructed the women in Japanese folk dances and the church held the summer Obon at Christie Pits. The event quickly grew in popularity, moving first to Dufferin Park and then to City Hall. Joining the dancers from the church were the Sakura-kai and Ayame-kai from the Japanese Canadian Cultural Centre, the Hamilton Buddhist Church, and Hamilton's Suzuran-kai. Kunio Suyama, a president of the TYBS, the congenial and distinctive emcee, soon became known as the "voice of the Japanese-Canadian community."

The Sangha remained remarkably cohesive until 1977. It oversaw the main activities of the church, from fundraising to social events. Perhaps its most lasting contribution was Camp Lumbini, a campground about one hundred miles north of the city, at Wasaga Beach. In July 1964, the Gomonshu and Lady Ōtani officially opened the camp. The Dana, formed in the early 1960s out of the Sangha Women's Division, became socially active under Mary Ishiura's influence. Its members raised money for, among other things, a scholarship fund (with the Gomonshu and Lady Ōtani as patrons), the Nagoya Relief Fund, and the adoption of first one, and eventually three, Tibetan orphans.

By the time of Reverend Ishiura's arrival, over two hundred students in eight grades were enrolled in the Sunday school. Throughout the minister's tenure, the school was a beehive of activity. The youth department carried on with the Junior Young Buddhists Association, a Boys Club, Girls Club, and Taruna, a group for young teenagers. These groups were largely social but they did keep the young in the church after finishing Sunday school. The students and the members of Taruna participated in *Hanamatsuri*, field trips, and interfaith seminars.

During this period, the duties of the priest evolved into a rather complex job, so much so that the church added two more full-time priests. Reverend Ishiura also brought with him his own agenda: one of social activism. "In my case, I liked to be involved in various civil rights movements ... I got involved ... with the Indians, Inuits, the Ainu people from Japan, and the Hiroshima Peace Day. Of course my wife was all for it. During the Vietnam Era, there were many kids coming from the States, underground, AWOL, 18, 19 year old kids ... they'd come penniless, no home, no job, bewildered. So I was involved in helping them."[19]

Throughout the 1960s and on into the 1970s, the Toronto Buddhist Church enjoyed a period of growth and prosperity that was strengthened by a dynamic, committed minister and a congregation open to new ideas and willing to embrace society's need for the involvement of its citizens.

CONCLUSION

Racism against Asian and Japanese Canadians was rampant until well after World War II. But oddly, the federal government was relatively tolerant of religion, and Buddhism in particular. It did try to limit the number of ministers in Canada, but the British Columbia government granted official recognition to

Buddhism in April 1909. The following month, Reverend and former Abbot Komyo Ōtani (father of the 23rd Abbot Kosho of the Nishi Hongwanji) left Japan and travelled to London via the Siberian Railroad to study various religions in Europe and the world. He also visited Jerusalem, toured South Africa, and visited sacred Buddhist remains in India, and on his way home came to Vancouver. Over one hundred devoted Buddhists met him at the train station. At a gala banquet held in his honour, he spoke of his happiness with the situation and acceptance of Buddhism in Canada.

Not all was as rosy as the former Abbot had thought, however, for Japanese Canadians. Restrictive employment laws, punitive licensing practices for fishing, and the denial of naturalization privileges impeded the Japanese and "Asiatics" from prospering in their new home. Much of this acrimony led to various race riots in the province. Later, prejudice and government restrictions hampered the *nisei* from developing careers in their chosen fields of study. There was also an attempt to prevent the second generation from serving their country by at first forbidding them from joining the military.

Still, Buddhists were generally left to their own devices. Since the religion posed little threat to the Christian status quo and interracial marriage was uncommon (the government also established anti-miscegenation laws to guarantee this outcome), Canadians staged no overt protest against the "alien" religion. Pressure did come to bear on individual Japanese Canadians to convert as *nisei* Dorothy Kagawa of the Toronto Buddhist Church relates in an interview. "We had many Buddhist friends as well as Christian friends and many of my parents' Christian friends tried to persuade my dad to convert to Christianity. He would always say very strongly, 'No never! I was brought up a Buddhist and I will never renounce my Buddhist faith'" (Watada 1996, 35).

Despite efforts such as a campaign of persecution by Christian Japanese Canadians against Buddhist Japanese Canadians in Alberta shortly after the war, the Jodo Shinshu Buddhists were too strongly tied into the religion to give it up. The church represented their culture and traditions – their "*Nembutsu* so to speak," Kagawa went on to say.

During World War II, British Columbia politicians railed against Buddhism, calling it a "major obstacle to assimilation" but, by and large, the mainstream citizenship remained uninvolved, perhaps too ignorant of Buddhism to care. Only one church was looted, the Steveston Buddhist Church, during the war. But as Alex Johnson, the son of the Steveston chief of police at the time, tells it, the looters' motivation was not racial hatred or religious intolerance, but pure avarice. "Two days after the Japanese Canadians left Steveston, the beer parlour gang ... decided to break into the church because they were looking for gold. They had heard the Buddhists were rich, sort of like the Catholics" (Watada 1996, 119).

The Jodo Shinshu Buddhists in Canada were sustained by their faith and the absence of serious opposition from the public. Given the immigrant and internment experiences and subsequent banishment, they of course did not have an easy go of it. Ultimately, their dedication carried the church through times of persecution and into the years of prosperity and expansion. In 1967, the Eastern Canada Sangha Dana League was organized to knit together the churches in Ontario and Quebec. It paved the way for collaboration with churches in the United States to celebrate the Buddha-dharma.

The following year, the Buddhist Federation of Canada was officially re-established as the Buddhist Churches of Canada, independent of the Buddhist Churches of America, a move that would tie the Canadian Buddhist churches together in a profound way. Thus in 1968, for the first time, Canada gained its own bishop, Bishop Newton Ishiura. Jodo Shinshu Buddhism arguably reached its apex in Canada during the 1970s. Japanese Canadian Buddhist communities settled in across the country, from Vancouver to Montreal. The BCC served as the central link with the Nishi Hongwanji in Kyoto. Challenges and decline confronted the various churches in the years to come but, as Japanese Canadian Buddhists had been doing since the beginning, congregations continually rose to those challenges, meeting them in order to maintain their Buddhist traditions in Canada.

NOTES

1   As will be explained later in this essay, Shin Buddhists in both Canada and the United States used Christian vocabulary to translate Japanese terms, so that, for example, the Japanese *otera* became the Buddhist "church." Although in later years terms like "temple" would come to be preferred, this account will use the Christianized language favoured by the early Shin Buddhists in Canada – church, priest, reverend, etc.

2   For a detailed account of the effects of the evacuation and internment see Adachi (1976), Miki (2004), and Shimizu (1993).

3   Note that all the Japanese Canadian names in this essay will be given following North American naming conventions, that is, with family name last, and without diacritical marks. However, Japanese names will be given in accordance with Japanese conventions,

that is, with surname first and with diacritical marks, if the person in question is based in Japan. For example, names of early ministers, such as Sasaki and Katō, who were born in and returned to Japan after short stays in Canada, are given in the Japanese order.

4 Jodo Shinshu in Japan is divided into two major wings – the Nishi Hongwanji-ha (West Hongwanji School) and the Higashi Hongwanji-ha (East Hongwanji School). Shin Buddhists in Canada have always fallen under the wing of the Nishi Hongwanji-ha, or Western School.

5 It appears that this consisted of taking in a woman from the congregation and her two children during a period when the woman's husband was unable to provide for them because of his own mental illness, and sheltering the same family during the flu epidemic of 1918. For more on these events, see Watada (1996, 54–7).

6 Reverend Shigeno was relieved of his duties in 1924, but he moved to Toronto and lived out his days there rather than returning to Japan. This is why his name follows Canadian convention of surname last unlike Reverend Katō who returned to Japan in 1925.

7 The *Tairiku Nippo* (Continental Daily News), *Kanada Shinbun* (Canada Daily News), and *Nikkan Minshu* (The Daily People). For more on these newspapers, including the interesting fact that readership tended to divide along religious lines, see Gonnami (2005, 13–27).

8 Two hundred volunteers served with the Canadian forces in France; fifty-four were killed and ninety-four wounded. Veterans were finally enfranchised in 1931.

9 This title, which is an honorific version of "*monshu*" (His Eminence), is commonly used by members to refer to the highest official of the entire Nishi Honwanji branch of Jodo Shinshu.

10 Initially, and until the British government forced a change, Japanese Canadians were barred from serving in the Canadian military during World War II, regardless of citizenship, although many tried to volunteer even after the evacuation and internment.

11 Personal interview with Terrie Komori, conducted by Jesse Nishihata and Harry Yonekura, Toronto Buddhist Church, Toronto, 1990.

12 Personal interview with Toshio Mori, conducted by Hideo Yoshida and Gloria Sumiya, Toronto Buddhist Church, Toronto, 1991.

13 RCMP, Alberta Division "K," Lethbridge Sub-Division, 21 June 1946, Section 9 – Report RG 36/27/30/F1613.

14 Personal interview with Rev. Yutetsu Kawamura, conducted by Dorothy Kagawa and Harry Yonekura, Lethbridge, Alberta, 1992.

15 It has been suggested that some organizers intended the garden as a memorial, constructing it as an expression of sympathy for the members of a local Japanese Canadian family, victims of violence. To support the project was thus to bring up the tragic incident again, resurrecting the pain and shame attached to it.

16 Leslie Kawamura gives an account of these events and their significance from his per-
    spective in "Changes in the Japanese True Pure Land Buddhism in Alberta – a case
    study: Honpa Buddhist Church in Alberta" (L. Kawamura, 1978).

17 Letter to F.Y. Okimura from Howard, Cate, Ogilvy, Bishop, Cope, Porteus, and Hansard,
    Advocates, Barristers, and Solicitors, 17 January 1966.

18 Personal interview with Rev. Kenryu Tsuji, conducted by Jesse Nishihata and Harry
    Yonekura, Toronto Buddhist Church, Toronto, 1990.

19 Personal interview with Rev. Newton Ishiura, conducted by Jesse Nishihata and Terry
    Watada, Toronto, 1991.

Buddhism after the Seventies

HENRY C.H. SHIU

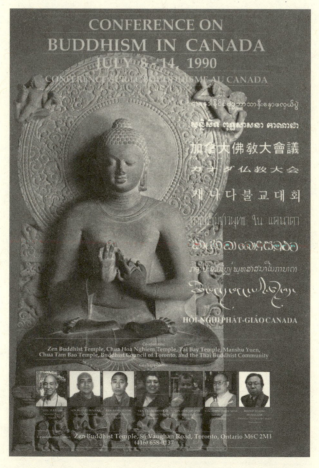

Poster of the 1990 Conference on Buddhism in Canada, held
at the Zen Buddhist Temple, Vaughan Road, Toronto

Terry Watada, in his essay in this volume, has described the the first sixty years of Buddhism in Canada as basically the history of the Japanese Jodo Shinshu (Pure Land) school in Canada. Then, during the 1960s and 70s, other schools of Buddhism started to arrive and take root. Buddhism took root in two patches of ground – among newly arrived immigrants and among native-born Canadians. In 1967, Canada abolished its race-based immigration laws and adopted a race-neutral, points-based system. Points were given for level of education, ability to speak either English or French, type of occupation, etc. If immigrants amassed enough points, no matter what their race, they were given permission to enter the country. Thereafter from Hong Kong and Singapore, Vietnam and Thailand, Korea and Taiwan, Burma and Laos, the newly arrived brought their Buddha from home.[1]

While legal and political changes initiated by the Canadian government opened up the ground for immigrant Buddhism, cultural and social changes opened up the ground for Westerners' Buddhism. The sixties and seventies constituted an era of political rebellion, cultural experimentation, and social innovation. During the Vietnam War in the late 60s and early 70s, student activists mounted strong opposition to the American government, targeting the war and demanding changes in the educational system. While Canada was not directly involved in the Vietnam War, students in this country led many large-scale protests. The baby-boomer generation attending universities demanded that their society be founded on the ideal of democracy. Although nothing in Canada corresponded to the Civil Rights Movement in the United States, the gap between rhetoric and social reality prompted young Canadians to cry out for a society that provided justice for all. American student activism was more politically driven, while, in comparison, Canadian activism was more sociological. On the other hand, many young Americans who were not supportive of the American military involvement simply left the United States to settle in Canada.

It was, furthermore, a time when many Americans not only mistrusted the government because of its involvement in Vietnam but also lost their faith in Christianity and turned to Asian religions for an alternative view on life. But as Richard P. Hayes observes, "[a]mong the American war resisters in Canada, experimentation with drugs and alternative forms of sex were fairly common, and the majority of people I knew who were interested in Buddhism were also interested in hallucinogenic drugs and free sex" (Hayes 1998, 19). To many, therefore, Buddhism was affiliated with escapism, the use of drugs, the loss of Christian faith, an indulgence of the sexual appetite, and a detestation of consumerism.

In the 1970s, Buddhism lay on the fringes of mainstream society. Immigrants brought it as part of their cultural baggage. Countercultural types dabbled in it as part of their social rebellion. Mainstream Canada knew the name of Buddhism and nothing more. No one could have predicted that in the following decades, Buddhism would grow both in numbers and in social acceptance to the point where today it is beginning to rank beside Christianity and Judaism as a mainstream religious option.

BUDDHIST GROUPS

By the 1990s, Buddhism had become a significant presence in the Canadian religious landscape; it constituted the largest group of non-Western religious communities in Canada, as well as the fastest developing. In Toronto, for example, within the span of forty years, the number of Buddhist temples has increased from one in 1965 to over seventy in 2005. The upsurge in the number of Buddhist temples is, in part, the result of the diversity of immigrants from various parts of Asia and Southeast Asia who brought into Canada their respective traditions of Buddhist practice. The ethnic diversity of the immigrant groups means that Theravada, Mahayana, and Vajrayana Buddhism can all be found in Canada in a variety of lineages, teachings, ritual forms, and practices.

Japanese Buddhism

The Japanese Jodo Shinshu community is the oldest Buddhist organization in Canada (Watada 1996). However, this group has also earned much criticism from other Buddhist groups who are concerned that the sect emulates the rituals, forms, and terminology of Christian churches at the expense of traditional Buddhist meditation and philosophy. While it is true that a Protestant Christian social and cultural ethos permeates many Jodo Shinshu congregations, it should be noted that the highly particularized practice of the Canadian Jodo Shinshu Buddhists that we observe today is a result of a series of historical factors, including the pressure on the first generation of Japanese immigrants to convert to Christianity (the principal form of institutionalized religion, required in order to gain access to and acceptance in mainstream society), the attempt of the subsequent generations (the *nisei* and the *sansei*) to reclaim their ethnic identity, and the process of acculturation (see the discussion in McLellan 1999, 35–73). Indeed, all Buddhist groups in Canada, not only the Jodo Shinshu, continue to change in order to accommodate the spiritual needs, culture, language, and interests of Canadians.

Chinese Buddhism

Several waves of Chinese immigrants, following the implementation of the new point system in 1967, make this group the largest of visible minorities. (For a more detailed historical account of Chinese Buddhism in Canada, see Liu 2005). A great number of Chinese from Hong Kong came to Canada after 1984 when Margaret Thatcher, then British prime minister, went to China to sign the Sino-British Joint Declaration which committed China to taking over Hong Kong after 1997 under the "One Country, Two Systems" policy. Another wave of Hong Kong immigrants followed after 1989 when the violent crackdown on student protests and demonstrations in Tiananmen Square in Beijing shocked the world and instigated international condemnation of the Chinese regime. People emigrated from Hong Kong for a better education for their children, a more stable environment (socially and politically), and a safer investment climate; they feared that Hong Kong might be converted into a communist system. The desire for freedom of speech and religion were also motives. Ironically, after the transfer of Hong Kong to China, the number of immigrants dropped significantly from close to ten thousand per year before 1997 to only a few hundred. However, Chinese immigration continued in great numbers from mainland China and Taiwan. Inevitably, Chinese Buddhism has come to play a significant role on the Canadian religious stage. The number of Chinese immigrants passed the one million mark in 2002, and Chinese Buddhists comprise more than half of Buddhists in Canada. (See Table 2 from Peter Beyer's chapter in this volume.)

Many of the Chinese Buddhist temples are branches affiliated with a large-scale Chinese Buddhist group outside Canada. For example, the Dharma Realm Buddhist Association, founded by Venerable Hsuan Hua in California in the early 1960s, has seventeen branches in North America and Asia. Its two Canadian centres, the Gold Buddha Monastery and the Avatamsaka Sagely Monastery, were opened in Vancouver and Calgary in 1984 and 1986 respectively.[2] The principal Taiwanese Buddhist groups also established branches throughout Canada: Ven. Hsing Yun's Fo Guang Shan Temple of Toronto[3] and the Vancouver International Buddhist Progress Society opened in 1997 and 1994 respectively, and branches in Montreal and Ottawa were opened. Ven. Cheng Yen's Tzu Chi Buddhist Compassion and Relief Foundation established the Tzu Chi Foundation of Canada in 1992, with one branch in British Columbia, two in Alberta, five in Ontario, and one in Quebec (see the chapter by André Laliberté and Manuel Litalien in this volume). More recently, Ven. Sheng Yen's Dharma Drum Mountain has also opened branches in Vancouver and Toronto.[4] Other major Chinese temples include the Cham Shan Temple, the oldest Chinese Buddhist temple in Toronto, which was established in 1973. The temple has expanded into a three-acre temple complex and has developed a number of affiliated Buddhist groups, including the Hong Fa Temple, the Cham Shan Buddhist Learning Centre, and the Cham Shan Library in the Greater Toronto area. In addition, Cham Shan has also built affiliated temples in other parts of Ontario to serve the Chinese community outside Toronto, including temples in Hamilton, Maple, Niagara Falls, and four other locations.[5] Other popular Chinese Buddhist temples include the Montreal Chinese Buddhist Society,[6] the Amitabha Society of Canada, the Universal Buddhist Temple in Vancouver, the Tai Bay Buddhist Temple in Toronto, and the Mui Kwok Buddhist Temple in Edmonton. (See the chapter by Tannie Liu in this volume for further details.)

Buddhists from South and Southeast Asia

The Sri Lankan community was the first to establish a Theravada temple in Canada, the Canadian Buddhist Vihara Society in Scarborough, Ontario, in

1978.[7] The Sri Lankans were immigrants who had decided to leave their country voluntarily and come to Canada. But during the 1970s, many of the groups who came to Canada from Southeast Asia were refugees driven out of their own countries by political turmoil. In 1975, Vietnamese escaped to Canada after the communists took over Saigon and Cambodians fled Pol Pot and his Khmer Rouge communist movement. In the late 1970s, Laotians fled from the Pathet Lao, the communist political movement which was closely associated with the Vietnamese communists. And in 1979 refugees arrived from Burma fleeing domestic conflicts resulting from that country's long struggle for stability in the wake of independence from British colonial rule.[8]

Of the Southeast Asian Buddhists, the Vietnamese are the largest group. However, a significant number of this group are Vietnamese by national origin but Chinese by ethnic origin. Furthermore Vietnamese Buddhism is a branch of Chinese Mahayana Buddhism, unlike the Buddhism of the other Southeast Asian nations which practise Theravada Buddhism. This further blurs the boundary between Vietnamese and Chinese Buddhism making it difficult to get an accurate estimate of the size of the Vietnamese Buddhist population. Because Vietnam was a French colony until the end of World War II, a sizeable proportion of the early immigrants were attracted to French-speaking Quebec. On the Buddhism in Quebec website, of the fifty-four Buddhist temples and meditation centres listed, thirteen – about one-quarter of the total – are Vietnamese related.[9] Because of the diverse political views and regional divisions among the Vietnamese refugees, the Vietnamese Buddhist groups remain more fragmented than any other in Canada (Dorais 2006).

In the decades since the first wave of refugees in the late 1970s, there has been a significant increase in the number of Southeast Asian immigrants (see Tables 2 and 3 of Peter Beyer's article in this volume). All these refugee communities are building temples. Thai Buddhist temples include the Wat Buddha Sodhara in Montreal, the Wat Ratchadham Viriyaram Temples in Kanata and Niagara Falls, Ontario, and the Wat Yanviriya in Vancouver. Among Cambodian Buddhist temples, the Pagode Khmer du Canada in Montreal is the oldest and largest, supporting the largest number of resident monks. Several other temples were built by Cambodians fleeing the "killing fields" of Pol Pot. These temples include the Wat Khmer Krom Buddhist Temple in Stoney Creek, Ontario; the Wat Khmer in London and Windsor, Ontario: the Khmer-Canadian Buddhist Society of Calgary; and the Wat Khmer Saamakii of Edmonton. Given the tiny Laotian population in Canada, Lao Buddhist temples are surprisingly numerous. There are at least three Laotian temples in Quebec: Wat Thepban-dol, Société Bouddhique Laotienne, and Wat Lao Samakhidhammaram. On-tario has several Laotian temples (See Marybeth White's field report on Wat Lao Veluwanaram in Caledon East), and there are Laotian temples in Winnipeg, Calgary, Edmonton, and Vancouver. These Lao Buddhist communities are attended almost exclusively by the Laotians, and rarely provide programs in English for local Canadians. However, out of Southeast Asian Buddhism have sprung the modern vipassana movement and Thich Nhat Hanh's Order of Interbeing, both of which have attracted significant followings among native-born Canadians. These movements are discussed below.

Tibetan Buddhists

In 1971 the Tibetans were the first group of Buddhist refugees seeking resettle-ment in Canada. Despite the small Tibetan population in Canada, all four major orders of Tibetan Buddhism (Nyingma, Kagyu, Sakya, and Gelug) are found in here. (Sarah Haynes gives a more complete account of the establish-ment of Tibetan Buddhist groups in her chapter in this volume. See also McLellan 1999, 74–100.)

In recent years, Tibetan Buddhism has eclipsed Zen as the form of Bud-dhism most attractive to Westerners. Arguably Canada was ahead of the trend. One of the first established Tibetan Buddhist organizations was the Dharma Centre of Canada in Ontario, founded in 1966 by a Canadian of Irish-Scottish descent, Leslie George Dawson, who received the title Karma Tenzin Dorje Namgyal Rinpoche from H.H. the 16th Karmapa, head of the Karma Kagyu tradition of Tibetan Buddhism. Dawson, like Robert Thurman in the United States, was a member of the first generation of North Americans who were ini-tiated as Buddhist monks in the Tibetan tradition. He was one of the first teachers to adapt Tibetan Buddhist teachings for Western students.[10]

After Dawson established the Kagyu order in Canada, well-known Tibetan Karma Kagyu lamas such as Kalu Rinpoche and Karma Thinley Rinpoche established various Karma Kagyu centres, including the Kampo Gangra Drubgyud Tekchen Ling in Toronto in 1973 and the Marpa Gompa Changchub Ling Buddhist Meditation Society in Calgary in 1979. However, the first native-Tibetan lama to visit Canada was the Venerable Gyaltrul Rinpoche of the Nyingma tradition. He went to Winnipeg in 1972, at the request of the Dalai Lama, to aid in the resettlement of the first groups of Tibetans in Winnipeg.

Buddhist groups of the Nyingma order in Canada include the Vajrayana Buddhism Association with centres in Toronto and Vancouver, headed by Tam

Shek-wing. Tam is a disciple of the late supreme head of the Nyingma school, Dudjom Rinpoche, who conferred on him the *vajrācārya* title in 1972. Tam is also a professor in Buddhist studies at the Renmin University of China in Beijing and a prolific writer whose publications include both scholarly and general books.

In Vancouver, the Orgyan Osal Cho Dzong of the Nyingma Palyul tradition was founded in 1984 under the direction of Venerable Peling Tulku and Lama Jigme Chokyi Lodro, both Caucasians who received full ordination as Tibetan monks in the late 1970s. Further, the Riwoche Tibetan Buddhist Temple in Toronto, led by Venerable Khenpo Sonam Rinpoche, preserves a peculiar lineage that fully integrates the Taklung Kagyu line with Nyingma teachings.

Besides the Nyingma and the Kagyu schools, there is the Sakya Thubten Kunga Choling, founded in 1974 in Victoria by Geshe Tashi Namgyal, which follows the Sakya lineage. And lastly, the Gaden Choling Mahayana Buddhist Meditation Centre (headquartered in Toronto with affiliated centres in Vancouver, Ottawa, Thunder Bay, and Longueuil), the Tengye Ling Tibetan Buddhist Temple in Toronto, and the Thubten Choling in Duncan, British Columbia, carry on the Gelug order of Tibetan Buddhism in Canada.

One cannot discuss Tibetan Buddhism in Canada without mentioning the controversial figure of Chögyam Trungpa. Lynn Eldershaw in this volume tells the story of his "crazy wisdom" teaching, his alcoholism and sexual activities, and the scandal associated with his successor who knowingly transmitted AIDS.

Zen

With the popularity of the works of D.T. Suzuki, Alan Watts, and Philip Kapleau in the 1960s, the Zen boom in the United States reached Canada at about the same time. Zen centres of both Japanese and Korean traditions were established throughout the country. Many Canadian Zen centres now follow the teachings and organization of "Americanized Zen," particularly in the authorization of Western roshis, or "old teachers," to guide Western students. Founded in 1970, the Zen Centre of Vancouver exemplifies this trend, with the centre's abbot, Eshin John Godfrey, a Westerner who studied at the temple of Rinzai-ji in Los Angeles.[11]

By contrast, Toronto's Zen Buddhist Temple (formerly Zen Lotus Society) is an example of a Buddhist association led by a Korean monk with a large number of non-Asian adherents. (Patricia Campbell's chapter in this volume is a study of practitioners at this temple.) Samu Sunim founded the temple in 1979 and remains its spiritual head. Sunim moved to Canada in 1968, settling first in

Montreal, then relocating to Toronto in 1971. In 1974, Samu Sunim revived the Zen Lotus Society and began to offer Korean Zen (Son) meditation classes first to the Korean Canadian community and then to the wider Canadian community. The Zen Buddhist Temple is active on many fronts in its efforts to further Samu Sunim's mission to cultivate a community of living Bodhisattvas. In 1981, the temple launched a non-sectarian quarterly newsletter, *Spring Wind*, which was renamed *Spring Wind: Buddhist Cultural Forum* in 2001. In 1986, Samu Sunim founded the Buddhist Institute of Canada, which continues to engage scholars from the University of Toronto and York University, and in 1989, shortly after the Dalai Lama received the Nobel Peace Prize, the institute held an interreligious service and a seminar on non-violent social action in his honour.[12] These activities culminated in the week-long "Conference on Buddhism in Canada," convened in 1990, which brought together for the first time a majority of the clergy and lay leaders involved in establishing and maintaining over one hundred Buddhist temples, churches, centres, and monasteries across Canada. Scholars and students from a number of Canadian universities also attended the conference, which aimed to promote greater understanding among different Buddhist traditions, to strengthen relations among Canada's various Buddhist communities, and to foster better understanding of Buddhism in the academic sphere. A few graduate students who presented papers at that conference are now tenured professors in Canadian universities.[13]

The Vipassana Movement and Soka Gakkai International

The "vipassana movement" is practised in two major branches: the Insight Meditation movement founded by Joseph Goldstein (1940–), Jack Kornfield (1945–) and Sharon Salzberg (1952–), and the Vipassana Meditation movement led by Satya Narayan Goenka.[14] Both branches arose outside the sectarian and religious context of Buddhism as modernized forms of Theravadin practice and were introduced to Canada in the 1980s. The traditional rituals and chanting are replaced by more psychotherapeutic concerns that allow the practice to be adopted widely in hospitals and prisons. The movement has spawned a wide following in meditation centres and affiliated groups of various delineations across Canada. There are currently five Satya Narayan Goenka's Vipasanna Centres (Dhamma Torana) in Alberta, Ontario, British Columbia, Manitoba, and Quebec. The Insight Meditation centres, more loosely organized but generally following the meditation programs established by Kornfield, Salzberg and Goldstein, are found in British Columbia, Saskatchewan, Ontario, and Quebec.

Soka Gakkai ("Value Creation Society") originated as a lay movement closely affiliated with the Buddhist school Nichiren Shōshū in Japan.[15] In its early days during the immediate postwar period, Soka Gakkai attracted much criticism for its aggressive proselytization. Eventually it developed an international arm, Soka Gakkai International (SGI). SGI now identifies itself as an NGO with particular concerns for world peace, humanitarian relief, education, human rights, cultural exchange, and interreligious dialogues. In many ways, SGI is now a more important organization than its parent. It focuses, at the heart of its practice, on chanting because chanting the title of the *Lotus Sūtra* is thought to lead to world peace and personal happiness. SGI Canada was established in 1976, and its centres can be found in Vancouver, Calgary, Edmonton, Winnipeg, Toronto, Ottawa, Montreal, and Quebec City. During the 1980s and 1990s, the Canadian branch of SGI participated in various peace movements. In 1986, major Canadian universities in Montreal and Toronto co-operated with SGI Canada, the United Nations Educational, Scientific and Cultural Organization (UNESCO) and the Canadian government to mount the touring exhibition "Nuclear Arms: Threat to Our World," and in 1993, a second exhibition, "Toward a Century of Humanity: An Overview of Human Rights in Today's World." In addition, SGI clubs exist in many Canadian universities. In 1991, after a long period of conflict, the Nichiren Shōshū officially excommunicated Soka Gakkai. As an independent organization, the SGI continues to grow, although its present leader, Daisaku Ikeda, and his organization have been severely criticized as a personality cult.

Demographic Makeup of the Buddhist Groups

In contrast to the traditional Chinese, Vietnamese, and Laotian Buddhist temples that serve as meeting and worship places primarily for these ethnic groups, the Tibetan and Zen traditions in Canada are predominantly supported by Westerners. The Tibetans, as Janet McLellan observes, attend Tibetan Buddhist temples for monthly social and religious gatherings. Furthermore, the native Tibetans have minimal communication with the non-Tibetan Canadians who use the same temples (McLellan 1999, 88–94). Paul Numrich calls such a phenomenon "parallel congregations" (Numrich 1996, ch. 4). Another tradition that attracts a high percentage of Westerner participation is the Order of Interbeing (*Tiếp Hiện* Order). Fourteen communities in various provinces of Canada are dedicated to the tradition of mindfulness practice in daily life established by the Vietnamese Zen master Thich Nhat Hanh. These communities are concerned with the peaceful and mindful daily living resulting from the various forms of sitting and walking meditation. Also connected with Thich Nhat Hanh's Order of Interbeing is the Vietnamese Zen Meditation Group, which is more engaged with social activism in Vietnam, providing social services to those who are in need.

In addition to Chinese immigrants and South and Southeast Asian refugees, the 1980s also saw significant emigration from Singapore, Sri Lanka and, more recently, Korea. Moreover, Thai and Sinhalese have settled in Canada, as have Punjabi-speaking Buddhists fleeing persecution in India. It should be noted, however, that the majority of Punjabis in Canada are Sikh, so the number of Punjabi Buddhist refugees in Canada remains small compared with other South Asians. Although profoundly shaped by the social and cultural traditions of Buddhism, many of these newcomers were unfamiliar with the tradition's religious teachings. And yet, perhaps as a way of maintaining identity in a strange environment, many have turned with renewed vigour to the moral values and spiritual ways of their forebears, and hence contribute to the great variety of lineages of Buddhist practice in Canada.[16]

ATTEMPTS AT ORGANIZING THE BUDDHIST COMMUNITY

A great diversity of Buddhist practices is to be found within many Canadian cities. Unprecedented in the history of Buddhism, this rich variety of practices, originally developed over the centuries in many different cultures and countries, can now be found within the same mosaic. Attempts have been made to bring together the various Buddhist groups to form a unified Buddhist identity in Canada.

Suwanda Sugunasiri was pivotal in the first joint effort, the formation of the Toronto Buddhist Federation in 1979, with sixteen Buddhist groups participating (see the article by Hori and McLellan in this volume). The formation of this federation was inspired by an interfaith meeting Sugunasiri attended in the same year at the World Conference on Religion for Peace (WCRP), which Canada had joined in 1978. The WCRP Toronto chapter initiated the interfaith meeting to help build community links among peoples of diverse faith traditions. Soon after attending the meeting, Sugunasiri and the head minister of the Toronto Buddhist Church, Rev. Orai Fujikawa, met to plan a formal organization of various Buddhist communities in Toronto. The formation of the Toronto Buddhist Federation was immediately followed by the celebration of

Vesak (or Wesak), the commemoration of the birth, the enlightenment, and the *parinirvana* of the Buddha according to the Theravada tradition (McLellan 1999, 31–4). The celebration of *Vesak* in 1981 in Toronto with various Buddhist groups of different traditions participating was the first of its kind in North America. In 1981, Louis Cormier in Montreal formed the Montreal Buddhist Council (Conseil Bouddhique de Montréal) with twelve Buddhist groups participating. This lasted until 1986 when Cormier joined forces with Suwanda Sugunasiri to form the Buddhist Council of Canada, which was meant to function as a national representative for Buddhism in interviews with newspapers and on interfaith television and radio programs. The Toronto Buddhist Federation, on the other hand, adopted a new official name as the Buddhist Communities of Greater Toronto in the same year 1989, and then was replaced by the Sangha Council of Ontario Buddhist Ministry in 1994 (McLellan 1999, 31–3). These attempts were all unsuccessful in providing a unifying force or a feeling of a common religious identity within the diversity of Buddhism.

The recent phenomenon of many diverse Buddhist groups coming together to celebrate Vesak (Wesak, *Vaisakha*) is itself a symptom of globalization. Vesak, which falls on the full moon day of the fifth month, is the Theravada commemoration of the birth, the enlightenment, and the death of the Buddha, all of which are said to fall on the same day. In large cities that have many different Buddhist groups, it is the one event during which all Buddhist groups can gather together, despite differences in language and culture. Since Mahayana groups celebrate the birth of the Buddha on 8 April, approximately the same time of year, the Vesak celebration often incorporates the Mahayana ritual of bathing the baby Buddha. In Singapore, Borobudur in Indonesia, Chicago, Toronto and other sites where Buddhism is a minority religion, Buddhists are using Vesak to declare their common identity as Buddhists (Turpie 2005).

Other Buddhist institutions, such as the Buddhist Churches of Canada (BCC) and the Buddhist Association of Canada (BAC), despite their names which suggest a unified representation of Buddhists in Canada, indeed represent nothing other than specific groups of Japanese and Chinese Buddhists respectively. The International Buddhist Foundation of Canada in Calgary and the International Buddhist Friends Association in Edmonton are similarly associated only with their regional Buddhist groups. In 1980, Steven K.H. Aung, a professor at the University of Alberta and a family physician who was awarded the Order of Canada in 2005 in recognition of his efforts to integrate traditional Chinese medicine and Western geriatric medicine, founded the

International Buddhist Friends Association (IBFA) in Edmonton, with a vision to "realize the unity, strength, purity and compassion" of the Buddhist teachings.[17] The IBFA initially aimed at bringing together various Buddhist groups in Alberta, by means of regular meetings, the annual Vesak celebration, sponsoring Buddhist events, and so forth. The organization has expanded in terms of its function to provide social services and charitable works and it has also developed a mission that goes beyond its geographical locality to promote Buddhist teachings "around the world." It is currently applying for membership with the World Fellowship of Buddhists. However, like other attempts mentioned earlier, the IBFA has never really succeeded in bringing together the many traditions of Buddhism under its umbrella in order to act as representative of the diverse community groups. Most temples prefer to stay independent in their celebrations and rituals, as well as in their social and charitable services to the community. Janet McLellan notes, "An interesting development among Buddhist groups in Toronto is that, as particular temple groups and communities increased numerically and attained favourable social, political, and economic conditions of recognition and representation, their involvement with other Buddhist groups and communities in coreligious activities decreased" (McLellan 2006, 100).

After twenty years of celebrating an all-Buddhist Vesak together, the Buddhist groups in Toronto have discontinued the annual event. The same can be said of Buddhist groups in other parts of Canada and, indeed, of most Buddhist traditions in general.[18] In Asia, Buddhist groups even of the same tradition tend to stay independent from one another, with different focuses in establishing presence or recognition. For example, in Taiwan Fo Guang Shan and Tzu Chi have been seen by some as "rivals" or "competitors." Although both groups claim to practice the ideal of "Humanistic Buddhism" (*renjian fojiao*) envisioned by Master Taixu, they differ in their methods and emphases: Fo Guang Shan is known more for its educational application, while Tzu Chi is renowned for its charitable and medical services (Chandler 2004). The distinction between the two groups can also be observed in the branches they established in Canada. With no unified presence or identity, Buddhism in Canada continues to flourish and develop, harnessing a wide range of adaptations and integration with mainstream Canadian society.

It should also be noted that many Buddhist groups in Canada have been influenced by Christianity in making themselves viable religious traditions within a Western society dominated by Christians. The Fo Guang Shan Temple of Toronto, for example, not only provides Sunday service and Sunday school, but also a youth group, a choir, discussion gatherings, a scout group, and diploma programs on doctrinal teachings. The organizational structure of Fo Guang Shan bears striking similarity to the papal hierarchy of the Roman Catholic Church, with a central body, the Religious Affairs Committee, supervised by a head abbot selected on rotation every six years through a democratic election (Chandler 2004, 70–1.). In other cases, rituals and ceremonies are also transformed to meet the spiritual and social needs of Canadians, as evidenced in the widely publicized Buddhist wedding ceremony of Sakyong Mipham Rinpoche (the spiritual leader of the Shambhala International) and Tibetan Princess Tseyang Palmo, in Nova Scotia in 2006. Other Buddhist groups form a network of social relationships, again similar to that of the Christian traditions, to offer support for the refugee Buddhists (Canda and Phaobtong 1992, 61–6). To cope with the need of the second and third generations of immigrants, whose first language is English or French, many Buddhist groups also find ways to transform their activities and programs, most successfully in the case of the century-long development of the Buddhist Churches of Canada.

SOCIALLY ENGAGED BUDDHISM AND NEW MOVEMENTS

From the 1960s onward, more and more Canadians, whether Buddhist or not, have generated a concern for and interest in the various contemporary Buddhist movements throughout Asia led by the Dalai Lama, Thich Nhat Hanh, Sulak Sivaraksa, Aung San Suu Kyi, and others. Many were also drawn to Buddhist environmental activism and inspired by the relevance of Buddhist teachings to Deep Ecology. All these attempts to revitalize the Buddhist tradition in ways that respond directly to the social and political needs of the contemporary age for a just and non-violent society are collectively known as "socially engaged Buddhism," a term coined by Thich Nhat Hanh in 1963. In recent years, "socially engaged Buddhism" has also been more broadly understood as Buddhists' engagement in caring and service with active social compassion, as well as in bringing together world peace and inner peace. The emphasis on peace and non-violence distinguishes socially engaged Buddhism from other forms of social activism whose confrontational tactics at meetings of the G8 and other world bodies seem driven by anger and the urge to violence.[19]

In the last four decades, the work of Thich Nhat Hanh has expanded from Vietnamese engaged Buddhist practice during the Vietnam War to a global movement emphasizing mindfulness practice and engaged practices such as peace movements to encourage a non-violent approach to social-political problems. In Toronto, closely related to Thich Nhat Hanh's Order of Interbeing, the Vietnamese Zen Meditation Group provides a range of social services and engages in social activism in Vietnam, in addition to regular meditative practices and retreats.

With a small population in Canada, the Tibetans have been seen participating mostly in homeland-oriented gatherings and protests. They take to the streets and demonstrate outside the Chinese consulate and the parliament buildings annually on 10 March, Tibetan National Uprising Day. Hundreds of Tibetans also gather to protest against the visits of Chinese leaders and to castigate the federal government for its reluctance to officially recognize the Dalai Lama as head of a state. The Canada Tibet Committee (CTC), in particular, is committed to "end the ongoing destruction of the Tibetan culture, alleviate the suffering of the Tibetan people, and restore Tibet to its status as an independent state within the family of nations" (Canada Tibet Committee). The Committee initiated the Canadian Parliamentary Friends of Tibet (PFT) in 1989, with some thirty members from all political parties. The PFT invited the Dalai Lama for his first visit to Ottawa in 1990. The Dalai Lama's visits to Canada have always been regarded as a political issue by the Chinese government. When the Dalai Lama was presented with an honorary Canadian citizenship in 2006, the Chinese government issued an official complaint to the Canadian government and warned that such a decision could harm relations between the two countries. Canada's Department of Foreign Affairs responded that Canada recognizes China as the legitimate government of China and Tibet, but the decision to grant the Dalai Lama citizenship was determined by Canada's great respect for him.

It should be noted that Canadian Tibetan Buddhist temples have other social concerns beyond protests for the autonomous status of Tibet. Gaden Choling, for example, is particularly notable for its "socially engaged practice" as fundamental for the members of this group. In 1988 the temple established a project named Gaden Relief,[20] which serves to raise funds for relief work and other charitable causes, and provides health care and cultural reconstruction work in Tibet, India, and Mongolia.

Although there is a tradition of social engagement, rarely do Buddhists engage in direct political confrontation. Yet this happened in Myanmar (formerly Burma) in 2007. With an estimated 400,000 Buddhist monks in the country,

Myanmar's soldiers under the command of the ruling junta barely exceed the number of monks. When the military junta took power in 1988, Aung San Suu Kyi, the Nobel Peace Prize winner, founded the opposition National League for Democracy (NLD), inspired by the Buddhist principle to fight for democracy with non-violent resistance. She was placed under house arrest in the following year and is still in detention. The soldiers' violent crackdown on the protestors in 1988, however, ended in bloodshed and massacre. Mass public demonstrations, led by well-known political and social dissidents, erupted again nine years later in 2007, occasioned by the government's raising the price of diesel oil by 500 per cent.[21] Though this round of protests was quickly suppressed by the military, it was soon followed by the peaceful protests of the Buddhist monks and nuns, who were led by an underground organization known as the All Burma Monks' Alliance which called on people to "struggle peacefully against the evil military dictatorship"[22] through their prayers and chants. The numbers of clergy protesting were far greater than in the late eighties, and the participating monks have discouraged the public from joining them. They have also excommunicated the military by refusing to accept alms from them. This time the images of the *tatmadaw* (armed forces) arresting and beating monks were captured on video and quickly spread on the Internet and news reports, alerting not only the predominantly Buddhist public in Burma but also catching the attention of the United Nations and people worldwide. Burmese monks in Canada responded swiftly to the junta's violent military crackdown and urged Ottawa to impose sanctions on Burma and support the call for democracy.

In addition to political and social activism, Buddhist groups in Canada have become increasingly aware of the possibilities of providing services of various kinds to the community. The Calgary Myanmar Buddhist Temple, for example, has stated on its website that its mission includes collaborating "with other communities and vulnerable groups" to respond to social needs and "assist the reform of social protection"; it also participates in the Calgary Multicultural Centre in order to strengthen "Canada's cultural diversity."[23] Bhikshu Tenzin Sherab, born Sean Hillman, a Canadian Buddhist monk ordained in the Tibetan tradition, is also a nursing assistant involved in hospice service at a hospital in downtown Toronto.[24] In addition, one can find Buddhist hospice care in the Greater Toronto Region, as demonstrated by research conducted by Jasmine Baetz and Susanna Redekop of the University of Toronto in 2006.[25] Related to hospice care is cancer care service; a free Cancer Care Meditation program for cancer patients and survivors is offered by the Vajrayana Buddhism Association in Scarborough, Toronto.[26] Though the program was given a rather modern title, the association maintains that the principle behind the meditative practice stems from "a systemic, holistic approach to meditation based on the teachings of H.H. Dudjom Rinpoche, the late supreme head of the Nyingma tradition of Tibetan Buddhism."[27] This practice does not draw on the faith of the participants in the Buddhas and Bodhisattvas for healing power. Rather, the practice is taught to patients from all cultural and religious backgrounds, emphasizing and using the traditional meditative techniques to reach a state of equilibrium in which the immune system functions at its optimum level so that cancer goes into and remains in remission, co-existing with the healthy cells. It is therefore not about eradicating the cancer cells through prayer for some miraculous compassionate healing power through faith. A similar meditation program is offered at the Vancouver branch of the Vajrayana Buddhism Association, where teachings are modified to assist people suffering from multiple sclerosis.

In general, different Asian Buddhist groups exhibit different interests in their participation in socially engaged activities. Chinese Buddhist temples raise money to provide relief for those who suffer from natural disasters like earthquake, drought, or flood in their home countries. For example, the Tzu Chi Foundation Canada has been providing funds in the areas of medicine, education, humanitarian and international relief. Over the years, the foundation has donated an astonishing $16 million to various organizations in Canada, including major universities, hospitals, food banks, cultural societies, and libraries, and relief funds in response to the South Asia tsunami, earthquakes in Taiwan and Turkey, and so forth.[28] Karuna Community Services, a Buddhist group affiliated with the Hong Fa Temple in downtown Toronto under the guidance of a Canadian Buddhist, Michael Kerr, serves as the "engaged Buddhist branch" of the traditional Chinese temple groups, including Hong Fa Temple and Cham Shan Temple, all led by Ven. Sing Hung, Shing Cheung, and Lok To, who are considered the founders of Chinese Buddhism in Toronto. Karuna Community Services has provided funding for tsunami relief, endorsed open letters to the Canadian prime minister and provincial premier to urge them to cosponsor the China resolution at the UN Commission on Human Rights in 2000, supported the inclusion of same-sex couples in civil marriage, expressed concern with human rights issues in China and Tibet, and been active in other social and political concerns (http://www.ccednet-rcdec.ca/?q=en/node/3634).

Founded in 1979 in Scarborough by Darshan Chaudhary, the Ambedkar Mission Canada is the Canadian adaptation of the social teachings of Dr Bhimrao Ramji Ambedkar, known to the world for his fight against the caste system in India and the mass conversion of the Untouchables to Buddhism in 1956. The 50th anniversary of this event was celebrated in the central Indian city of Nagpur in 2006. While there is no caste system to fight against in Canada, the Ambedkar Mission focuses on the promotion of social justice and peace. The mission published a biannual magazine that sought to give a voice to the oppressed in Toronto from 1982 to 1991. A seminar on "Ambedkar's Social Justice and Peace" was held in the Department of South Asian Studies at the University of Toronto in 1993, coordinated by Joseph O'Connell with papers presented by Paul Younger, Richard Hayes, and Barbara Joshi.[29]

The Sarvodaya Shramadana Movement, which began in 1958 in Sri Lanka, originally with the goal of learning from long-established village work in order to use that knowledge to improve rural life, also sows its seeds in Canada (http://www.sarvodaya.org/). The founder of this movement, Dr A.T. Ariyaratne, who borrowed the concept *sarvodaya shramadana* (the awakening of all in the sharing of labour) from Mahatma Gandhi (1868–1948) but modified and adapted it according to the Buddhist teachings, visited Toronto in 2006 when he received the Acharya Sushil Kumar International Peace Award at the University of Toronto. He subsequently gave a talk, "Sarvodaya in Sri Lanka – Past Challenges and Future Visions," at the university's Centre for South Asian Studies. A charitable trust named Sarvodaya-Canada was soon established to promote social and economic justice in Canada.[30] In 2006, the trust donated $200,000 over five years to New College of the University of Toronto to fund a new undergraduate course on the history of social change. To successfully complete the course, students are required to work with a local non-governmental organization in order to practically apply the skills they learned in the classroom. Top students are also funded to work abroad with Dr Ariyaratne on a peace project in Sri Lanka.

BUDDHIST EDUCATION IN CANADA

The late 1960s and early 1970s also marked the beginning of an era when Canadian universities increased their support for Buddhist studies. Following the earlier, comparative religion scholarship after the Second World War, many universities across Canada began to support academic research in Buddhist studies and produced significant scholars from their graduate programs. Faced with an immense increase in enrolment as the baby boomer generation began to attend university, governments increased their funding of post-secondary education, enabling universities to expand their programs. Many included the study of Buddhism as a response to the upsurge in interest in Eastern philosophy and religions, Zen experience, and spiritual cultures that lie outside the Judeo-Christian tradition. The inclusion of Buddhist studies also fits in well with the policy of multiculturalism.

Pre-1980

During the first half of the century, the University of Toronto amassed a quite large collection of manuscripts and artifacts from South and East Asia which provided a research base for its Department of Sanskrit and Indian Studies. At McGill University, Robert Lawson Slater, formerly a Christian missionary with decades of experience in South Asia, published in 1951 *Paradox and Nirvâna,* probably the first academic book on Buddhism to be written by a Canadian. Slater went on to become the first director (1958–1964) of the Center for the Study of World Religions at Harvard University. As John Harding has noted in his essay in this volume, in this early period the Japanese Pure Land Buddhist community contributed several important scholars. Richard Robinson, who in 1961 started the first Buddhist studies graduate program in the United States at the University of Wisconsin, had earlier led discussions in the basement of the Toronto Buddhist Church on Bathurst Street in Toronto. Masatoshi Nagatomi, the son of a Pure Land missionary, was named Harvard's first Professor of Buddhist Studies in the Department of Sanskrit and Indian Studies in 1969; over a career of thirty-eight years, he produced an entire generation of Buddhist scholars. Leslie Kawamura, a Pure Land minister himself, studied in Japan and became a professor of Buddhist studies at the University of Calgary in 1976, where he still teaches.

The scholars in this formative period include A.K. Warder, a distinguished scholar in Pali and the history of Indian Buddhism, Bimal Matilal, professor of Sanskrit, and Leonard Priestley, a student of Warder specializing in early Indian Buddhism, including Abhidharma, the Pudgalavāda tradition, and Nāgārjuna's philosophy, all at the University of Toronto; Mervyn Sprung, a specialist in Mādhyamika philosophy, at Brock University; Herbert Guenther, renowned scholar at the University of Saskatchewan, specializing in the Buddhist tantric tradition, especially in the Nyingma school of Tibetan Buddhism, as well as Abhidharma literature; Leon Hurvitz, Iida Shotaro, Arthur Link,

Daniel Overmyer, and Michael M. Ames at the University of British Columbia; Jan Yün-Hua, a leading scholar in Chinese Buddhism, and Paul Younger, in the area of Indian Buddhism and the role of women in Buddhism, at McMaster University; and Bruce Matthews at Acadia University specializing in the Buddhism of Burma/Myanmar.

Between 1980 and 2000

As the study of Buddhism became more established, Canadian universities appointed more scholars to traditional Buddhist studies positions; meanwhile scholars in other disciplines, such as philosophy, history, and anthropology, developed major interests in the study of Buddhism. Among the scholars prominent in this period were Richard Lynn, Sonya Arntzen, and Eva Dargyay at the University of Alberta; A.W. Barber at the University of Calgary; Julian Pas and James G. Mullens at the University of Saskatchewan; Kate Blackstone at the University of Manitoba; Yuan Ren at the University of Regina; Roy Amore at the University of Windsor; Chan Wing-cheuk and Michael Berman at Brock University; Graeme MacQueen, Phyllis Granoff, and Koichi Shinohara at McMaster University; Mavis Fenn at the University of Waterloo; Kay Koppedrayer and Janet McLellan at Wilfrid Laurier University; Julia Ching, Timothy Brook, and Neil McMullin at the University of Toronto; Judith Nagata and Penny Van Esterik at York University; Peter Beyer at the University of Ottawa; Arvind Sharma, Richard Hayes, and Victor Sōgen Hori at McGill University; Mathieu Boisvert à l'Université du Québec à Montréal; Leslie Orr and David Miller at Concordia University; Edward Chung at the University of Prince Edward Island.

After 2000

A new generation of younger scholars is currently being appointed. Scholars joining Canadian universities since the year 2000 include Martin Adam at the University of Victoria; Chen Jin-hua, who assumed the Canada Research Chair at the University of British Columbia; John Harding at the University of Lethbridge; James Apple and Shinobu Apple at the University of Calgary; David Quinter at the University of Alberta; David Drewes at the University of Manitoba; Kevin Bond at the University of Regina; James Benn, Mark Rowe, and Shayne Clarke at McMaster University; Frances Garrett, Christoph Emmrich, Juhn Ahn, Amanda Goodman, Vincent Shen, and Henry C.H. Shiu at the University of Toronto; Barbra Clayton at Mount Allison University; Marc Des

Jardins at Concordia University; Lara Braitstein at McGill University; Alexander Soucy at Saint Mary's University.

As the number of graduate programs in Buddhist studies continues to grow, the number of students and scholars graduating from these programs with either an MA or PHD continues to increase. Scholars who have completed their doctoral studies in Canadian universities have moved seamlessly into the North American academic community in Buddhist studies and can be found teaching and doing research outside of Canada.

A number of MA theses and doctoral dissertations on the study of Buddhism in Canada have also been written in recent years,[31] although far fewer than the number of dissertations produced on American Buddhism in universities in the United States.[32]

Funding from Buddhist Communities

In a few cases, funding from Buddhist communities outside the university has begun to play a pivotal role in supporting the vitality of the study of Buddhism at academic institutions. This is an occasion when the "insiders" of the tradition joined with the "outsiders" who critically examine the history and teachings of Buddhism. A recent example is the University of Toronto, where concerned students feared that Buddhist studies would disappear by 2003 when all tenured professors would have retired. The Buddhist Education Foundation for Canada (BEFC), founded by the Ching Kwok Temple and the Ching Far Temple in Toronto, was established in 2001 with the objective of raising funds for promoting Buddhist studies at Canadian universities, and it has committed itself to sponsoring some courses and lecture series over a five-year period at the University of Toronto.[33] In 2002 the University of Toronto Buddhist community also rallied support from faculty members from various departments for the establishment of a Centre for Buddhist Studies. Although the centre is still under development, the University of Toronto has since hired three tenure-stream professors, made one spousal appointment, and appointed one contractually limited assistant professor in Buddhist studies. In 2005, the Scarborough campus of the University of Toronto received a $4 million gift from Tung Lin Kok Yuen, a Hong Kong-based non-profit Buddhist organization, which also donated another $4 million to the University of British Columbia, resulting in the establishment of a Buddhism and Contemporary Society program in 2006. In addition, the Numata Foundation established Numata Chairs at the University of Calgary, McGill University, and the University of Toronto, in 1987, 1988, and 1999 respectively; the grants usually support an annual visiting scholar in Buddhist studies.[34] If government funding continues to dwindle, Buddhist studies in Canadian universities may have to rely more on funding from research grants and Buddhist organizations.

Buddhist Studies in Public Schools and Post-Secondary Education

The study of Buddhism was also introduced to the public school curriculum in the early 1970s, usually as part of an elective course on world religions. A neutral approach to all religions was adopted by the school board as part of education at the secondary level. Minority religious groups in British Columbia, Alberta, Manitoba, and Quebec are currently entitled to apply for provincial funding for the establishment of religious schools.[35] However, no Buddhist elementary or secondary school has yet been established in these provinces.

In Ontario, where almost half of the Buddhist population resides, Suwanda Sugunasiri established the Nalanda College of Buddhist Studies in 2000, after he failed twice to launch a Buddhist studies program at the University of Toronto. In 2006, he applied to the Ontario provincial government for accreditation for Nalanda College but the application was eventually refused. (More detail on this is contained in the chapter by Hori and McLellan on Sugunasiri in this volume.)

It should also be briefly noted that with the current and ever-increasing influence of the Internet, one can easily find journal articles, Buddhist scriptures, discussion groups and forums, language courses, and other online resources (Poceski 2006). The Internet has changed not only our methods of communication but also the way we learn about an ancient tradition and its contemporary development. Buddhism in Canada is a website created in 1995 and maintained by Canadian lay Buddhist practitioners George Klima, Chris Ng, and Mathieu Ouellet. It provides a directory of the Buddhist organizations across Canada, frequently updated news about Buddhism in Canada and worldwide, and announcements of Buddhist events in Canada.[36]

THE SEVENTIES AND THE POLICY OF MULTICULTURALISM

The vision of building Canada as a country with individual rights and cultural pluralism is captured by Pierre Trudeau's statement that "although there are two official languages, there is no official culture, nor does any ethnic group take precedence over any other. No citizen or group of citizens is other than

Canadian, and all should be treated fairly."[37] The intention behind the implementation of the policy of official multiculturalism can be seen as a tactic to protect the incoming cultures brought by the immigrants and, at the same time, to prevent these cultures from creating social confusion within the existing conflict between the English and French cultures in Canada. It is, therefore, a policy designed, ideally, to allow the incoming cultures to remain vital, without losing their identities in the process of cultural exchange, and to enable them to overcome cultural differences without being absorbed, rejected, or replaced by the host cultures. The Multiculturalism Act states that the Canadian government is determined to maintain the policy "designed to preserve and enhance the multicultural heritage of Canadians while working to achieve the equality of all Canadians." The policy is also seen to provide Canada with economic, social, and cultural dynamic forces. Indeed, multiculturalism has been seen as one of the ways Canadians are distinguished from Americans. Due to this policy, Canada does not seem to exhibit some of the extreme views one sometimes finds in America.

It was a change in the Canadian immigration policy that fostered the sudden increase of Asian immigrants and allowed large numbers of refugees into Canada, many of whom were practising Buddhists. Since the 1970s, Canada has experienced a transformation of its demographics. Immigrants coming from Asian countries have increased, while those from European countries have relatively decreased. However, according to Reginald W. Bibby, the religious makeup of Canada has not changed greatly, since most immigrants identify themselves with Christianity (Bibby 1987). Caution should be used when studying the figures in Statistics Canada, for it is apparent that the census, among other limitations discussed by Peter Beyer in this volume, assumes that Canadians, immigrants or not, are affiliated with only one religious tradition. Such a view of exclusive affiliation in religious practice, however, does not reflect the reality. Studies have already shown that there are in North America those who have a "double-identity" as Hindu-Christians (Duraisingh 1979) or Confucian-Christians (Berthrong 1994). The Canadian census also overlooks the fact that Asians have a long tradition of engaging themselves in more than one religious activity, sometimes even at the same time. Penny Van Esterik states, "the Lao argue there should be no conflict between Christianity and Buddhism. In fact, many of them attend Buddhist merit-making services on Saturday and Christian services on Sunday" (Van Esterik 1992). The census cannot account for those who are Buddhist-Christian or Buddhist-Hindu, and so forth.

Michelle Spuler makes a similar observation that "[b]lack and white classification systems are no longer correct, particularly not politically" (Spuler 2003, 136). The classification models proposed by Charles Prebish, Jan Nattier, and others are not only misleading but also, as Victor Sōgen Hori argues in his chapter, are imprecise and harbour racist presuppositions. These models, as I argued in an earlier paper (Shiu 2005, 86), are conventional by nature and have their own limitations; they were developed out of the context of American culture, which does not necessarily apply to Buddhism in Canada. Janet McLellan further calls our attention to the distinction between "immigrant Buddhists" and "refugee Buddhists" in Canada. Once again, such a distinction is helpful in recognizing that not all Asian Buddhist groups should be discussed under the same rubric, and yet, such a model also works on a conventional level. Among the refugee Buddhists in Canada, for example, there are great differences between Vietnamese and Tibetan Buddhism, and even within the Vietnamese group one finds great diversity resulting from Vietnamese regionalism and differing political affiliations. In approaching the literature on Buddhism in North America, it is important to bear in mind the various limitations of the different models drawn, and assess under what circumstances these models can be most useful.

CONCLUSION

In the 1960s and 70s, Buddhism lay far removed from the mainstream of Canadian culture. It was practised by small immigrant groups who barely spoke either of the two official languages of Canada. Most Canadians born in Canada had little interest in Buddhism; it was the object of romantic imagination for only a small minority who read D.T. Suzuki or Alan Watts and were fascinated by Eastern religion. It was studied by a small handful of academics who studied Sanskrit and Pali in order to read ancient texts.

Now barely forty years later in the year 2009, the cultural landscape is quite different. The immigrant groups are more numerous and much larger. The Buddhist temples being constructed in the immigrant communities are often the local branches of sophisticated organizations who decades ago developed a modernized Buddhism. Those organizations are now sending their missionaries to promulgate their Buddhism in Canada and the other countries of the West. Among Canadians born in Canada, those interested in Buddhism are still a minority, but it is a serious minority whose needs are no longer satisfied by D.T. Suzuki and Alan Watts. On the Buddhism in Canada website, the page for the British Columbia Lower Mainland (centred around Vancouver) lists eighty-one Buddhist temples and meditation centres. The page for central Toronto (excluding Toronto-East and Southwest Ontario) lists sixty-seven Buddhist temples and meditation centres. The page for Quebec, centred around Montreal, lists fifty-four Buddhist temples and meditation centres. In each case, about half the temples and centres are Western Buddhist centres. They direct themselves to a Western audience. Their first language is English or French. The teacher is often a Westerner, not an Asian. Their practice is continually being adapted for a Westerner's needs, lifestyle, and frame of mind. Buddhism is now constantly present in the media, in films, in schools, in magazine advertising, in the culture in general. Almost always Buddhism is depicted as gentle, non-violent, "nice," so much so that there is a danger that an overly positive stereotype is being created. Nevertheless, it is clear that today, for more and more people, Buddhism is a choice within the cultural mainstream of Canada.

NOTES

1   See Jean R. Burnet with Howard Palmer (1988) for a detailed description of the several waves of immigration to Canada after 1967.

2   See http://www.cttbusa.org/cttb/relatedlinks&branches.asp.

3   See http://www.fgs.ca/english/index.html.

4   See http://www.dharmadrum.org/map-directions/maps-directions.aspx.

5   Cham Shan Temple also publishes a quarterly journal, *Buddhism in Canada*, which chronicles the early development of the temple in Toronto.

6   See Dickson (2002).

7   The first meeting of the Canadian Buddhist Vihara Society took place in 1973, with fifteen committee members elected and the society officially registered. See the history section of the Toronto Mahavihara website at http://lankanstyle.com/mahavihara/history1.htm.

8   In 1976, the Canadian government broadened the definition of "refugee" to allow greater numbers of persecuted South Asians to come into Canada. See Tepper (1980, 138).

9   See http://bouddhisme.buddhismcanada.com/quebec.html.

10 For further information, see the website of the Namgyal Rinpoche Stories Project at http://namgyal.wikidot.com/.

11 See Zen Centre of Vancouver, at http://www.zen.ca/.

12 Suwanda Sugunasiri has published the personal anecdotes of Samu Sunim in *Thus Spake the Sangha* (2008b, 127–60).

13 Among the scholars who participated in this conference are Janet McLellan, Richard Hayes, Leonard Priestley, Roy Amore, Robert Sharf, Victor Sōgen Hori, and Peter Timmerman.

14 The study "Insight Meditation in the United States" by Gil Fronsdale (Prebish and Tanaka 1998, 164–80) is mainly about the Americanized Insight Meditation movement, although there is mention of Goenka. Thibeault (2005) also studies the Goenka movement, mainly in Quebec.

15 There is a great deal of scholarship on Soka Gakkai and Soka Gakkai International. On SGI in the United States, see Hurst (1992). One of the few studies of SGI in Canada is Daniel Metraux's article, "The Soka Gakkai in Australia and Quebec: An Example of Globalization of a New Japanese Religion" (2004).

16 McLellan has written about the role Buddhism plays in the immigrant attempt to maintain ethnic identity in the Canadian milieu (1999, 192–5).

17 See IBFA's website: http://www.aung.com/ibfa.asp.

18 An exception is the Buddhist Council of the Midwest, first formed in 1984, which represents more than eighty Buddhist groups in the Chicago area and has ties to several dozen more groups in Indiana, Wisconsin, and Michigan (http://buddhistcouncilmidwest.org/members.htm). It continues to hold an annual Wesak celebration.

19 On the defining traits of "socially engaged Buddhism," see Queen (1996), and King (1996b).

20 See http://www.gadenrelief.org.

21 See BBC News (2007).

22 See the cover report in *The Economist* (24 September 2007, 29–30).

23 See the Calgary Myanmar Buddhist Temple website.

24 An educational conference on palliative care, entitled "Caring for the Dying in a Multicultural Society: Ethical, Religious, Social and Cultural Perspectives," took place in Toronto in April 2006, with Tenzin Sherab addressing the audience from a Buddhist perspective.

25 See http://www.chass.utoronto.ca/~fgarrett/hospice/.

26 See http://www.vbatoronto.org/en/lesson/CCpamphlet.pdf.

27 See http://www.vbatoronto.org/en/lesson/cancercaring.aspx.

28 See http://en.tzuchi.ca/canada/files/other/tcc-Smile-20060405-StatsSheet.pdf.

29 See http://www.ambedkarmission.com/.

30 In comparison, Sarvodaya USA was formed much earlier than Sarvodaya Canada. Dr
    Ariyaratne authorized the establishment of Sarvodaya USA in late 1995. See the Sarvo-
    daya USA website.

31 These dissertations include Janet McLellan (1993), Angie Danyluk (2003), and Tannie
    Liu (2005). Three MA theses on Buddhism in Canada were written: Alexander Soucy
    (1994); Patricia Campbell (2004), and Kelly Braun (2004). It should be noted that these
    theses deal particularly with Buddhism in Canada. There are many more theses dealing
    with Buddhist studies in general.

32 According to the list of dissertations and theses on the study of American Buddhism
    from 1937 to 1997, compiled by Duncan Ryūken Williams, some seventy-five works, in-
    cluding doctoral dissertations and MA and BA theses, can be found. See Williams and
    Queen (1999, 262–6).

33 See http://www.buddhistedufoundation.com/.

34 See Karunadasa (2001); McGill University; and U of T/McMaster Numata Program. See
    http://www.chass.utoronto.ca/buddhiststudies/numata/index.html.

35 Cf. S. Swift (1993).

36 George Klima reviews the history of his website in an appendix chapter of *Buddhism in
    Canada* (Matthews, 2006)

37 See Pierre Trudeau's speech to the House of Commons, found in the *Report of the Royal
    Commission on Bilingualism and Biculturalism,* (Laurendeau and Dunton, 1971).

Buddhism in Canada
A Statistical Overview from Canadian Censuses 1981–2001[1]

PETER BEYER

Bodhisattva of Compassion, open house weekend
at Monastère Tam Bảo Son, Harrington, Quebec, 2006
Photo by Alexander Soucy

In terms of the number of declared adherents, Buddhism is now the fourth largest religion in Canada, surpassing 300,000 people in the 2001 Canadian census. Although that number represents only a tiny 1% of the overall Canadian population, it is more than double what it was as recently as 1991 and almost six times the figure for 1981. By the next decennial census in 2011, if the pattern of the last thirty years continues, the current number will in all likelihood have doubled or more as the result of continued high levels of immigration from areas of the world where Buddhism is a dominant religion. And Buddhism will have attained the number three position behind only Christianity and Islam. As is almost always the case, however, such inclusive statistics hide as much as they reveal. Above all, they tell us nothing about the nature of this Buddhism, its depth, its personal and institutional strength or weakness. These are, of course, the topics of most of the other essays in this volume. The Canadian census question from which the statistics derive asks only to what religion a person adheres, irrespective of whether or how they actively practise that religion. It is a subjective identification that is being measured, nothing more. Nonetheless, by looking more closely at various other characteristics of its adherents over the last few decades, ones targeted by other census questions, it is possible to gain a somewhat more complex, if not clearer, picture at least concerning such issues as the national origin of Canada's Buddhists, their gender distribution, their level of education, and the patterns of identification among the Canada-born children of these Buddhists. In addition, one can look at where adherents live in Canada, where they are concentrated, and thereby have an idea of where the possibilities for further institutional growth are highest, namely in the areas of highest concentration. This article is devoted to this sort of contextual analysis.

Canada has been asking census questions about religious identification since the 1840s. During the nineteenth century, the categories recorded were all varieties of Christianity, with the single exception of Judaism. In the 1901 census, two additional non-Christian religious identifications make their appearance in the statistics, Confucianism and Buddhism. These reflect the then significant numbers of migrants who had arrived in the late nineteenth century in western Canada from China and Japan respectively.[2] Buddhism is in fact a heavily "Japanese" category until well after the Second World War, a fact well reflected in the two chapters in this volume that focus on Buddhism in Canada before 1970: Terry Watada and John S. Harding both treat exclusively Japanese Buddhist organizations. As late as the 1971 census, almost two-thirds of Buddhists in Canada gave Japanese as their ethnic origin. This strong relation between religious and ethnic identification is further revealed in that the number of Buddhists in 1951 was roughly half of those recorded in the 1941 census – dropping from about 16,000 to about 8,000 – a probable consequence of the harsh treatment of Japanese Canadians during this global conflict.[3] Among the implications of these earlier statistics is that the story of Buddhism in Canada, both statistically and more generally, will be dramatically different after the change in Canada's immigration laws in the late 1960s. With the end of the exclusionary policies that essentially restricted immigration to Europeans, people have been coming to Canada from all over the world. Large numbers of self-identified Buddhists are emigrating from the various Buddhist heartlands of South, Southeast, and East Asia, China and Vietnam in particular. As Henry C.H. Shiu details in his chapter, this pattern has resulted in a significant variety of Buddhist organizations, movements, traditions, and directions developing in Canada and being imported to Canada over the last forty years. The face of Canadian Buddhism is now much more complex and varied, and this is evident from the census statistics.

A look at the Buddhist growth patterns and the ethnic composition of that growth since 1971 can put some flesh on this observation. Table 1 shows the overall situation clearly. We note very low numbers of no more than 15,000 until 1971. Then in only three decades, the numbers climb to the aforementioned 300,000 of the 2001 census. In terms of ethnic origin, already by 1981, the percentage of Japanese Buddhists had declined to roughly 20% of the total. This figure then shrinks to 8% in 1991 and only 4.5% in 2001, a reflection of the fact that few immigrants in recent decades have come from Japan and many more from other Asian regions. Correspondingly, the percentage of Bud-

TABLE 1
Buddhist population of Canada, 1901–2001

Year	1901	1911	1921	1931	1941	1951
Buddhists	10,407	10,012	11,281	15,784	15,635	8,184

Year	1961	1971	1981	1991	2001	
Buddhists	11,611	16,175	51,955	16,3415	300,345	

Source: Canada. Dominion Bureau of Statistics n.d; n.d; Statistics Canada 1980; 2003a

dhists of Southeast Asian origin (mostly Vietnamese at this point; later these are joined by Cambodians and Laotians; see McLellan [1999] and Marybeth White's chapter in this volume) increases from negligible numbers in 1971 to 39% in 1991, only to give way slightly to the ever increasing numbers of Buddhists of Chinese ethnic origin. This latter category went from about 14% of Buddhists in 1971 to almost 55% by 2001. Given the sheer number of immigrants coming to Canada from China, this Chinese dominance is almost certainly still increasing, inevitably lending Canadian Buddhism at the level of the general population an increasingly Chinese flavour. Whether this will lead to Chinese dominance of Buddhist institutions in Canada remains to be seen. Certainly the population base for such ascendancy is there.[4]

Looking at the ethnic composition of Canada's Buddhists somewhat further, Table 2 shows some additional significant trends over the last three decades. These have to do with the increasing and significant minorities of Buddhists who consider themselves ethnically Canadian, the consistent and growing presence of "Western European" Buddhists, and the growth in South Asian (mainly Sri Lankan) and Korean Buddhists. The table gives the raw numbers in addition to percentages so that the growth of these minority categories will be more evident. In particular one notes the significant growth in the ethnically European Buddhists, not in percentage but in absolute terms. Also quite evident is the large increase in ethnically Canadian Buddhists from 1991 to 2001. While not unimportant, the increase probably has more to do with the increasing popularity of this ethnic category in the overall Canadian population – in part a somewhat delayed response to permitting multiple answers for the ethnic identity question as of 1991 – than with the conversion of longstanding Canadians to Buddhism or a change in ethnic identification among the Canadian-born children of immigrant Buddhists.[5] I deal with the issues of "Western Buddhism" and the Buddhist second generation in greater detail below. By contrast, Korean and South Asian Buddhists, while still tiny

TABLE 2
Ethnic composition of Canada's Buddhists, 1971–2001

	1971		1981		1991**		2001**	
Chinese	2310	(14.3%)	15,520	(29.9%)	74,715	(45.7%)	163,570	(54.5%)
Southeast Asian	n/a		19,285	(37.1%)	63,265	(38.7%)	100,635	(33.5%)
Japanese	10,320	(63.8%)	10,510	(20.2%)	13,320	(8.2%)	13,380	(4.5%)
Korean	n/a		495	(1.0%)	1,060	(0.7%)	3,875	(1.3%)
South Asian	285	(1.8%)	1,050	(2.0%)	3,290	(2.0%)	7,105	(2.4%)
Western European	2,210	(13.7%)	4,040	(7.8%)	10,795	(6.6%)	22,215	(7.4%)
Canadian	65	(0.4%)	105	(0.2%)	1,570	(1.0%)	15,685	(5.2%)
Totals	16,175	(100%)	51,955	(100%)	163,420	(100%)	300,345	(100%)

n/a = not available
**includes single and multiple ethnic origins; therefore totals of individual categories are more than overall total
Source: Statistics Canada 2003a

minorities, are clearly increasing both in absolute and percentage terms. Their comparatively small numbers nonetheless point to two of the many peculiarities of recent Canadian immigration patterns: immigrants from Sri Lanka have been overwhelmingly Tamil Hindus, not Sinhalese Buddhists; and Korean immigrants still, as it were, "self-select" for Christianity.[6]

An examination of Canada's immigrant Buddhists in terms of country or region of birth reveals another significant dimension. Among the increasingly dominant ethnically Chinese component, as Table 3 shows, the single largest group here is actually those who were born in Southeast Asia, mostly Vietnam, not China. Even though the sheer numbers of immigrants from the People's Republic, from Taiwan, and from Hong Kong are eroding the percentage dominance of these Chinese Southeast Asians, in 2001 they still constituted over one-third of all Chinese Buddhists. In fact, if we add these Southeast Asian Chinese Buddhists to the ethnically Southeast Asian Buddhists, the degree to which Canadian immigrant Buddhism is still a heavily "Vietnamese" Buddhism becomes even more evident. Instead of the distribution between Chinese and Southeast Asian Buddhists being 54.5% to 33.5% of all Buddhists, it reverses to a ratio of 38.5% to 49.5%. Currently, about half of all immigrant Buddhists in Canada are Southeast Asians, either ethnically or in terms of place of birth.

To a certain degree, this continued Southeast Asian dominance is also a reflection of how people from different world regions typically characterize themselves, and not just or not simply a difference in religious adherence and

TABLE 3

Country of birth of ethnically Chinese immigrant Buddhists in Canada, 1981–2001

Born in	1981		1991		2001	
(PR) China	2,885	(20.1%)	20,930	(31.6%)	45,520	(33.0%)
Taiwan	2,760	(19.2%)	5,130	(7.8%)	22,270	(16.1%)
Hong Kong	1,095	(7.6%)	8,025	(12.1%)	18,285	(13.3%)
Southeast Asia	6,720	(46.8%)	30,415	(45.9%)	47,975	(34.8%)
Elsewhere	910	(6.3%)	1,790	(2.7%)	3,855	(2.8%)
Total	14,370	(100%)	66,290	(100%)	137,905	(100%)

Source: Statistics Canada 2003a

practice. When immigrants from different regions read the Canadian census question "What is your religion?" they will tend to understand it in different ways, at least initially. People from parts of the world where a particular religion or particular religions are an accepted aspect of general cultural identification are more likely to give those religions as their religions, even if their level of involvement or practice is marginal or minimal. In Canada, for instance, it is still the case that far more people identify themselves as one or another variety of Christian than actually practise that religion with any depth or regularity (see, e.g., Bibby 2002). Something similar might be said about people from Muslim majority countries and the identification as Muslim. In many countries of Eastern Asia, by contrast, this kind of "cultural" identifying of oneself as the adherent of any particular religion is far less prevalent. Thus, in China (including Taiwan), Japan, Korea, or Vietnam, the percentage of people who identify as having no religion is much higher than it is in most other places in the world (Pas 1989; Reader 1991; *The Republic of China Yearbook* 2002; Cho 2004). We may interpret this simply as a comparative lack of religiousness but it is probably more accurate to say that the standards for considering oneself an "adherent" of a religion are different. Nonetheless, even among these countries, there are differences in how strong this penchant toward non-identification is. Of those mentioned it appears to be strongest in China, and then in descending order, less strong in Japan, Taiwan, Korea, and finally Vietnam. Accordingly, we should expect these differences to be reflected to some degree among immigrants to Canada who come from these countries. Table 4 shows how this is the case. There we see that the tendency to identify with no religion is strongest among all the ethnically Chinese except those who were born in Southeast Asia. It is comparatively weaker among the Japanese and then

TABLE 4
Religious identity of selected immigrant ethnic groups in Canada, 2001

	Chinese				Japanese	Southeast Asian	Korean
Born in:	PR China	Hong Kong	Taiwan	SEAsia	Japan	Southeast Asia	Korea
Buddhist %	13.0	7.7	31.7	37.8	26.7	53.3	4.3
Christian %	15.7	34.3	20.1	31.7	13.5	25.3	75.0
No religion %	70.6	57.4	47.4	29.7	56.9	19.4	20.3
Other %	0.7	0.6	1.8	0.8	2.9	1.3	0.4
Population	348,915	236,375	70,285	126,980	25,170	141,725	81,575

Source: Statistics Canada 2003a

even more so among the Koreans and Southeast Asians. The ethnically Chinese from Southeast Asia almost seem to be influenced by both elements in that designation, being less nonreligious than the other Chinese but more so than the other Southeast Asians. With the Koreans, their historical self-selection for Christianity must be kept in mind. This is a factor for all the groups listed, but it is strongest among the Koreans. Most important for our purposes here, however, is that the two subgroups born in Southeast Asia are those that identify most readily with Buddhism. Thus the Southeast Asian dominance of Canadian immigrant Buddhism may be as much a matter of differing habits of identification as it is something that will be reflected at the institutional and personal practice level.

This subjective component of Buddhist identity among Canada's immigrants is further evidenced by changes in patterns of religious identification over time once people have arrived in Canada. Table 5 shows such changes for Chinese ethnic immigrants who arrived in Canada between 1981 and 1990. It compares their religious identification in 1991, from one to ten years after their arrival, with that of 2001, after they had been in Canada from ten to twenty years. Although these changes can and should in part be attributed to actual changes in religious identity through conversions or greater involvement in religion – and it is well established that immigrant populations often increase their level of religious involvement as an aspect of their adaptation to new circumstances and a different societal context – the consistency of the change in pattern across groups from different regions or countries of birth signals that we are probably also dealing with a simple shift in subjective identification, in other words, a shift in how the census question is understood and how "approved" answers are perceived. Accordingly, whether these immigrants were

TABLE 5

Religious identification of ethnically Chinese immigrants by place of birth, 1991 and 2001 (immigrated to Canada between 1981 and 1990)

	1991				· 2001			
Born in:	PR China	Hong Kong	Taiwan	SEAsia	PR China	Hong Kong	Taiwan	SEAsia
Buddhist (%)	13.8	5.0	30.1	34.4	19.0	8.4	33.0	42.6
Christian (%)	14.4	32.3	21.0	25.1	16.6	38.4	26.6	26.3
No religion (%)	71.4	62.4	48.5	39.5	63.9	52.4	39.6	30.5
Population	69,695	89,905	11,450	48,735	63,255	65,055	8,450	52,140

Source: Statistics Canada 2003a

born in Taiwan, the People's Republic, Hong Kong, or Southeast Asia, in each case Buddhist and Christian identifications increase from one census to the next and "no religion" identification decreases correspondingly.

These different and changing religious identifications among these immigrant groups lead to questions of the overall numerical strength of Buddhism in Canada and its geographical distribution. A look at these dimensions will prepare the ground for a subsequent and more detailed consideration of the issues of the second generations and levels of education among Canada's Buddhists.

As noted at the outset, Buddhism in 2001 ranked fourth among Canadians in terms of identification with generally recognized world religions. Christianity, of course, was by far the most common such identity, with 77% of the total population of a little under 30 million still declaring themselves Christian in one form or another. Among Christians, as has historically been the case since the arrival of Europeans in Canada, Roman Catholics are the dominant group. In 2001, about 43.5% of the Canadian population said they were Roman Catholic, while Protestants constituted a further 32%, and Eastern Christians a modest 1.5%. As for non-Christian identities, Muslims had risen to around 2% of the population (about 580,000), while Jews (about 330,000), Hindus (about 300,000), and Sikhs (about 278,000), like Buddhists, hovered in the range of 1% each. To say that Buddhists ranked fourth, therefore, is to put them in a group of minority religions, each with similar numerical strengths.

Leaving aside Christians, who make up a substantial majority in almost all parts of the country – the one notable exception is the greater Vancouver area where Christians in 2001 were a bare majority of the population – a look at the geographical distribution of the adherents of the five other world religions reveals some notable concentrations. Overall, Canada's Jews, Muslims, Buddhists,

Hindus, and Sikhs are overwhelmingly concentrated in the major urban areas, especially Vancouver/Abbotsford, Calgary, Edmonton, the Golden Horseshoe (Hamilton to Oshawa, including Kitchener/Waterloo, Guelph, and the Greater Toronto Area [GTA]), Ottawa-Gatineau, and Montreal. In 2001, around 90% of the adherents of each of the five religions lived in these six urban areas. Within those overall figures, however, we find some interesting distributions, including some relating to Buddhists. Table 6 summarizes the statistical picture. Of potential significance is that Buddhists are disproportionately located in Western Canada. Even though a greater number live east of the Manitoba-Ontario border than west of it, 43% of Buddhists live in the west, yet only 30% of the Canadian population does. Moreover, the Vancouver area has 70% as many Buddhists as does Toronto, and yet the Toronto region has almost three times as many inhabitants. The only religious group more heavily western is the Sikhs, 60% of whom live in the west. There are more Sikhs in the Vancouver region than in the entire Toronto area. The adherents of the other three non-Christian religions are all more heavily concentrated in the eastern half of Canada. Over two-thirds of Hindus live in the Toronto region alone; and 80% of Jews are located in either Montreal or Toronto. Even 80% of Muslims, the second largest religion in Canada by number of adherents, live in the east, again, especially in the Montreal and Toronto urban areas.

When populations migrate, especially voluntarily, they often do not do so in equal gender proportions. Historically, in the Canadian case, migrants from Asia – the continent of origin of most Buddhists – were until recently in sometimes great majority male, due to the primarily economic reasons for migration and because Canada's highly restrictive immigration policies before the late 1960s made family unification or the subsequent arrival of wives and families difficult. Although there has been a significant change in this regard in the recent period of a relatively open immigration policy, Muslims, Sikhs, and Hindus in Canada were still in slight majority male in 2001. In 1981, 53.6% of all Muslims were male; in 2001 that figure was still 52.4%. For Sikhs the corresponding figures are 51.6% and 50.7% and for Hindus, 51.5% and 50.5%. Somewhat in contrast, Buddhists were majority male in 1981, but had become majority female by 2001. The corresponding male percentages were 52.1% and 47.4%, the most significant shift in either direction among the four religions. In fact, this shift to majority female has been an accelerating process. The small numbers of Buddhist immigrants who arrived before 1961 were in majority men. Thereafter, the majority are women. Between 1961 and 1970, 54.3% of the

TABLE 6

Geographic distribution of religious identities in Canada, 2001
(Muslims, Jews, Buddhists, Hindus, and Sikhs)

	Muslims	Jews	**Buddhists**	Hindus	Sikhs	Total
All of Canada	579,645	329,990	**300,345**	299,655	278,415	29,639,035
Toronto†	280,670	170,705	**107,530**	203,240	97,980	6,146,450
Vancouver*	53,030	17,435	**75,630**	28,430	115,785	2,112,465
Montreal	100,185	88,765	**37,840**	24,185	7,930	3,380,640
Calgary	25,915	6,530	**16,640**	7,315	13,320	943,310
Edmonton	19,580	3,980	**14,045**	7,920	9,405	927,020
Ottawa‡	41,725	11,325	**9,985**	8,215	2,645	1,050,755
Rest of Canada	58,540	31,255	**38,675**	20,355	31,350	15,078,395
Eastern Canada**	466,820	283,710	**172,325**	244,245	113,505	20,696,525
Western Canada**	112,820	46,285	**128,030**	52,960	164,900	8,942,500

* includes Vancouver and Abbotsford
† includes Golden Horseshoe area including Hamilton, Kitchener-Waterloo, Halton, Peel, York Region, Metropolitan Toronto, and Oshawa
‡ includes Gatineau
** east and west of Manitoba/Ontario border
Source: Statistics Canada 2003a

very small numbers of Buddhist immigrants were women. Between 1971 and 1980, only 51.2% were women, but thereafter the percentage of female increases along with the absolute number of Buddhist immigrants: 52.4% of the 78,000 who arrived in 1981–1990 were women, as were 57.0% of the 84,500 who arrived in 1991–2001. By contrast, Muslim immigrants have been in majority male throughout the post-1970 period, while Hindus and Sikhs have been fairly evenly divided between the two sexes. In addition, the Buddhist gender imbalance also appears to be slightly more of a western than eastern Canadian trend: Buddhists in Vancouver/Abbotsford, for example, were in 2001 over 55% female and immigrants were consistently over 56% women for every decennial cohort after 1960. The Toronto region really experienced the shift only in the most recent decade, when 57.5% of Buddhist immigrants were female. The numbers hover less dramatically just over 50% in the three preceding decades. As the research reported in several of the chapters in this book attests – for instance Tannie Liu's chapter on Chinese Buddhists – Canadian Buddhism leans in the direction of being, at least at the level of practice if not leadership, more female than male; and it clearly shares this characteristic with the still dominant Christianity in practically all its forms.

The reasons for all these imbalances and differences must remain speculative in the absence of focused research on the question, but given that gender in matters religious, as in most other domains of life, tends to make a difference, they are worth keeping in mind. This is especially the case when we consider that overall, 52.1% of Canada's immigrants in the post-1970 period have been women as were about 51% of the total population in 2001. Table 7 summarizes the overall national picture with respect to the four religions and the overall population.

One of the more common questions asked in research on religion and migrant populations is what happens among the second, native-born generations. In the case of Canada's Buddhists, the vast majority are either first generation or the relatively young second generation. This latter group, demographically, is becoming increasingly important. In 2001, 24.4% or 73,350 of Canada's Buddhists gave Canada as their country of birth. Although a sizeable minority of these are not the children of more recent immigrants (I discuss "Western Buddhists" below), the clear majority are. Thus, breaking this group down by declared ethnic origin, we find that 25,700 are of Chinese ethnic origin, 23,300 of Southeast Asian origin, and a further 7,000 or so of either Japanese or South Asian origin.[7] Together these constitute about three-quarters of the Canada-born Buddhists. Here I will concentrate only on those of Chinese and Southeast Asian origins since they are the most significant, making up two-thirds of the overall group; and because the vast majority of Canada-born Buddhists of Japanese background (about 6,300) are not the children of more recent immigrants.[8] A closer look at religious composition, educational attainment, and, in the context of these two, gender, will give a sense of how this generation is different from their parents.

The first observation to make in this regard is somewhat obvious but needs to be underlined: the overwhelming majority of this generation was still quite young in 2001. As concerns the second generation Chinese and Southeast Asian Buddhists, over half were still 10 years old or younger and over 90% under the age of 21. It therefore remains to be seen how they will finally relate to this religion of their heritage when they, in turn, raise the succeeding generation. Some indication emerges from very recent research conducted by me and several colleagues on second generation Buddhists, Muslims, and Hindus in Canada.[9] With very few exceptions, the relation of these young adults (18–27 years old) to Buddhist heritage was minimal. Many of them did not identify themselves personally as Buddhist, most had little knowledge of Buddhism, and those that

TABLE 7
Post-1970 immigration gender balance in Canada, 1981–2001
Percent female*
Overall population, all immigrants, and selected religious identifications

	1971–80	1981–90	1991–2001	Total Population in 1981†	Total Population in 2001†
Canada	–	–	–	50.3	50.9
All immigrants	51.1	51.0	52.3	51.1**	52.1**
Muslims	*47.6*	*44.7*	*48.2*	*46.4*	*47.6*
Sikhs	51.1	*49.8*	51.2	*48.4*	*49.3*
Hindus	50.7	*49.7*	50.4	*48.5*	*49.5*
Buddhists	*48.5*	52.4	57.0	*47.9*	52.6

* when less than 50% and thus majority male, figures are in bold + italics
† includes those born in Canada
** post-1970 immigrants only
Source: Statistics Canada 2003a

did consider themselves – as opposed to their parents or grandparents – to be Buddhist engaged in little meaningful Buddhist practice. Most, however, were also open to future exploration of Buddhism and, given that they had not yet embarked on their careers nor founded their own families, it is possible that at least a sizable minority will in the future reidentify and become involved in some sort of regular Buddhist practice. That, of course, from a Buddhist perspective, is an optimistic scenario.

Although the future may thus be uncertain with regard to the relation of the second generation to Buddhism, what is far more secure is their level of education. Looking at only the small percentage of the Canada-born Buddhists who were over 20 years old in 2001, they appear to be at the leading edge of a generation with very high levels of formal education. Overall, over 80% of this older age group had at least some post-secondary education by 2001, a significant contrast with the Buddhists of the first generation in this regard. Table 8 contrasts the level of post-secondary exposure of Canadian Buddhists, restricting itself to those over 20 years old and those of declared Chinese or Southeast Asian origin. It breaks down the overall pattern to show some very significant intra-Buddhist variations. Perhaps the most obvious fact that reveals itself is how small the Canada-born group was in 2001, especially among Southeast Asians. And among these, a potentially troubling difference is the relatively low level of post-secondary attainment among Southeast Asian, Canada-

TABLE 8
Post-secondary education for Buddhists in Canada according to sex and place
of birth, 2001
Percent with post-secondary education, over 20 years old
Southeast Asian or Chinese ethnicity

	Chinese ethnicity		Southeast Asian ethnicity	
Place of birth	Post-secondary	Total number	Post-secondary	Total number
	%		%	
Women				
China (PRC)	23.7	25,295	–	–
Taiwan	71.3	9,415	–	–
Hong Kong	49.5	9,140	–	–
Southeast Asia	34.7	23,845	36.0	35,455
Canada	85.8	1,755	83.8	340
Average				
(all religious identities)	58.1	71,000	36.5	36,200
Men				
China (PRC)	33.1	17,800	–	–
Taiwan	78.9	7,765	–	–
Hong Kong	61.3	6,750	–	–
Southeast Asia	42.1	20,935	46.2	32,390
Canada	80.1	1,555	63.8	345
Average				
(all religious identities)	66.2	56,350	46.4%	33,050

Source: Statistics Canada 2003a

born males. This group had only about 64% post-secondary education, whereas
the corresponding figure for Chinese and Southeast Asian Canada-born fe-
males and Chinese Canada-born men was 80% or more. A further gender difference is that first generation women in all the categories listed have less
post-secondary exposure than their male counterparts, whereas the women of
the second generation are reversing that trend. The fact that Canada-born
women in these groups have higher levels of post-secondary education than
the men conforms to the overall Canadian pattern in the younger age groups
(Beyer 2005b). It is a small indication of how well integrated the second generation is becoming into the general Canadian social and power structure.

The data in Table 8 also show various differences with respect to the first generation Buddhists of these two ethnic backgrounds. Two seem of particular note. First, in terms of place of birth, the two largest subgroups, those born in Southeast Asia and on the Chinese mainland, are both the largest subgroups and the ones with the lowest percentages of post-secondary education. The majority of them are also women, who have the lowest levels. Second, the Chinese born in Southeast Asia have similar levels to those of Southeast Asian ethnicity (again, to be noted, these are mostly Vietnamese), indicating that it is probably the relative lack of opportunity for post-secondary education in these regions that is making this difference, again especially for women. Correspondingly, those born in Hong Kong and especially Taiwan show much higher levels. For the Southeast Asians, the fact that many of them were refugees and entered Canada as such would also have to be taken into consideration, but further analysis reveals that even those arriving from Southeast Asia well after the era of the "boat people" show lower percentages of post-secondary education than other immigrants (see Beyer 2005b).

Finally, the contrasts between the first and second generation are also reflected in differences in overall religious composition. Again staying with only the majority groups of ethnically Chinese and Southeast Asians, it is notable that the presence of self-identified Buddhism is significantly lower in the second generation than it is in the first. Table 9 shows the contrast in summary fashion. It gives data for first and second generations of the ethnically Chinese or Southeast Asian and parallels the data presented in Table 4 for the first generation. Beside the lower percentage of Buddhists among the Canada born, one also notes a corresponding increase in Christian identification. With respect to those that declare no religious identity, this figure increases for the Southeast Asians and decreases very slightly for the Chinese. One must, however, be careful in how one interprets any of these differences. Since the second generation is still so young, their religious identities are more likely to reflect that of their parents, and therefore the changing composition of successive immigrant cohorts must be taken into consideration. In particular, ethnically Chinese immigrants are arriving less and less Christian in percentage terms in favour of either Buddhist or no religious identity. The more Christian earlier cohorts may well account for more of the Canada-born generation and therefore have passed their religious identities on to them, a fact that would in part explain the higher percentage Christian and lower percentage Buddhist in that Canada-born group. Further analysis of the census data would be required to

TABLE 9

Religious identities of first and second generation Chinese and Southeast Asians in Canada, 2001

	Chinese		Southeast Asian	
Born:	Outside Canada	In Canada	Outside Canada	In Canada
Buddhist (%)	16.6	9.1	51.9	37.7
Christian (%)	26.6	35.4	25.7	33.1
No religion (%)	55.9	54.3	19.9	27.1
Other (%)	0.8	1.2	2.5	2.1
Population	829,130	283,125	148,880	61,895

Source: Statistics Canada 2003a)

know how much this is the case. As concerns no religious identity, this category over the past three decades has been on the rise in the overall Canadian population, and therefore the second generation, being more integrated into the dominant culture as a result of their socialization, may be more likely to reflect that increase than their parents' generation. Yet all this in no way excludes more obvious explanations, especially that there may be a net conversion of the second generation to the dominant Christianity and a net abandonment of Buddhist identity, the latter perhaps for the reasons mentioned above and reflected in the qualitative research project on second generation immigrants: the Canada-born are simply not being socialized as effectively into Buddhist identification and practice.

Any attempt to isolate the "Western" Buddhists from among Canadian Buddhists is fraught with certain difficulties relating to both the nature of the statistical data here under review and the category itself. On the one hand, it is relatively clear that Buddhism, especially of the Tibetan and Zen variety, has been enjoying a period of significant growth in Western countries like Canada over the last few decades (see, e.g., Prebish 1998; Prebish and Baumann 2002), specifically among those of non-Asian cultural and ethnic backgrounds. On the other hand, this "Western" Buddhism does not exclude people of Asian backgrounds, in particular not those of the second and subsequent generations. Quite aside from the question of precisely what forms of Buddhist institutions, movements, and practice should actually count as Western Buddhism, it is not nearly as clear as observers might sometimes assume as to *who* should count as a "Western" Buddhist.[10]

In the context of those questions, the Canadian census statistics at least have the advantage that they cut through all these ambiguities because they are based on a single question that asks only subjective identification: people are listed only as Buddhist, not according to whatever subtype they may or may not have also included on their census form. In most cases, one can safely assume that the response was "Buddhism, not otherwise specified." Nonetheless, that virtue becomes somewhat tempered when we then ask which of those Buddhists might count as Western from a cultural or ethnic perspective. There are three Canadian census variables that one could use, namely ethnic identity, place of birth, and what is called "visible minority" status. But each of these is not clear enough by itself. Thus, for instance, Buddhists who give Canadian as their ethnic identity might still have significant Asian background, whether because they are multiply ethnic or because they simply choose to declare themselves Canadian, as anyone who lives in this country can do. Something similar, but less so, goes for those who give one of the variety of European ethnic identities. Place of birth is the least reliable because one cannot separate the Canada-born second generation of Asian immigrant Buddhists from other Canada-born Buddhists. In addition, those born outside both Eastern/Southern Asia and Canada could also be of Asian Buddhist background. And finally, although "visible minority" is in certain ways more promising in that one could focus especially on "white" (i.e., non-visible minority) Buddhists, it is less reliable than one might think given evidence that some people whom one might consider "objectively" Asian will "subjectively" identify themselves as "white" on the census. Indicatively, therefore, in 2001 there were somewhat fewer "visible minority" Chinese in Canada than "ethnically" Chinese; somewhat fewer "visible minority" Southeast Asians than "ethnically" Southeast Asian; and so on for Koreans, Japanese, South Asians, and most other categories (Statistics Canada 2003a; 2003b).

To "find" the numerical strength of Western Buddhists, therefore, one must of necessity guess a bit or get at the number indirectly. It thus seems advisable to approach the question using all three of the ethno-cultural variables. Table 10 gives statistics for the number of Canadian Buddhists in 2001 who gave various answers for these three. There are few consistencies here, but the one exception is the roughly similar numbers for "white" and ethnically "European" Buddhists, both of which are in the low to mid 20,000s. Place of birth seems entirely unreliable. If one had to guess, therefore, a conservative estimate of the number of Western Buddhists in Canada in 2001 would be somewhere in

TABLE 10

"Western Buddhists"

Buddhist in Canada by ethnic identity, place of birth, and visible minority categories, 2001

	Buddhists
Visible minority*	
"White"	24,070
Other "non-Asian"	2,340
Ethnicity	
European	22,215
Canadian	15,685
Place of birth	
Europe	3,135
Other "non-Asian"	1,435
Canada	73,350

* excludes "multiple" visible minority
** "non-Asian" = not East, South, or Southeast Asian
Source: Statistics Canada, 2003a; 2003b

the low 20,000s, a greater number by far than similar categories of "white" and "European" Muslims, Sikhs, or Hindus.[11] Overall, then, one can tentatively conclude or confirm from the statistics what the qualitative literature indicates as well: Euro-Canadian Buddhists (to use another title) are still a statistical minority in Canada when compared to those Buddhists who are of recent immigrant origin, but the former nevertheless constitute a significant number which is apparently growing; in 1991, there were, for instance, only 10,800 ethnically European Buddhists in Canada (Statistics Canada 2003a). Moreover, if our current research on second generation immigrants of Buddhist background is any indication, then it is unlikely that this group will contribute significantly either to the Buddhism of their parental generation or to the "Western" Buddhism of their co-citizens. The second generation functioning as a kind of bridge between the two categories of "Western" and "Asian" therefore seems equally unlikely – at least for the time being.

Attempting overall conclusions from the 2001 Canadian census data is somewhat risky given the sorts of ambiguities in the numbers that I have reported here. Nonetheless, some conclusions do seem quite solid, even if their significance will have to await the future and further, more focused research. They can be summarized as follows:

- Numerically, Buddhism is growing in Canada, at least doubling in number of declared adherents every ten years, even though in 2001 they still constituted barely 1% of the Canadian population.
- The bulk of this growth reflects continued high levels of immigration from regions of the world where Buddhism has historically been a strong presence.
- Since the source of Canada's immigration is a modest reflection of the distribution of world population, it is unsurprising that Buddhism is demographically increasingly dominated by people from China or of Chinese ethnic origin. In this context, immigrants from the People's Republic of China will probably constitute an ever larger portion of Canada's Buddhists simply because that country has so many people, regardless of religious identity. In the meantime the large influx of refugees from Southeast Asia during the late 1970s and the 1980s still gives Canadian Buddhism a decidedly "Vietnamese" flavour, whether ethnically those Buddhists are Vietnamese or Chinese.
- The Canada-born children of self-identified Buddhist immigrants in large proportion do not appear to be retaining or carrying forth their parental Buddhist identity, with the qualification that this generation is still quite young and may, in its more mature years, evidence a different pattern.
- Using education as a measure, the children and youth of Canada's immigrant Buddhists are integrating rapidly into the mainstream, showing high levels of post-secondary exposure as well as reflecting the overall Canadian situation in which women have post-secondary education in greater percentages than do men, both measures in express contrast to the immigrant generation of their parents.
- Canada's Buddhists live disproportionately in the western part of the country, even though a majority live in the eastern part, mainly because of large numbers in the two largest urban areas of Montreal and Toronto.
- So-called "Western" Buddhism is a significant, if minority, aspect of Canadian Buddhism, probably constituting from 6 to 9% of self-identified Buddhists, and thereby making Buddhism the Canadian religion attracting the highest number of outside converts in absolute numbers or in percentage terms, after Christianity.

Each of these conclusions is, if perhaps intriguing, only a surface measure. As is usual with such statistics, they do not answer questions so much as frame them. And it is in this spirit that they are offered here. Further research and careful observation is needed in order to discover what patterns of institutions, practice, and transformation are behind these numbers. The remaining chapters in this volume make their contribution in this direction.

NOTES

1 The data reported in this article derive substantially from the results of a research project, *Trends in Religious Identification among Recent Immigrants to Canada, 1961–2001*, conducted by the author in collaboration with John H. Simpson, Leslie Laczko, Wendy Martin, Kyuhoon Cho, and Rubina Ramji. The project was financially supported by the Social Sciences and Humanities Research Council of Canada. This chapter is a slightly amended version of Beyer (2006a).

2 Of note is that migrants of South Asian origin who arrived during the same period, especially Sikhs, are not similarly recognized in the 1901 census. Along with Islam, Hinduism, and various other religions, Sikhism had to wait until 1981 before its census numbers were recorded and published by the Dominion Bureau of Statistics/Statistics Canada.

3 A parallel phenomenon can be observed in the number of ethnic "Germans" recorded before and after the First World War. In 1911 Canada had about 400,000 people who declared themselves as German. In 1921, this number had decreased to around 295,000 only to rebound to slightly over 470,000 in 1931. Meanwhile, the number of "Austrians" jumped from 44,000 to 108,000 between 1911 and 1921, only to descend again to 49,000 in 1931. The situation demonstrates that the "subjective" component of all these identifications must always be kept in mind (Statistics Canada 1980).

4 As various chapters in this volume reveal (see, for instance, those by Alexander Soucy, Lina Verchery, Tannie Liu, and André Laliberté and Manuel Litalien), there is correspondingly an increasing presence of Chinese Buddhist movements and organizations in Canada, but not to the exclusion of an increasing number that are not. The trend toward Chinese dominance is therefore, at least to date, more a demographic than an institutional one. The reasons behind this are complex and cannot be broached here adequately.

5 See Victor Sōgen Hori's discussion of this issue in his introductory chapter. This chapter's extensive discussion about the difficulties inherent in the categorizations that Statistics Canada and all the rest of us use should be read in conjunction with the analysis here.

6 Thus, in 2001, of the 101,715 ethnic Koreans in Canada, only 3.8% declared themselves Buddhist, while 75.2% were Christian, with "no religion" taking up the remaining fifth

(Statistics Canada 2003a). By contrast, in Korea, Christians make up only some 25% of the population and about half declare that they belong to no religion (see Cho 2004). The custom data from which the Canadian figures are calculated do not allow me to isolate Sri Lankans from South Asians more generally. From other available data, however, we see that 87,000 immigrants said they were born in Sri Lanka and about 65,000 identified themselves as ethnically Sri Lankan or Sinhalese. Even if all the South Asian Buddhists noted in Table 2 were among these, that is still a small minority of this group.

7 Not surprisingly perhaps, given the dominance of Christianity among them, there were in 2001 only a very insignificant number of Canada-born Korean Buddhists (260) (Statistics Canada 2003a).

8 The Canada-born children of post-1970 immigrants could be no older than about 30 in 2001. In that year, 26,500 of the 56,000 Canada-born and ethnically Japanese in Canada were over 30; and of the 6,300 Japanese Buddhists, almost 4,700 were over 30 and of those, more than 3,200 were over 50. Since, however, only 1,740 of the Canada-born Japanese Buddhists also had parents who were both born in Canada, the second generation story of Canada's Japanese Buddhists is simply a rather different story compared to the one that I am addressing here. See Makabe (1998).

9 *Religion among Immigrant Youth in Canada* was funded by the Social Sciences and Humanities Research Council of Canada and carried out by the author in collaboration with Shandip Saha, Rubina Ramji, Nancy Nason-Clark, Lori Beaman, John H. Simpson, Leslie Laczko, Arlene Macdonald, Carolyn Reimer, and Marie-Paule Martel Reny. It interviewed about 200 youth from the three religious backgrounds, youth who grew up in or were born in Canada to immigrant families. A little less than a quarter of these youth were of Buddhist background. The interviews were conducted between spring of 2004 and spring of 2006 predominantly among current university students in Ottawa, Toronto, and Montreal. For a partial report on the male Buddhists from this research, see Beyer (2008).

10 This is a recurrent theme in a number of the other chapters in this book, but see especially the introductory chapters by Victor Sōgen Hori and Alexander Soucy.

11 The number of "white" and "European" Hindus and Sikhs is far lower than the number of Buddhists in these categories, but neither of these has a reputation or a self-identity as a proselytizing religion. For Islam, which does actively seek converts, the situation is somewhat more complicated because many people who identify as Arab ethnically do not categorize themselves as Arab visible minority, but rather, it seems, as "white." These will therefore increase the number of "white" Muslims, but will for the most part not be converts, especially when one considers the sizable number of Muslims from ex-

Yugoslavia in Canada, who are "white" but also not generally converts. Thus, the number of "white" Muslims, 82,000, is much higher than the number of "white" Buddhists, but the number of ethnically "Western European" Muslims, 18,000, is quite a bit lower when one considers that there were almost twice as many Muslims in Canada in 2001 as Buddhists (Statistics Canada 2003a; 2003b).

PART THREE From Global to Local

Jodo Shinshu in Southern Alberta
From Rural Raymond to Amalgamation

JOHN S. HARDING

Ministers from across Canada and children in
Ochigo procession for the BTSA's New Temple
Dedication Service on 26 April 2009
Photo by John S. Harding

Yutetsu Kawamura and his wife, Yoneko,
with their three children, Leslie (Sumio)
in the middle, Rosie (Yukiko) on the left,
and Cathy (Yoriko) on the right, in front
of the Raymond Buddhist Church
in the late 1930s
Photo courtesy of Rosie (Yukiko) Marano

On 4 July 2004, members of the Raymond Buddhist Church[1] along with family and friends filled their historic building to capacity for an Obon service. They came to commemorate the 75th anniversary of this cultural and religious hub of the Buddhist community in southern Alberta. Yutetsu Kawamura, then in his mid-nineties, was the first of several ordained Jodo Shinshu[2] ministers to approach the image of Amida Buddha and take his seat for the service. The first and second generation members who had led the congregation for most of its seventy-five-year span sat quietly in the pews. The presence of some younger families, the third and fourth generation descendants of the first Japanese immigrants, as well as a few non-Asian Buddhists, offered glimpses of potential enduring vitality. The dharma talk – given in unaccented English by Michael Hayashi, a young minister with a good sense of humour whose cultural references were eminently Canadian – further reinforced the sense of ongoing transformation from earlier decades when services were in Japanese and all ministers had been born and trained in Japan.

Despite these signs of youth, vitality, and transformation, the commemorative events emphasized this important community's past more than its present. At a banquet that weekend, representatives from several generations gathered and reminisced about the history, developments, and various activities that made their beloved Buddhist temple central to their community. Speakers at this event also expressed appreciation for the pioneers whose vision and dedication, in difficult circumstances, successfully established the Raymond Buddhist "Church" in 1929 within an overwhelmingly Christian landscape. First and second generation members were praised for supporting Buddhism in southern Alberta through the Great Depression, forced internment, and a range of challenges and celebrations. Whereas the wealth of stories testified to the deep roots of Jodo Shinshu in this rural area of Canada, the vitality of the community for that special commemoration dissipated in later regular services.

The core membership in Raymond proved to be only a small fraction of the several hundred in attendance on 4 July. Moreover, the average age of the regular members was considerably older than that of the multi-generational crowd, which had included children and grandchildren who had come from nearby cities and more distant locations. Demographic shifts common to other rural settings had resulted in few of the younger generations taking over their parents' roles in the temple, the closing of the Sunday school, and related signs of decreased participation and diminished vitality in the 1990s.[3] Dwindling numbers of younger members compounded by the deaths of aging members in its last two decades foreshadowed the Raymond Buddhist Church's own demise.

In 2006, less than two years after the 75th anniversary events, the Raymond church building had been sold. It was the oldest Buddhist temple in the region, a provincial historic site, and a multifaceted centre of Buddhism for several generations. However, the centre had become increasingly peripheral. During the final service, on 21 May, Rev. Leslie Kawamura, who was born in the Raymond temple when his father, Yutetsu Kawamura, was the minister, offered a moving eulogy for the building itself (Nishiyama 2006).[4] In the context of Buddhist notions of rebirth, where causes and conditions that determine a new birth are understood to be rooted in earlier cycles of existence, the closing of this centre of Buddhism in southern Alberta was a planned prelude to, and one of the conditions for, the rebirth of a new temple to serve an amalgamated congregation consisting of several communities in southern Alberta.

On Remembrance Day, 11 November 2007, Rev. Yasuo Izumi, the local Jodo Shinshu minister, and other dignitaries and Buddhist officials broke ground in Lethbridge at the site of the future Buddhist Temple of Southern Alberta (BTSA).[5] This new centre ushers in a new era, a new building, a newly combined congregation, which includes Raymond's Buddhists, and a newly articulated vision, mission, and set of guiding principles.[6]

This chapter tells the story of the old church and the new temple. The present amalgamation marks a transition from the trials and triumphs of early Buddhists in Raymond and related congregations to a new phase of hope and anxiety as the old churches have been sold and a new temple has been built. The Jodo Shinshu communities of southern Alberta have lost members and vitality, but they hope that the newly amalgamated congregation will restore both. Jodo Shinshu no longer dominates the Buddhist scene in Canada, but this relatively rural community was strikingly influential in shaping the early contours of Canada's Buddhist landscape.

Whereas the majority of Buddhists in Canada today are relatively recent immigrants from China and Southeast Asia, who came after the change in immigration laws in 1967 and settled in Canada's largest cities, the multi-generational Jodo Shinshu communities in southern Alberta stem primarily from much earlier immigration patterns.[7] Starting in the late 1800s, immigrants came from Japan, and some moved to rural settings. Peter Beyer's chapter in this book provides statistical data and analysis that indicates how anomalous this scenario is in Canada; in the 2001 census less than 5 per cent of Buddhists declared Japanese ethnic origin and less than 13 per cent lived outside six metropolitan areas. This community represents a small and steadily decreasing percentage of the population. Nonetheless, Jodo Shinshu Buddhists' contributions have been impressive.

This case study complements several other chapters in *Wild Geese*. Terry Watada includes some of the history of Raymond and Lethbridge in his overview of Jodo Shinshu in Canada up to the 1970s. Henry Shiu's chapter brings the larger story of Buddhism in Canada up to the present and includes the role of scholars from the Jodo Shinshu community. And Victor Hori's critique of categories such as Asian/ethnic and Western/convert highlights their limitations and the implicit value judgments that render such categories inadequate for describing and understanding this Buddhist community.

ORIGINS OF THE COMMUNITY[8]

Jodo Shinshu Buddhism did not arrive in rural Alberta due to a missionary campaign but instead followed young Japanese men who emigrated from Japan in the late 1800s and early 1900s. Moreover, the institutional support of priests and temples did not accompany these men, who typically intended to return to Japan after making their fortunes. The majority of these early Japanese immigrants were from rural settings in Japan and were not first sons, who customarily would inherit their parents' household.[9] Although many came for economic reasons, they generally were not destitute economic refugees. Iwaasa indicates that his interviews and research revealed that immigrants needed sufficient status and means to afford the journey and to be allowed by the Japanese government to represent their homeland (Iwaasa 1972, 4–6). Although economic motivations for immigration were important, the lowest socio-economic strata would have been doubly hindered, lacking both means for the voyage and the backing of the Meiji government, which was striving to bolster its image abroad. The Meiji Restoration had opened Japan to global markets of information, technology, transportation, and labour – prompting a group of Japanese emigrants to leave for Hawaii in 1868 without official sanction. However, that early experience of Japanese workers overseas was not positive and the Meiji government allowed its citizens to legally seek employment abroad only from the middle of the 1880s (Gall 1995, 100).[10]

The young men who left Japan for the mainland of North America settled primarily along the west coast. Canada received Japanese immigrants as early as 1877 with surges from 1899 to 1900 and 1906 to 1907. Due to increasingly restrictive Canadian immigration policies in the first half of the twentieth century, numbers decreased until there was only a slight influx in the 1930s, primarily of spouses (Boisvert 2005, 72).

The reception extended to the immigrants was mixed. Canadian Christian organizations and individuals sent a full range of signals, from offers of assistance and social services to aggressive proselytizing and overt prejudice (Takata 1983, 30–1).[11] Japanese Christian organizations also offered services to these immigrants and sought converts from among them. The Japanese Methodist Church in Vancouver was established in 1896 and the United Church of Canada, which included the Methodists after a 1925 merger, boasted the most Japanese Christians in Canada (Takata 1983, 32). Nonetheless, most immigrants remained Buddhist and began to receive institutional support from Japan soon after the turn of the century. The Nishi Hongwanji[12] headquarters of Jodo Shinshu Buddhism in Japan actively reached out to communities of Japanese abroad. By 1905, a Buddhist temple opened in Vancouver, where there was a significant concentration of immigrants, complete with a minister, Reverend Sasaki.[13]

Smaller numbers of Japanese immigrants began to settle in rural areas of southern Alberta from around this time through to the middle of the twentieth century. Caldarola reports that approximately forty Japanese immigrants arrived in Raymond in 1903 to work for the Knight Sugar Company and by 1908 the Canadian Pacific Railway employed many of the six hundred Japanese workers in southern Alberta (2007, 5). Although growing, this community was considerably smaller and less established than Vancouver's. There would be no temple or full-time minister during the first quarter of a century; nevertheless, small towns such as Raymond became surprisingly influential centres for some of the oldest Buddhist communities in Canada.

The transformation from a collection of young, single, male workers planning to return to Japan to a community of families striving to establish a Buddhist temple took time. Some immigrants returned to Japan, others moved to America, and still others decided to stay in Canada or felt they had not attained the fortune or glory necessary to return to Japan honourably. As it became clear that they would not be returning to Japan, many married and began to raise families. Some returned to Japan to wed and others were united with "picture brides"[14] in Canada, since travel back and forth was expensive and made more difficult by increasingly restrictive and racist immigration laws.

When the Japanese shifted their intention from returning to Japan to raising families in Canada, they also reoriented their identity from Japanese temporarily abroad to Japanese Canadian increasingly at home. The evolving identity of this community is typically differentiated by successive generations: *issei*, who were born in Japan and generally held fast to the culture, language, and values that had shaped them; *nisei* (second generation), who at times straddled both cultures and languages; and the typically quite integrated and assimilated *sansei* and *yonsei* (third and fourth generation), who identified most strongly with the English language and Canadian culture and values. There is, of course, a wide spectrum of variation among and within these generations.

Unlike the *sansei* and *yonsei*, who are very well represented in a wide variety of professions, *issei* and *nisei* "pre-War Japanese Canadians were largely concentrated occupationally in farming, logging, fishing, grocery, small hotels, and were restricted legally from certain professions" (Hirabayashi 1978, 63). Whereas many who settled in cities initiated businesses, those who came to rural southern Alberta before the war worked as farmers in towns such as Raymond and as railroad workers and coal miners in towns such as Hardieville and Coalhurst (L. Kawamura 1978, 42). These towns included substantial numbers of Okinawan settlers, some of whom had been recruited as railroad workers but transitioned to coal mining.[15] Watada reports that many Okinawan settlers may have chosen southern Alberta over "concentrated areas of Japanese settlements in B.C." due to concerns that those larger Japanese groups may have maintained an anti-Okinawan bias (Watada 1996, 134–5).

ESTABLISHING A BUDDHIST CHURCH

While rural southern Alberta is better known for its influential Mormon population, the Japanese pioneers forged a significant Buddhist presence as well. Japanese immigrants in the small town of Raymond formed a Japanese Society in 1914. By 1929, Jodo Shinshu members were sufficiently settled in Raymond to purchase a suitable structure for religious services, a former school and Mormon meeting house.[16] One hundred and twenty-four community members from Raymond, Coalhurst, and Hardieville committed almost $7,400 to cover the $5,000 purchase price and to provide additional support as part of a one-hundred-year plan for the new church (LDJCA 2001, 97; Watada 1996, 136). Their success in establishing the first Buddhist temple in southern Alberta is all the more impressive in light of their limited resources and the financially strained circumstances at the onset of the Depression. A concerted effort led to payment of these pledges by 1940 (Watada 1996, 139).[17]

The building was for sale because the Mormon community needed a larger space for worship.[18] While this reinforced the minority status of the Japanese immigrant community, the willingness of the Mormon Church to sell to them, their own ability to purchase the building, and the increasing prominence of the Buddhist community in the 1930s suggest that the Japanese immigrants had achieved a certain level of acceptance relative to the discriminatory immigration laws in the 1920s and forced internment in the 1940s. Discrimination was not unheard of in southern Alberta – and it would intensify in the 1940s – but it appears to have been less prevalent than in British Columbia. This impression of broader community support and acceptance is buttressed by newspaper articles and anecdotes related by Buddhist residents in Raymond.

The Raymond Buddhist Church gained its first resident minister with Shinjo Nagatomi's arrival on 4 June 1930. Visiting ministers had performed services for the Raymond community before this; in fact, one account credits Rev. Taga's visit from the Honpa Buddhist Temple in Vancouver for an Obon service on 1 July 1929 as being a catalyst for establishing a temple in Raymond (L. Kawamura 1978, 43–4). The addition of resident ministers, naturally, increased the vitality and centrality of the new church and of Buddhist services and organizations in this widely dispersed, rural community. Rev. Nagatomi's wife, Sumi, joined him soon after his arrival and taught Japanese lessons to the *nisei* children (Iwaasa 1972, 49).

After Rev. Nagatomi's departure in 1934, Rev. Yutetsu Kawamura and his family joined the community. Although Rev. Kawamura left Raymond in 1940 intending to return to Japan, circumstances redirected him first to an interim position with Maple Ridge temple in British Columbia and then, with Canada's entry into World War II and the forced relocation of Japanese immigrants and their descendents away from British Columbia's coast, back to southern Alberta.

Rev. Yutetsu Kawamura's return to southern Alberta in early May of 1942 was followed almost immediately by the arrival of Rev. Shinjo Ikuta and his family. Both ministers were central to Buddhist developments in southern Alberta throughout the 1940s with Rev. Ikuta leading the Raymond Church and Rev. Kawamura moving to Picture Butte in October of 1942, where members of the Picture Butte Bukkyokai (Buddhist Society) provided a house that was at once a residence, the church, and a co-op store (Watada 1996, 139–53).[19]

FORCED RELOCATION

The government-mandated relocation dispersed all Japanese communities beyond coastal strongholds in British Columbia. It was a profound hardship and the culmination of a series of discriminatory policies. The relocation also precipitated a transitional moment for Shin Buddhism in southern Alberta, bringing these ministers to Raymond in 1942 and resulting in the spread of Jodo Shinshu throughout Canada.

Japanese *issei* pioneers had established and led the communities and temples through the difficult years from the late 1920s to the end of racially biased laws following World War II. The First World War had not presented particular obstacles to acceptance of Japanese immigrants because Japan was an ally in that conflict. However, with the shift of Japan's status to an enemy nation in 1942, Japanese and Japanese Canadians were forced to relocate, transported to internment camps, and forced into specific areas of labour. Thousands of these so-called "enemy aliens" chose southern Alberta from quite limited options, often because evacuation to Alberta allowed the families to stay together.

The forced relocation sent approximately 3,000 evacuees to southern Alberta at a time when there were fewer than 600 Japanese residents in the entire province. This influx coincided with a shortage of labourers on southern Alberta sugar beet farms, a shortage exacerbated by the loss of young men who enlisted in the war effort, including more than a half dozen local Japanese Canadians. Many of the relocated Japanese were put to work on beet farms in various rural communities. Caldarola states that from April to June of 1942 approximately "2,250 Japanese (370 families) were settled on sugar beet farms and other irrigated lands throughout southern Alberta, particular[ly] in Taber and Raymond" (2007, 6). The Minister of Labour, Humphrey Mitchell, credited the Japanese with having "saved the sugar beet industry" but also stated, "I do not see any chance of Southern Alberta getting any more" (Iwaasa 1972, 81).

At the end of World War II, some Japanese immigrants were deported and many Japanese Canadians discovered that their property and possessions in British Columbia had been taken with little or no compensation. A significant number of those who had been relocated to southern Alberta chose to remain in the area. This was, in large part, because a Japanese community was already well established, well respected relative to the times, and had Buddhist temples and organizations in place. In fact, the Raymond Buddhist Church was the only active temple with a resident minister in all of Canada during much of 1942 when ministers in British Columbia were relocated and some of their temples vandalized (Watada 1996, 118–20).

The forced relocation to southern Alberta included some positive developments for Buddhism in the area. Although the surge in population was not permanent, it prompted the construction of a number of Buddhist churches and the development of related organizations. In his carefully researched 1994 article, Akira Ichikawa shows how Canada's discriminatory wartime policies both inflicted injustice upon Japanese Buddhists in Canada and inadvertently helped to spread Jodo Shinshu more widely throughout the country. He asserts that "The Buddhist ministers' well-being and that of the faith, at a time when animosities toward them were rife, were linked to an ironic twist of priorities wherein the Canadian government highlighted religious tolerance even as it had made a shambles of due process" (Ichikawa 1994, 59). Discriminatory policies, while leading to inadvertent spread, also resulted in the deportation of most Jodo Shinshu ministers in Canada and accelerated assimilation.[20]

RAYMOND BUDDHIST CHURCH AS HUB

Raymond's Buddhist church had served as the centre of all sorts of religious, recreational, and cultural activities for children and adults for more than a

decade before the forced relocation. It continued on during the war with ver-
satile functions from Sunday school to innovations supported by Reverend
Ikuta, such as a daycare and martial arts dojo for kendo and judo (Watada
1996, 142–3).[21] Moreover, after the war, the Raymond Buddhist Church became
the headquarters for the Buddhist Foundation of Canada (BFC), which was
formed in 1946 to "raise money and oversee the administration of all Buddhist
churches in Canada" (Watada 1996, 146). Ichikawa notes that the original full
name of this new organization was the "Canada Bukkyo Fukyo Zaidan (Canadian Buddhist Propagation Foundation)" and that its objectives included
"financially helping new temples in central and eastern Canada and recruiting
second-generation ministers" (1994, 59). Its power over ministers, however, was
quite limited. These appointments were made by the Nishi Hongwanji head
temple and administered in North America through the newly renamed Buddhist Churches of America (BCA) until the Buddhist Churches of Canada
(BCC) formed in 1967.

In addition to providing an organizational hub, Raymond's relative stability
furthered its status as a central repository for valuable religious items during
and after the war. Rev. Shinjo Ikuta had arranged for the shipment of "approximately 200 urns containing the ashes of church members to the Raymond
Buddhist Church for storage" during the wartime relocation in British Columbia. Rev. Toshio Katatsu brought Steveston temple's statue of the Buddha
to Raymond in February 1946 before he returned to Japan. And the altar from
the Royston Church arrived in Raymond two months later (Watada 1996, 118,
143). Raymond's church was the oldest Buddhist temple in southern Alberta,
but a half dozen others followed from the influx of Japanese families into other
rural southern Albertan towns from 1942 until the founding of Lethbridge's
second temple in 1970.

Through the movements and activities of Shin family members and ministers, the influence of the Raymond Buddhist community spread to these new
congregations as well as to other Buddhist churches and Shin groups in North
America. Descendents of early ministers in Raymond helped shape Buddhism
in Canada and beyond through religious and academic pursuits. For example,
Shinjo Ikuta's son, Kyojo Ikuta, was the minister for the Calgary Buddhist Temple from 1972, became the first Canadian-raised sōchō (Bishop) of the Buddhist
Churches of Canada from 1998 to 2002, and returned to lead the Calgary community until his retirement in May 2008. His son, Grant Ikuta, has extended

this role to a third generation. He led the large Toronto Buddhist Temple before assuming ministerial duties at the Steveston Buddhist Temple in July 2008,
several months before the 80th anniversary celebration of that temple.

Yutetsu Kawamura's son, Leslie Kawamura, also followed a ministerial path
with training at Ryūkoku University in Kyoto and an active role as a minister
in Raymond and Lethbridge. His contributions have spanned the academic
study of Buddhism as well. He pursued graduate work at Kyoto University and
the University of Saskatchewan before becoming a professor of Buddhist
studies at the University of Calgary in 1976. He is a renowned Buddhologist
specializing in Indian Yogācāra Buddhism – including the relevant Sanskrit,
Tibetan, and Chinese source texts – as well as an influential force behind many
Asian and Buddhist studies initiatives at and beyond the University of Calgary,
including the establishment of Calgary's Numata Chair in Buddhist Studies.[22]

Shinjo Nagatomi's son, Masatoshi Nagatomi, studied first at Ryūkoku and
then pursued Indian philosophy and Buddhism at Kyoto University. He became one of the best-known scholars of Buddhist studies during his almost
half-century affiliation with Harvard until his death in 2000. Because of his
facility in all major Buddhist languages, wide-ranging expertise, and enthusiastic dedication, an overview of his life and accomplishments at Harvard notes
that "after his retirement, no fewer than three searches were launched to replace his contribution"(Carman et al. 2005).

Admittedly, Masatoshi Nagatomi was a young boy during his father's time
in Raymond before the latter moved on to other ministerial posts in the United
States. In fact, many influential Jodo Shinshu ministers, whose careers span
multiple roles and positions in North American Buddhism, began careers in
Raymond or served a significant term in southern Alberta. The tradition of
sons taking over their father's temple or at least following in their father's religious occupation is as old as Jodo Shinshu.[23] The careers of these sons of early
ministers epitomizes the wide-ranging influence radiating out from Raymond
to Jodo Shinshu practice in North America and to the newly emerging field of
Buddhist studies.[24]

SPREAD AND SPLIT

Whereas southern Alberta Buddhists in small communities other than Raymond had conducted services and gatherings in members' homes before
World War II, the 1942 surge in population led to the establishment of four

additional churches in Picture Butte (1942), Coaldale (1943), Taber (1950), and Rosemary (1958).[25] The locations for these religious and cultural centres reflect the largely rural distribution of Japanese families, many of whom were involved in agriculture. Increasing freedom to adopt a wider range of professions followed the end of World War II. Nonetheless, Raymond remained attractive, even to many Jodo Shinshu members who were not tied to the land, precisely because of the well-rooted Japanese community and the relatively supportive relationships cultivated with residents beyond that community. In contrast, city officials in Lethbridge had imposed discriminatory restrictions aimed at preventing the Japanese from settling within city limits. After this barrier was removed in 1946, increasing numbers moved to the city from rural towns. A Buddhist church opened in Lethbridge within a decade with another joining it by 1970.

In 1966, an institutional split divided Jodo Shinshu communities in southern Alberta. Caldarola, on the basis of his fieldwork with this community in the 1970s, asserts that "personality conflicts" led to the split, and that these were rooted, in part, in "generational differences ... among the congregations over the importance of tradition in the church, and the degree of lay control the congregation should exercise over its minister" (2007, 12). Discussions I have had with members directly involved with the difficulties in the 1960s, and the resulting division in the community, reinforce the centrality of these personal dynamics and the marginality of doctrinal differences (Caldarola 2007, 12). The split resulted in a realignment of organizational affiliations and ministerial duties. The newly formed Honpa[26] Buddhist Church of Alberta included several branch temples, such as the Lethbridge Honpa Buddhist Church, which was established in 1966, the Raymond Buddhist Church, the Rosemary Buddhist Church, and portions of other Jodo Shinshu communities in southern Alberta. This group supported its own ministers separately from the Alberta *kyōku*, which remained the administrative authority for the other Jodo Shinshu churches and congregations.

In terms of institutional authority, both groups were ultimately aligned with the mother temple in Japan – the Nishi Hongwanji. However, the Alberta *kyōku* remained under the intermediate authority, leadership, and organization of the BCA and later the BCC. The Honpa group was associated with the head temple in Japan but made most of its own decisions directly within the community. Leslie Kawamura, who had returned from his studies in Japan in 1964 to become the minister of the Raymond Buddhist Church, became the minister of the Honpa Buddhist Church of Alberta for its first six years, which included construction of the new Lethbridge branch temple in 1970 (LDJCA 2001, 91, 101).

The succession of other ministers included James Burkey (1972–1976) and June King (1976–1981), the only two Caucasian Jodo Shinshu ministers in Canada until decades later (LDJCA 2001, 93). Such innovations are best understood against the backdrop of the Honpa Buddhist Church of Alberta's freedom to make its own hiring decisions locally and its willingness to experiment with new forms deemed appropriate to its Canadian environment. The experiment ended in 1981 when Honpa members joined the BCC and were once again assigned ministers from that institutional authority.

Despite the split in the 1960s, the various Jodo Shinshu temples in southern Alberta were still flourishing in the 1960s and 1970s with active Sunday schools (also known as Dharma Schools), a vibrant women's auxiliary (*Fujinkai*), and other vital organizations. Caldarola provides examples of religious practices performed at home, as well as church rites, festivals, and commemorations (2007, 17–25). His analysis indicates adaptation of religious and cultural practice to Canada. For example, he describes a Buddhist marriage ceremony in Canada – including the Buddhist content but Christian form of the priest's address to the couple, the exhortation, and the marriage vows – even though marriages in Japan do not usually fall within the scope of Buddhist rituals (Caldarola 2007, 23–4). Caldarola's ethnographic observations from the 1970s extend to dharma talks, *gāthās* (Buddhist hymns), *ikebana* (flower arrangement), ceramics, woodblock printing, painting, sports, martial arts, doll making, apparel, home furnishings, food, folk medicine, folktales, poetry, proverbs, songs, and other aspects of Japanese and Japanese Canadian culture in southern Alberta (Caldarola 2007, 25–71).

Accounts of important annual temple services during this active period often refer to a cycle where each Buddhist church would hold its own commemoration on successive Sundays. For example, Caldarola reports that "in order to ensure the largest participation of believers," *Hōonkō* (the service commemorating Shinran's death) was "celebrated in each temple of the Japanese community in southern Alberta on Sundays between December and January," and *Hanamatsuri* (the "Flower Festival" commemorating the birth of the historical Buddha, Siddhartha Gautama) was celebrated on four consecutive Sundays in April (2007, 21).

DECLINE AND RECENT EVENTS: RELOCATING THE CENTRE

In more recent years, the special services have instead been offered to a combined congregation rather than performed serially at each church. Although a combined service can be a special occasion and symbol of unity, it is the result of diminishing membership and fewer Buddhist churches in southern Alberta in the past fifteen years. Each successive decade saw demographic changes as members died or moved away.

Temple closures in Rosemary and Picture Butte illustrate contrasting responses by congregations whose numbers had dropped below a critical mass. Faced with declining numbers and costly renovations, Rosemary Buddhist Church decided to sell its property in March of 1999 and continued to meet in members' homes while renting facilities for occasional special services (LDJCA 2001, 104). Picture Butte, on the other hand, addressed its dwindling membership earlier by deciding in 1992 to amalgamate with Lethbridge Buddhist Church. Although the Picture Butte congregation still had forty members, almost twice the size of Rosemary's congregation, they decided on this course of action in January, celebrated their 50th anniversary in March, and joined Lethbridge Buddhist Church by the April 1992 *Hanamatsuri* service (LDJCA 2001, 96). Ideas for a more thorough centralization were already present, and the Lethbridge Buddhist Church passed a resolution that same year to address the related issues of dwindling membership and centralized alternatives to the struggle of maintaining six churches with limited financial and ministerial support (LDJCA 2001, 89–90).

The exodus from rural communities and a declining Jodo Shinshu membership dispersed across multiple locations in southern Alberta posed persistent difficulties. However, celebratory occasions and instances of more dynamic vitality also persisted. Conferences, commemorations, and special services brought the larger community together and signalled that the community's centre was shifting from rural Raymond to Lethbridge, a small but growing city with a 2008 population of approximately 84,000.

CENTENNIAL COMMEMORATION

The 75th anniversary commemoration of the Raymond Buddhist Church occurred at a time when the centre of the community was progressively shifting away from Raymond to Lethbridge. In a similar tension between the old base and the new frontier, there have been special occasions that have drawn the highest dignitaries from the headquarters in Japan, even as the Japanese identity of Jodo Shinshu members in Canada has become more tenuous with each successive generation. On 22 August 2005, His Eminence (*monshu*) Ōtani Kōshin, who is the leader of the Nishi Hongwanji branch of Shin Buddhism, as well as Lady Ōtani and several other Jodo Shinshu officials, visited Lethbridge to commemorate the one-hundred-year anniversary of Buddhist churches in Canada. The presence of the highest abbot of the head temple in Japan prompted questions about the nature of the relationship between the Hongwanji headquarters and the contemporary Shin members, who have been influenced by living in Canada for generations and by the unique history of their tradition in Canada.

Public presentations were delivered to commemorate the centennial anniversary and to coincide with the dignitaries' visit. The first three presentations emphasized religious teachings of Jodo Shinshu, World War II policies that were formative to its development in Canada, and questions about whether its present forms have adapted enough to ensure its future survival.[27] The current minister of the Buddhist Federation of Alberta, Rev. Yasuo Izumi, gave the first talk, focusing on Shinran and Shinran's religious teachings without special reference to Canadian identity or developments. Whereas Rev. Izumi was born and trained in Japan – though he has served numerous congregations in Canada for almost four decades – the next two speakers were born in North America and are prominent local Jodo Shinshu lay members. Akira Ichikawa, professor emeritus from the University of Lethbridge, addressed some of the difficulties that Jodo Shinshu ministers and members faced in the 1940s stemming from distrust of Canadians of Japanese descent. He also pointed out that unintended consequences, such as the spread and growth of Jodo Shinshu in Canada, followed from government policies that discriminated against Japanese but generally tolerated religious freedom. Ichikawa reaffirmed conclusions from his 1994 article, in which he asserted that the tireless work of Shin members, including seven ministers, "and a government commitment, however lukewarm, to a basic freedom in wartime helped maintain a Buddhist foothold in Canada during a dark period in the history of both the country and the sect" (1994, 61).

In the third presentation, Robert Hironaka, chancellor emeritus of the University of Lethbridge, suggested that too great an attachment to Japanese institutional authority and traditional forms limits Jodo Shinshu's growth. Hironaka asserted that Buddhism must adapt to its host culture and to current circumstances to survive and thrive just as it has in other cultures in the past.[28] With the Japanese institution's top authority in attendance, as well as other high officials, this was a remarkable challenge. However, it did not provoke protest, reprimand, applause, or discussion. The basic, long-standing tension seemed to be recognized by all parties, even if few would voice it as boldly.

TRADITION AND INNOVATION

During the following year there were two well-attended events, a *Hanamatsuri* service in the spring and a conference in the fall. The final *Hanamatsuri* service at the Raymond Buddhist Church, 9 April 2006, once again demonstrated how even that rural community, which had closed its Sunday school for lack of children in the 1990s, could fill its building with children and other generations of family members for such special occasions. This joint *Hanamatsuri* included children, many from Lethbridge and Calgary, who celebrated the birth of the historical Buddha by offering flowers to and pouring sweet tea over a statue of the baby Buddha before receiving gift bags and listening to a short, friendly address about Buddhism from James Martin, who was then a minister-in-training.[29] *Hanamatsuri* celebrations exemplify the family-centred traditional forms of Japanese Buddhist practice for which Jodo Shinshu is well known.

In contrast, the annual Alberta Buddhist Conference (ABC) illustrates innovations devised for Jodo Shinshu in North America. The theme for the 28th Annual ABC, which was held in Lethbridge in November of 2006, was Buddhism Now (*Bukkyo Ima*) with an advertised subtheme, "Meditation and Jodo Shinshu." Meditation epitomizes the type of Buddhist practice that has been most attractive to interested Westerners. It is more closely associated with the Japanese Zen, rather than Jodo Shin, tradition. The subtheme suggested that the southern Alberta Buddhist community might be looking to other Shin practices and, arguably, to other forms of Buddhism in North America for assessing Jodo Shinshu's present and strategizing for the future. Posters for the ABC event state that "In preparation for the conference and if you've a chance, please read 'Meditation Compromise: Buddhist Sect Joins Trend,' *New York Times*, June 13, 2006; and 'Ordinary Struggles' (An interview with sōchō Koshin Ogui of the Buddhist Churches of America) in *Tricycle* (Summer 2006:42-45)" and note that copies of these articles were distributed to the temples.

Meditation, which is not traditionally central to Jodo Shinshu (in fact, not especially central to most lay Buddhist practice in Asia), has been such a dominant feature for attracting interest among Western sympathizers and practitioners that there has been growing acknowledgment in Shin communities that offering meditation as part of their practices might assist in reaching out to non-Asian North Americans. However, since the conference, I have heard little about meditation in the community beyond the short meditation period already employed at the beginning of a service.[30]

There have been thoughtful reflections on this issue in other forums. For example, a Fall 2005 special issue of *Pacific World: Journal of the Institute of Buddhist Studies*, edited by Richard Payne, focuses on "Meditation in American Shin Buddhism." Articles indicate diverse forms of Shin practice and of Buddhist meditation through time as well as the intersection between the two in both early and contemporary periods. The conclusions are by no means unanimous. Lisa Grumbach's engaging contribution demonstrates that contemplation, devotion, meditation, and faith are overlapping categories and that a strong case could be made for emphasizing or further incorporating meditation into Shin Buddhism. However, even after collapsing some of the assumed differences in ideas and doctrine between Shinran and Dōgen – and between the practices associated with each – she resists calling on Shin to incorporate seated meditation. Instead, she argues that sociological differences here are more important and that it might be "counterproductive, to both Jodo Shinshu specifically and to the maturation of Buddhism in America generally" to add Zen meditation to a Shin service even though she argues for the "compatibility – even identity – of practices labelled meditative versus devotional, or contemplative versus faith" (Grumbach 2005, 101). Most Buddhism in Asia, including Jodo Shinshu, is family-based with little or no Zen-style meditative practice; thus, perhaps increased demand for Shin "as a family-based Buddhism, including Dharma School for kids" might accompany a maturing of Buddhism in North America (Grumbach 2005, 102).

AMALGAMATION

Pure Land communities in North America are concerned about the future of Shin and the steps most appropriate for its development in the West. Reflections about the state of Buddhism's present and future in southern Alberta were heightened during the *Hanamatsuri* and the ABC conference in 2006 because that was the year when the seventy-seven-year-old Raymond Buddhist Church was sold. Meetings, plans, and conversations regarding amalgamation took on a new sense of urgency. On 18 December 2006, the two Lethbridge temples – Honpa and Lethbridge North (which already included Picture Butte) – along with Taber and Raymond, officially merged their members and assets into the newly created Buddhist Temple of Southern Alberta (BTSA).[31] Momentum gathered inexorably behind the plan to build a new temple rather than renovate an existing one. The groundbreaking ceremony took place in November 2007, both older Lethbridge temples sold in a three-day span in January 2008, and construction was scheduled with the hope of moving into the new temple by late 2008. By early fall of 2008, the BTSA congregation had vacated the now sold Honpa temple and had begun meeting at the Coaldale temple while awaiting the completion of their new building, which was delayed to January 2009. Many members have expressed excitement about the new organization, temple, and future it embodies. However, others have acknowledged trepidation concerning the future of the group and doubts that the current and future number of members will sustain the new temple.

These concerns stem, in part, from witnessing the decline in membership among important rural temples and questioning the possibility and likelihood of implementing changes that might slow, stop, or reverse diminishing membership. In the case of Raymond and similar Buddhist churches in smaller towns, issues of age and vitality may relate as much to demographic realities in rural Alberta as to the challenges faced by a primarily "ethnic" religious community that has over several generations become well assimilated and integrated with the surrounding dominant culture. The recent events described in this section illustrate the acceleration of a shift in the Jodo Shinshu community of southern Alberta. The sale of multiple small churches and move to one amalgamated temple completes the relocation of the community's centre from Raymond to Lethbridge. The community's commemorations, conferences, and concerns also reflect the ongoing shift from Japan to Canada, which is evident in the language, practices, preferences, and perspectives of successive generations.

DISCRIMINATION, ASSIMILATION, AND MULTICULTURALISM

Recent Buddhist immigrants from Asia have been, for the most part, welcomed into Canada in a context of multiculturalism and an official pluralistic policy that does not demand assimilation. However, this was not the case for early Japanese Buddhists. For them, discrimination was closely linked with assimilation. Some of the consequences have been surprising and even ironic:

discrimination spurred on the spread and growth of Jodo Shinshu while as-similation "succeeded" at the cost of decreased membership and vitality. Whereas in the early decades anti-Japanese discrimination caused a more than fivefold increase in rural southern Alberta's Jodo Shinshu population, the greater freedom of more recent decades has diminished the Jodo Shinshu population in these smaller towns. Demographic shifts and relocation for educational and professional opportunities have reduced the rural population, and assimilation of Japanese-Canadians and absorption through intermarriage have disrupted the continuity of religious and cultural identity.

Jodo Shinshu has been in Canada for more than a century and aspects of assimilation have been well documented, from the weekly rhythm of Sunday services to the incorporation of hymns, choirs, Sunday (Dharma) school, pews, and so forth. In the face of discrimination, not appearing too foreign provided motivation for early assimilation. Other changes were practical accommoda-tions to the lives and needs of members in North America. The assimilation of these members into wider society led to further adaptations of religious practices to meet the changing needs and expectations of the congregation. The shift from using Japanese language exclusively, to a blend of the two (or separate services or talks), to English exclusively signals one of the most obvi-ous transitions, and one that mirrors the abilities and preferences of each generation from the Japanese-born *issei* to the fourth generation *yonsei*.

Whereas services that have moved from Japanese to English are unlikely to reverse direction, such a reversal has occurred with the recent use of the term "temple" rather than church. The use of this term exemplifies a step back from assimilation, which had been accelerated by discrimination, to an em-brace of tradition sanctioned by pluralistic multiculturalism. The use of the term "church" became more common than "temple" in the wake of World War II as part of an effort to blend in more closely with the norms of the dominant culture. The 1944 decision to rename the Buddhist Mission of North America (BMNA) the Buddhist Churches of America (BCA) was part of a more self-con-scious effort to redefine Buddhist organizations in terms less likely to be per-ceived as foreign or threatening. Raymond's temple had used the term "church" in its title for more than a decade before World War II (see note 1). Japanese Canadians oscillated between adopting forms less alien to Christianity, such as "church" rather than "temple," and attempting to more closely replicate Japan-ese tradition, by using the term "*otera*" or its English translation as "temple" rather than "church." "Our Beloved Otera: Memories of Raymond Buddhist

Temple" illustrates this reversal. The narration and title of the DVD use "*otera*," the label and opening preamble refer to the Raymond Buddhist Temple, and the earlier publications, pictures, and signs shown in the DVD use "church." Moreover, the new Buddhist Temple of Southern Alberta provides further evidence that "temple" is enjoying resurging popularity in contemporary, pluralistic Canada. The sequence of the oscillation between the terms suggests a complex movement of partial assimilation followed by partial reclamation of tradition rather than a steady movement toward assimilation.

Based on what appears to be an inverse relation between assimilation and the growth of the community, slowing or interrupting some patterns of assimilation might provide a useful tonic. However, assimilation is only one factor in the community's ongoing vitality. Younger generations move away from small towns whether or not these former residents continue to practise and identify with Buddhism. In order to thrive, the communities would need to grow or at least maintain a critical mass to sustain a temple, a minister, and a community. Chinese traditions continue to expand in major cities due to an ongoing influx of Chinese immigrants; there is no similar wave of Japanese immigrants. Therefore, the vitality of the community, as measured by numbers of adherents, will be best assured by retaining as many members as possible while attracting new members. The search for new members includes the potential for converts from among Canadians who did not grow up Buddhist or as part of a family with roots in Japan.

ATTRACTION AND RETENTION

Yutetsu Kawamura, an especially influential Buddhist minister and member of the Order of Canada who died in 2005, recognized the need for converts and ministers from North America. In his memoirs, *The Dharma Survives with the People*, Yutetsu Kawamura includes a chapter on "An Outlook for the Pure Land School in America and Canada." He writes, "now that we are in America and Canada, we should spread the Buddhist teachings to Americans and Canadians" (1997, 49). He acknowledges that maintaining the ongoing vitality of the core community is itself a great challenge, expansion of the community through attracting converts an even greater challenge: "When one considers how difficult it is to pass on the True Pure Land Buddhist teachings to one's own children, one can see how bleak it is to pass on the True Pure Land teaching to the non-Japanese people" (1997, 49).

In his call to spread Jodo Shinshu more widely in North America, Yutetsu Kawamura wrote that *issei* priests "like myself came here to do missionary work among the Japanese people. We had neither the courage nor the ability to spread Buddhism among the Caucasians. But now ... there is very little excuse to maintain the same old attitude that the first-generation priests held" (1997, 49). He goes on to point out structural and financial obstacles, notes the skepticism of some people about the possible appeal of Jodo Shinshu to "Caucasian believers," and insists that it may be necessary to have "Caucasian Buddhist priests to do missionary work" (1997, 50). In acknowledging – but then looking to overcome – various obstacles, Yutetsu Kawamura saw opportunities in such unlikely places as the practices of the surrounding Mormon community and the high rate of exogamy among Japanese Canadians.[32] Mormon support of young missionaries provided "a model from which the Buddhists could learn," and the frequency of marriages outside the Buddhist community was turned to advantage as "a great opportunity to spread the Buddhist teachings among Canadians" (1997, 50, 53).

Mullins's research confirms the exceptionally high rate of exogamy,[33] over 70 per cent according to data he obtained from various BCC communities, but suggests that these marriages typically result in a loss of adherents rather than a gain (1988, 227–8; 1989, 119–21).[34] His study "Life-Cycle of Ethnic Churches" asserts that intermarriage and other forms of structural assimilation in the monolingual third generation extends the cultural assimilation of the bilingual second generation to the point where the "ethnic" church either abandons its function of "maintaining ethnic customs, language, and group solidarity" or faces being abandoned by these later generations (1987, 322–4).

NORTH AMERICAN CONVERTS AND MINISTERS

Yutetsu Kawamura's progressive views were directed to the ideal of a vital religious community expanding explicitly beyond ethnic boundaries and not restricted to cultural preservation. To this end, he called for opening opportunities for ministerial training beyond the traditional system, which still required training and being ordained in Japan. The Institute for Buddhist Studies (IBS) in Berkeley has expanded opportunities for North American ministerial training, but formal ordination is still done only in Japan. In contrast, "The ideal situation would be to train North Americans to become priests right here in North America without having to send them to Japan for training" (1997, 50).

James Martin's recent case illustrates developments in the direction of this ideal. Martin, a Caucasian minister at Calgary's Jodo Shinshu temple, trained at IBS and recently passed his *kyōshi* training at the head temple in Kyoto in December 2007. This intensive ten-day session emphasizes traditional rituals and liturgy, but has also adapted to contemporary challenges and opportunities by inviting foreign ministers-in-training along with those who were born in Japan.[35] Martin's experience indicates that there is increasing accommodation at the head temple.

There are also signs of adaptation to contemporary dynamics within Canada's Jodo Shinshu institutional authority. In 2008 the BCC changed its name to something more tradition-specific. It is now known as the Jodo Shinshu Buddhist Temples of Canada. The change further reinforces the shift to "temple" from "church" and makes clear that this is a Jodo Shinshu organization rather than an administrative head or representative of other Buddhist traditions in Canada, much less of all Buddhism in Canada. The name change is in keeping with Yutetsu Kawamura's concern that "Perhaps such a title [the old BCC] was acceptable a half century ago when there were no other major Buddhist organisations here, but times have changed. To be more accurate, we should refer to ... ourselves as the True Pure Land Buddhist School ..." (1997, 51).

Despite challenges, incomplete adaptations, and loss of members, Jodo Shinshu has attracted some converts. In fact, the Honpa Buddhist Churches of Alberta – including the Raymond Buddhist Church, the Lethbridge Honpa Buddhist Church, the Rosemary Buddhist Church, and other members of this group – was the first in Canada to hire a Caucasian minister, Rev. James Burkey, who served from 1972 to 1976, and the first to hire a female minister, Rev. June King, who served from 1976 to 1981.[36] Members of this community recognized the importance of helping to train English-speaking ministers, including individuals who are not of Japanese descent.[37]

James Martin's recent ministerial training and ordination epitomizes this aspiration at the Calgary temple as well. Mullins reports that the Calgary Buddhist Church, which dates back only to the 1970s, was never primarily shaped by Japanese speaking *issei*. It has attempted to appeal to a broader Canadian audience with less explicitly Japanese characteristics (Mullins 1988, 229). There is, however, an earlier history of *issei* meeting at members' homes in the late

1930s and early 1940s as well as the "Calgary Hoyuu-kai" established by *issei* and *nisei* members who later formed the Calgary Buddhist Church.[38] Nevertheless, this church has become known for its innovative efforts to broaden its appeal within and beyond a Japanese Canadian audience. Since 2006, it has sponsored the Calgary Buddhist Film Festival, demonstrating that it is open to attracting an audience to Buddhism in general without specific reference to Jodo Shinshu. It is difficult to assess the success of such initiatives, but James Martin's conversion and ordination fulfill two goals articulated by Yutetsu Kawamura earlier in this section: attracting Canadian converts and Canadian ministers.

CHALLENGES

The challenges religious leaders face are inextricably linked to the sustainability of the Jodo Shinshu community in Canada. Mullins details various organizational dilemmas, among them the relationship of language and religious leadership. All the ministers before 1940 were born and trained in Japan. From 1945 to 1983, almost 70 per cent of the Jodo Shinshu priests in Canada were *issei* as well (1988, 221). Their move to Canada meant the loss of financial security, status, and power in predominantly lay-organized communities. In the temple system in Japan, the priest would inherit the temple and control its considerable income. Jodo Shinshu ministers from Japan had to learn English and otherwise accommodate *nisei* and *sansei* members while still performing services in Japanese and conducting more traditional rituals for the lay *issei* members (Mullins 1988, 225). On average *issei* priests have served as resident ministers in Canada for shorter durations than *nisei* religious leaders not only because of the difficulties they encounter in Canada but also because some return to Japan to take over their fathers' temples in Japan's hereditary Jodo Shinshu system (Mullins 1988, 221, 224).

The situation for lay members involves the interrelated obstacles of insufficient numbers of ministers and varying degrees of satisfaction, often falling along generational lines, with the language, form, and emphasis of Buddhist practices. Lay leadership has been critical for Canada's Buddhists who have never enjoyed the levels of institutional support found in Buddhist countries in Asia. As a result, many groups have been without a minister or have had to share a minister who rotates among temples and congregations. This remains the case for southern Alberta. Rather than increasing the number of ministers to solve this problem, several older temples have been consolidated into one new temple with an amalgamated congregation. However, the leadership role of lay people extends beyond staffing social groups or filling in and making do in the absence of a minister. Lay people have also engaged directly with questions of their tradition's future, such as how to retain young members of their community and attract outsiders. For example, lay leaders in Lethbridge have demonstrated their openness by hosting less formal gatherings for anyone interested in discussing Buddhism and related topics.[39] Nonetheless, Western ministers and lay converts are not aggressively recruited because Jodo Shinshu does not share Soka Gakkai's proselytizing zeal or tactics.

Moreover, Jodo Shinshu has not garnered the same level of interest from Western convert Buddhists as have Zen, Tibetan, or Insight Meditation traditions.[40] Members and ministers in southern Alberta have long acknowledged this situation. Fifteen years after the institutional split and the formation of the Honpa Buddhist Church in the middle of the 1960s, the annual Alberta Buddhist Conference (ABC) began as a unifying and informative event for all members in Alberta. It is also a forum to test new ideas, such as considerations during the 2006 ABC of the merits of adding meditation to enhance Jodo Shinshu's appeal. Although there are no clear signs that Jodo Shinshu in southern Alberta will make this type of change in an effort to attract new members, the sale of old churches and establishment of the new amalgamated BTSA temple demonstrates that change is underway to address the reality of declining memberships in small towns.

CONCLUSION

Jodo Shinshu is the formative school of Buddhism in Canada. It is also held up as the early example, par excellence, of Asian/ethnic Buddhism. It entered Canada as a tradition from Japan that accompanied Japanese immigrants and has remained central to families, often of Japanese descent. Its Asian/ethnic category is further reinforced by the perception that Jodo Shinshu does not significantly overlap with the Western/convert category. "Western" Caucasian converts and sympathizers, from meditation practitioners to "night-stand Buddhists,"[41] have more often shown interest in other forms of Buddhism and the writings of charismatic Buddhists outside the Shin tradition. However, as Hori and others clearly show, the accuracy and explanatory power of these categories break down after the first generation Asian immigrant or Western convert. The families of Japanese descent are no longer immigrants. The third generation and beyond are most often culturally quite fully Canadian or American with widely varying links to an "ethnic" Japanese identity. Moreover, some Jodo Shinshu ministers have been born and trained in North America. Jodo Shinshu churches have had male and female Caucasian ministers as well as members. In short, the case of the Buddhist community of southern Alberta highlights fundamental flaws in the categories of "Asian/ethnic" vs "Western/convert."

Although it is currently undergoing an uncertain transition to an unknown future, Jodo Shinshu in southern Alberta is instructive. Jodo Shinshu was dominant in early Buddhist developments in Canada; its relatively rural and well-established roots present an important anomaly that reinforces the diversity of the contemporary Canadian Buddhist landscape; and over generations it has produced scholars in the academic study of Buddhism and developed in ways that challenge academic assumptions and categories about Buddhism in the West.

Raymond's church had been the first Buddhist temple east of British Columbia, a historic landmark, the administrative centre of Buddhism in Canada immediately following World War II, and the locus of many activities, memories, and events for the community of Buddhist Japanese immigrants in southern Alberta for several generations. Its sale completed a dramatic transition for this community, which had grown in the face of discrimination but then gradually lost members and some of its cohesive vitality after decades of assimilation and demographic shifts as young people moved out of rural towns and married outside the Japanese Buddhist community. The sale of the old church and subsequent amalgamation in a new temple also begins a new chapter of adaptation in contemporary multicultural Canada where Jodo Shinshu is now a well-established but relatively small minority tradition within Canadian Buddhism as well as within southern Alberta.

The Jodo Shinshu Buddhist community continues to transform and is attempting to direct some of the changes by reaching out to their own members through amalgamation and to new members by continuing to reflect on the ideal balance for assimilation to Canadian culture. Of course, such adaptation has been the norm throughout Buddhist history in Asia as well as in the West. Just as Buddhism both influences and is influenced by the surrounding culture, changing practices shape identity and vice versa. It is too soon for definitive conclusions.

In late April 2009 the amalgamated congregation held dedication events for the new Buddhist Temple of Southern Alberta.[42] At a banquet dinner, several hundred in attendance watched a film that interspersed slides and narration reflecting on the history of each local church that had been sold in preparation for the new temple and amalgamated BTSA congregation. The next morning, the dedication service began with a ceremonial procession of at least ten ministers from across Canada interspersed with more than twice as many children resplendent in traditional Japanese costume. The presence of ministers and other members from all Jodo Shinshu temples across Canada and hundreds of local supporters signalled a certain unity and vitality. Messages of support ranged from written encouragement sent by His Eminence (*monshu*) Ōtani Kōshin to a series of short speeches from local politicians, including the mayor of Lethbridge and ministers and senators involved in provincial and federal government. These speeches expressed the esteem within the wider community for this long-standing Buddhist group and also revealed how early friendships had fostered favourable opinions among local politicians toward descendants of Japanese immigrants. Several noted that the BTSA congregation is not composed exclusively of Japanese-Canadian members; however, dignitaries' comments and repeated reference to the injustice of forced relocation and internment during World War II also reinforced the sense of a dominant narrative and relatively unified ethnic, cultural, and historical identity among many in southern Alberta's Shin community.

The Ochigo parade of children, who moved carefully to keep their elaborate headgear from toppling, delighted the hundreds in attendance. In addition to their contribution in the present, their participation was simultaneously symbolic of the community's past and future. The procession linked the opening of this new temple to celebrations that have marked the founding of previous temples in Canada – including those that have now been sold as part of the formation of the new BTSA – as well as to related occasions in Japan. The children's participation in this event prompts hope, but does not guarantee, that they will remain involved in the temple and ensure its future. The ceremonial procession inaugurated a new phase for Shin in southern Alberta, but it is uncertain whether there will be subsequent parades, celebrations, growth, and survival.

The events surrounding the BTSA dedication were well attended, well supported, and widely enjoyed; however, the difficulties and demographic trends that prompted amalgamation remain. The composition of the BTSA's future membership remains partially unknown, although amalgamation became complete when Coaldale joined the BTSA in late 2009.[43] Similarly, relationships and interactions among different groups represent another dynamic and uncertain factor. After all, the new temple is not for a new community. Instead, this amalgamated community spans multiple generations and the new BTSA combines numerous related but formerly separate congregations. It is also unclear whether this recently combined community will succeed in attracting new members. Nor is it known whether Jodo Shinshu in Canada will significantly modify and reshape its identity in an attempt to become more attractive to potential members and segments within its current community.

The tale of the new temple has only begun to be written, but Raymond's old church, from its establishment in 1929 to closure in 2006, has already contributed an especially rich, multi-generational narrative to the story of Buddhism in Canada. Raymond's Buddhist heritage continues to offer valuable resources. While this is most evident through the ongoing participation of people whose formative Buddhist education took place in Raymond, special events at Calgary's Glenbow Museum illustrate a new legacy linked to this pioneer community. Reverends Leslie Kawamura and James Martin conducted ceremonies on 3 May 2009 at the museum before an audience of well over one hundred people, including many former members of the Raymond Buddhist Church who had come to see their former shrine blessed at its new home in the museum. Like many of Raymond's congregants, the shrine and statue of Amida Buddha had come to Raymond's temple from British Columbia communities – Royston and New Westminster respectively – in the aftermath of World War II and forced relocation. Rev. Kawamura and his wife, Toyo, donated the shrine to the Glenbow Museum, and it is now placed beside an impressive variety of Buddhist statues and related artifacts as a physical illustration of the place and importance of Jodo Shinshu in Buddhism and of this religious community within southern Alberta. The challenge for the new temple is to continue to build on this legacy and remain vibrant in the present and future rather than being honoured and displayed primarily as important to Canada's past.

NOTES

1   Although it is also accurate to refer to this centre of Buddhism in Raymond as a temple, I primarily use "church" in this chapter, particularly for the proper name "Raymond

Buddhist Church," to more accurately reflect how this structure has been designated by signs and most printed material throughout its history. For example, programs for major events, such as the 50th, 60th, and even the more recent 75th anniversaries list it as the Raymond Buddhist Church as does the 1984 sign designating it a provincial historic site. Nonetheless, many members use "temple" or even the corresponding Japanese term "*otera*" to describe this Buddhist religious centre in more traditional terms. *Hikari – The Light,* the newsletter of the Buddhist Federation of Alberta, now uses "temple" to designate all the member organizations. Of course, names are only conventions. However, an examination of names and changes of terminology can provide insight into changing ideas, institutions, and social and cultural dynamics.

2 Jodo Shinshu is the True Pure Land sect, also known as Shin Buddhism. It is the largest Buddhist denomination in Japan and was also most influential in the first half of the history of Buddhism in Canada.

3 Reyko Nishiyama, in LDJCA (2001, 102). In the 2006 DVD "Our Beloved Otera: Memories of Raymond Buddhist Temple," Nishiyama describes the activities of the Sunday school until it closed due to a lack of children. Around this same time, she reports a shift to using prerecorded sutras and *gāthās* for services when no minister was available.

4 Nishiyama, in "Our Beloved Otera," describes the final services including this "eulogy" for the temple and the process of dispersing temple possessions. The altar (*naijin*) was entrusted to Rev. Leslie Kawamura and is now at the Glenbow Museum in Calgary.

5 Orai Fujikawa, the *sōchō*, or bishop, of Buddhist Churches of Canada, David Major, the president of the board of trustees for the BTSA, and Bridget Pastoor, a local politician and MLA for Lethbridge East, joined Rev. Izumi in the ceremonial groundbreaking. Other politicians would have attended, reflecting the importance of this group in the community, but Remembrance Day obligations limited them to sending congratulations. Dozens of members and supporters watched the ceremony and participated in an official group photo on the construction site near a sign that included the artist's depiction of the future BTSA temple.

6 The January 2008 issue of *Hikari – The Light,* the newsletter of the Buddhist Federation of Alberta, gives the vision, mission, and guiding principles above an artist's rendering of the new temple. Vision: "The Buddhist Temple of Southern Alberta is dedicated to being an open Jodo Shinshu Sangha organization that appreciates, promotes, preserves and practices the Buddha Dharma teaching." Mission: "The mission of the Buddhist Temple of Southern Alberta is to gratefully promote and practice Buddha Dharma teaching through: Communication, Community, Tradition, Education, Resource Development." Guiding Principles: "A response by the BTSA must always involve the following key factors: Ensure that our motivation is a sense of gratitude and compassion; Take into account the widest possible perspective; Be vigilant in ensuring that we remain honest,

self-aware, unbiased and trustworthy; the danger otherwise is that we may fall victim to self-delusion; In the face of any real ethical challenge, respond in a spirit of humility; Ensure our interaction with the community by promoting dedication, commitment and involvement; Strive to keep in mind the primary goal of the wellbeing of humanity as a whole and the planet we inhabit."

7   There are records of Japanese workers immigrating to rural southern Alberta from 1903 (LDJCA 2001, 97 and Caldarola 2007, 5). This chapter addresses the best-known and most influential Japanese Canadian Buddhist communities in southern Alberta, which were well established before World War II and augmented due to the forced relocation of Japanese immigrants and their descendants from British Columbia in 1942. There were also Japanese Christians among early immigrants, including those who converted at various times after arriving in predominantly Christian Canada. Moreover, there have been more recent immigrants from Japan to southern Alberta; however, they have received comparably little attention. This is likely due, in part, to their small numbers relative both to early Japanese immigrants and to waves of more recent immigrants from other countries in Asia.

8   This section of the chapter draws from John Harding, "Jōdo Shin-shū Buddhism in Southern Alberta," *Our Diverse Cities* 3: 140–4, with permission.

9   In contrast, Audrey Kobayashi notes that at the turn of the millennium current immigrants coming to Canada from Japan are women. Moreover, most of them are unmarried, thirty years of age on average, living in major cities, and "generally highly educated, inclined toward professional careers, and disinclined toward the role of the traditional Japanese housewife/mother" (2002, 205). Boisvert notes that more recent immigrants from Japan included more "young urban candidates who were highly educated" because immigration policy after 1967 favoured these applicants "based on their education level and professional qualifications" (2005, 73).

10   This group of 150 workers were "artisans, criminals, former soldiers, intellectuals, farmers, and women who had been recruited off the streets of Yokohama" to work on plantations in Hawaii; mistreatment led many to move to Honolulu and only about fifty returned when ordered to do so by Japan's government (Gall 1995, 100). See also Azuma (2002, 1) and Befu (2002, 6).

11   Takata provides examples from the Methodist "Oriental Home" shelter and the Catholic "day nursery for working and ailing mothers of Japanese settlement" to refusals to condone interracial marriages and related prejudicial treatment as well as Rev. H.W. Fraser's role in instigating the Anti-Asiatic Riot of 1907 (1983, 30–1).

12   This spelling may appear outdated to those more familiar with "Honganji"; however, our policy in this book is to consistently follow the version used by the organization it-

self (see http://www2.hongwanji.or.jp/english/). For similar reasons, we use "Jodo Shinshu" rather than "Jōdo Shinshū."

13 Although early developments in British Columbia are relevant to all Japanese Buddhist communities in Canada, the focus of this chapter allows for only brief reference to developments outside Alberta. Terry Watada's chapter offers more thorough treatment of this history.

14 Yamagishi's book offers first-person perspectives from Japanese immigrants and their descendents in southern Alberta. The chapter "Picture Bride – Hiro Komatsu" describes a picture bride's desire to emigrate to North America, her hope to save money and return to Japan, her voyage across the Pacific with other eager brides, her arrival during the winter of 1916–1917, and her surprise at the harsh realities of farming life in southern Alberta (2005, 29–40).

15 Conversation with Dr Robert Hironaka on 13 January 2008. He recalled how his father-in-law was the youngest of a group of Okinawan men recruited to railroad work, housed in box cars near Fort Macleod for the winter, and understandably motivated to shift to the better pay of coal mining in the small towns near Lethbridge.

16 Nishiyama's "Our Beloved Otera" relates how the building's history as the former "Four-Room School" with 300 pupils in 1903 as well as its subsequent Mormon then Buddhist religious identities contributed to its 1984 designation as a Provincial Historic Site. When it was a school, it was used for church services on Sundays. It was still a Mormon meeting house after a new school was built and then it assumed its most lasting identity as a Buddhist church after the Church of Jesus Christ of Latter-day Saints community built a larger meeting house and sold this building to the Japanese Buddhist community in 1929.

17 Watada provides examples of sacrifices made to make this payment, from Rev. Kawamura's donation of 10 per cent of every $30 paycheque and farmers' donations of crops to President Hironaka's unique sacrifice and donation (1996, 139). His son, Robert Hironaka, tells the story of this last contribution: "my dad gave up smoking and drinking and gave the money that he would have spent on tobacco and beer to the church" (27 February 2008 email correspondence).

18 This became the model for several other Buddhist churches in southern Alberta each of which purchased a building that had been used as a Mormon meeting house. While "church" and "temple" work as virtually interchangeable terms for the Buddhists in this region, they are not interchangeable for the Mormon community, for whom temple refers to a relatively rare and especially sacred religious centre, which would not be sold in this way.

19 Watada describes many of the initiatives of these Buddhist communities including the

ministers and the lay families who spearheaded them. He also notes that the temple in Picture Butte changed name to "the Picture Butte Buddhist Church" in 1945 (1996, 153).

20 Ministers Kawamura and Ikuta were first ordered deported but objections from community leaders and political intervention saved them. Reverend Tsuji, the first Canadian-born Buddhist minister, was protected from deportation by citizenship.

21 Raymond's church housed the first judo club in Alberta, and southern Alberta remains a prominent centre for judo in Canada. Sensei Yosh Senda came to southern Alberta during the wartime forced relocation in 1942 and he became the judo assistant to Yoshio Katsuta at the Raymond Buddhist Church the following year. He founded the Lethbridge Judo Club in 1952 and continued to teach and practise judo until his death on 9 September 2009. His coaching, including duties as the national coach at three Olympics Games, and the success of his program in Lethbridge, which has produced Olympians, are widely recognized. He was named to the Order of Canada in late December of 2007 which was the same year he opened the Kyodokan Judo Club and became the only Canadian to receive *kudan*, a ninth-degree black belt.

22 The establishment of this Numata chair is a testament to the dedication and ingenuity of lay Shin members in southern Alberta. Robert Hironaka reports that he was asked by Leslie Kawamura to quickly raise $33,333.33 in order to secure twice that amount in matching funds from Alberta's government and thereby meet Numata's requirement for an endowed chair. To his great surprise, Hironaka succeeded in securing $35,000. The Numata foundation contributed $300,000 and the government supplied the rest of the $1 million fund (email correspondence 20 February 2008). Many Numata scholars over the ensuing years have come to southern Alberta to give a talk during their visiting fellowship.

23 Shinran (1173–1262) broke from tradition by marrying and having children, who in turn became influential in the development of this largest sect of Japanese Buddhism.

24 Contributions have also been made by scholars of Buddhism, such as Richard Robinson, who was not born into this community but grew up in Calgary and visited Raymond's church somewhat frequently while learning about Buddhism with Rev. Yutetsu Kawamura and later with Rev. Tsuji and others in Toronto. He founded the Buddhist Studies program at the University of Wisconsin in Madison, which was the first in North America (Nagatomi's program at Harvard was the second).

25 Leslie Kawamura provides an insightful account of Jodo Shinshu in these communities as well as at the two Lethbridge churches (1955 and 1970) through expansion and up until later closures beginning with Picture Butte and Rosemary (2006, 31). He describes Shin beliefs, changing practices that evolved with the shift from a Japanese-speaking

and more traditional community to English-speaking and decidedly Canadian later generations, and the succession of ministers including concomitant changes in their duties and support.

26 Honpa is an abbreviated form of Hongwanji-ha, which means the [Nishi] Hongwanji side of Jodo Shinshu Buddhism.

27 These presentations, "What is Jodo Shinshu Buddhism" by Yasuo Izumi, "Jodo Shinshu Buddhism in Canada during the Pacific War, 1941–1945" by Akira Ichikawa, "The Self-Corrective Way" by Robert Hironaka, as well as a fourth, "Jodo Shinshu, Japan and the West" by John Harding, appear in *Dharma: My Guiding Light*, no. 5, printed by the Jodo Shinshu Buddhist Federation of Alberta.

28 Robert Hironaka's talk and his other presentations and writings about "New Directions" for Jodo Shinshu reflect on the issues of vitality, transformation, identity, directions of influence, and the desire to attract more adherents – of Japanese descent as well as other Canadians. In 2009 Hironaka wrote *Now is the Moment*, a self published book about Buddhism that combined new reflections with some of the essays he had written over the years for discussion groups, community members, and people curious about Buddhism.

29 The joint *Hanamatsuri* celebrated one year later, on Easter Sunday 2007, at the north Lethbridge Buddhist Temple was similarly full and celebratory, demonstrating the ongoing vitality of these traditional special occasions. These joint services prefigured the amalgamation to a single entity, the Buddhist Temple of Southern Alberta.

30 This does not require a different posture, etc., but is instead a time of quiet reflection, awareness, and gratitude while seated in chairs before recitations and the dharma talk.

31 To create this new organization out of several old ones, the BTSA had to be incorporated under the Religious Societies Land Act as a new entity. Lethbridge North was in this category already while Lethbridge Honpa was unincorporated. Taber and Coaldale are incorporated under the Societies' Act as charitable organizations.

32 In his 1997 memoirs, Kawamura can recall only one or two cases of marriage within the Japanese-Canadian Jodo Shinshu community from 1964 to 1975. Even these, he notes, might not have "taken place in a Buddhist church without the persuasion of their parents" (1997, 49).

33 See also Ram (1990) for data supporting much higher rates of marriage outside one's ethnic community among Japanese in Canada relative to other Asian immigrants.

34 Mullins cites analysis by Montero (1980, 72–3): "Exogamous Sansei are less likely to retain their traditional religion, Buddhism. Only about one in ten … as against over four in ten of their endogamous peers."

35   Conversation with Rev. James Martin on 13 January 2008. He noted that there were sixteen non-Japanese ministers (most from the United States) at this session, four female and twelve male, in a group of approximately eighty.

36   Rev. June King's dates are listed as 1976–1981 in Watada (1996, 216) and combined with Yutetsu Kawamura's dates of 1975–1982 in LDJCA (2001, 93). Both sources note that Rev. Nobuyuki Kasagi also served as a minister during James Burkey's tenure and Rev. Yutetsu Kawamura also served as a minister for the Honpa Buddhist Churches of Alberta during the 1975–1982 span that coincided with June King's tenure. Reyko Nishiyama recalls that Rev. Kasagi left Canada in order to return to Japan and take over his father's temple.

37   One particularly influential example is Fred Ulrich, who was supported by the Honpa Buddhist Church of Alberta in his summer session studies at IBS before becoming the minister of the Manitoba Buddhist Church.

38   Leslie Kawamura provided this information about the early formation of the Calgary Buddhist community and noted that he served this group twice a month when he was the Honpa Buddhist Church of Alberta minister. He identifies "Mr. Kuwahara's house" as the main meeting venue for the early Shin community in Calgary (email correspondence 20 February 2008).

39   For example, Dr Robert Hironaka hosts a group as often as every two weeks and Mac and Reyko Nishiyama have hosted occasional gatherings to informally discuss Buddhist topics.

40   For analysis of this relative neglect of Jodo Shinshu by the group he refers to as "non-Asian American Buddhists," see Galen Amstutz (2002).

41   Thomas Tweed introduced the term "night-stand Buddhists" as part of a more concerted emphasis on various "sympathizers" who may not identify themselves as Buddhists but are sympathetic to the tradition and may incorporate a variable range of Buddhist practices and perspectives into their lives.

42   The annual general meetings of the Jodo Shinshu Buddhist Temples of Canada (JSBTC) and the Ministerial Association and Women's Federation of this organization, which had been known as the Buddhist Churches of Canada until 2008, were held in Lethbridge in the days preceding a banquet with approximately 430 participants on 25 April and the official dedication ceremony with still more in attendance in the new temple on 26 April.

43   Some members joined early and others expressed reluctance to amalgamate. By the time of the BTSA dedication ceremony on 26 April 2009, the Coaldale congregation had sold its temple and it seemed clear Coaldale would be joining the BTSA soon. Even before

the sale, due to similar pressures that had led to the same outcome for the other small-town Shin congregations in southern Alberta, there had been strong signs of interest in joining the BTSA. For example, a group from Coaldale visited an amalgamated BTSA service in February 2008, the Coaldale Buddhist Church donated $50,000 to the BTSA, and they hosted BTSA members briefly later in 2008 before the new amalgamated temple's first service on 18 January 2009. On 18 November 2009, members of the Coaldale Buddhist Church signed a merger agreement to join the amalgamated BTSA.

That Luang
The Journey and Relocation of Lao Buddhism to Canada

MARYBETH WHITE

Wat Lao Veluwanaram, Caledon, Ontario

That Luang Replica, Caledon, Ontario
Photos by Marybeth White

Religious men and women are continually in the process of mapping a symbolic landscape and constructing a symbolic dwelling in which they might have their own space and find their own place.

THOMAS TWEED, *Our Lady of the Exile*

INTRODUCTION

That Luang is Laos' most renowned stupa and is located in the heart of Vientiane. It is visually stunning, towering fifty metres into the air and encased in layers of gold leaf. The stupa sits on a square base in the centre of an enclosed grass area. Around its perimeter is a portico that is opened toward the stupa yet closed along the exterior wall. On the outside of the wall are palm trees and lush shrubs. From the courtyard area at the base of the stupa there are access points to the walkway that circles the stupa. On this pathway Buddhist practitioners circumambulate the golden tapering tower in a clockwise fashion.

Stupas had been burial mounds for rulers, sages, and other people of note in South Asia during the time of the Buddha. That Luang is believed to contain relics of the Buddha. For Lao Buddhists, the stupa is a reminder of Siddhārtha Gautama's ability to achieve enlightenment and a location where the perceived powers radiating from the relics are experienced. From a doctrinal vantage point, the stupa holds no suprahuman powers; yet, for many practitioners it is imbued with them. Consequently, since the time of King Aśoka stupas have become sites of pilgrimage where people seek aid or protection and the accumulation of merit (Swearer 1995, 64–77; Boord 1994, 16–20).

Prior to the current Lao People's Democratic Republic (LPDR) government, That Luang was incorporated by the royal family as a visual sign of the king's protection and power, in addition to being a locus of Buddhist merit (Evans 1998, 46–7). For Buddhists, the predominant religious group in Laos, this stupa provided the Lao people with protective elements, politically, spatially, psychologically, and spiritually. Following the overthrow of the Royal Lao Government, over 400,000 Lao crossed the Mekong River between 1975 and 1980 to the perceived safety of Thailand (Van Esterik 1992, 11). When they left Lao soil, they left behind the spiritual protection offered primarily by That Luang as well as other smaller stupas and local protective *hos* or spirit houses (Van Esterik 1992, 45 and 132; Condominas 1975, 255–7).

In this essay, I examine the spatial relocative journey of Lao Buddhism onto Canadian soil and explain why That Luang is still a relevant symbol for the Lao community of Caledon, Ontario and the role it plays in creating a Lao Buddhist place in Canada. While there are Lao Buddhist communities in Winnipeg, Regina, Calgary, Edmonton, Vancouver, Ottawa-Hull, Kitchener, Windsor, St Catherine's, Quebec City, and London, I will focus primarily on the Greater Toronto Area group[1] and the initial group that arrived in the Montreal area. Thomas Tweed's concept of "dwelling" in his recent work *Crossing and Dwelling: A Theory of Religion* (2006) will be employed to understand how Lao Canadian Buddhists are creating a place in Canada for their religious tradition.

CROSSINGS AND DWELLINGS: TWEED'S THEORY

Tweed develops a theory that makes "sense of the religious life of transnational migrants and addresse[s] three themes – *movement, relation,* and *position*" (2006, 5 – emphasis in the original text). Theories themselves, in his view, are transitory glimpses from a particular vantage point at a particular juncture in time. They are not absolutes, not rigid or static, but rather signposts posited by academics to give meaning or direction to their observations (2006, 7 and 8). Tweed's theory endeavours to situate academics within the historical action of recording and making sense of the data to which they have been exposed, while simultaneously recognizing the life experiences which have potentially biased and shaped their observations. In this way Tweed attempts to avoid what he perceives to be a blind spot in constructionist and critical theories. The key components of Tweed's theory are crossing, dwelling, and the relationship between the two.

For Tweed, crossing is not merely terrestrial but also corporal and cosmic (2006, 123). His research observations of the community of Cuban transnational migrants reveal the simultaneous experience of homeland, diaspora community, and the multifarious crossings between them. Tweed propounds that religions "are not only about being in place but also about moving across [places]" and that these movements are both enabled and constrained by the religions themselves (2006, 123). Tweed employs the themes of movement, position, and relation when recognizing that within the concept of crossing there must, necessarily, be found the concept of dwelling.

In speaking about the consecration of a Cuban shrine in Miami, Tweed states that the ceremony is "as much about settlement as about migration" (2006, 81). Even though the consecration of the shrine would appear to be an act of dwelling, Tweed observes that within transnational religious groups there are crossings occurring in the very action of dwelling, thus pointing to the relational nature of crossing and dwelling. He uses James Clifford's term "dwelling" but draws on the sense of impermanence contained in the term, citing its Sanskrit etymological roots that invoke the notion of action. This provides the reader with the understanding of continual remapping or repositioning through space and time. In this way Tweed articulates the dynamic and relational nature of creating place. To convey a sense of active dwelling Tweed employs the phrase "kinetics of dwelling" (2006, 83).

For Tweed, "locative" means locating one's place within the flux and flow of ongoing crossings and dwellings. Within the relationship of these nodes and flows are the formations of a sense of individual and communal place. Tweed shuns the supralocative, "bird's eye view" as a static concept of place preferring to offer a concept that is fluid and dynamic. Tweed also proposes that religion has the ability to provide this sense of place, locating oneself among the nodes of countries and communities and the multiple levels of crossing between these boundaries.

CROSSINGS

Tweed's theory provides a lens through which the religious lives of transnational migrants may be understood. His theory involves three components: position, relationship, and movement. Although the core of this essay will focus on the spatial component of "position," in terms of Lao Buddhism's settlement in Canada, this section will narrate the journey, or the movement, of the practitioners of Lao Buddhism from Laos to Canada.

In 1975 there were approximately two hundred Lao in Canada (Dorais 2000, 6). Most were students attending various universities in Toronto, Montreal, and Quebec City. After the fall of the Lao Royal Government in 1975, many bureaucrats, military personnel, and professionals from major Lao urban centres sought asylum in other countries. Dorais calls this initial group of Lao migrants the first wave (Dorais 2000, 6). They were academically accomplished, financially prosperous, and fluent in French.[2] Most migrants settled in Quebec where the French language is prominent. The second wave of refugees to arrive in Canada was the business class, many of whom were Sino-Lao who were experiencing hardship because of the increased nationalism of the Pathet Lao (Dorais 2000, 7). The final group of Lao, arriving between 1979 and 1982, consisted of 7,700 people who were sponsored by either the government or the private sector. Most of these people came from Thai refugee camps as opposed to other camps found in Southeast Asia. These Lao faced greater challenges than the previous two waves of immigrants because they were less educated, had fewer monetary resources, fewer job skills, and spoke neither of Canada's two official languages (Dorais 2000, 7).

The Lao had access to Buddhist monks while in the refugee camps, but once the refugees came to Canada there was a period of two years before the first monk arrived in Montreal. During this time the Lao were forced to grapple with multiple issues with profound emotional consequences – leaving the protection of their homeland, spending years in a refugee camp, and adjusting to the radically different environment of Canada. Within the Theravada tradition, Buddhist monks offer counselling and support, provide spiritual and emotional guidance, and are thought to give protection through blessings or amulets. Furthermore, Theravada Buddhist adherents believe that Buddhist monks are karmic "fields of merit," who enhance the lay practitioner's own personal karma. The relationship between Theravada monks and the laity in Southeast Asian Buddhist countries such as Sri Lanka, Thailand, Cambodia, Myanmar (Burma), and Laos is one of reciprocation. The monks rely on the laity for the physical necessities of life; the laity in return depend on the monastic field of merit to generate positive karma in order to allow for a better rebirth in the next life.

Given the importance of monks in the spiritual journey of Lao Buddhists, the absence of a monk was taxing for the community but not incapacitating. During this time of transition, devoid of ritual specialists, Lao refugee communities drew on the strengths of those who had previously been monks.[3] These lay members were available to the community to help with some rituals such as chanting. Without Lao Buddhist monks, the group continued to practise within their homes.[4] The emphasis on home ritual continues to be an important element of Lao Buddhist practice in Canada. With or without a resident monk, community members are able to continue their personal observance and maintain their identity as Buddhists by keeping the five precepts. A room or an alcove is set aside for prayers and chanting and a small- or medium-sized statue of Buddha is placed in a prominent location.[5]

The success of the Lao in finding and sustaining employment (Dorais 2000, 15; cf. Portes and Rumbaut 2001) in the mid-1980s led to the sponsorship of family members and the initial planning for a resident Lao monk in many Lao communities across Canada. But until the group had the monetary and organizational resources to sponsor a permanent monk, some Lao communities shared religious implements and personnel with the Khmer community (Dorais 2000, 25), who were experiencing even greater adaptive challenges (McLellan 1999). Both communities relied heavily on lay leaders with excellent knowledge of Pali and ritual procedures. These leaders were able to perform ceremonies, such as officiating at marriages and leading the community in chants. These religious specialists are known as *achaa* among the Khmer, and *moh phon*[6] within the Lao community.[7]

The process of sponsoring monks is not as straightforward as sponsoring fellow relatives. It is in the interest of both the government and private sponsors to encourage and assist refugees in becoming self-sufficient. Buddhist monks of the Theravada lineage observe a precept preventing them from handling money and participating in the broader paid labour force. From the government's point of view, the sponsored monk is considered "unemployed" and not financially contributing to society, therefore posing a risk in a system driven by the principles of productivity rather than by the principles of a contemplative life. Sponsoring a monk becomes a difficult task because the monk is dependent on the religious community to provide for his needs, which can only be accomplished after the basic needs of individual families have been met.

The Montreal community was the first to be able to sponsor Lao monks from refugee camps in the early 1980s. Because of this group's fluency in French and familiarity with bureaucratic circles, as many had held government jobs in Laos prior to the takeover of the LPDR government, they possessed the organizational skills required to navigate the sponsorship of monks. The Montreal community was able to amass sufficient funds in order to support a group of monks and procure a temple, which was initially an apartment in the Laval area of Montreal. Many of the monks who originally came to the Montreal *wat* (temple) were relocated within Canada to other communities, such as Toronto, Winnipeg, Regina, Calgary, Edmonton, Vancouver, Ottawa-Hull, Kitchener, Quebec City, and London.[8] The relocation of monks occurred once a community had the resources in place to receive them and permission granted by the head monk of the sending community. Monks were in great demand among various Lao groups in order to provide emotional and spiritual support,[9] as well as to help provide religious instruction to the generations of Canadian-born children, who would not experience a life immersed in Buddhism as their parents had in Laos.

A split in the Montreal lay community during the early 1990s resulted in the elderly, first generation Lao leaving the downtown community and purchasing a piece of land in Sainte-Julienne, approximately one hour north of Montreal. Disagreements over how to respond to the new Canadian context were responsible for the division of the community. The members who formed the Ste Julienne community held that traditional ways should be maintained. Not all the monks who relocated to Ste Julienne were in agreement with the group of lay leaders who formed the new community. It was from this rural location that the monks sought to reconcile the two communities.[10] In 1992 the Ste Julienne community suffered a great loss when the main building, used as a *sala* (the ritual space of a temple complex), burnt to the ground, reducing four large Buddha statues to melted pools of metal. The house that was used for accommodation remained untouched, but to date the community has insufficient resources to rebuild the *sala*; consequently, a renovation to the farmhouse has transformed the accommodation building into a multipurpose design that now houses a *sala* as well. Presently, there are three resident monks at Ste Julienne and four resident monks in the urban Montreal temple.[11]

The Toronto group was able to persuade one of the monks from the original monastic community in Montreal to come to assist their community. As Penny Van Esterik notes, the Lao who arrived in the Toronto area took years to become sufficiently established and able to provide accommodation and the basic necessities for a full-time resident monk. Nonetheless, in 1984 this community elected a board of directors for the newly established Wat Lao Toronto of Ontario and purchased a small two-bedroom apartment situated in an area where many Lao refugees lived. This group intended to entice one of the resident monks from the Montreal community to move into the Toronto suburb, as the act of sponsoring a monk from overseas would require greater language proficiency in order to negotiate the complex government forms and bureaucracy that sponsorship would entail.

The Toronto Lao have had a resident monk since 1984 (Wat Lao 2006, 20), although the turnover of monks has been great as they, in turn, relocated to other urban centres throughout Canada. As of 1986 there were a total of at least five monks in residence at Wat Lao in the Toronto area. Until 1998, when Wat Lao sponsored two monks directly from Laos, all the previous monks had come from Southeast Asian refugee camps via the Montreal and Winnipeg communities. While further establishing themselves within Canadian society, this community has simultaneously supported its own household, assisted others in the community, and financed a temple whether it be a permanent structure, such as an apartment or house, or the rental of a community hall for conducting ritual events. This has been a challenging process. The relocation of the temple four times between 1984 and 1988 added to these responsibilities (Wat Lao 2006, 20–1). A house in suburban Toronto was the final location prior to the purchase of property in Caledon in 1997.

Orchestrating the temple moves and sponsoring monks were not easy feats. A steep learning curve in language and bureaucratic channels was successfully negotiated in concert with accumulating the financial resources in order for Lao Buddhist refugee communities to establish their religion in Canada.[12] Increased understanding of the Canadian environment also led to the establishment of Wat Lao Toronto of Ontario as a registered charitable organization. With this official designation the Toronto group commenced a property saving plan. In 1997, after years of fundraising efforts, the Lao of the Greater Toronto Area (including Newmarket, Aurora, Bradford, and Brampton, as well as Hamilton, Guelph, St Catherines, and Niagara Falls), purchased seventy-three acres in Caledon, one hour northwest of Toronto, for the purpose of building what is currently the only traditional style Lao *wat* in Canada.[13] The building of the temple was delayed because of grievances – ultimately unfounded – by local residents. This resulted in years of litigation and legal fees. The community reports that the hostility took its toll and at one point some considered selling the property to prevent further suffering on both sides. In April 2001, following a year of hearings at the Ontario Municipal Board, Wat Lao received permission to carry on with its original intention of constructing a temple (White 2006). Currently, this *wat* houses six resident monks, one of whom is a trained artist from Laos and another, the most recent arrival, is American-born and fluent in both Lao and English.

The Lao Buddhist community's crossing to Canada was rife with challenges. The flight from the homeland and its subsequent emotional, financial, physical, and spiritual toll; the time spent without access to the "field of merit" believed to surround a monk; the pragmatic need to secure their own resettlement prior to sponsoring a monk; the competition between communities for resources such as ritual specialists and monks; the fundamental questions of community direction which divided the Montreal group; and the external resistance from host communities are some of the situations confronted by the Lao diaspora. The obstacles encountered in a difficult crossing inform the experiences of dwelling. For the Lao community of Caledon the challenges inherent in their journey to Canada manifest in the difficulties the community has had in establishing a dwelling. Moreover, there would appear to be a direct relationship between crossing and dwelling; the more hardships encountered in the crossing the more imperative is the need to establish a dwelling in the new homeland in order to recreate and shore up communal notions of identity, and specific to Lao Buddhism, the notions of protection and lineage.

DWELLINGS

This section will narrate how Lao Canadian Buddhists are recreating their spiritual space within North America. Tweed's concept of dwelling is a lens through which the religious settlement of the Lao community can be viewed. Again, Tweed's theory consists of three components: position, relationship, and movement. While the prior section retold the journey of the Lao to Canada, this part will concentrate on how Lao Buddhists who settled in the Greater Toronto Area transformed a Canadian space into a place for their tradition.

A miniature scale reproduction of That Luang, constructed of plywood and a plaster/concrete mixture, was the first symbol to be erected on the temple property in Caledon by one of the community members. The stupa in Vientiane has a square base from which a central spire rises 50 metres. The base perimeter is lined with thirty-two smaller gilded spires.[14] The smaller model is approximately three metres square and has been painted bright yellow to represent the gold-tipped stupa in Vientiane. The smaller points surrounding the central and taller spire correspond to the number of stupas throughout Laos.[15] When asked why this was the first piece of artwork undertaken on the site, two board members responded that this is a symbol that all Lao would recognize as their own.[16]

The original That Luang was constructed in 1566 as a Buddhist stupa, legitimating both the spiritual power of the Buddha and the political power of the monarch, who was believed to be a *buddharāja*, that is, a king ruling in accordance with the dharma. Within Laos, the significance of That Luang is immense: "[it] symbolizes the structure of the world; it is the center of power, a source of merit, and a symbol of Buddhism" (Evans 1998, 47). The stupa radiates the authority of the king, in concert with the dharma, through the surrounding environment (Harvey 1984, 68–70).

It is significant that this stupa was chosen by the Toronto group as the first symbol to be reproduced in Canada signifying recollection, remembering, and relocation. The practitioners are reminded of the veneration ceremonies that occur at home, the importance of the symbol, and the representation of legitimation.[17] Van Esterik, whose research predates the purchase of this property, reflects that it is surprising that the *Phrathatluang* celebration has continued in Canada as it is intimately connected with Laos's geography and the Lao royal family neither of which are directly applicable to life in Canada (1992, 78). Nonetheless, the That Luang celebration continues to be one of the highlights of the religious calendar for this community. During this November celebration special bouquets consisting of two incense sticks, a small tapered candle, and a silk flower are placed between the palms of the hands. The participants, led by some of the monks, circumambulate a copper relief of That Luang placed in the centre of the room. During the procession a gong is sounded in a rhythmic fashion. Some of the participants chat amicably with others, some look solemnly at the floor. The participants are sprinkled with lustral water as they pass a monk near the riser at the front of the temple. After three circles around the relief, the procession ends with the participants converging on the relief. Half prostrations are performed and the bouquets offered to That Luang.[18]

The symbolism of That Luang is important for the successful establishment of Lao Buddhism on Canadian soil for three reasons: it offers protection, legitimation of this tradition's monastic lineage, and group identity. All three are essential for the relocation of Lao Buddhism in the new spacio-temporal context of Canada and have parallels with Tweed's observations about dwelling. For Tweed, dwelling elicits connotations of mapping, building, and inhabiting (Tweed 2006, 82). These are similar to my observations of what the Lao Buddhist community is setting out to achieve by installing That Luang. They are mapping the protective elements of Lao Buddhism on Canadian soil, building a Lao Buddhist monastic lineage, and inhabiting a space that they identify as a Lao Buddhist place within Canada's multicultural mosaic.

THAT LUANG: THE RELOCATION OF LAO BUDDHISM TO CANADA

The Protective Element of Lao Buddhism

Lao Buddhism is a combination of various beliefs. Most notable are the overtones of Brahmanism, animistic traditions from the mountains of Laos, and Theravada Buddhism transported to Laos from Myanmar, Cambodia, and Sri Lanka (Van Esterik 1992, 40–1, 67 and 127; Gunn 1982, 81). These main components of what has come to be known as the tradition of Lao Buddhism all bear references to the notion of protection.

First, Theravada Buddhism speaks of taking refuge in the triple gem as a way of offering protection to the laity. This is not considered to be an external source of protection, but rather refuge through the knowledge and practice of the Buddha, dharma, and sangha – giving protection against delusion. The Buddhist practice of "chanting … [the triple gem], is often used as a form of protection" (Harvey 1990, 180). It is believed that the monks generate a "field of merit" because of their commitment to living according to the *vinaya* (precepts). Therefore, when monks chant protective *suttas* it is thought that they can pass along this protection to the laity. This is done through the "blessing" of amulets and strings, which are tied around the wrists of practitioners who seek protection.

Second are the animistic characteristics of Lao Buddhism, represented by belief in a spirit realm. There are evil spirits and spirits that protect. In Laos it is thought that each household, community, and territory is protected by spirits; thus there are multifarious layers of protection (Boord 1994, 14–17 and Condominas 1975, 255–72). The establishment of a spirit house to ward off evil is tended to by one member of the community, who brings offerings to entice protective spirits (Condominas 1975, 261).

Third, the influence of Brahmanism is found in Lao Buddhism through the notion of the *buddharāja*. The king of Laos is considered to rule in conjunction with the dharma, thus representing, although not a manifestation of, the Buddha in this earthly realm. This concept of kingship is based on ancient Vedic notions of divine rule. Certain symbols are believed to legitimate the king's rule; for example King Aśoka (third century BCE) erected stupas throughout the extensive areas he ruled (Boord, 1994, 14–21; Swearer 1995, 92–5; Harvey 1984, 68). The king of Laos would renew his relationship with his subjects through a ritual ceremony which occurred at the That Luang stupa. This rite revalidated the rule of the king and acknowledged the right of all subjects to protection from the *buddharāja*.

Van Esterik, writing at the beginning of the Lao refugee experience in Canada, notes that by leaving what they consider to be the overarching protected lands of Laos as well as the protectorate spirits of their own region and community, the Lao refugees find there is "no substitute" in North America for the "territorial based guardian spirits of Laos" (1992, 45). Muecke's case study of a Seattle community of Lao refugees demonstrates the spiritual and mental anguish of leaving what is considered the protective homeland of Laos. She reports that this community experienced haunting episodes during their resettlement. They were, however, able to find solace through ritual action which was reinterpreted in order to regather and protect the community from outside forces and spirits, such as those believed to be doing the haunting (1987, 273–89).

As with the Lao in Seattle who inform Muecke's study, the Lao refugees who established their community in Caledon draw on ritual practice to regather the community. The symbol of That Luang is used in order to recollect and remember the security of Laos under the guardian spirits, the protection of a king, and the perceived powers of the stupa, establishing an environment conducive to Lao Buddhist ritual practices. The Lao community desires to create and maintain a place of protection resonating with Lao Buddhist cosmology. Future plans involve moving the That Luang reproduction in order to construct a *sim* building. This structure will be used for ordination ceremonies and will be the most sacred space on the temple property.[19] It is therefore important to ensure that the surrounding environment is able to contribute to the continuation of the Lao Buddhist lineage in Canada.

Legitimation: The Importance of the Lao Buddhist Lineage in Canada
The reciprocity between Lao monks and laity is a key component of Lao Buddhism. The monastics are a field of merit that is vital to lay ritual practice as well as a source of aid in times of suffering. It is, as Van Esterik emphasizes, key that the community maintain a legitimate lineage in order to firmly establish Lao Buddhism in Canada (1992, 82). Therefore, the acquisition of a senior Lao Buddhist monk is of primary importance for Lao Canadian communities because of their experience and requirement, in order to conduct full ordinations. Once the *sim* building is constructed this obstacle will be removed and

all Lao diaspora communities will be able to send their novice monks to the temple in Caledon to undertake full ordination.[20]

In 1988, the community of the Greater Toronto Area was able to sponsor two monks directly from Laos. The most senior monk has extensive experience, as he was ordained in Laos prior to 1954. He draws on his immersion in Lao Buddhism in order to accurately recreate ritual ceremonies on Canadian soil.[21] This negotiation, between memories of past ritual actions that occurred in Laos and those that are being performed in Canada, constitutes the dynamic relationship between crossings and dwellings that Tweed refers to in his theory.

The representation of That Luang plays a significant role in preparing the temple grounds for the construction of a *sim* building by acting as a mnemonic device to aid in the recollection of Buddhist traditions specific to Laos, such as Lao Buddhist notions of protection, rituals performed in Laos, and monastic/laity relationships of reciprocity. But most important for continuing and legitimating the Lao Buddhist lineage is the connection with the home country of Laos. Through the image of That Luang, the link with Laos is enhanced for the lineage of Lao Buddhist monks presently residing in Canada.

Identity: Finding a "Sense of Place"

One of the three aspects of dwelling which Tweed's theory observes is the act of inhabiting – the others being mapping (as seen in the remapping of protection onto Canadian soil) and building (for example, the essential quality of ensuring a legitimate Lao lineage). These are not mutually exclusive but rather "overlapping processes" that together enable practitioners to orient themselves in time and space much as a "watch and compass" (Tweed 2006, 82 and 83).

The Lao community in Caledon declared their identity as Lao Buddhists by marking their property with the image of That Luang that identified them as Lao, Buddhist, and in relationship with Canadian society.[22] That Luang acts as Tweed's "watch and compass" assisting the Lao Canadians in reaching simultaneously backward and forward across space and time, between Laos and Canada, between past, present, and future, in order to firmly place themselves within Caledon, Ontario. From this place Lao Buddhists of this community interact with others in their community during ritual celebrations, or with members from outside the community, such as area neighbours, passersby who drop in to explore the temple, and other groups within the diaspora. By declaring their presence in the multicultural society of Canada they are engaging with other cultural communities around them. This speaks directly to the creation of identity as explained in Charles Taylor's *Sources of the Self*, where Taylor analyses the formation of the modern identity, emphasizing the hermeneutical relationship between self and other. In the act of recognition a community finds its identity confirmed or challenged by other members of society. The installation of That Luang is one of the key features that initiated a process of settlement.

The marking of space is usually carried out with the intention of making something permanent, even if the reality over time is its impermanence.[23] It is with a sense of permanency that the temple space is constructed. Lao Canadians, who arrived as refugees, are recreating their Buddhist tradition within multicultural Canada by seeking to make a permanent location for their tradition within the social, political, and geographical landscape of Canada. As one young adult explained in her speech during the opening ceremonies of Wat Lao Veluwanaram, it is up to future generations of Lao Canadian Buddhists to sustain what their parents have built.[24] The community projects itself into the space through activities, such as planning the site, obtaining building permits, and tendering construction companies. The process of preparing space with the intention of "moving in" and making it their place is in this sense "re-locative," in that it is making the physical space adhere to, conform with, and echo the recollections and reinterpretations of the diasporic community. The diasporic community has moved in, politically and physically, to what had been considered a host country, mapping their space within Canadian society.

CONCLUSION

Traditionally, Lao Buddhism, especially prior to 1975, was intimately connected with the land. The *nāgas* and tutelary guardian spirits protect designated areas of land and water. When 400,000 Lao left the protective space of Laos they also left the most significant symbol of guardianship, national and Buddhist identity – That Luang. Although Van Esterik was surprised that this symbol retained its relevance in the new homeland of Canada (1992, 78), it has translated well in its new context, becoming the first piece of iconography created on Canadian soil that was owned by the Lao Buddhist community.[25] The intimate blending of symbols that have since been crafted at Wat Lao Veluwanaram and the presence of Lao Buddhist monks continually embodies and inscribes meaning onto the physical space of the property, temple, and practitioners in such a way as to transform this Canadian space into a Lao Canadian Buddhist "place."

In addition to being a source for recreating the protective cosmology of Lao Buddhism on Canadian soil, That Luang acts as a symbol on other levels. It is a beacon for group identity and a mnemonic device which acts as a reminder of the homeland and ritual ceremonies practised there, and it provides a context for their recreation here to ensure a valid lineage. The symbol of That Luang is not a static object of plaster and cement. But as Tweed's notion of dwelling suggests, the community's active participation with the symbol is ongoing through space and time. Actions and memories are recollected, moving between the past, present, and future, as well as crossing space between their present location in Caledon, the homeland, and other diaspora communities.

Evans has noted that That Luang "symbolizes the structure of the world; it is the center of power, a source of merit, and a symbol of Buddhism" (Evans 1998, 47). It is possible that these are the facets of Lao Buddhism that the Lao Canadians in Caledon, Ontario wanted to relocate. While the geography of Laos cannot be mapped onto Canadian soil, the protective elements and spiritual guardians of the homeland's geography can be. Tweed's theory supports such an observation. The relationship between dwelling and simultaneously traversing is ongoing and fluid. For the Lao in Caledon, dwelling is symbolized in the replica of That Luang that elicits notions of group identity, legitimation, and protection, while the act of traversing space and time maintains the relevance and significance of the symbol. The annual celebration of *Phrathatluang* and veneration of the copper relief, the regular offerings made at the replica stupa on the property, and the memories of the protective elements that the stupa elicits are all examples of the ongoing active crossings which occur in order to create a dwelling for Lao Buddhism in Canada.

This essay has focused on Tweed's notion of dwelling and the creation of a Lao Buddhist place in Canada rather than the specifics of the ongoing crossings of the Caledon community. However, the recreation of a Lao Buddhist cosmology, the embodied recollections and performances of specific ritual actions, and the ongoing relationship with the homeland and diaspora in order to send familial remittances, procure ritual supplies, and have access to monks ordained in Laos, exemplify various forms of crossings that enable the community to dwell in Caledon.

The Lao Buddhists are currently (and will always be) in the process of recreating their religious tradition. For this reason, That Luang continues to be significant for Lao Canadian Buddhists at this juncture in space and time. In order to successfully establish their tradition in Canada the community recognizes the need to relocate their protected space, establish a Lao Buddhist monastic lineage, and mark their group identity on Canadian soil, all of which are symbolized in That Luang. Moreover, That Luang is not a static symbol of innate meaning; rather, it is a representation imbued with fluid and multiple meanings. The That Luang representation located on the property in Caledon elicits different responses and meaning than does the actual stupa in Laos because of the migration experiences of this community of Lao Buddhists.

The history of Lao Buddhists who came to Canada in the 1970s and 1980s as refugees is one of resilience, hard work, and co-operation. When compared to other Buddhist communities, such as the Chinese or Thai, Lao social capital is relatively low (McLellan and White 2005). In spite of this, Lao communities across Canada have pooled their resources in order to establish a *wat* and maintain a resident monk. The Caledon area group has had greater success than some other Lao Canadian communities because of fewer internal struggles, relative affluence of some of the members, and the willingness of the majority of the members to donate large amounts of their time to fundraising efforts and the monies raised to the temple.[26]

The place has been created in Canada for Lao Buddhism. That Luang is the initial symbol that provided the visible marker for Lao Canadians of the Greater Toronto Area. It assists in the recreation of a Lao Buddhist cosmological view of protection and guardianship in the new homeland of Canada. The symbol has translated well onto Canadian soil where protection and refuge was and continues to be sought by the Lao people. By creating a Lao Buddhist "place" the community has formed a relationship with Canadian space, an action that involves crossings and dwellings but also roots and a sense of permanency. This is a move abounding in meaning; Canada is not a "host" country to this Buddhist community; it is another home.

NOTES

1 I have been a participant-observer at Wat Lao Veluwanarm since October 2004. To date I have spent approximately 160 hours attending regular annual religious ceremonies,

special ceremonies such as house blessings, and the preparations for these events as well as the temple's opening, and two major cultural celebrations hosted by the temple.

2 Laos was a French Protectorate from 1893 to 1954.

3 It is common in Theravada Buddhist countries for young boys and men to take temporary ordination lasting a few days, through the summer months, or a few years.

4 Van Esterik conducted a survey which found that prior to the arrival of Lao monks the community continued to practise: 82 per cent continued to pray at home, 35 per cent meditated, and 39 per cent continued to keep the extended eight precepts on certain auspicious days of the year (1992, 116).

5 Email correspondence, August 2007. My respondent also suggested that these areas are more prevalent in homes with seniors.

6 As Grant Evans states, there are many variations in the spelling of Lao words and currently "there is still no standardized way of spelling Lao words in English" (1998, 193).

7 Although the two groups are linguistically distinct, the majority of Lao having descended from Tai-speaking tribes and the Khmer from Mon, the two groups share the ancient scriptural language of Pali through their Buddhist roots. Khmer and Lao Buddhist rituals and chants share many common elements even though there are different cultural nuances.

8 The final destination point of refugees is frequently dependent on the location of their sponsors. For example, many Lao who were sponsored by Mennonite individuals and communities settled in Kitchener and Winnipeg. This is how many Lao came to be settled across Canada.

9 Edward R. Canda and Thitiay Phaobtong, in their study of Southeast Asian refugees, note the importance of ritual specialists in assisting refugees to maintain their emotional health. They state that "studies have suggested that religiously based indigenous healers and helpers [such as Buddhist monks] are important sources of support for many Southeast Asian refugees" (Canda and Phaobtong 1992, 61).

10 Interview conducted in Lao through a translator with a Ste Julienne monk, July 2007, during which he mentioned his use of intense meditation whereby he would meditate for almost twenty-four hours on a constant basis. The two groups were gravely concerned for his well being and made efforts to reconcile. Today the two groups enjoy a better relationship.

11 Interview conducted in Lao through a translator with a Ste Julienne monk, July 2007.

12 Another complex task is learning how to organize the purchase of religious goods from overseas. For example, the Toronto community arranged for the purchase and shipping of two Buddha statues from Thailand in 1994. There was also the overseas purchase of statues and books for various Southeast Asian refugee camps (Van Esterik 1992, 25 and

60) as well as ritual implements for the Toronto group itself. Many of these arrangements involved shipping fragile or large items such as the intricately carved six-foot candles purchased from Thailand. More recently, two hand-carved wooden doors arrived for installation as the main doors of the newly built temple in Caledon. These transactions involved many steps of negotiation and logistics before the doors arrived at the temple.

13 Wat Lao Veluwanaram is the only Lao Buddhist temple on Canadian soil that is built in accordance to the Lao tradition. It occupies 465m² of soil and is visible from a main roadway leading north from the Toronto/Brampton area. It is a beacon for many Lao Buddhists who travel from across Canada to see the new temple. Many combine a visit to the temple with a large Lao festival that is hosted every summer and draws Lao from all over North America.

14 The number 32 is significant in the Buddhist tradition. It symbolizes something that is complete. It is believed that Siddhārtha Gautama had the 32 marks of an important person and in Lao Buddhism there are 32 spirits that gather in the crown of a person's head.

15 Conversation with the senior monk of Wat Lao Veluwanaram, March 2005.

16 Field notes, July 2007.

17 Grant Evans notes how the LPDR have appropriated the symbol of That Luang along the lines of the Royal Lao Government before them. Each draws on the stupa's perceived ability to legitimize their powers and efforts, as rulers, to unify the various ethnic groups within Laos (Evans 1998, 42).

18 Field notes, November 2004 and November 2006.

19 The term "sacred space" is not found in the traditional Lao Buddhist lexicon. By sacred space I mean a special space which can be transforming. This is where it is believed that the Buddhist practitioner can generate merit, for example, a site of pilgrimage such as a stupa. It is a location that is pure or with "no sin" (Field notes, March 2005). Chidester and Linenthal (1995) suggest that American sacred space is created through contested space. Elements of this theory are evident in the Toronto community's struggle with a group of neighbours who attempted to block municipal approval of the temple's site plan (White 2006).

20 A full ordination is required to take place within a *sim* building or over flowing water. A *sim* building must have its boundaries marked by *sima* stones and its space prepared through ritual. In addition five monks are required to be present, one of whom must be a senior monk (Van Esterik 1992, 82; and e-mail correspondence August 2007).

21 An example of the importance of this experience can be seen in the ritual actions that were involved in the ceremony to open the newly constructed temple in July 2006. These actions involve both mental and physical acts; ritual actions had to be first mentally

recollected and remembered as they had been performed in Laos in the past, and only then physically performed.

22 By placing the stupa replica in a highly visible location along a major roadway, the Lao were engaging with the broader Canadian society and declaring their presence. The neighbours in the surrounding area responded by challenging the building of a temple on the site as well as questioning the legitimacy of this form of Buddhism. For more on the challenges this community experienced, see White (2006). For more information on how social capital can affect a community's ability to engage in the politics of recognition, see McLellan and White (2005).

23 One aspect of Tweed's theory that is problematic is his emphasis on dwelling as "always 'for a time'; it is never permanent or complete" (2006, 81). While I agree with Tweed from a philosophical perspective, and acknowledge the ever-changing nature of religious community as suggested in the symbol of That Luang, nonetheless, the physical structure of Wat Lao provides the community with a relatively permanent space. It is this notion of a relatively permanent space which I think Tweed does not adequately address with his notion of dwelling. He states that he is considering the "kinetics of dwelling" as an orientation process which "allow the religious to map, construct, and inhabit ever-widening spaces: the body, the home, the homeland, and the cosmos" (Tweed 2006, 84). This echoes Jonathan Z. Smith's (1978) somewhat evolutionary perception of space as ever widening to the point of transcending physical, geographical space altogether. Embodiment to the point of disembodiment is a concern as it does not reflect the reality of numerous hours of thought, discussion, work committees, physical labour, and money that Lao diaspora communities spend in creating a place for their community's cultural and religious tradition in Canada. In his defence he quotes James Clifford's *Routes;* "I'm not saying there are no locales or homes, that everyone is – or should be – traveling, or cosmopolitan, or deterritorialized" (Clifford quoted in Tweed, 80). Yet, Tweed does not address this in his own words; my observation of the Lao community is that there is an intention of permanence, even if philosophically one can make the argument for the impermanence of things.

24 Field notes, 1 July 2006.

25 Jonathan Z. Smith suggests that among diasporic communities there will be a "lessening of concern" over time with the relationship between the community's religious tradition and a tie to the homeland. Smith predicts that a diasporic community will eventually embrace a transcendent form of their tradition, severing ties with previous geographical connections of the homeland (1978, xiv). How much of a connection will remain between this community and their Buddhist tradition's intimate ties to native soil is yet to be seen.

26 Conversation with translator, July 2007.

Transforming Ordinary Life
Turning to Zen Buddhism in Toronto

PATRICIA Q. CAMPBELL

Members sitting in meditation, Zen Buddhist Temple, Toronto
Photo courtesy of Toronto Zen Buddhist Temple

At the corner of College and Spadina, near Toronto's Chinatown district, a large yellow brick building houses the Zen Buddhist Temple of Toronto (the ZBT). Founded by Korean Zen teacher Samu Sunim, the temple offers meditation services, courses, retreats, and community events for temple members and visitors. Public services held on Sunday mornings and afternoons include short meditation sessions, dharma talks, and a number of different chants. Wednesday evening services, which are reserved for members, include three thirty-minute meditation sessions and some chanting in Korean and English.

A steady stream of new visitors encounters the temple through its public services, meditation courses, rummage sales, Buddha's Birthday celebrations, or New Year's Eve services. The introductory meditation course, offered several times a year, is the prerequisite for membership. Members pay monthly dues and have access to all the temple's regularly scheduled events. Some choose to formalize their involvement by taking the precepts. This involves a formal ceremony in which practitioners agree to follow five guidelines based on the traditional five lay precepts.[1] Founder and head teacher Samu Sunim, who officiates at these ceremonies, gives each participant a dharma name. For those interested in an even deeper commitment, the ZBT offers its Maitreya Buddhist Seminary, an intensive training program for members interested in becoming dharma teachers.

This chapter is based on ethnographic interviews, conducted in Toronto from June to October 2003, with twelve members of the ZBT. Like the majority of ZBT members, all were from non-Buddhist familial and cultural backgrounds; none had ethnic or cultural ties to Korea. The stories of how they came to Buddhism and the significant themes that arise within these stories provide some interesting insights into the process of becoming involved in Buddhism in Canada. Primarily because respondents use, and are familiar with it, the problematic term "Western Buddhist," is retained here. As Victor Hori argues, this group should be regarded as its own cultural expression, one among many present in Canada. "Western Buddhism" is also not intended as an ideal category exclusive of any others. In this chapter, references to Western practitioners have less to do with genetic or cultural heritage than with participants' experiences of beginning to practise Buddhism in the Canadian cultural setting.

The question underlying this study originated with a reading of *Sources of the Self* by Canadian philosopher Charles Taylor (1989). Taylor describes a trend he calls "the affirmation of ordinary life," which he says has gained "unprecedented importance" in modern Western societies, particularly in North America (Taylor 1989, 13). Religious values and goals frequently demand a sacrifice of the goals and benefits of everyday life. One response to this dilemma has been to strip away religious values that require any form of self-sacrifice in favour of the more worldly or ordinary values of human prosperity (Taylor 1989, 519). The affirmation of ordinary life includes a tendency to stress vocation and family over religious goals and values. The life of work and the family becomes the *sole* locus of the good life, and new, utilitarian values are created based only on the objectives of ordinary life (Taylor 1989, 13). Utilitarianism, in this sense, is a tendency to stress practicality or utility over other values. Despite this trend in modern societies, the values associated with traditional ethical systems such as religion are still highly regarded. A conflict thus exists between the need to elevate the goals of career and the family and to live up to one's religious values (Taylor 1989, 23–4). The question becomes, how do we balance ordinary life with religious commitment?

Taylor writes primarily about Catholicism, but in many Buddhist schools, too, the model practitioner is one who renounces many of the ordinary goals of everyday life. For North American Buddhists raised in a culture unfamiliar with Buddhist tradition and one that affirms vocation and family over religious values, balancing the two may be difficult. Practitioners thus need to negotiate a balance between the kinds of Buddhist teachings and practices that they adopt and their everyday Canadian lifestyles. The process of negotiating this important balance is evident in respondents' stories of beginning to practise Buddhism. While adaptations were going both ways – Buddhism was being adapted to them as they were adapting to Buddhism – respondents indicated that Buddhist values helped them inform and transform their ordinary lives in significant ways. Their affirmations, therefore, were not only of ordinary life.

Conversion theory can be a fruitful framework for exploring the experiences of Western practitioners, but referring to the process of taking on Buddhist practices as "conversion" is not always accurate. Beginning to practise Buddhism in Canada (which I define as adopting, to varying degrees, Buddhist practices and world views) does not necessarily mean leaving something else entirely. Many regard Buddhism as a nonexclusive religion, and many who follow teachings or practices they identify as Buddhist also maintain affiliations with other religious traditions. Moreover, as Angie Danyluk (2003) has shown, taking on Buddhist practice does not necessarily mean fully accepting a Buddhist identity. Some long-term practitioners with whom she spoke were either uncomfortable calling themselves Buddhists, or placed certain qualifiers on that identity.

Respondents involved in this study had been members of the ZBT from one to twenty years. All had taken precepts at the temple, and all self-identified as Buddhists. Many respondents indicated a broad but superficial understanding of Asian Buddhism. They were, rather, attracted to a Westernized form of Zen that is still developing here. What emerges from these responses is a picture of religious or spiritual seeking, specific to these particular practitioners but having certain characteristics in common with broader conversion theories. While it is too complex to explore in its entirety here, Lewis Rambo's model of religious conversion (1993) contains several categories that can illuminate respondents' stories of discovering Buddhism. Four common themes emerge from these stories which correspond to Rambo's discussion of crisis, apostasy (a subcategory of crisis), encounter, and quest. These themes are

1) discovering Buddhism at a time of crisis or personal need,
2) having reservations about mainstream religions or religion in general,
3) discovering affinities with certain Buddhist teachings or principles,
4) shopping around when looking for a Buddhist group or teacher.

Each theme represents a circumstance or orientation that influenced respondents' decisions to become involved with Buddhism. Each also served as an important step whereby respondents began to integrate Buddhist principles and practices into their lives. The remainder of this chapter explores each theme in turn.

TIME OF CRISIS

Not everyone who adopts a new religious or philosophical affiliation does so because of a crisis. According to Rambo, however, most scholars of religious conversion claim that "some form of crisis usually precedes conversion" (1993, 44). Five of twelve respondents in this study noted that their initial involvement with Buddhist teachings and practices either coincided with or came as a direct result of a crisis in their lives. Nathan's story is a good example.

Nathan[2] was a legal services professional who was thirty-four at the time of his interview. When asked how he came to Buddhism, he replied:

[In] late 2000, early 2001, I started reading some material by the Dalai Lama. I was dealing with a lot of stressful issues from work and relationship issues, and I was trying to find a way to focus more on myself. And I think I read his book entitled *New Ideas for a New Millennium* ... I read that over Christmas. My father was terminally ill at the time ... So, I was at home over Christmas time with my mother and father, and I was actually using my reading as a manner of escape. And I was trying to understand these concepts that I was reading, and I realized that they were making sense to me. So, [for] my birthday in 2001, one of my friends bought me *The Art of Happiness* by the Dalai Lama, and that sort of furthered me down the path. And while I was in Korea in August and September of 2001, I went to the Buddhist temple established by my assistant's ... great-uncle. And that was two days before September the eleventh ... I had to spend another week in Korea after what happened in New York City, because no planes would land in Toronto. So I had time to think a little bit more. I wanted to start working more towards this. So, from there on I started focusing on trying to meditate at home and I came to the Zen Buddhist Temple primarily by accident in September of 2002. And in October of that year I did their introductory meditation seminar. And then from there I started going as regularly as possible.[3]

Nathan was facing at least two crises in his life: his father's illness and the fallout from the terrorist attacks in the United States. He connected each crisis to a step that he had made toward a commitment to Buddhism. In each of these parallel incidents there was a crisis and an exposure to the Buddhist tradition that first initiated and then intensified Nathan's interest. He specifically emphasized, however, that he had not been actively looking for a Buddhist community when he found the ZBT.

Nathan said that several crises in his life were pulling him in different directions, and his private life was consuming him. When he started investigating Buddhism, he was looking for a way to "focus more on myself." He said, "I find that the teachings and the practices and the rituals are something that foster self-hope and that you work on your own self and try to perfect yourself, which is what I believe we should all try to do more."[4] While it may appear that his initial interest in Buddhism focused on practical solutions to his immediate personal needs, his interest was also based upon a spiritual search. At thirty-four years of age, he saw himself at a time of life when people begin to contemplate mortality and wonder about their legacy in the world. Nathan believed that this was why people often start looking to religion. Facing mortality through his father's terminal illness and the terrorist attacks on Washington and New York, in his words, "made a few spiritual changes."[5] He said that he had entered into a "self-destructive cycle," and in order to break it, he had to begin with himself before being able to address larger spiritual questions.

The desire for transcendence is one of the motivations for conversion that Rambo lists among other conversion crises. He describes it as a need humans have to "seek beyond themselves for meaning and purpose" (Rambo 1993, 50). Nathan experienced three crises identified in Rambo's model: illness and healing (i.e., his father's illness), externally stimulated crises (i.e., the terrorist attacks), and the desire for transcendence (Rambo 1993, 48–55). In Rambo's perspective, any one or a number of different crises may create tensions that initiate a spiritual quest. This represents a different perspective from that of Taylor, who is concerned that a commitment to religious values can itself create tension in our lives and that we too often sacrifice those values in favour of more worldly concerns. Nathan's quest to find spiritual answers to his life crises indicates that he was not concerned about these kinds of tensions or sacrifices. Rather, crises motivated him to seek answers in new religious orientations and experiences. Nathan was not only looking for short-term, practical solutions to these crises that would alleviate his personal suffering; he also sought a spiritual path that would uncover a sense of meaning that went beyond himself.

While it is the case that five of twelve respondents came to Buddhism as a means of alleviating psychological suffering, each of them expressed an attachment to the tradition's spiritual aspects. Mary, a fifty-six-year-old business researcher and writer, had suffered a severe stroke when she was in her thirties. Facing serious physical limitations, she discovered that she had to learn to be patient with herself and control her anger during her recovery. Then she discovered, in some contemporary books on Buddhism, some of the same lessons she had begun to learn on her own.

> I still think of myself as a real shadow of what I was: not accomplished, not articulate. Now, everything is hard. If I didn't bother with things that weren't easy, I'd sit in my room, you know. So, it gives you a new patience. And then I discovered one day [that] the things that I habitually reacted to with anger, which sort of made me miserable, didn't necessarily make anybody else miserable. They made me miserable, and that I had a *choice*. You know, I didn't *have* to do that. And if I chose not to do that, I was a lot happier. And when I finally started to read some Buddhist books, there's quite a bit about anger. Thich Nhat Hanh talks a lot about it in his books, about how you do have seeds of anger and the more you water anger the faster it comes up. And I realized I'd been watering it regularly over little things. And you can choose not to do that. And so it takes a lot more now to make me angry. But that was an insight before I'd read about [Buddhism]. So as I started to read [books on Buddhism], it just was like a light going on. There's a whole system that deals with the things that I've been trying to deal with, or discovering in my own life.[6]

Mary had been reading contemporary Buddhist teachers, from whom she learned that the qualities she found most helpful in her recovery were also valued in the Buddhist tradition. The lessons she learned provided practical answers for her situation. In her view, however, they were also spiritually significant because of their correspondence to certain Buddhist teachings.

Michelle, a doctor who was thirty-six at the time of her interview, had been suffering from, in her words, "a pretty serious eating disorder," and attributed much of her recovery to Buddhist meditation. She had been reading about meditation in some books by Thich Nhat Hanh, and had been meditating on her own for a time before she became ill.

> I just kind of dabbled for a few years, until a lot of stuff happened to me in residency, some very heavy-duty bad stuff that was very difficult to go through and I ended up being quite ill. I had to take an entire year off last year. So I thought: How can I fix it? I'm working too hard, and dealing with

a lot of personal things. But, over the past year I started doing meditation taught [at a resource centre] by somebody who actually knows what he's doing. It's Buddhist meditation for the non-Buddhist. So, I tried a little of that, and in the hospital some people also tried to guide me through that. I said, you know what? I think there's something to this that can really help me. And meanwhile, I was reading, from the intellectual standpoint, just eating up those books – Jon Kabat-Zinn, Robert Thurman – and so, intellectually it totally appealed to me, the philosophy of it. And, the two sort of *merged* through my recovery.[7]

Like Mary, Michelle had been reading contemporary teachers. The philosophical and practical aspects of these writings and of meditation initially appealed to Michelle. But her involvement eventually went beyond the more secular style of meditation taught at the resource centre. She travelled to Thailand, where she did an intensive meditation retreat. When she returned to Toronto, she took the precepts at the ZBT and later went on several lengthy retreats with another organization. Michelle's involvement in Buddhism as a distinctly religious practice increased over time and became an integral part of her ongoing recovery process. "A lot of Westerners like me come to it [Buddhism] through self-help … But then I adopted it really as a way of life, and it is vital to my being. I've never been happier; I've never been more grounded. It's just amazing."[8]

Michelle said that psychotherapy had been a large part of her treatment, without which she might not have recovered. But she believed that Buddhism was also critical to her recovery, not only because it helped to treat her illness, but also because she felt it gave her a new way to live.

This discussion has allowed for a separation between psychological health and spiritual health. Naturally, these are inextricably linked. The effects of identifying Buddhism with Western psychology or psychotherapy are open to debate. For good or ill, some people do turn to Buddhism as a means of overcoming personal difficulties. But respondents like Nathan, Mary, and Michelle believed that the solution to more immediate, worldly problems opened the door to a more spiritual way of living and understanding their worlds.

PERSPECTIVES ON RELIGION AND RELIGIONS

Some respondents in this study noted that they had fallen away from a previous religious affiliation, or that they were dissatisfied with religion in general. For most, existing opinions concerning religion had a part to play in their initial attraction to Buddhism. Deborah, a forty-eight-year-old information specialist, was one of four respondents who had been devout practitioners in another tradition before they came to Buddhism. Deborah had suffered a religious crisis at the age of ten when her father died. She felt that the Christian tradition in which she was raised failed to provide sufficient answers to that crisis. This left her feeling very suspicious of religion in general. She said that she was uncomfortable with what she called "institutional religion." Nevertheless, when she was very young, she had begun to develop an interest in certain concepts she identified with Buddhism, particularly its rebirth cosmology. Deborah later began to study karate and said she learned more about Buddhism from her martial arts teachers. But it was not until she suffered a second loss in her family that she considered pursuing her interests further. The death of her stepfather acted as a vivid reminder of her father's death.

> I think when people die – every time somebody kind of major dies in my life, it brings me back to that first death, at ten, and the feeling at that point – because I was an extremely religious Christian when I was young, and at that point at ten years old, when my father died, I couldn't believe that a god would do that. So that was a very big problem at that point in my life. Now, some people overcome it, but I never really overcame it, because at the point that he died, I actually believed he wasn't dead, or at least that he had been reborn. And I actually almost felt the turning, the whole rebirth cycle. And it was really weird, because I didn't know anything about Buddhism, I mean nothing about anything to do with rebirth or anything. I knew he had come back. And I was sure of it.[9]

The religious crisis Deborah suffered when her father died shook her faith in the tradition in which she was raised. She was initially attracted by the doctrine of rebirth, a religious aspect of Buddhism, as opposed to its philosophical or psychological elements. Despite this, her initial involvement at a Buddhist centre was not religious. Deborah was very reluctant to become involved with a religious organization. This, coupled with a strong curiosity about the tradition, led to a sort of flirtation with the ZBT before she finally decided to join.

> I had a friend at the time who was going to the temple … I had asked her a bit about it, but I was very leery of any kind of institutional religion, ever since my childhood. [But] this friend was saying, well, here's the [ZBT]. So I called the temple one day. I didn't want to come to a service; I didn't want

to come to meditation. I wanted to come and look at the bookstore. That's really funny; this was my round about way, right? So I called them up, and [asked] when is the bookstore open? And they said it's open just after services and such. So I went and I looked around at the bookstore, and I was feeling really awkward. And I sort of peeked in to the meditation hall, and I thought "this is a very odd place." And I sort of exited stage left. But I had picked up a couple of flyers.[10]

From the flyers, Deborah learned about a lecture series to be held at the temple on Saturday afternoons. "I was still leery. You know, I still wasn't really keen to get involved with any institutional anything, and I thought: I'll come to another lecture … And before I knew it I was at a rummage sale, and before I knew it I was doing the Sunday service. I finally got brave enough … It could have been as much as six months from the day I visited just on the excuse of looking at the bookstore to the time I went to a first service. I took precepts the next May [or] June."[11]

Rambo argues that leaving a religious orientation throws a person into a crisis that then initiates a search for new religious teachings and communities (Rambo 1993, 53). Apostasy, in his words, "inevitably" causes a convert to grieve over lost beliefs, rituals, and connections to friends and family, aspects of one's life that are difficult to leave behind (Rambo 1993, 53–4). In this view, there is a powerful pull of the past. In Deborah's experience, the pull was not from her past orientation but toward her new one. In Buddhist rebirth cosmology she had already found the religious answers she needed concerning her questions about mortality. She had only to overcome her wariness about religious institutions in general. The tension she felt was not between the new tradition's values and her ordinary life: it resulted from her earlier religious crisis and a reluctance to become involved in another religious tradition.

Like Deborah, most respondents were raised in another religious tradition. Eight of twelve respondents had a Christian background. Two were raised in Jewish families and two were raised with no particular religious affiliation. Ten of twelve, then, had either turned away from their religious background or were seeking something in addition to it. Several respondents indicated some discomfort with the teachings of mainstream Canadian religion. Reasons for this ranged from respondents' disagreements with religious views on homosexuality to their association of dominant traditions with hypocrisy or with historical religious violence. For the most part, however, respondents indicated that what they wanted was a sense of agency and direct religious experience, something that many believed was not offered by other religious traditions. David L. McMahan has noted that Zen has been interpreted in the West, by both Asian missionaries and its Western recipients, in ways that appeal to Western cultural ideals of democracy, individual freedom, and equality (2002, 218). This perception of Zen, and of Buddhism more generally, is among the reasons it appealed to participants in this study. But its appeal also had to do with perceived distinctions from mainstream theistic religions.

Buddhism is often regarded as an atheistic or nontheistic tradition. In actual fact, many schools, particularly in Mahayana, have a large pantheon of divine beings, including countless Buddhas and Bodhisattvas. Although it originated in Mahayana Buddhism, Zen tends to place less emphasis on Buddhist deities. At the ZBT, theistic elements are not emphasized. Its nontheistic attribute was one of the main reasons why some respondents in this study were attracted to Buddhism and to Zen in particular. For example, Mary explained why she felt Buddhism appealed to her more than theistic religions: "I just felt like there had to be some meaning, some force to all of this, which I didn't really see in conventional religion. I mean, the thing is … as I got older, a theistic religion where somehow someone outside of you took care of you seemed sort of silly. And, you know, if both football teams are praying that they win, how come one of them loses? … I really think in Western religions there's somebody else saying you shouldn't do this, you shouldn't do that. It doesn't have anything to do with coming from you, that somehow you're short-changing your own nature."[12]

Following her stroke, Mary discovered that her recovery depended upon her own strength and capacity to master her emotions. This discovery may account for her view that relying on an external deity is unnecessary, even "silly." That kind of reliance, in her view, is predicated on the idea that individuals lack agency. Mary believed that Zen and the practices followed at the ZBT emphasized her own power to care for herself. This reflects a common interpretation of Zen in the West: it is regarded as a tradition that allows for individual freedom and direct personal experience (McMahan 2002, 221).

Linda, who was fifty years old and a communications consultant by profession, said that she did not think of Buddhism as a religion. She explained this view in an email message:

My personal experience of religion, i.e. my Protestant tradition, is: it is theistic, full of contradictions (e.g., God loves you but is a tough cookie, often bringing good things to bad people and bad things to good people …). It's up to you to determine what kind of relationship you are going to have with God and Jesus. Buddhism: To me, it's more of a philosophy or a way of looking at the world. Buddha is not a god. You don't have to worry about the randomness of phenomena in the world (e.g., good things for bad people ... bad things for good people) ... it's all constantly changing and impermanent. It's not all being sent down to us from a father-figure ... There is no separation between us and Buddha.[13]

Despite viewing Buddhism as a philosophy rather than a religion, Linda's belief in "no separation between us and Buddha" indicates a felt connection with certain religious principles such as reverence for the Buddha. Linda said that, in the Protestant tradition, people have control over their relationship with God, indicating that, in her view, the practitioner has a degree of agency. But the idea that an external father-figure has influence over human lives was not appealing.

Like Linda and Mary, most respondents appeared to have been searching for practices and teachings that allowed for their own agency or their own active involvement in their spiritual path. Many were strongly opposed to the notion that the spiritual or religious life must rely on an external authority or power. This differs from the more devotional style of practice followed by many lay practitioners in Korea and other Buddhist nations. In many Asian Buddhist cultures, the laity provides physical, social, and financial support for the clergy (the sangha). In exchange, monastics, who are regarded as "fields of merit" because of their dedicated religious practice, will transfer some of that merit, through ritual observances and ceremonies, to the lay people who support them (Harvey 1990, 240). While members of the ZBT do support the temple financially and through volunteerism, respondents did not regard such practices as a means of spiritual attainment. Respondents aspired to be their own source of spiritual merit and the agents of their own spiritual growth and were less willing to rely upon external powers or authorities.

The focus on agency in respondents' religious path was evident when they answered questions about prayer. In *Restless Gods*, Reginald Bibby writes that, among the Canadians he surveyed, "there is an assumption that Someone or Something is hearing the prayer – that it is being *directed towards some Other*" (2002, 157 emphasis original). Bibby notes that 47 per cent of Canadians surveyed in 2000 said that they prayed either daily or weekly (Bibby 2002, 158). Unlike the trend Bibby discovered in his survey group, which was representative of Canadians from a variety of religious affiliations, all the respondents in this study said that they did not pray. Most of them did not believe that prayer was a Buddhist practice. Most indicated a belief that there were no deities in Buddhism and therefore no one to whom prayers could be directed. This is true despite the fact that members' services at the ZBT include a prayer sung in Korean to offer homage to the Buddhas. Nathan's comment was representative of many respondents' views on prayer. "Well, having been raised in a nominally Christian background, part of my path to self-discovery has been more coming to terms with myself and self-reliance. The notion of praying means you're giving over power, or you are acknowledging that there's something else above you to which you can transfer power, or you seek the help of something else, of some other being. And, ultimately, we're really only able to help ourselves. So I don't really see the purpose in praying."[14]

Agency or self-reliance was therefore an important aspect of many respondents' spiritual paths. Many of them felt that Buddhism offered practitioners a greater sense of agency in comparison to other religious traditions and this appears to be a key reason why many respondents were attracted to Buddhism and to Zen. This perception allowed them to regard themselves as the instrument of their own spiritual growth and to adapt the practices and teachings they learned at the ZBT to fit with their everyday lives. Agency in their religious path thus allowed respondents the latitude to negotiate their own balance between ordinary life and religious commitment.

AFFINITIES WITH BUDDHISM

Most respondents started practising Buddhism as a consequence of a conscious, self-directed investigation of the tradition. Ten of twelve had read books on Buddhism or encountered Buddhist teachings in nonreligious settings before they began looking for a community to join. If it can be said that they converted to Buddhism, they were, in Rambo's words "active agents in their conversion process" (Rambo 1993, 44). For the majority of respondents, their investigations into the tradition uncovered felt affinities with the teachings and practices, sometimes quite unexpectedly. Linda, for example, had developed an immediate, unanticipated affinity with a particular teaching after hearing one dharma talk.

At the time of her interview, Linda had been a member of the ZBT for four years. Before she came to Buddhism, she had known very little about it. In fact, she claimed to have had little interest in religion at all. "I sort of grew out of it," she said, "and thought organized religion was really not for me."[15] She encountered Buddhist teachings quite unintentionally, at a time when she had been facing some personal difficulties in her life. Someone told her about a retreat centre in Kinmount, Ontario and she went there for a few days just for a quiet getaway. Visitors were not required to participate in meditation or dharma talks, but they were welcome to do so if they wished. Linda was not at all interested in the Buddhist element of the centre. But on the third day she decided to look in on a dharma talk. Feeling uncomfortable, she went in and sat down. "As soon as the dharma teacher started talking," she reported, "I swear, within 30 seconds I was gone."[16] The talk was about the illusory nature of the things around us, a reference to Buddhist doctrines concerning *anicca*, impermanence, and the Second Noble Truth: attachment to things that will naturally cease to exist is the primary cause of human suffering. Quite to her surprise, Linda was suddenly introduced to a new perspective that she believed would help her face her problems and her everyday life. She made a very intriguing comment about the dharma talk: "I thought, if that were true, that would really be helpful. And then I thought, even if it weren't true, that would still be really helpful. Even if I were duped and thought that, it would be a better way to live."[17] Evidently, Linda was not looking for ultimate truth. She came to Buddhism out of a need to find a better life in the here and now, an immediate means of improving her circumstances and her outlook in this life. But the thing that she hit upon, that helped her redefine her life, was one of the most basic Buddhist doctrines: the Noble Truths. From this experience, Linda began to draw on this teaching in order to inform and transform her everyday life. The affirmation, in this case, was of ordinary life through religious teachings.

This ability to relate the teachings to the circumstances of their lives appears to be another reason respondents were attracted to Buddhism. As noted, many respondents were uncomfortable with external authority. Many were also uncomfortable with doctrines that seemed rigid or authoritarian. Some respondents indicated a belief that Buddhist teachings were more flexible than those of other traditions. Buddhist teachings, they believed, were open to adaptation and interpretation. This perception once again reflects the ways in which Zen has been, in McMahan's words, "re-packaged for the West." The strict hierarchies and the authority of the Zen Master, as well as the rigid routine of the monastery, are de-emphasized. Instead, Zen has been presented as iconoclastic and individualistic (McMahan 2002, 221). Its doctrines and practices are seen as being open to interpretation and adaptation. This perception of flexibility permitted respondents to relate its teachings and practices to modern Canadian life.

Macario was thirty-one years old and a musician by training. Like Linda and Deborah, he had had certain qualms about religion. He said that he was uncomfortable with the kind of doctrinal rigidity he saw in some religious traditions. "I think I still have some resistance to being enclosed in a religion, because I have never been a religious man … So, in the sense that I follow the teachings of the Buddha and I try to attain the goals of Buddhism, yes I can say I'm Buddhist. But also Buddhism, from my point of view, [is] a different religion. It specifically tends to break with these ideas of enclosing, making things rigid."[18]

At the time of his interview Macario was enrolled in the ZBT seminary program, was living full time at the temple, and following a rigorous schedule of meditation, chanting, prostrations, and manual work. He clearly was not averse to religious institutions or structures. Rather, it was a perception of Buddhist teachings as flexible and nonauthoritarian that appealed to him. Macario related the parable of the raft as an example. In it, the Buddha likens his teachings to a raft, which is useful for crossing a river but is left behind once one reaches the other shore. The river is samsara, the cycle of birth and death, and the opposite shore is nirvana or enlightenment. Through this parable, the Buddha counsels his followers not to become attached to the teachings. Macario found this attractive because, in his view, it indicates that Buddhism is less doctrinally rigid than other religious traditions.

Gordon, a mind/body therapist who was sixty at the time of his interview, said that Buddhism's doctrinal adaptability was what most attracted him to the tradition. "The thing that really set my heart with Buddhism is hearing the Buddha say: what I say isn't absolute. Question it. Learn what I say then question it. Take it apart, look at it. If you can see that it works for you, then great. If it doesn't, then find something else. And that, to me, always was very appealing, because a lot of belief systems, they're sort of very rigid and this is the only way you can see the world."[19]

Gordon was referring to a Buddhist text called the *Kālāma Sutta* in which the Buddha encouraged the Kālāma people to reflect upon the worth of the different religious teachings they had heard. In it, the Buddha tells the Kālāma people,

Now look you Kālāmas, do not be led by reports, or tradition, or hearsay. Be not led by the authority of religious texts, nor by mere logic or inference, nor by considering appearances, nor by the delight in speculative opinions, nor by seeming possibilities, nor by the idea; 'this is our teacher.' But, O Kālāmas, when you know for yourselves that certain things are unwholesome (*akusala*), and wrong, and bad, then give them up ... And when you know for yourselves that certain things are wholesome (*kusala*) and good, then accept them and follow them. (Rahula 1962, 2–3)

This sutra is often interpreted among Western practitioners as espousing the agency of the individual, upon whose authority it places the evaluation of teachings. Since it promotes the rejection of any religious teachings deemed inappropriate or unwholesome, it also appears to advocate the adaptability of all teachings, including those of the Buddha. It is worth noting, however, that this view of the Kālāma sutra has been contested. Bhikkhu Bodhi (1998), for example, argues that the sutra does not necessarily counsel questioning Buddhist doctrine. He argues that the Buddha advises the Kālāmas to question *other* religious teachings while simultaneously proving the validity of his own. Bodhi argues that the sutra promotes Buddhist doctrine *as it is*, based upon its intrinsic worth (Bodhi 1998). In this view, the sutra does not allow for the kind of doctrinal flexibility that many interpreters have drawn from it.

The perception of the adaptability of doctrine and/or flexibility of practice is quite common among Westerners. Whether or not this view is the one advocated in the frequently cited Kālāma sutra is a matter of debate. This discussion demonstrates, however, that 1) respondents believed in the adaptability of the teachings and practices they associated with Buddhism, 2) because of this belief they were attracted to the tradition, and 3) the belief allowed them to find ways of balancing their ordinary lives with their involvement in Buddhist practices.

SHOPPING AROUND

For most respondents, the decision to become involved in Buddhism was followed by a search for an appropriate community to join. This was another step on the path to adopting Buddhism, which for most respondents was an ongoing process. Respondents were continually re-evaluating their responses to the teachers and teachings they encountered, and were rediscovering teachings and practices that best fit into their lives. Many respondents visited and assessed several different groups, traditions, and/or teachers before they settled on one that best suited them. Linda referred to this process as "shopping around."[20]

Macario's story is representative of this kind of search. His quest for a Buddhist group took place in Mexico City, where he lived at the time. There were many different organizations for him to choose from, and he and a friend visited several.

> Well, first I tried this Western tradition, the Friends of the Western Buddhist Order. There is a group in Mexico City, so I went sometime and tried to practise meditation with this group, but maybe in that moment I didn't think it was serious enough for me. I don't know, but something was wrong with that group, so I started to look for another group and I found this Theravada group and also started to practise a little. I went just for two sessions of meditation, and they started to look more interesting. The insight was deeper in meditation. A friend of mine was also interested in Buddhism. Both of us were interested in Zen. I found in Zen art there was something very special: a special insight about life and about the nature of things … So we started to look for a Zen group in Mexico. We started to look on the internet for groups, and we found a list of Zen groups in Mexico and we started to make some calls. My friend went to one group but it started to mix Christianity with Zen and so we didn't like that group. In fact the teacher at the Friends of the Western Buddhist Order said if you want Zen, I can give you the number of a good teacher and a very good group. He said they really practice Zen.[21]

That group turned out to be the Mexican temple associated with the Toronto ZBT. Macario and his friend attended one of its five-day retreats. Macario's experience on the retreat left a profound impression on him and he decided to become much more involved. "I decided [to join the seminary] after the retreat, because it was a very great experience for me. It was so moving and it changed me a lot and started to open my eyes deeply. So I thought that I wanted to make a deeper practice, you know? And Sunim talked about the seminary and said if you want to have good training, you should come to Toronto."[22]

Shopping around from group to group, leaving behind the ones that do not appeal, may have less to do with religious commitment and more to do with utilitarian concerns, but for Macario, the search for an appropriate community clearly had religious significance. He indicated that he had been specifically looking for a deeper insight into the meaning of life, a committed practice, and serious religious training. By this, he meant a focus on meditation and the insights that come from that practice. It was clear that, like many Westerners, Macario regarded meditation as the true spirit of Zen. Mental cultivation through meditation was the "serious practice" he was looking for. When asked why he decided to become more committed to Zen, he replied, "The reason is the experience of meditation; experiencing the practice and how it can change the way you perceive everything, like your own nature and what surrounds you. It activates new perceptions that usually you don't have. It's like discovering something you were missing."[23] Macario sought an organization which would allow him to pursue these religious goals. In fact, that search took him out of ordinary life for a time. He left his career and his family to enrol in full-time seminary training in Toronto. He, thus, chose to affirm his religious values over those of ordinary life.

Two respondents, Alan and Michelle, moved on to other Buddhist organizations between the time of their first interviews in July and August of 2003 and their second interviews in October. Alan, who had also studied transcendental meditation some years before joining the ZBT, had moved on to a Tibetan-based group. He said that he and his wife had both found it difficult to relate to someone "as Asian" as they felt Samu Sunim was.[24] The Tibetan group they moved to was run by Westerners. Alan said that some of the Asian elements at the ZBT were "a little too alien."[25] Some Western Buddhists feel that Asian cultural elements, especially language, present a barrier to their involvement. Deborah was one respondent who insisted that the ZBT really needed to translate its services entirely into English. Other respondents, like Laura and Linda, appreciated the ZBT's Korean elements, particularly the Korean-language chants, because they felt those chants represented a link to a long-standing Buddhist tradition. For Canadian Buddhist organizations, these different preferences demand a delicate and often difficult balance of Asian and Western cultural elements if they are to attract committed, long-term practitioners. This is true among all the different cultural expressions of Buddhism in Canada. How many traditional elements, many of them considered sacred, should be retained in a new cultural environment? To what degree do practitioners born and raised in Canada find such elements alienating or attractive? These are significant questions that Buddhist teachers and their organizations currently face. McMahan notes that Zen in particular has been decontextualized in the West, removed from its traditional cultural expressions. He argues that this has resulted in a Zen that has been "re-mythologized" in terms of European and American attitudes (McMahan 2002, 219).

While some respondents moved from one Buddhist organization or tradition to the next until they found the right fit, others were drawing on practices and teachings from different traditions simultaneously. Peter, a fifty-six-year-old librarian, said, "What I found was, as I practise more, the traditions become less important and I tend to pick from a variety of traditions."[26] At the time of his first interview, though still a member of the ZBT, Peter was attending another group, founded by a Canadian monk trained in the Theravada tradition. Theravada, Peter said, "is not what I'm naturally inclined to, but the fact that I found this teacher is important, and not the Theravada tradition."[27] Peter said he had wrestled with the idea that "most accomplished Buddhists or authorities will say: choose a tradition or choose a practice and follow it. But what I've been doing over the last several years is picking and choosing, finding what works for me and following that."[28] Eclecticism of this sort is perhaps a predictable outcome of the process of religious shopping. Seekers find they can select different elements that best appeal to them. Picking and choosing allowed Peter to develop a practice that he believed was meaningful and relevant for his life and his spiritual needs. He said it was difficult to maintain Buddhist values in "big city life," but claimed that his practice allowed him to be kinder, more patient, and more compassionate.

Another respondent, Alan, also commented on the tendency to select from different traditions. He said, "Obviously because of upbringing and more freedom, call it whatever word you want, in the West we're more likely to pick and choose from any religion than somebody who's grown up in Korea or Japan with a very strict religious upbringing. And with Buddhism I'm picking and choosing things."[29] Alan touches on significant issues such as the desire for freedom of choice and the availability of religious choice in Canada. He believed that these resulted from the Western social environment, rather than any necessary development in Buddhism in Canada. Like Peter, Alan found that picking and choosing allowed him to negotiate his Buddhist involvement in terms that fit his Canadian lifestyle. Even so, he compared this approach unfavourably to the "strict religious upbringing" of Buddhists from Asian backgrounds. Buddhist scholar and convert Richard Hayes argues that there are deep connections to the symbols, rituals, and meanings of a tradition in which one was raised, connections that can be lost when one converts to an unfamiliar tradition as an adult (Hayes 2000, 45). This seems to have been the case in Alan's experience: "I'm torn at times between [Buddhist] teachings and reality in the Western world, and teachings and my upbringing and my long-held beliefs … It's not a tension, but there's a disagreement between the dharma … and what I believe and feel and do. Sometimes they're together and sometimes they're very far apart."[30] For these people, taking on Buddhist practices thus necessitates finding ways to balance those practices with their existing world views and lifestyle.

Respondents said they were looking for many different things when they moved from group to group: a teacher with whom they could connect; a serious or disciplined religious practice; a "spiritually uncluttered" atmosphere; an environment that is either connected to a long-standing Buddhist tradition, one that is culturally comfortable for Canadians, or one that is both. Some of these needs are practical, others more spiritual. Within this process of searching, it is therefore apparent that respondents were considering their ordinary, everyday needs along with their more spiritual needs.

Several conditions in the religious environment in Canada allow for and even encourage the process of religious shopping. For the first time in its history, numerous different branches of the Buddhist tradition are represented together in the same geographical regions. In the West, there is the unprecedented opportunity to try out different organizations and traditions. Where there is no family or cultural connection to a particular nationality or Buddhist school, and in a pluralistic society offering a variety of religious groups and traditions, those interested in beginning to practise Buddhism have the means and motivation to look around until they find the right teacher, the right tradition, the right group. With so much choice available, practitioners see little need to maintain involvement with a group that does not immediately fit their individual needs. Finding the perfect fit – if, in fact, they are able to do so – may enable them to become more involved and perhaps more devout than they would be otherwise.

Having the means and motivation, however, may not be enough of a justification for unlimited tradition-hopping. Certainly it is necessary for practitioners to find religious practices that fit into their lives. Moreover, the ability to adapt to Canadian culture and lifestyle is necessary if Buddhism is to succeed here. Adaptation of the tradition to Canadian needs and world views could allow the religious elements of Buddhism to become part of Canadian life. There is, however, a danger when many practitioners readily hop from group to group. The result may be that no one group will have a stable enough membership to succeed. Organizations lack a strong sense of community when their memberships suffer high rates of attrition. Without a stable and long-term membership, such organizations have difficulty establishing the strong lay community that is necessary for creating a viable monastic community in Canada. Since its beginning the tradition has relied upon the contributions of the lay community, in terms of both volunteering and financial resources, to support monastics and full-time teachers. All Buddhist traditions, and especially Zen, have long relied on transmission of the tradition from accomplished teachers to their students. Excessive mobility of practitioners will likely leave Western-based centres with weakened support systems for monastic practitioners as well as weakened lay communities.

CONCLUSION

High attrition rates at Western Buddhist centres, practitioners who do not identify as Buddhists, and a large number of unaffiliated Westerners interested in Buddhism (*cf*. Coleman 2001, 186–91 and Tweed 2002, 18) are noted time and again in studies of Western Buddhism in North America. These features may be temporary and possibly even necessary stages of the process of developing new, more stable forms of Buddhism in Canada. They may also be reflections of Westerners' tendencies to experiment and to shop around for Buddhist groups and practices. At the very least, such features indicate that Buddhism is still finding its way.

While we cannot extrapolate to all Western Buddhists from this small group, respondents' reflections do tell us what some people who were willing to become committed to certain Buddhist-based teachings and practices were looking for: a nontheistic tradition they regarded as adaptable, allowing for inquiry and experimentation as well as personal authority in their spiritual practice. Respondents indicated that certain teachers and groups catering to Western sympathizers have adapted to such needs and expectations. Such adaptations are shaping a form of Buddhism in Canada that both responds to and affirms those elements, carrying them forward to future generations of Western followers.

From the teachings and practices they encountered, respondents selected elements that fit, allowing them to find the balance between religious commitment and ordinary life that Taylor suggests is so crucial. A perception that Buddhism allows adaptation and agency in practitioners' involvement aided the negotiation of that balance. In their interviews, respondents stressed the importance of certain spiritual aspects of Buddhism: teachings like the Four Noble truths, Buddhist ethical precepts, or values such as compassion, mindfulness, and letting go. Time and again they reported the belief that Buddhist spirituality helped them inform and transform everyday life. Thus, shopping around and experimenting were the very things that enabled respondents to incorporate various Buddhist teachings and practices into their lives.

Respondents' experiences of beginning to practise Buddhism indicate that there are viable reasons for studying Western Buddhists as a distinct group, provided they are properly identified as only one among many different cultural expressions of Buddhism in Canada. There are common experiences, expectations, and obstacles among Buddhist sympathizers and followers whose primary cultural and/or religious influences are those of mainstream Canadian society. They therefore form a population distinct from those with more direct ties to Asian Buddhism.

Establishing Buddhism in Canada necessitates adapting traditional teachings and practices to a pluralistic and secular environment. The interaction of Buddhist values and Canadian secular society is an issue facing all Buddhist groups in Canada. The experiences of those from non-Buddhist backgrounds highlight this issue from a particular perspective, and can complement the study of Canadian Buddhist communities of Asian heritage. Together, such studies contribute to a better understanding of the influence of mainstream religion and culture on the development of Buddhism in Canada.

NOTES

1 ZBT wording of the precepts is as follows: Do not harm, but cherish all life; Do not take what is not given, but respect the things of others; Do not engage in sexual promiscuity, but practice purity of mind and self-restraint; Do not lie, but speak the truth; Do not partake in the production and trading of firearms and chemical poisons

that are injurious to public health and safety, nor of drugs and liquors that confuse or weaken the mind.

2 All names used for respondents are pseudonyms.

3 Interview conducted on 11 July 2003.

4 Ibid.

5 Ibid.

6 Interview conducted on 15 July 2003.

7 Interview conducted on 6 August 2003.

8 Ibid.

9 Interview conducted on 27 June 2003.

10 Ibid.

11 Ibid.

12 Interview conducted on 15 July 2003.

13 Email communication received on 17 October 2003.

14 Interview conducted on 11 October 2003.

15 Interview conducted on 22 July 2003.

16 Ibid.

17 Ibid.

18 Interview conducted on 5 August 2003.

19 Interview conducted on 28 July 2003.

20 Interview conducted on 22 July 2003.

21 Interview conducted on 5 August 2003.

22 Ibid.

23 Ibid.

24 Interview conducted on 10 October 2003.

25 Interview conducted on 10 July 2003.

26 Interview conducted on 18 July 2003.

27 Ibid.

28 Ibid.

29 Interview conducted on 10 July 2003.

30 Ibid.

The Woodenfish Program
Fo Guang Shan, Canadian Youth, and a New Generation of Buddhist Missionaries

LINA VERCHERY

Members of the Humanistic Buddhism Monastic
Life (Woodenfish) Program sit in meditation at the
Fo Guang Shan temple in Kaohsiung, Taiwan.
Photo courtesy of the Woodenfish Program

The Taiwanese Buddhist order of Fo Guang Shan (Buddha's Light Mountain) has attracted significant scholarly attention since the publication of Stuart Chandler's *Establishing a Pure Land on Earth* in 2001. Today, there is scarcely a publication on the topic of globalization and Buddhism that does not at least mention Fo Guang Shan (FGS). As Chandler states, "the Foguang 'empire' … is now arguably one of the most extensive and best-organised Buddhist groups in the world" (Chandler 2005, 162). With over 205 temples and lay chapters in more than thirty countries, Fo Guang Shan has circled the globe, ostensibly crossing national, linguistic, and cultural borders. Underlying this global expansion is an explicit missionizing mandate: Fo Guang Shan's founder, the Venerable Master Hsing Yun, holds that globalization, insofar as it makes the world smaller, rendering the division between nations increasingly fluid and permeable, presents an unprecedented opportunity for Buddhism to spread to people of all nations. In the words of Master Hsing Yun, "We are all global. We are all the same … If we could join together with one another with no regard to nationality or race, it would be wonderful. So [the] global character [of Fo Guang Shan] doesn't simply mean building temples in various places. We want to spread peace, equality, forbearance, friendship, respect, and tolerance everywhere to everyone" (in Chandler 2005, 180).

The impressive breadth of FGS's global expansion, however, raises a paradox. On one hand, Fo Guang Shan, with its globe-trotting, polyglot monastics running temples and lay organizations on six continents, seems to brilliantly fulfill its mandate of propagating the dharma across national, ethnic, and linguistic barriers. However, scholars conclude that despite its rhetoric of spreading Buddhism "everywhere to everyone," FGS has been unsuccessful in attracting non-Chinese followers in Canada. Instead, it has stayed within the rubric of what has been termed "ethnic" Buddhism[1] – a religious organization designed to serve a local ethnic community by providing an enclave where the rituals, language, and traditions of the homeland are preserved. This is the case of FGS branch temples from Ottawa to Vancouver. These temples practise a decidedly FGS Chinese style of Buddhism and have resisted assimilation into the Canadian cultural environment: their members are ethnically Taiwanese, religious and social functions are predominantly conducted in Taiwanese or Mandarin, the main shrine and adjoining rooms are decorated in the Chinese FGS style, and the food served at community functions is Chinese. One could describe FGS temples in Canada in the same way that Chandler describes FGS temples in the United States: "life in the temple is essentially the same as it would be if it were located in Taiwan" (Chandler 2005, 179).

Contrary to Chandler and other scholars who conclude that FGS has failed to attract non-Chinese Westerners to Buddhism, I hold that FGS is, in fact, successfully promoting Buddhism among an influential demographic of Canadians. The conduit for this dharma propagation is not, as one might expect, FGS's sophisticated international network of branch temples but, rather, the Woodenfish program: a one-month academic residency program held annually at FGS's monastic headquarters in Taiwan. Furthermore, I contend that the Woodenfish program is at the centre of the development and promotion of a distinctively "Westernized" – or to use FGS terminology, "localized" – form of FGS Buddhism in which a number of features of FGS Chinese-style Buddhism are de-emphasized and reinterpreted in order to appeal to Westerners. Moreover, I will argue that Canadian youth who work as Woodenfish staff are actively informing this localization process. Thus, an examination of the ways in which FGS is modifying its Chinese-style Buddhism in order to localize can offer insight into some of the ways in which today's youth are helping to change Buddhism in Canada.

This chapter will begin with an examination of Fo Guang Shan in Canada and the two-fold mandate that underlies its paradoxical missionizing agenda, followed by a description of the Woodenfish program based on my experience as a participant in 2005 and a staff member in 2006 in Taiwan, as well as on my continued involvement with the program through its various alumni branches in North America from 2006 to the present. I will suggest that the ways in which FGS Buddhism is localizing reflect trends in Canadian Buddhism as a whole, including an emphasis on individual practice rather than institutional affiliation, an increasing prevalence of "diffuse affiliation,"[2] and a recognition that youth are identifying as "spiritual" rather than "religious." I argue, moreover, that these trends must be reflected in our scholarly methodologies if we are to properly study the changing face of Buddhism in Canada.

FO GUANG SHAN'S DOUBLE MANDATE IN THE WEST

Fo Guang Shan's mandate in Canada is twofold. While serving members of the Chinese diaspora by acting as "a bridge back to the Chinese cultural homeland" (Chandler 2005, 178), FGS also aims to extend beyond Chinese communities and "feels called upon to energetically undertake foreign missionary work" (Chandler 2005, 171) among non-Chinese Canadians. FGS undoubtedly fulfills the first aspect of its globalization mandate, as illustrated by the relative ethnic and cultural homogeneity of Canada's FGS branch temples. To address the second aspect, FGS has developed a rhetoric of "localization." "[T]o lessen tensions with the mainstream society in each country in which Fo Guang Shan plants one or more temples, and to smooth the transition for those attracted to the Dharma ... customs which have been generated by Buddhists in China and other cultures over the centuries may be replaced by other customs more appropriate to each new region into which the Dharma is introduced" (Chandler 2005, 176).

In other words, by appealing to a rhetoric that separates the grain of Buddhist truth from the chaff of Chinese culture, FGS legitimates the de-ethnification process whereby it strips itself of its distinctively Chinese cultural elements in order to better plant the "seed of the Dharma ... in every nation, and not just among emigrants from Buddhist countries, but among the general populace" (Chandler 2005, 171). Despite this rhetoric of localization, however, Chandler concludes that Fo Guang Shan is unsuccessful in reaching non-Chinese Westerners, remarking that "over 99 percent of ... [FGS] members are ethnically Chinese ... [Fo Guang Shan] remains almost completely associated with one cultural group" (Chandler 2005, 167). Chandler suggests that this stems from the mutually exclusive nature of FGS's two main objectives in the West – serving as a cultural bridge for Chinese diaspora communities while also converting non-Chinese Westerners. That is, because the process of localization de-emphasizes the Chinese features of FGS Buddhism, it inevitably effaces those very elements upon which FGS's role as a cultural bridge to the homeland depends. Thus, FGS's "capacity to serve as a vehicle to preserve Chinese identity is directly undermined by any effort to localise practice" (Chandler 2005, 178). Since FGS cannot afford to alienate its Chinese devotees, Chandler concludes that FGS's efforts to transcend ethnic and cultural barriers in the West have failed.

While Chandler is correct in asserting that FGS's role as a cultural bridge to the homeland has taken precedence over its aspirations to attract non-Chinese Canadians to its branch temples, I contend that FGS's missionary efforts in Canada have not been unsuccessful. FGS is aware of the conflicting forces at work in its double mandate and has responded to this challenge by developing an entirely new avenue through which to propagate the dharma to non-Chinese Canadians: the Woodenfish program.

THE WOODENFISH PROGRAM: LOCALIZING BUDDHISM FOR WESTERNERS

The Woodenfish program takes place annually at Fo Guang Shan's international headquarters in Kaohsiung, Taiwan, and offers North American university students the opportunity to experience FGS Buddhism in its monastic context. Founded in 2001 by Venerable Dr Yifa, who was ordained under Master Hsing Yun in 1979 and received her doctorate in Buddhist studies from Yale in 1996, the month-long program combines academic study of Buddhism with participation in the various daily rituals and practices of the monastery. A number of extracurricular activities are also offered including classes in Tai Chi, Mandarin, traditional Chinese music, cooking, calligraphy, a five- to seven-day silent meditation retreat, and a cultural tour of Taiwan. In addition to providing all participants with a scholarship that fully covers room, board, and the cost of program activities, FGS offsets the cost of airfare to the island for most program participants. Because the Woodenfish program draws most of its participants from the United States and Canada, with two or three participants each year hailing from other parts of the globe, the program's influence is not limited to Canada but, rather, extends throughout North America. While many of the points discussed herein also apply in the American context, I limit the present discussion to the program's impact in Canada.

Localizing Buddhism in Taiwan: The Appeal of the Exotic
While the fact that FGS's localization of Buddhism for Canadians takes place in Taiwan rather than in Canada may seem ironic, I suggest that this geographical reversal is one of a number of key elements in the success of FGS's localiza-

tion project. Historically, the popularization of Buddhism in the West has involved adopting Western cultural values while maintaining, at least on the surface, a certain aura of Asian authenticity. The importance of assimilating without losing the appeal of the exotic is illustrated by the failure of a number of Buddhist organizations in North America to attract non-Asian devotees because they have either resisted assimilation or have assimilated too much. On one end of the spectrum, there are temples like Fo Guang Shan that have remained under the rubric of "ethnic" Buddhism: their devotees are ethnically Asian, their assimilation into non-Asian Canadian communities is minimal, and their temples function principally to maintain and preserve the culture, language, and religion of the homeland. These "ethnic" temples have failed to attract non-Asian Canadian devotees, leading scholars to conclude that they are too foreign to appeal to Western tastes. This stands in contrast to Buddhist organizations that have thoroughly assimilated into the Canadian cultural environment but have, paradoxically, also failed to attract Western devotees. As has been well documented, this is the case among many Japanese Pure Land Buddhist temples; having reorganized their practice on the model of Protestant Christianity in order to assimilate into the Canadian cultural milieu, they failed to attract non-Asian devotees because they appeared too similar to American Christianity to appeal to Westerners.[3]

The ability of the Woodenfish program to inscribe itself between these two poles[4] – namely, assimilating Western cultural values without losing the appeal of the exotic – is central to its success in attracting Western youth. While the Buddhism presented to Woodenfish participants is decidedly localized, the fact that the program takes place at FGS's international headquarters – a massive complex of impressive buildings that easily dwarfs FGS's comparatively modest branch temples in Canada – lends a powerful air of exoticism and authenticity to the program. That is, the program's symbolically significant location reinforces FGS's implicit endorsement of the distinctively localized Buddhism of the Woodenfish program, despite the fact that the latter differs significantly from the Chinese-style Buddhism of FGS monastics. In fact, the establishment of this symbolic continuity with Chinese-style FGS Buddhism leads many Woodenfish participants to believe that the Buddhism they encounter in the program is authentic FGS Chinese-style Buddhism. As scholars have observed, the Westernization of Buddhism often occurs under the guise of a sincere belief that one is following a traditional Asian practice.[5] The fact that participants are required to actively take part in a number of the highly institutionalized practices of daily life at FGS headquarters is a key element in establishing this perceived continuity between FGS Chinese-style Buddhism and the Wooden-fish program, as will now be discussed.

Daily Life as a Woodenfish

The most conspicuous way in which the Woodenfish program inscribes itself within the heavily institutionalized environment of FGS headquarters is through its dress code. Six days a week, program participants are required to wear an FGS uniform consisting of light-coloured loose-fitting pants and a large Chinese-style shirt with a high collar and mid-length sleeves. These uniforms resemble those of the students at the Buddhist College on the FGS headquarter grounds. "Monk's shoes," the standard closed-toe canvas sandal worn by all FGS monastics, are made available at minimal cost for program participants, although participants are allowed to wear their own shoes, provided they are closed-toe, neutral in appearance, and modest. Women are required to wear their hair off the face, and men are expected to shave regularly. Jewellery is generally discouraged. A strict dress code is even enforced on free days (generally Sundays) when uniforms are not required. Tank tops, low necklines, skirts, and shorts above the knee are prohibited. Shoulders must be covered and closed-toe shoes are required. Every year, the Woodenfish dress code elicits resistance from program participants. Many participants are not used to the sweltering heat and humidity of the Taiwanese summer and feel that full-length pants and sleeves are too hot. Some female participants have trouble adapting to Taiwanese standards of modesty that seem prudish when compared to acceptable summer dress for young women in Canada. The most serious and common complaint, however, is ideological: participants dislike how the uniform effaces their individuality. Venerable Yifa's standard response to such complaints is that clinging to individuality is, in actuality, a hindrance to progress on the Buddhist path, and that uniforms, insofar as they help dissolve one's notion of self, are a means of spiritual cultivation. While some participants come to accept this view, many others see it as an overly strict and authoritarian application of Buddhist doctrine, holding that individualism and Buddhism need not be mutually exclusive.

In addition to the strict dress code, Woodenfish participants are required to comply with other institutionalized rules of FGS monastic life. For the duration of the program, participants must take their meals in the FGS refectory alongside the entire community of FGS monastics, lay devotees, and visitors who, during peak visiting seasons at FGS, can sometimes number nearly two thousand. Meals at the FGS refectory are highly ritualized: they begin and end with chanting, bows to the Buddha, and sometimes a short Buddhist teaching delivered by the abbot. The meal itself is consumed in silence. Strict ritual protocol governs everything from how one must pick up one's chopsticks, to how plates of food are placed on the table, to how to position one's fingers when holding the rice bowl. The highly ritualized nature of meals at FGS requires participants to relinquish virtually all personal control over their consumption of food. Participants must eat at fixed times; they must finish their entire serving even when not hungry; and they cannot choose the types of food they eat. The last was an acute problem for many non-vegetarian participants who felt that the FGS vegetarian fare could not provide them with the nutrition they required. As FGS monastics emphasized, however, daily meals are meditations: monastics strive to eat without regard to whether the taste is pleasing or whether the quantity of food is sufficient in an effort to cultivate an attitude of nonattachment in their daily actions. This highlights an important difference between the FGS view of food and that of Woodenfish participants. For the latter, choices relating to food consumption lie in the private sphere of the individual. Participants eat for their own good, and consider it each person's right to make their own dietary choices. At FGS, however, food is a means of meditative practice and is, therefore, not consumed for one's own self but in order to cultivate selflessness.[6]

The strenuous schedule of the Woodenfish program is another way in which the program mirrors the highly structured and institutional nature of daily monastic life at FGS. A typical day for Woodenfish participants begins in much the same way as it does for FGS monastics. The sounding of the wooden board at 5:30 signals wakeup. Participants then line up at the strike of the bell at 6:00 and proceed to morning Tai Chi. A designated Woodenfish staff member rings this bell throughout the day to signal the beginning of each activity. The Woodenfish group goes everywhere in two silent, parallel lines, one for women and one for men. Tardiness at the lineup is not tolerated, and participants are not to speak while in line. Morning Tai Chi is followed by a thirty-minute meditation period. At 7:00, participants line up, bow, and proceed to breakfast. The day's first academic lecture runs from 8:00 until 11:00, with one or two short breaks punctuated by the ring of the bell. At 11:15 sharp, participants line up in silence to proceed to the refectory for lunch at 11:30, which is followed by walking and sitting meditation in the Main Buddha Hall from 12:00 to 1:00. A second academic lecture period runs from 1:00 to 3:00, and the time from 3:00 until 5:45 is dedicated to either communal chores, such as gardening and maintenance of the FGS grounds, or personal chores, such as handwashing one's uniform for the next day, cleaning one's sleeping quarters[7] and, if time permits, checking emails in the FGS computer lab or calling home. At 5:45, participants line up for the evening medicinal meal, followed at 6:15 by a forty-five minute class on a range of topics, including Mandarin, sutra study, calligraphy, Chinese music, and additional meditation instruction. Nightly dharma talks are offered by FGS monastics through an interpreter from 7:00 to 9:00. At 9:00, participants line up for evening vespers. The final bell of the day is rung at 9:30. Participants generally manage to squeeze in a few minutes for laundry and other tasks before crashing into bed in time for lights out at 10:00.

The Meditation Retreat

A notable exception to the aforementioned schedule[8] is the five- to seven-day silent meditation retreat during the last week of the program. As noted above, meditation training is a daily part of the Woodenfish curriculum. During the first week or so of the program, Venerable Yifa and Woodenfish staff provide basic meditation instruction for program participants who have no prior meditation experience. As the program progresses, sitting sessions become gradually longer to prepare participants for the retreat. Woodenfish participants then move into the meditation hall for the duration of the retreat, sleeping in the group dormitories adjoining the shine room. Participants wear a special tag inscribed with the Chinese characters "not talking." This indicates to those of the wider FGS community that the badge-wearer has taken a week-long vow of silence. The day runs from 5:00 am to 11:00 pm, and includes ten one-hour sessions of sitting and walking meditation, as well as meals in the refectory, a few hours of silent chore time, and an evening dharma talk. Significantly, the retreat is led by one or two FGS monastics with the help of an interpreter; Venerable Yifa and Woodenfish staff are generally not present. An FGS meditation instructor remains with the participants in the meditation hall for the retreat and maintains the schedule and rules of conduct. The meditation retreat is, thus, the first extended period during which participants are truly immersed in the heavily ritualized and institutionalized world of FGS Chinese-style Buddhism without easy recourse to Venerable Yifa or Woodenfish staff. In many ways, the meditation retreat, more than any other activity in the Woodenfish program, demands the highest degree of submission to authority and relinquishment of personal autonomy.

At the end of the meditation retreat, there is an informal question-and-answer session with the other participants, retreat leaders, Woodenfish staff, and Venerable Yifa. The question-and-answer marks the end of an entire week of silence for the participants, who share their thoughts on the lessons and challenges they encountered during the retreat. The benefits gained from the retreat vary greatly among individual participants: some emphasize the psychological and stress-relieving effects of meditation, while others relate discoveries of a decidedly spiritual nature. Regardless, the majority of participants express an overwhelmingly positive response to the meditation retreat. This enthusiastic response is especially interesting when considered in light of participants' initial resistance to other aspects of daily life at FGS, such as the dress code, ritual meals, and strict schedule that required the same kind of compliance to authority and sacrifice of personal autonomy as did the meditation retreat. This evidences a significant change in attitude among participants over the course of their stay at FGS. Although some outside observers and probably many FGS monastics would like to conclude that this attitude shift demonstrates that participants gradually come to accept and even embrace FGS Chinese-style Buddhism as the program advances, I contend that this shift in attitude has less to do with participants acclimatizing themselves to FGS Chinese-style Buddhism than it does with how FGS adapts itself to accommodate Woodenfish participants. The various ways in which FGS effects this adaptation are the topic of the following section.

SEPARATING THE WHEAT FROM THE CHAFF: TECHNIQUES OF LOCALIZATION

Fo Guang Shan's efforts to localize FGS Buddhism for Westerners can be saliently illustrated by two important features of the Woodenfish program. First, the Woodenfish program places significant emphasis on academics. Much of the program consists of scholarly classroom work which, I suggest, constitutes an important break from the ritual formalism of FGS Chinese-style Buddhism. This creates a much-needed space within the Woodenfish program for participants to engage Buddhism in a typically Western way, thereby advancing the localization process. Secondly, Venerable Yifa and the Woodenfish staff encourage a decidedly localized interpretation of the Five Precepts and Triple Refuge ceremony that reflects the particular socio-cultural realities of Western youth.

*Different Styles of Teaching and Learning: Academic Discourse
and Ritual Practice*

A predominant feature of the Woodenfish program is its decidedly academic flavour. All program applicants must submit university transcripts with their application and the majority of those accepted are high-performing students. The Woodenfish program also involves considerable classroom work, averaging six to seven hours of academic lectures per day. These lectures are often conducted in English by either Venerable Yifa or members of the Woodenfish staff. The latter are Woodenfish alumni who, for the most part, are graduate students enrolled in Buddhist studies programs at top North American universities, including McGill, University of Toronto, Harvard, Columbia, and Stanford. The lectures cover a range of topics, such as women in Buddhism, the democratization of Buddhism, Buddhism and human rights, and Buddhism and biomedical ethics. These themes could be lecture topics in any North American university-level religious studies program and happen to coincide with topics that scholars have identified as areas of major interest in the study of contemporary Western Buddhism.[9] The discussion format, consisting of formal lectures followed by lengthy question-and-answer periods, is analogous to that of a Western academic setting. In both form and content, therefore, the academic portions of the Woodenfish program reflect a style of "rational learning" that is distinctively Western, in which students are taught "to 'analyze,' 'explain,' 'articulate,' 'generalize,' 'contextualize,' and 'apply to concrete situations'" (Hori 1994, 8). This can be contrasted with the methods of instruction used by FGS monastics when leading the practice portions of the program, which are characterized by ritual formalism, a form of learning that is prevalent in Asian Buddhism and is based on "repetition, rote memorization, behaving according to traditional prescription ... [in which] students imitate form without necessarily understanding content or rationale" (Hori 1994, 5). The emphasis FGS monastics place on ritual formalism offends many Woodenfish participants who feel that the requirement to simply "go through the motions" of Buddhist ritual actions violates their sense of individual and intellectual autonomy.

I suggest that the academic focus of the Woodenfish program helps to localize FGS Buddhism by emphasizing rational teaching and learning over ritual formalism. The Woodenfish program seems to understand that the ritual formalism of FGS Chinese-style Buddhism can alienate Woodenfish participants.

Consequently, the program creates a rhetoric in which ritual formalism can be replaced with rational teaching and learning without compromising the essential truth of the dharma. By transplanting the essential core of Buddhist truth into another type of cultural soil – one which reflects the Western propensity for rational teaching and learning methods over Asian ritual formalism – the academic portions of the Woodenfish program help to make FGS Buddhism more appealing to Westerners.[10]

Localizing the Five Precepts and Triple Refuge

During the practice portions of the Woodenfish program, FGS monastics instruct Woodenfish participants as they would any other group of lay FGS devotees, based on the assumption that the Woodenfish participants are at FGS in order to become Buddhists.[11] Some in my cohort of Woodenfish participants worried that FGS monastics were trying to convert them, and expressed their concerns to Venerable Yifa and the Woodenfish staff. The staff responded to these concerns with the suggestion that, although participants were required to show respect by outwardly complying with the FGS monastics' instructions, participants could inwardly choose whether to absorb the teachings of FGS monastics into their personal understanding of Buddhism. Venerable Yifa and the Woodenfish staff reassured participants that the Chinese-style practice of FGS monastics is but one expression of the dharma and that this particular expression can be selectively reinterpreted to suit Western laypeople. For example, although the precepts are strictly enforced on FGS property, Venerable Yifa and Woodenfish staff are aware that, upon returning home after the program, participants resume their normal lifestyle. For some, this includes activities FGS cannot condone, such as eating meat, drug use, and premarital sex. In light of this, Venerable Yifa and Woodenfish staff encourage participants to adopt more lenient interpretations of certain precepts, such as the prohibition against intoxicants and the requirement of vegetarianism, rather than to abandon the precepts altogether. This lenience reflects the Woodenfish program's stance that reinterpreting the precepts is an integral part of localizing FGS Buddhism for Western youth.

Similarly, although the Three Refuge ceremony is generally considered the determinative moment of conversion when one officially becomes a Buddhist, many Woodenfish participants are reluctant to adopt such a concrete notion of Buddhist identity for themselves, either because they already have a religion or because they want to stay away from religious labels altogether. In response, the Woodenfish program emphasizes that taking the Triple Refuge (in Buddha, dharma, and Sangha) does not preclude having other religious identities, echoing Master Hsing Yun's own claim that "Buddhism is different from other religions in its lack of exclusivity" (Master Hsing Yun, in Chandler 2005, 175). Moreover, it is emphasized that one need not necessarily call oneself a Buddhist after taking the Triple Refuge. Living according to the *spirit* of Buddhism is more important than identifying with the religious label. These reinterpretations of the Buddhist Precepts and the Triple Refuge ceremony were so effective in appealing to Westerners that most of the participants in 2005 (approximately two-thirds) took the Triple Refuge at the end of the program, despite having initially expressed fear of being proselytized by FGS monastics.

Fo Guang Shan's localization agenda, however, raises an important problem. As Chandler states, "[the] difficulty in applying the [localization] method lies in determining just where core truth ends and custom begins" (2005, 176). In response to this issue, Master Hsing Yun suggests that those best qualified to negotiate the tension between core truth and extraneous custom, or between preservation and assimilation, are natives of the countries where FGS is trying to localize. The need to find Westerners who can take on this role – we might call them "localizers" – illuminates another way in which the Woodenfish program benefits FGS's globalization endeavour. In the past, FGS has tried to train Westerners for ordination at the FGS headquarters in order to fulfill this role, but these attempts have been unsuccessful. Of "the approximately one dozen Europeans and Americans who tonsured under Master Hsing Yun, only two can still be found in the Fo Guang Shan order as of the year 2002" (Chandler 2005, 177). By contrast, Woodenfish participants are ideally suited to act as localizers, especially those Woodenfish alumni who return to the program as staff members and, thus, become active agents in the localization process for each new generation of Woodenfish participants. This formula is working very well. Each year, the number of Woodenfish participants who express a desire to become future staff significantly exceeds the four or five available positions.[12] This has a potentially exponential outcome. As the Woodenfish program gains popularity in the West and increases its enrolment, the number of Westerners available to act as FGS localizers and ambassadors in the West also grows, increasing, in turn, both the popularity of the program and FGS's visibility in the West.

Fo Guang Shan Localizers: Buddhist Missionaries Who Are not Buddhists?
As discussed, FGS's localization project involves the modification of a number of core elements of FGS Chinese-style Buddhism to reflect Western culture and values. The Woodenfish program's lenient interpretations of the Five Precepts and the view that taking the Triple Refuge does not require Westerners to give up their inherited religious identity are cases in point. In practical terms, this means that some Woodenfish alumni who took the Triple Refuge do not self-identify as Buddhists. One wonders whether these non-Buddhist localizers can be of any value as ambassadors for FGS in the West. I suggest, however, that the powerful ambassadorial role that Woodenfish alumni play in representing FGS in the West has more to do with their influence in academic circles and among their peers than it does with their personal religious convictions.

Master Hsing Yun's understanding of *jieyuan*, or "links of affinity," can be helpful in elucidating the somewhat unintuitive claim that non-Buddhists can be useful in furthering FGS's missionary project. Master Hsing Yun explains that "planting the seed of the dharma in a person's consciousness usually will not lead to that person's attaining enlightenment in the present life, but such a seed of wisdom can bear fruit in a subsequent rebirth" (Chandler 2005, 171). FGS has applied this principle in cultivating relationships with prominent politicians in both Taiwan and the United States who, even if they are not Buddhists themselves, can nevertheless benefit the religion. "If the act of *jieyuan* with a member of the elite does not lead to the person taking Triple Refuge, it may nonetheless trigger merit, for the recipient is in the position to benefit the tradition even as a non-Buddhist. A wealthy person, for instance, may donate considerable funds for a charitable drive, or a politician may help to pass legislation advantageous to the religion" (Chandler 2005, 172).

I contend that Woodenfish participants, regardless of whether they take the Triple Refuge, are seen by FGS in much the same light. That is, the main contribution Woodenfish alumni make for FGS in the West is not in a religious capacity but, rather, consists in popularizing FGS in Western universities. In the short term, Woodenfish alumni increase FGS's visibility through the various academic and extracurricular activities they organize at their home universities, such as recounting their experience of the program to their peers, making class presentations and writing papers on their time at FGS, encouraging professors to publicize the program, organizing Woodenfish group reunions, and creating

Woodenfish alumni associations at their local universities.[13] In the long run, since Woodenfish participants are selected based on academic potential, it is likely that many Woodenfish alumni will end up as scholars of Buddhism. For Fo Guang Shan, fostering a strong bond with these future representatives of Buddhist studies in North America can be considered, like cultivating *jieyuan* with wealthy philanthropists and politicians, of service to the dharma.[14] As Master Hsing Yun points out, these "links of affinity" are always beneficial, placing FGS in a win-win situation since all Woodenfish participants are potentially influential ties for Fo Guang Shan in the West regardless of whether they convert to Buddhism.

WOODENFISH IN CANADA: THE GENERATION GAP IN CANADIAN BUDDHIST SCHOLARSHIP

It seems that Fo Guang Shan's outreach efforts to non-Chinese Westerners have been largely invisible in the current scholarship on FGS. Experts such as Chandler and Learman have concluded that, despite its missionizing rhetoric, FGS suffers from a "lack of success in reaching beyond [its] ethnic communities" (Learman 2005, 13). This invisibility, I suggest, is simply due to the fact that scholars are not looking in the right places.[15] If one's investigation is limited to FGS's official avenues in Canada – for example, its branch temples and cultural centres – then one may conclude that FGS has failed to cross ethnic and cultural barriers. But looking beyond FGS's official avenues, we see that FGS is, in fact, reaching non-Chinese Westerners through different routes. A perusal of the hugely popular internet socializing forum Facebook reveals that upon returning to Canada Woodenfish alumni are organizing Woodenfish reunions and other activities at their universities, promoting the program through online forums, recruiting new applicants, and enlisting past participants interested in becoming future Woodenfish staff. Several alumni have gone on to found Buddhist initiatives which, significantly, reflect the openness that FGS localized Buddhism displays toward diffuse or non-affiliation, such as the Dharma Bum Centre, the Red Lotus Society, and the Matrix Mandala Garden project.[16]

That scholars interested in Fo Guang Shan have not discovered the expansive network of Woodenfish alumni operating under the auspices of FGS reflects the fact that the methodologies traditionally used to study Buddhism in Canada are now inadequate to identify the ways in which Canadian Buddhism is changing. The features that have rendered the Woodenfish network largely invisible to Buddhologists – namely, that it emphasizes individualism over institutional affiliation, operates through channels other than FGS's branch temples, and understands Buddhism in a largely nonsectarian way that is open to both diffuse affiliation as well as non-affiliation – are illustrative of the ways in which today's Canadian youth are helping to reshape Buddhism. An examination of the Woodenfish program, therefore, may offer insight into how scholarly methodologies must evolve if they are to adequately study the changing face of Canadian Buddhism.

Blurring the Lines between "Ethnic" Buddhism and "Convert" Buddhism
The study of Buddhism in Canada has historically relied on the categories of Asian/ethnic Buddhism and White/convert Buddhism. As pointed out by several scholars, however, these categories disintegrate as soon as one attempts to apply them to Canadian youth. For example, they cannot describe non-Asian Canadians born to convert parents – as in the Shambhala Buddhist community in Halifax, Nova Scotia – who are, therefore, white but not converts. They also fail to describe the Canadian-born children of, for example, Taiwanese FGS devotees who, although they are born into Buddhist families, do not necessarily practise the Asian/ethnic Buddhism of their parents. The Woodenfish program offers an especially interesting example of this latter case.

In recent years, in addition to the regular Woodenfish program, Venerable Yifa and members of the Woodenfish staff have run a second, slightly shorter and less intensive summer program for elementary school-age children. For the purposes of this paper, I will call this second FGS summer program the mini-Woodenfish program. In contrast to the regular Woodenfish program, the mini-Woodenfish program caters principally to the children of FGS's international branch temple devotees. In other words, the participants of the mini-Woodenfish program are second generation North American-born Chinese. On the surface, it appears that the mini-Woodenfish program affords these children a chance to reconnect with their roots by spending two weeks living in an FGS Chinese-style monastery learning about Buddhism. It is crucial to note, however, that, as in the regular Woodenfish program, the principal instructors in this program are Venerable Yifa and her staff, made up of Woodenfish alumni. The latter have inherited a localized version of FGS Buddhism through the Woodenfish program, and some instructors, although considering themselves spiritual, do not even identify as Buddhists. The ways in which these instructors present Buddhism to the mini-Woodenfish participants inevitably reflects a heavily localized version of Buddhism. Mini-Woodenfish participants are not learning the FGS Chinese-style Buddhism of their parents but, rather, they are assimilating a type of Buddhism that has been already localized for Westerners. Thus, this is not a return to their roots; it is the growth of an altogether new form of Buddhism.

Trends in Canadian Buddhism: Individualism, Diffuse Affiliation, and Non-Affiliation

Several trends can be identified among Woodenfish participants that, I suggest, also reflect trends occurring in Canadian Buddhism as a whole: the move away from institutional affiliation, the phenomenon of diffuse religious identity, and the popular rhetorical separation of spirituality from religion. These trends, moreover, pose serious challenges for the study of Buddhism in Canada.

Scholars have remarked that, although lay Buddhist organizations imported from Asia have proliferated in Canada since the 1960s, Buddhist monastic practice does not seem to have caught on.[17] This trend in Canadian Buddhism, I suggest, is related to the Western emphasis on individualism over institutional affiliation. Nattier's comment that Americans are "notorious non-joiners" (Nattier 1998, 185) can apply to Canadians as well. Although some Canadian Buddhists may join lay Buddhist organizations, many choose not to join a religious community at all, as is the case among many Woodenfish alumni who are not part of FGS's branch temples or formal members of any Buddhist organization. Thus, as the Woodenfish example illustrates, if we try to describe Canadian Buddhism by looking only to those practitioners who go to temples and belong to lay groups, we will miss an important demographic of Canadian Buddhists.

The phenomenon of diffuse affiliation (Tanaka 1998, 296) – namely, the fact that many Westerners simultaneously identify as adherents of more than one religion – adds another layer of complexity to the multi-faceted character of Canadian Buddhism. The diffuse affiliation model describes, for example, the many Woodenfish participants who come from Jewish or Christian religious backgrounds, and also take the Triple Refuge at Fo Guang Shan. Despite the now widespread recognition within the academy that the notion of religion as a reified category reflects Judeo-Christian biases that cannot be applied cross-culturally, the exclusivity of religious identity is still presupposed in many statistical and sociological tools used to study religious populations in Canada. Statistics Canada's census questions on religious identity, for example, require participants to indicate only one religion in describing themselves. This methodological presupposition of exclusive religious affiliation makes diffuse affiliation statistically invisible. While StatsCan could better measure diffuse affiliation by using a model of hyphenated religious identity similar to that of hyphenated ethnic identity (i.e., Italian-Canadian, Japanese-Canadian), implemented in order to more accurately reflect the ethnic diversity of Canadians, this still cannot measure how those who identify with a single Judeo-Christian tradition may have absorbed and been influenced by Buddhist practices and beliefs. As Verhoeven aptly remarks while discussing the influence of Buddhism in the North American Judeo-Christian landscape, just as

> 'Protestant Buddhism' evolved in Ceylon in response to the Western missionary and colonial presence, might not America be undergoing a parallel development, 'Buddhist Protestantism'? Could changes in areas of Christian thought and practice reflect an assimilation of certain Asian influences? The interest in meditation, comparative religion, Buddhist-Christian dialogues, as well as the "immanentist" and psychological orientation of modern liberal Christianity, and even the "New Age" phenomenon – all could be read as Christian attempts to accommodate Eastern religion or, in some cases, to undercut its appeal. (Verhoeven 1998, 223)

For many Woodenfish participants, for instance, taking the Triple Refuge at FGS was not so much about converting to a new religion or taking on a new religious identity as it was about enriching their existing religious identity by supplementing it with various aspects of Buddhist doctrine and practice. By presupposing exclusive definitions of religious identity, StatsCan neglects the ways in which different religions in Canada interpenetrate and influence each other. In other words, we must not limit our study to how Canada is changing Buddhism; we must examine how Buddhism is changing Canada as well.

A third trend in Canadian Buddhism might be termed non-affiliation. That is, while the diffuse affiliation model describes Canadians at one end of a spectrum – those who take on many religious identities – there is also a need to develop a model that can describe the opposite end of the spectrum: Canadians who, although identifying as spiritual, do not belong to any religious tradition. The distinction between religion and spirituality has been an issue of debate, and these terms have yet to be properly defined. Despite the strict divide that this rhetoric sets up between spirituality and religion, one is hard pressed to find examples of "spirituality" that are not, at least to a degree, informed by elements drawn from "religion." Many aspects of Buddhism, especially meditation, have been extremely influential in shaping Western ideas of spirituality, as evidenced by the popularity of non-denominational, non-religious forms of meditation, such as Transcendental Meditation (TM) and forms of meditative practice, such as Insight Meditation, that emphasize the psychological and spiritual benefits of meditation without necessarily having ties to Buddhism or any institutionalized religion.[18] Ascertaining the place of Buddhism in the lives of individuals in this category – we might call them non-affiliated or "spiritual" Buddhists – is doubly difficult. Not only do these spiritual Buddhists steer away from institutionalized organizations (where official documents might record their numbers) but, additionally, they may not even self-identify as Buddhists. While the distinction between "religion" and "spirituality" is difficult to establish, there is nevertheless an acute need to study what Canadians *mean* when they draw this distinction, and why this distinction is becoming such a popular rhetorical tool in helping many Canadians define themselves. By blurring the lines between "religion" and "spirituality," moreover, this group raises important questions surrounding what it means to be Buddhist and what qualifies as Buddhist activity.

What Makes a Buddhist?
As the trends of diffuse affiliation, non-affiliation, and individualism move Buddhism beyond the scope of our traditional methodologies, several taxonomical questions come to the fore. First, there is the thorny question of who is a Buddhist. As the above case of non-affiliated or spiritual Buddhists illustrates, an important demographic of those Canadians whose spirituality is heavily informed by Buddhist ideas and practices does not identify as Buddhist, feeling that the very category of "Buddhism" smacks of institutionalization. Because these individuals do not fit our traditional definitions of what makes one a religious adherent – namely, one who self-consciously identifies with an organized, and generally exclusive, religious group – are we to neglect studying them altogether? Buddhism's history is one of adaptation and syncretism. Many suggest that the Westernization of Buddhism in Canada is no different from the changes and localization of Buddhism in its move from India to China, or from Korea to Japan. Just as no one would dispute the fact that Zen – despite its significant differences from Indian Buddhism of the third century BCE – can be rightly considered Buddhism, one should be wary of dismissing Bud-

dhism's new expressions in Canada on account of their dissimilarity with our limited definitions of religion and religious adherence.

A second, tangentially related question is what constitutes Buddhist activity. Just as non-affiliated or spiritual Buddhists cannot be found in the places where scholars have traditionally looked for Buddhists – in temples and Buddhist organizations – many of these individuals also do not engage in what has been traditionally considered Buddhist activity. Many Woodenfish participants, for example, consider the academic study of Buddhism in graduate school to be more than simply an intellectual pursuit; they see it as a kind of Buddhist activity. In pondering what makes a person a Buddhist, one must ask whether a definition of Buddhist identity is even possible. Are there readily identifiable necessary and sufficient conditions that differentiate true Buddhists from non-Buddhists? For example, must one meditate to be Buddhist? Take the Triple Refuge? Call oneself a Buddhist? Similarly, one wonders whether there are incontrovertible elements that circumscribe what exactly counts as Buddhist activity. Must Buddhist activity occur within the context of a sangha? Can mundane activities, such as community outreach or academic study, count as meditation? Can Facebook replace the Buddhist temple as a legitimate venue for Buddhist activity? All these questions raise an overarching problem, namely, who has the authority to answer them. If we are to seriously consider Master Hsing Yun's response to the question of who should determine how far Buddhism can adapt to better integrate into new cultural contexts, then we must allow that Western practitioners have the authority to redefine notions of Buddhist identity and praxis as they see fit. However, given the vastly different understandings of religion and religious identity put forward by Woodenfish participants – to whom, as I have argued, we can look for a sample demographic of Canada's upcoming generation of Buddhists – Buddhism in Canada is likely to evolve in a multiplicity of unanticipated ways. Soon, the category of Canadian Buddhism will be obsolete; there will be only Canadian Buddhisms.

CONCLUDING REMARKS: BIFURCATING THE BUDDHA'S LIGHT

Fo Guang Shan in Canada is unique in that it simultaneously presents two distinct – and, as Chandler suggests, mutually exclusive – versions of Buddhism. On the one hand, there is what I have called FGS Chinese-style Buddhism – namely, the Buddhism practised in Canada's FGS branch temples which functions principally as a cultural bridge to the homeland for members of the Chinese diaspora in Canada. Because non-Chinese Canadians often find the particularly Chinese cultural elements of these temples to be foreign and alienating, FGS branch temples have failed to attract non-Chinese members. On the other hand, as I have argued, FGS is also actively propagating a localized version of Buddhism that reflects the needs and tastes of non-Chinese Westerners. Being cognizant, moreover, of the mutually exclusive nature of these two forms of Buddhism, FGS has developed two distinct avenues through which to propagate the dharma in the West. While FGS's Chinese-style Buddhism goes through FGS's network of Canadian branch temples, FGS's localized Buddhism is promulgated through the Woodenfish program and the mobilizing efforts of young university students in their academic and online communities.

The fact that Fo Guang Shan in Canada simultaneously upholds these two very different and perhaps even mutually exclusive forms of Buddhism begs the question of how long the two can coexist, and what will happen when they meet. Although the language barrier in Taiwan limits the possibility of informal interchange between the Woodenfish program participants and the rest of the FGS monastic community, the Canadian environment is quite different. These two Buddhisms are bound to eventually cross paths, as has, indeed, already begun to happen through the mini-Woodenfish program. How will the localized Buddhism of the children attending the FGS mini-Woodenfish program differ from the Buddhism of their parents? And perhaps most importantly, will one of these versions of Buddhism overtake the other? Although FGS officially asserts the complementarity of tradition and modernity, it nevertheless warns against the danger that "occurs when either one of these polarities eclipses the other" (Chandler 2005, 168). Given the increasing popularity of the Woodenfish program, the important influence that Woodenfish alumni are liable to have in the future of Buddhist studies in Canada, and especially the role of Woodenfish staff in localizing FGS Buddhism for a new generation of North-American-born Chinese, it seems to be only a matter of time before FGS localized Buddhism overtakes FGS Chinese-style Buddhism in Canada. The complementarity between modernity and tradition to which FGS aspires is a tenuous balancing act. Through its missionizing efforts in Canada, FGS Chinese-style Buddhism has sown the seeds of its own demise: the more successfully FGS localizes, the more the scales tip away from FGS Chinese-style Buddhism toward the localized Buddhism of Canada's next generation.

NOTES

1 In order to avoid the racist assumptions implicit in the word "ethnic," which takes "whiteness" to be normative by sweepingly categorizing all non-whites as ethnic, I will henceforth use the term "FGS Chinese-style Buddhism" when describing FGS temples in the West whose members are Chinese and whose practices are directly modelled after those of FGS in Taiwan. I say Chinese rather than Taiwanese to reflect the fact that many Taiwanese self-identify as Chinese, taking China – not Taiwan – as their cultural homeland (see Chandler 2005, 169). Moreover, I specify that we are dealing with FGS Chinese-style Buddhism to show that it differs from other types of Chinese Buddhism. It is also important to note that, although the term "ethnic Buddhism" has historically connoted that ethnic religions are more primitive than modernized non-ethnic ones, this is not the case in FGS Chinese-style Buddhism. Fo Guang Shan in Canada is not an archaic, traditionalist religion "directly lifted from the rice paddies of Asia" (Hori, in this volume); it is an extremely modernized, globalized, and technologically savvy Buddhist organization.

2 Tanaka uses the notion of "diffuse affiliation" to describe Buddhists "who have had affiliation with more than one form of Buddhism as part of their spiritual journey … [or who have] concurrent multiple affiliation, whereby an individual maintains active ties with more than one temple or centre" (Tanaka 1998, 296). This notion can be extended beyond the intra-Buddhist context to describe Buddhists who are also affiliated with non-Buddhist religions. The coining of terms like "Jubu" – designating those who identify as both Buddhist and Jewish – is an example of this phenomenon.

3 As documented by scholars such as Payne 2005a, Tweed 2000, and Seager 1999 among others, the assimilation of the Protestant liturgical model by many Buddhist groups in North America involved adopting pew-style seating and organ music, conducting sermon-style dharma talks on Sundays, singing Buddhist songs as Western-style hymns, and creating Buddhist weddings. In most cases, these Buddhist groups assimilated mainstream Protestant norms so thoroughly that they failed to attract non-Asian devotees who, initially drawn to Buddhism because of its apparent exoticism, found it too similar to Western Christianity.

4 Fo Guang Shan has demonstrated awareness that leaning too far toward either of these extremes – assimilating too much or too little – is counterproductive in attracting non-Chinese members. While, on the one hand, FGS holds that "too strong a sense of foreignness can repel people" (Chandler 2005, 176), it has also made efforts to attract non-Chinese devotees by "purposely play[ing] up the appeal of the exotic" (Payne 2005a, 113) by, for example, building opulent Chinese-style temples in the West – such as Hsi

Lai Temple in California – which, FGS holds, will arouse Westerners' curiosity, eventually drawing them to the dharma (Chandler 2005, 175).

5   Although examples of this trend – that the Westernization of Buddhism operates under a veneer of Asian authenticity – can be found throughout Canadian Buddhist organizations whose devotees are principally non-Asian Canadians, I will here cite only the salient example of Gampo Abbey, the Shambhala Buddhist monastery in Cape Breton, Nova Scotia. Many features of life and practice at the abbey, such as the use of Tibetan monastic terminology rather than English terms, and the use of traditional Asian-style religious iconography and art throughout the abbey and the shrine rooms, reinforce the Asian roots of the Buddhism practised there. This creates a perceived continuity between Tibetan Buddhism and the Buddhist practice at Gampo Abbey, thereby bestowing upon the latter the same aura of authenticity and legitimacy that is attributed to Tibetan Buddhism. Despite this apparent continuity, however, Gampo Abbey has developed a number of rituals and practices that have never been practised in Asia. By ostensibly tracing the roots of its Buddhist practice to Asia, Gampo Abbey establishes an implicit rhetoric of Asian authenticity that legitimates the authority of its practice, while also creating an aura of exoticism that appeals to Western practitioners.

6   The evening medicinal meal and the transfer of merit are further illustrations of how FGS considers food consumption an exercise in cultivating selflessness. Not wanting to disregard the Vinaya's admonition against eating after noon but knowing that the extremely active lifestyles of FGS monastics demand more calories than can be provided by breakfast and lunch alone, FGS instated the evening medicinal meal – a practice that is common in many Chan monasteries. As its name indicates, the underlying rationale for this meal is that it keeps monastics healthy, not for their own sake, but so they might better serve the community, which FGS considers an integral part of the bodhisattva vow. The transfer of merit, through which monastics transfer the merit generated by their consumption of food to others, also highlights the FGS view that food consumption is a selfless and compassionate act. This attitude toward food is part of a greater mandate at FGS that asserts the importance of practising Chan in daily life: "Chan must be integrated into everyday living if it is to have any relevance. As [the Master] phrases it, formal sitting is worthless unless one is able to experience 'a taste of Chan in daily life'" (Chandler 2004, 45).

7   Participants generally share a comfortable – albeit small by Canadian standards – four-person room, which they must keep tidy according to specific instructions. Bed linens must be folded "tofu-style" and are subject to daily inspection. Participants are instructed on how to properly make their beds, roll their towels, and so forth until they sufficiently master the standard FGS techniques of housekeeping. Many participants find

this aspect of the program difficult. In contrast to North America, where the bedroom is considered an almost inviolable sanctum of privacy, at FGS, even private space is, to a degree, public.

8 In addition to regularly scheduled activities, it is worth noting that, every year, the Woodenfish program arranges one or two private audiences between the Woodenfish group and Master Hsing Yun. These private meetings are very special events – especially considering that, even for FGS monastics, the chance to meet with the extremely busy Master in such an intimate setting is considered a rare honour. These meetings generally consist of a dharma talk given by the Master, followed by questions from the Woodenfish participants and a customary group photograph. Prior to the meetings, Woodenfish participants are instructed to be particularly courteous and to demonstrate heightened etiquette while in the presence of the Master. Interestingly, these meetings with the Master tend to spark contention among Woodenfish participants who, although they might accept many other features of the FGS institution, criticize FGS for being a kind of idolatrous "cult of the personality." For these participants, the Master's charismatic and highly public persona makes him more of a celebrity than a spiritual teacher. Even at the end of their one-month stay at FGS, many program participants identify this feature of FGS Chinese-style Buddhism – the degree to which FGS centres itself around the veneration of a single charismatic figure – as the most difficult aspect of FGS Buddhism to accept.

9 Tanaka, among others, lists a number of areas that call for immediate consideration in the burgeoning field of Buddhism in the West. These include the place of women in Western Buddhism, Buddhism and pluralism, Buddhism and ethnicity, and the democratization of Buddhism, which Tanaka explains as "a shift away from hierarchical to more egalitarian structures within the Buddhist tradition … [and] the involvement of Buddhism in the promotion of the inclusive and egalitarian ideals in American society" (Tanaka 1998, 289). William LaFleur and Damien Keown have also done extensive work on Buddhism and biomedical ethics.

10 Incidentally, this is not the first instance in which Buddhism has emphasized its intellectual proclivity and rational nature in order to appeal to Westerners. Other examples include the missionizing work of Shaku Sōen, D.T. Suzuki and others who presented Buddhism to the West as a rational and scientific religion that rejects superstition and blind ritual formalism.

11 One Woodenfish staff member, who has been with the program since its inception, explains, "[i]t is easy to come to the program believing that you will be able to fit in sufficiently and satisfy the instructors simply by performing the required ritual movements and utterances, but in fact [FGS monastics] are going to be telling you how you

should adjust your mind; they're going to ask you to change your beliefs and your very attitudes, indeed, to alter your personality fundamentally and permanently. This is a very hard thing for most students to accept" (J. Clower, Interview 2005).

12 Of the thirty-seven program participants in 2007, twenty-two expressed a desire to return to FGS as Woodenfish staff, fourteen asked to return as staff for the mini-Woodenfish program, and sixteen said they would staff a similar monastic life program offered in China (2007 Woodenfish Participant Feedback Report).

13 As a fellow Woodenfish staff member remarked to me, nearly all program applicants hear about the Woodenfish program through their university. In a survey conducted among 2007 Woodenfish participants, twenty out of thirty-seven participants first heard about the program through announcements made in their universities; five participants found out about the program via the Woodenfish Internet recruitment forums and website; and the remaining participants heard about the program through a variety of different means, predominantly in their universities: a poster on the Religious Studies Department announcement wall, a Religious Studies listserv, etc. (2007 Woodenfish Participant Feedback Report).

14 Fo Guang Shan is not the first to recognize the value of training North American youth to act as ambassadors of Asian culture in the West. This is also the rationale behind a number of prestigious government-run programs in several Asian countries, such as Japan's Ship for World Youth, or the Japan Exchange and Teaching (JET) program and Korea Exchange and Teaching (KET) program. Ostensibly, programs like JET, which gives young Westerners work placements to teach English in the Japanese public school system, improve the education of young Japanese students. Some argue, however, that the even greater value of the program is that, every year, over 5,000 JET alumni return to their home countries with an understanding and deep appreciation of Japanese culture and language. These alumni, moreover, are likely to move on to positions of influence in business, government, and academia. Since its inception in 1987, an impressive 46,000 young people have participated in the JET program. These JET alumni stay actively involved in promoting Japanese culture and the JET program through alumni organizations and local JET chapters in their hometowns. Canada boasts provincial chapters in most provinces and major cities: Ottawa, Toronto, Montreal, Manitoba/ Saskatchewan, Northern Alberta, Southern Alberta, and Vancouver.

15 It is interesting to note, moreover, that this invisibility affects not only scholars; many senior FGS monastics fail to see the impact of the Woodenfish program because they, too, measure the program's success according to traditional categories: namely, whether participants go on to take ordination. Since very few participants pursue formal ordina-

tion (at present, only one Woodenfish alumnus has enrolled at the FGS Woman's College in preparation for possible ordination), these older monastics, unaware of the alternate avenues Woodenfish alumni have developed for promoting FGS apart from monastic ordination, assume the program is unsuccessful in propagating the dharma.

16 In its mission statement, the San Diego-based Dharma Bum Centre describes itself as "inspired by the experimental Buddhism described in Jack Kerouac's 1958 autobio-graphical novel 'Dharma Bums' ... embrac[ing] the free spirit of the beat generation and their artistic approach to religion and spirituality" (Dharma Bum Centre website). The Red Lotus Society is a non-profit, non-sectarian organization whose mission is "to promote the practice and awareness of meditation for the improvement of mental health and environmental well-being" (Red Lotus Society website). Similarly, the Ma-trix Mandala Garden is a non-profit, non-sectarian organization that aims to promote "meditation throughout North America ... [and] combine the knowledge and wisdom of the world's religious traditions to open new paths and possibilities for enlightenment" (Matrix Mandala Garden website).

17 Gampo Abbey is a fascinating case study in relation to this point. The abbey generally houses several dozen Western Buddhist practitioners. These residents identify as monas-tics, don maroon robes, shave their heads, and live according to a highly regulated and ritualized daily schedule. The majority of these monastics, however, are temporary or-dinands – meaning that, after a stay of one to three years at the abbey, they will all return to secular life. This is a salient example of a trend that might be termed lay monasti-cism in Canada.

18 Tanaka's example of the Insight Meditation West Centre is a case in point. He writes, "just as the name of the organisation exhibits no explicit identification with Buddhism (Insight Meditation), its adherents are not required to claim Buddhist identity. In fact, the majority of their teachers elected not to be identified with the ancient Theravada lineage. Many are attracted by the psychological insights and benefits of vipassana med-itation" (Tanaka 1998, 296).

Shambhala International
The Golden Sun of the Great East[1]

LYNN P. ELDERSHAW

Funeral procession of Vidyadhara Chögyam Trungpa Rinpoche,
26 May 1987 at Karmê Chöling, Barnet, Vermont
Photo by Ray Ellis

Shambhala was his [Chögyam Trungpa's] secular program, a vehicle for teaching and serving a large number of people and preparing them for the spiritual path. He was hoping that it would be helpful to the people like sunshine from the East.

GEHLEK RIMPOCHE, "Chögyam Trungpa: Father of Tibetan Buddhism in the U.S."

Although Tibetan Buddhism has had a place in Canadian society since the early 1970s, arguably the most prominent sangha in North America is Shambhala International. Based in Halifax, Nova Scotia, the community was founded by the late Chögyam Trungpa Rinpoche (1939–1987)[2] a much-admired yet unconventional and controversial Tibetan *tülku* (an incarnated being).[3] Originally known as Vajradhatu, the community was renamed Shambhala International in 1994 by the current leader, Sakyong Mipham Rinpoche.[4]

In the early 1980s, Chögyam Trungpa relocated the sangha's main administrative offices to Halifax, Nova Scotia from Boulder, Colorado. One long-time member explains the reason for the move: "Well, I heard him say at one point he thought it was good because it was away from the dizziness and the sometimes borderline aggression of the United States, but not completely in the middle of nowhere. It's a real city, it has culture, universities and so forth. So, it's somewhere in-between; off the beaten track, but not too far off" (Eldershaw 1994, 89).[5]

Throughout the early 1980s, approximately five hundred members of the American sangha immigrated to Nova Scotia. Today, the Shambhala sangha is firmly entrenched in Maritime culture, the members bringing with them their entrepreneurial spirit, developing businesses, buying real estate, raising families, and participating in local cultural and civic life (Swick 1995).[6] The Halifax base is the nexus of a global community of Shambhalians, a multi-faceted organization that offers Buddhist and secular teachings, referred to as Shambhala Training, as well as an array of arts and educational programs. Of the approximately 170 centres Shambhala operates worldwide, thirty are located in Canada, with several major "land centres" (retreat centres), including a monastery,

Gampo Abbey, in Cape Breton. Shambhala publishes two highly successful magazines for Buddhist practitioners, the *Shambhala Sun* and *Buddhadharma*, and is associated with Naropa University, an accredited postsecondary institution located in Boulder, Colorado.[7]

The establishment of Shambhala International in Canada and the unique manner in which this sangha presents the Buddhist teachings are the products of interconnecting forces at play in the contemporary engagement with religion and the transmission of Buddhism to North America. Buddhism in particular is noted for its ready adaptation to the cultural contexts of the countries to which it migrates. The development of Shambhala Buddhism is one expression of the Buddhist tradition in the context of Western culture.

The community's presentation of its teachings has changed dramatically since its inception in the early 1970s. Originally Chögyam Trungpa set up Vajradhatu as a Tibetan Buddhist practice (specifically grounded in the Kagyu and Nyingma traditions),[8] and Shambhala Training as a secular, non-Buddhist, contemplative practice. Today, the two practices are being merged[9] and the community reflects a synthesis of Trungpa's secular teachings, Tibetan Buddhism, and shamanic rituals associated with the Bön[10] and Rimed[11] traditions of Tibet. Elements of Zen Buddhism, Shinto, and a selection of British, North American, and Asian cultural practices are also present. In 2000, Sakyong Mipham Rinpoche (literally, "Earth Protector") assigned the name "Shambhala Buddhism" to represent this particular assemblage of teachings and practices.

Academics studying the evolution of religion have long observed the slow (and occasionally rapid) transformation of religious traditions. Noted historians Eric Hobsbawm and Terrence Ranger (1983) have termed the process whereby movements modify, adapt, and reshape over time "the invention of tradition": "'Invented tradition' is taken to mean a set of practices, normally governed by overtly or tacitly accepted rules and of a ritual or symbolic nature, which seek to inculcate certain values and norms of behaviour by repetition, and which automatically imply continuity with the past" (Hobsbawm 1983, 1).

The transformation reflects a sometimes deliberate, sometimes unconscious, effort to reconstitute traditions to make them resonate with changing circumstances. This can also imply a connection with a "suitable historical past" as a means to legitimate innovations and adaptations. Augmentations in traditions can also arise in order to engender cohesion among the members of a community. The cultural integration of transplanted religions is particularly ripe for these kinds of adjustments. As with the telling of history, often what is presented as centuries old is, in actuality, a recent interpretation designed to meet contemporary needs. The degree of change and the extent to which adaptations are *validated* by legendary, historical, and sometimes mythical associations is a matter of great debate and contention. Stephen Vlastos elaborates on this contentious aspect of invention, saying that it has a double meaning which "signifies imagination and contrivance, creation and deception." He continues, "Every tradition trades between these two poles; and if traditions are to retain their vitality under changing historical conditions, one can expect to find constant shifting and overlapping of signifying positions" (1998, 6).

As Hobsbawm points out, in essence all traditions are social constructs and thus social inventions. Of significance are the innovations themselves which, according to Hobsbawm, are important indicators or "evidence" of changes in the wider culture (1983, 12). Scholars mapping the changing shape of religion and religious practices in contemporary society emphasize the need for more detailed ethnographies of this adaptive evolution. As Rodney Stark and Roger Finke (2002) observe, what is needed is a body of research that plots the pattern of religious variation and tries to explain the cultural climate that precipitates change.

The concept of invented traditions is a useful lens through which to situate ideological adaptations associated with Shambhala International's presentation of Tibetan Vajrayana Buddhism, Trungpa's creation of a separate Shambhala Training, and the Sakyong's integration of these two "traditions." These innovations and adaptations are considered in the context of contemporary religious pluralism and privatized spiritual interests, as well as of events unique to the history of this sangha.

The findings reported here are derived from extensive participant-observation primarily at Shambhala International headquarters in Halifax, Nova Scotia; Shambhala Mountain Centre, Red Feather Lakes, Colorado; and Dechen Chöling, Limoges, France. Fieldwork was augmented by ongoing content analysis of the community's substantial publications. In addition, in-depth interviews were conducted with eighteen long-term members.[12] This chapter provides a descriptive overview of the history and evolution of this unique sangha, including discussion of some of the more pronounced adaptive measures undertaken since its inception. The chapter begins with an examination of the life of the founder, Chögyam Trungpa, in the context of the evolution of the sangha he inspired. Emphasis is on the Shambhala teachings conceived by Chögyam Trungpa and the sangha's current incarnation as Shambhala Buddhism under the Sakyong's leadership. The details of this analysis expose some of the tensions and creative resolutions faced by transplanted traditions.

CHÖGYAM TRUNGPA RINPOCHE: A BRIEF BIOGRAPHY

The story of Chögyam Trungpa's early life and appearance in the West has come to be fairly well known, first told in his autobiography *Born in Tibet* (1985). Like all noteworthy charismatic figures, his story has taken on the hagiographic quality of legend: a mixture of documented fact and allegory. Scholarship is divided, with some electing to emphasize the more controversial episodes (Beit-Hallahmi 2001, 61; Lewis, 1998, 121–3) and others stressing Trungpa's mastery in translating the esoteric Tibetan Buddhist teachings for Westerners (Coleman 1999, 91–8; Prebish 1999, 159). This chapter attempts to provide balanced interpretation reflecting the multiple layers that informed his public personality and the manner in which he presented the Buddhist teachings.

Chögyam Trungpa was born in 1939 in a remote village in eastern Tibet. At an early age, Trungpa was recognized to be a *tülku*, the eleventh incarnation of a great lineage within the Kagyu school of Tibetan Buddhism.[13] As tradition dictated, he was enthroned as the Supreme Abbot of the Surmang monasteries and raised in the rigorous tradition of a Tibetan *tülku*. Trungpa lived as a monk for twenty years until the Chinese incursion into Tibet forced the exile of many religious leaders, including the Dalai Lama. In 1959, Trungpa fled Tibet, scaling the Himalayas to cross into India.

In 1963, Trungpa moved to Great Britain to attend Oxford University where he studied, among other subjects, comparative religion, philosophy, and English. During this period he developed his vision to transmit the Buddhist teachings to Westerners. Part of this vision involved the relinquishing of his monastic vows and an immersion in the new culture in which he found himself. In 1969, Trungpa married a young British woman, Diana Pybus,[14] and moved to the United States with the express purpose of fulfilling his mission to teach Buddhism.[15]

Trungpa's arrival in the West coincided with the religious ferment of the 1960s and 1970s. He travelled extensively throughout North America offering teachings on Tibetan Buddhism and meditation. He published two important texts that were widely read, *Meditation in Action* (1969) and *Cutting through Spiritual Materialism* (1973). In a relatively short time he had garnered a significant following and established centres in several major North American cities.

I have written elsewhere about the unique confluence of factors that led to Trungpa's positive reception (Eldershaw 2007). Western fascination with Eastern cultures, in particular that of Tibet, added to Trungpa's appeal among the youth of the period. As an acknowledged high spiritual leader from this exotic tradition, Trungpa was a credible candidate in the market of spiritual seekers. Adding to his appeal was Trungpa's young age and fluency with the English language. Even more so, perhaps, was his personal style and the unique methods by which he transmitted the Tibetan Buddhist teachings.

Trungpa's particular manner in conveying the Buddhist teachings challenged many Westerners' expectations of an Eastern Holy man. He smoked, drank, and was known to have sexual relations with his female students.[16] Defenders attributed his behaviour to "crazy wisdom," associating him with the tradition of *mahāsiddhas*[17] extending back to Padmasambhava (eighth century CE) and Milarepa (ca 1052–1135), renowned for their wisdom and outlandish behaviour.[18] Emulating the *mahāsiddha* ethos, Trungpa employed eccentric and often radical means to "stop short the conventional mind" (Hayward 1995, 215). Trungpa's whimsical behaviour and apparent disregard about being favourably received was further evidence of his authenticity as a legitimate teacher according to his followers. As one member said, "He would frequently blow his chances at having a good reputation. He didn't seem to care."[19] That Trungpa made no attempts to hide his drinking or womanizing was part of his appeal. "I would have been more stung and hurt by the sexual conduct of my teacher if I had been the student of a teacher who gave one appearance in public but acted oppositely in private" (Gross 1998, 241).

Looking back, his students believe that Trungpa explicitly adopted this mode of presentation in order to make a connection with Westerners. If he had presented himself as a monk, he would not have been so enthusiastically received by the counterculture youth. One long-time student reflected on Trungpa's approach during this period:

First, I think his way of connecting with his students was to actually immerse himself in their world. But secondly, I think because it was the '70s –

it was the time of what was called the spiritual supermarket and a lot of us had some pretty silly ideas about all kinds of things. We'd been exposed to this Hindu teacher and that Sufi dancer and this psychic blah, blah, blah – not to mention I was doing mescaline, you name it. There were a lot of fairly silly ideas – at least from Rinpoche's perspective about what spirituality was or could be. Certainly for me, I showed up extremely confused … At that time he talked a lot about what's called "cutting through spiritual materialism."[20]

Similar to the impulse of material consumption in the pursuit of happiness, spiritual materialism is the propensity to randomly acquire religious teachings and practices which, according to Trungpa, works to magnify the ego rather than reduce it. "Walking the spiritual path properly is a very subtle process; it is not something to jump into naively. There are numerous sidetracks which lead to a distorted, ego-centered version of spirituality; we can deceive ourselves into thinking we are developing spiritually when instead we are strengthening our egocentricity through spiritual techniques. This fundamental distortion may be referred to as spiritual materialism" (Trungpa 1973, 3).

A significant part of Trungpa's success was his ability to present Buddhist doctrine in a way that appealed to Western audiences. It is significant that Trungpa was among the first high Tibetan lamas to appear in the West. In this respect, Trungpa was introducing a new and esoteric form of Buddhism that, apart from sketchy accounts, was previously not available outside Tibet.[21] Using Western jargon, including psychological terminology and imagery to express the Tibetan Vajrayana teachings, Trungpa was able to convey the esoteric teachings in a way that resonated with Westerners' experiences. Trungpa also devised a secular meditation program called Shambhala Training which he began introducing in the late 1970s. These teachings are compiled in his book *Shambhala: The Sacred Path of the Warrior* (1984). Shambhala Training is primarily a meditation program that incorporates teachings dealing with life in contemporary society. Its principles are applied to daily living including how one dresses, eats, speaks, decorates one's home, chooses a livelihood, and relates to others interpersonally. A long-term student explains the Shambhala world view: "This includes our individual sitting practice on our zafu [meditation cushion], to how we dress, eat, and speak, to how we conduct our households, our businesses, or relate to our government, our world at large. It has been said that Shambhala vision teaches one how to brew a cup of tea and how to rule a nation. The collective manifestation of those principles is enlightened society" (McKeever 1980, 10).

Central to the Buddhist and Shambhala paths that Trungpa introduced was the practice of meditation. Although not traditionally practised in Tibetan lay culture (lay practice consists primarily of maintaining shrines and reciting mantras), Trungpa perceived that meditation would be highly beneficial for Westerners. In fact, research has shown that "in contrast to the motives of most traditional American religious congregants [which placed social over experiential aspirations], the central focus and *raison d'être* of the new Buddhists is direct religious experience and the personal transformation it produces" (Coleman 1999, 98). Trungpa encouraged his Western students to sit, "sit a lot." Most members of the community practise meditation daily, often for several hours.[22] As one student remarked, "It wasn't necessarily Buddhism, it was the practice of meditation that struck me. I had an inclination that that was the only way to go about things … just to sit down and make some space."[23] Extended sitting practices (referred to as *Nyinthuns, Weekthuns,* and *Dathuns*; day-, week-, and month-long meditation intensive retreats) were initiated. These involve eight to ten hours of daily meditation practice, punctuated by walking meditation and a formal Japanese style of eating referred to as *ōryōki*.

As the community expanded in numbers, an administrative organization evolved to orchestrate the sangha's growing activities. Numerous ritual formalities were inaugurated and Trungpa's teachings became more clearly structured into a series of courses and programs.[24]

Trungpa's unusual methods and adaptation of the teachings were explained in terms of his special status as a *tertön*. Chögyam Trungpa was recognized by His Holiness Dilgo Khentse Rinpoche, former head of the Nyingma school (Hayward, 1995), as possessing the rare ability to discover "hidden teachings."[25] Tibetan lore claims that various teachings remain hidden, "buried in the subconscious mind," and are accessed or "received" when the time is right for them to be uncovered (Trungpa 1999, 217). According to members of the community, the Shambhala teachings are regarded as *terma* (literally "hidden treasure") revealed to Trungpa in a series of dreams and visions.[26] In short, the Shambhala teachings are regarded as a vehicle for the Buddhist teachings for the present time.

The *tertön* tradition within Tibetan Buddhism is a legitimating vehicle for innovation and invention. Within the context of Buddhism in North America, the Shambhala teachings represented something radically novel and their reception both within and outside the community has been mixed. Trungpa's personal secretary, David Rome, recalls this period:

His behaviour – then and later – was controversial among Tibetans and Westerners, and for a few years he was really on his own. To me there was a heroic quality to his journey, as he continually left behind his connections and reference points for periods of isolation and rejection. Having shed everything and joined into the hippie lifestyle for a while, he began to create a structure from a clean slate and draw on a combination of Tibetan heritage and Western resources. We had reveled in his outrageousness and unusualness, and we were shocked to discover that he represented an establishment and tradition, though in an anti-establishment and non-traditional way. (Graham 1990, 188)

Although Trungpa's behaviour appealed to some who saw him as authentically manifesting his esoteric brand of Buddhism, his conduct often proved to be too controversial for others. One long-time student explained it this way: "His behaviour was so outrageous that you would just reject the whole thing together and become a Christian or just walk away from it and shudder. *Or*, you would be so shocked that you would lose some of your own views, which is really losing your own egohood."[27]

But it was an incident that became known as "the Snowmass affair," more than Trungpa's unusual behaviour or teachings, that generated extensive negative attention for the community. In 1975, during an exclusive retreat for advanced practitioners, at Trungpa's command, two participants were forcibly taken from their room and stripped naked in front of the entire assemblage after refusing to attend the evening's festivities. While the act was interpreted by members as a lesson in giving up of "self," the event was widely publicized. Judith Simmer-Brown, a long-time student of Chögyam Trungpa, explains teachings such as these within the Tibetan Vajrayana, crazy-wisdom framework.

Whatever act is motivated by compassion or transcendent knowledge carries a liberating power. No matter how scandalous, it can liberate if the mind of the teacher and student are in harmony. In this context, Buddhism has a rich heritage of seemingly abusive acts: Tilopa slapping Naropa in the face, Unmon giving Tozan sixty blows, Gutei cutting off his student's finger, Yeshe Tsogyal's husband offering her as a gift to his teacher, Guru Rinpoche. These acts taken in a conventional way are nothing short of outrageous. But for the student trapped in samsara, they are experienced as acts of great kindness, motivated by deep wisdom and compassion. For many of us, only the most direct communication has the ability of cutting through ego and its deceptions. (1994, 41–2)

The Snowmass affair caused a tremendous amount of public criticism and scrutiny. It conjured up associations with Jonestown and raised questions about seemingly blind obedience to spiritual authority. Public attention to the episode was so heightened that it became the subject matter of two books and a feature-length article in *Harper's Magazine.*[28]

Following this controversial period, Trungpa decided to relocate his headquarters to Canada. Throughout the late seventies and early eighties Trungpa had taken a number of extended retreats, two of which were spent in the Maritimes.[29] His experiences in the region may have influenced his subsequent decision to relocate to Nova Scotia. A small party was sent to begin resettlement, followed by several hundred members, primarily from the United States. By 1986, when Trungpa himself had relocated to Canada, the community had established its main administrative offices and spiritual centre in Halifax, and had purchased land throughout the province. A large tract was obtained in Cape Breton for the construction of a monastery,[30] and an elegant home in an upscale neighbourhood in Halifax was purchased to serve as Trungpa's residence. The opening ceremonies of the main centre in Halifax were attended by over five hundred guests, including the city's mayor, the archbishop of Nova Scotia, and a number of invited regional business and political figures.

Within a year and a half of moving to Nova Scotia, Chögyam Trungpa died. His health had been failing since the mid-eighties, largely, some believe, due to his lifestyle. During the last few years of his life he made fewer public appearances and his talks became increasingly enigmatic. He would lapse into lengthy silences emerging for only brief periods of lucidity. According to Tibetan Buddhist lore, Trungpa passed into *parinirvana* ("total extinction" or "full enlightenment") following cardiac and respiratory arrest in the Halifax Infirmary on 4 April 1987, at the age of forty-seven.

Analogous to the stories of the lives of great spiritual masters, the passing of realized beings are often claimed to be accompanied by miraculous signs. Several accounts surfaced of great storms, clocks stopping at the moment of

Trungpa's death, and rainbows encircling the sun at his cremation. As is the case with hagiographies, these stories came to be viewed as confirmation of Trungpa's enlightened nature. The following account appears as text in a photo essay depicting Trungpa's life and death: "A few days before his death, for the first time in many years, black icebergs came into the Halifax Harbour. The day that he passed away was a cloudless, warm and beautiful day. The Vidyadhara died in the early evening and a heavy mist and fog came into the city and remained for a number of days."[31]

Although Chögyam Trungpa's death had a profound impact on his sizable following, his students seemed determined to continue his vision and many more moved to Nova Scotia following his death. A member who relocated to Nova Scotia during this period offered this explanation: "I think a lot of us came up right after he died because you felt like you had to because he wanted us to and now he was dead. You would do whatever he wanted you to do."[32]

As if beset by ill fortune, the community was soon facing another unexpected challenge. Leadership in the community was vested in the Regent, a well-regarded American student named Thomas Rich, whom Trungpa had appointed to be his successor. In December of 1988 the community learned that the Regent had developed Acquired Immune Deficiency Syndrome and that, knowing of his illness, had had unprotected sex and infected a male partner who inadvertently infected a female partner. The scandal was reported to the world in an article in the *New York Times* (Zaslowsky 1989). Although married, the Regent was openly bisexual and known to be promiscuous, behaviour which the members of this community tolerated without judgment. Worse still, knowledge had surfaced that many in the administration had long known of the Regent's illness but failed to make this information public. The community called for the immediate dismissal of the Regent and the resignation of the board of directors. The crisis polarized the community into pro-Regent and anti-Regent factions. Upon the recommendation of His Holiness Dilgo Khyentse Rinpoche, the Regent went into retreat in Ojai, California surrounded by a group of supportive students until his death in 1990.[33]

In what has been referred to as the "biggest crisis" (Coleman 2001, 87) in North American Buddhism, the events surrounding the Regent's leadership seriously threatened the stability of the sangha. Although many left, a significant number remained in order to continue the vision initiated by Chögyam Trungpa Rinpoche. The controversy cast a pall over the reputation of the community. A letter to the board of directors drew a vivid parallel; "Clearly the only comparable parallel people will have is to Jonestown, and Jonestown will not fade from memory for generations. Nor would the infamy of Vajradhatu, and then how will Vajradhatu be able to fulfil its charter?"[34] Since this period, the community has worked to re-establish itself. Among other modifications, the name has been changed from Vajradhatu to Shambhala International, and there has been a change in leadership.

The period following the death of a founding leader is considered to be an important time in the development of a religious community. Many observers of new religious movements[35] predict disruption, the forming of factions, dispersal, or eventual collapse of the movement (Madsen and Snow 1991; Melton 1991; Miller 1991). Although the death of Chögyam Trungpa impacted his followers greatly, the community had in place a solid organizational network and provisions for the eventuation of his death. With centres in most major cities in North America and throughout Europe, including an accredited university, a monastery, several major retreat centres, and a publishing house, and with numerous internal support structures such as day cares, grade schools, and so forth, the institutional framework was well able to maintain itself in the absence of Chögyam Trungpa.

The scandal involving the Regent threatened to undermine this framework. Under intense media and public scrutiny, the sangha became polarized, many left the community, financial donations diminished, and the main administrative body was disbanded. The survival of the movement was a genuine concern. But, while trust in the central administrative body and the leadership of the Regent had been undermined, the smaller regional centres were able to preserve the semblance of unity. With the dissolution of the main administrative branch, one member explained, "everything kind of fell down on the local centres." The allegiance to the regional centres is a central reason why the community persisted during this time.

Shambhala International's survival can be attributed to a number of interconnecting factors related to commitment, devotion, and adaptation. In the twenty years since the crisis, the members of the Halifax community have established strong bonds of commitment based on shared experience. They have worked, volunteered, married, practised and studied Buddhism together, creating deep attachments. Although shattered by the betrayal of the Regent and those in the administration who knew that the Regent had HIV, the bonds connecting the larger membership together were too long established to allow the complete dismantling of the network. Despite the departure of many members, enough of a core group remained who were invested in the continuance of the community. Perhaps a more significant aspect of the complexity and endurance of Shambhala has been a deep, abiding commitment to Chögyam Trungpa. As stated earlier, many followers moved to Nova Scotia *after* his death because they believed part of his vision was the establishment of their main headquarters and nexus in Canada. This core group has been a solidifying force in the community, often serving central roles as teachers and in the administration.

Although the leadership of Shambhala International has been troubled by controversy, Chögyam Trungpa remains an acknowledged and influential Buddhist authority. More than twenty years after his death, his books continue to sell in the several thousands. Annual sales of *Cutting through Spiritual Materialism* (1969) number roughly 100,000, and *The Sacred Path of the Warrior* (1984) continues to sell about 15,000 per year. These and his other texts, *Meditation in Action* (1969) and *Myth of Freedom* (1988), for example, have been recognized as "classics" in the early North American Buddhist literature market.[36] Several of Trungpa's early students have become acknowledged scholars and teachers of Buddhism in North America, constituting another part of his legacy; figures such as Judith Simmer-Brown, Rick Fields (now deceased), Jeremy Hayward, Rita Gross, Robin Korman, and Reginald Ray have all had a marked influence on Western Buddhism.

The endurance of this community may also be attributed in part to the adaptive measures undertaken since the crises. Following the brief and controversial leadership of the Regent, Trungpa's eldest son was appointed head of the community. In an elaborate ceremony in March 1995, he was enthroned as Sakyong Mipham Rinpoche (literally "Earth Protector"). Under his leadership the community has undergone a series of organizational and ideological adaptations in order to regain the trust of the wider sangha and to draw in much needed new membership. The community has developed a variety of innovative ways to convey its unique teachings and practices. Perhaps the most significant shift has been the adoption of the title Shambhala Buddhism to express its unique combination of teachings. The following section provides an overview of this path, highlighting the Shambhala teachings devised by Chögyam Trungpa and the more recent innovations, including the Shambhala School of Buddhist Studies which attempts to integrate the Shambhala teachings with Tibetan Vajrayana Buddhism. Added to these bodies of teachings are numerous arts and educational programs. These adaptations and augmentations reflect the process of tradition building. In the context of Shambhala, they serve as a mechanism to overcome controversies in the history of this sangha and as a strategy to make the teachings more resonant with contemporary privatized spiritual practices.

THE SHAMBHALA TEACHINGS: THE WARRIOR'S PATH

Tibetans consider history progressively improving and leading to the flowering of Shambhala, a time in the near future when all on earth will be devoted to the quest for enlightenment.

ROBERT THURMAN, *Inside Tibetan Buddhism: Rituals and Symbols Revealed*

When Chögyam Trungpa first came to the West, he taught primarily from the Tibetan Vajrayana Buddhist tradition. In the mid-1970s he began introducing a secular set of teachings referred to as Shambhala Training which he devised exclusively for Westerners. The name Shambhala is derived from the legend of Shambhala and the rulers of this kingdom, the Rigdens. *Acharya* (elder) John Rockwell explains the historical and mythical origins of this tradition:

> King Suchandra came from the central Kingdom of Shambhala to southern India where Shakyamuni was dwelling at a famous stupa. It's said that King Suchandra requested teachings from the Buddha and that the Buddha asked, "What kind of teaching would you like?" Suchandra's reply was very specific. He said, "I'd like teachings such that I don't have to give up my kingdom, my wives, or sensory enjoyments." Accordingly, the Buddha sent his monastics out of the room and empowered the king to practice the Kalachakra Tantra. So the connection between Shambhala and the vajrayāna teachings started right there. (2001, 7)

Most regard this earthly paradise as metaphor, but many Tibetans and spiritual leaders believe in its current existence. According to Chögyam Trungpa, "the kingdom of Shambhala itself is not some mysterious heavenly realm. It is the realm of the cosmic mirror, the primordial realm that is always available to human beings if they relax and expand their minds" (Trungpa 1984, 145). In another passage he writes that Shambhala is "the expression of a deeply rooted and very real human desire for a good and fulfilling life" (Trungpa 1984, 7). According to the Shambhala teachings, in order to realize the existence of

Shambhala, one must first have attained an advanced level of spiritual awareness. "Shambhala lies hidden as a state of mind that must be awakened so that the kingdom can be found in the world outside" (Bernbaum 1980, 62). Chögyam Trungpa adapted the legend of Shambhala to symbolize the ideal of a "secular enlightenment" (Goss 1999, 218). Long-time personal attendant to Chögyam Trungpa, The Dorje Löppön Lodrö Dorje (Dean of Practice and Study) explains his vision:

> Although he founded Gampo Abbey, it was not his primary project. His primary idea was to create a western tradition of lay yogin practitioners, people who were involved in work and in family life and in that context also practised the Vajrayāna teachings. In line with that, he presented the Shambhala vision that dharma should not only be a religious affair of monastic people, but also carry a complete social vision. It needs to infiltrate society. In early years he talked a lot about infiltration, which was partly motivated by political vision. He knew what had happened in Tibet, where [sic] after 150 years of Buddhism, underwent a period of persecution, and the monasteries were particularly vulnerable. He said that you have to create a lay yogin society so that if Buddhism is ever persecuted in the West, it is hard to wipe out. It is invisible; it is everywhere. It is integrated into the fabric of the culture, and therefore it will take root and be sustained. (Dorje Löppön 2001)

The body of teachings associated with the Shambhala tradition is covered in a series of weekend programs referred to as Shambhala Training. The training consists of five introductory, or "undergraduate," courses, collectively referred to as "The Heart of Warriorship." The warrior archetype is prominent throughout the Shambhala teachings and may be said to parallel the bodhisattva ideal within Buddhism. In Shambhalian terms, the warrior symbolizes the "courage" to confront habitual patterns and to expose oneself to the phenomenal world directly, with clarity, precision, and compassion. Trungpa recast the conventional notion of warrior into a new framework to express these teachings. "Warriorship here does not refer to making war on others. Aggression is the source of our problems, not the solution. Here the word 'warrior' is taken from the Tibetan *pawo*, which literally means 'one who is brave' ... The key to warriorship and the first principle of Shambhala vision is not being afraid of who you are. Ultimately, this is the definition of bravery: not being afraid of yourself" (Trungpa 1984, 8).

Some aspects of the Shambhala teachings readily juxtapose with Buddhist principles. For example, the qualities associated with warriorship correspond to the Buddhist characterization of egolessness: *karuṇā*, gentleness or compassion, and *upāya*, wisdom, or skilful means. "The compassion aspect is connected with oneself, and the skilful means aspect is connected with how to deal with others. Compassion and skilful means put together is what is known as *egolessness*" (Trungpa 1991b, 211). The means to this awareness is the discovery of what Trungpa referred to as "basic goodness" – "acknowledging that we are intrinsically good, that we possess within ourselves an undiluted, unconfused, healthy and energetic quality ... That's the basic idea" (Fields 1981, 375).

Other aspects of the tradition Trungpa devised appear to be entirely novel. Emulating a Western curriculum format, Shambhala Training continues at the "graduate" level with a series of six weekend sessions entitled the "The Sacred Path: The Great Eastern Sun," and introduces students to more esoteric teachings unique to Shambhala. Practices developed by Trungpa, known as "raising windhorse, or *lungta*" are said to rouse "the energy of basic goodness into a wind of delight and power" (Trungpa 1984, 132). A core set of teachings in this series are the Four Dignities, characterized by the "virtues" meek, perky, outrageous, and inscrutable. Symbolized as Tiger, Lion, Garuda, and Dragon respectively, the Four Dignities constitute familiar images in the community's iconography. Trungpa describes these four states: "Meekness is basically experiencing a humble and gentle state of being, while perkiness is connected with uplifted and youthful energy. Outrageousness is being daring and entering into situations without hope or fear, and inscrutability is the experience of fulfilment and uncontrived, spontaneous achievement" (1984, 133). The goal of *lungta* and the dignities teachings is to develop "authentic presence."

Other important teachings include *Drala* and *Ashe* and represent advanced practices in the Shambhala tradition. Literally, *drala* means "energy beyond aggression" (Trungpa 1984, 108) and is said to reflect the "living energy" beyond common awareness, yet not beyond our potential experiential realization. In Buddhist terms, the practice of *drala* is oriented to the cultivation of egolessness, a state beyond the delusion of self.[38] Shambhala Training culminates with "Warrior Assembly" where participants are introduced to the practice of *ashe*, also known as "stroke," a calligraphic execution considered to evoke nondualistic action. Postgraduate programs include "The Practice of Authentic Presence" and "Kalapa Assembly."

Integrated throughout the Shambhala teachings are various well-attended arts programs,[39] most notably *Kyūdō* (Zen archery), *ikebana* (a traditional form of Japanese flower arranging), calligraphy, Miksang photography,[40] dressage, *chanoyu* (Japanese Tea Ceremony), and the Mudra Space Awareness program that teaches performance postures based on Tibetan monastic dance form. Broadly, the aim of these aesthetic programs is to bring the meditative state of awareness to the practice of the arts.

Two additional forms associated with the Shambhala tradition, the Dorje Kasung and Monarchy Principle, merit mention here as much for their originality as for their controversial character. Patterned after the British regimental system, the Dorje Kasung resembles a paramilitary-style guard. During large gatherings, members of the Dorje Kasung are positioned at key locations to monitor the audience. Beyond protective services, the Kasung is viewed as another vehicle through which Trungpa's teachings may be realized. "People who needed to work with aggression or who had a passion for order joined the guards; their job was to relate to the boundaries of situations" (Leontov 1991). The more combative aspects commonly associated with the military are minimized in the Dorje Kasung while more affirmative qualities, such as "discipline," are accentuated. Over the years, a comprehensive body of teachings and practices has emerged around this position referred to as Kasungship.[41]

The Monarchy Principle may be said to represent a Western format for the guru/disciple relationship. Chögyam Trungpa was regarded as Lord Mukpo, the Dorje Dradul ("indestructible warrior"), and treated in the manner of a sovereign, which included personal attendants, a chauffeur, and a residence referred to as Kalapa Court. The court was described by one member as representing "the really regal display of one's domestic situation. You had servants and guards, and chauffeurs, and cooks and nannies and people to walk your dog, and secretaries and social secretaries. They were all for one house! (Laughs)."[42] These attendant positions were primarily voluntary and valued for the access they afforded to Trungpa and his inner circle. The extravagant treatment was explained in the following way. "Here's this guy who really doesn't want to be served, he just permits it so many people will have access to him. It's paradoxical really."[43] Another member explained, "Much of what he was presenting was how to present oneself in a dignified way in ordinary life from a Shambhalian point of view. So, things like how to speak, how to dress, how to eat ..."[44] Additional practices in this context included Oxonian elocution lessons and ballroom dancing.

The Shambhala Buddhist teachings follow a path of self-reflection and contemplation through the practice of meditation, offering a set of guidelines on how to live life according to the warrior principle and how to develop authenticity and confidence through the practices of *lungta*, the four dignities, and teachings on basic goodness. The collective goal is the establishment an enlightened society. Long-time Shambhalian, Jeremy Hayward elaborates on this aim: "An enlightened society is not a utopia by any means ... An enlightened society is one where people are *willing* to practice, to let go of their fear, to be genuine and kind to each other ... The purpose of the Shambhala teachings is not merely to provide another path of personal spiritual development. The purpose is to provide a means by which we can begin, together, to build a community of warriors" (Hayward 1995, 235).

The structural foundation for this society includes schools (elementary, secondary, and post-secondary),[45] businesses, practice centres in most major cities in North America and Europe, and an international network of relationships that connect this global community of Shambhalians. Reflecting the principles of Shambhala, the community has, largely on the initiation of Chögyam Trungpa, designed a whole culture of symbols and terminology, including holidays, songs, stories, flags, banners, uniforms, and so on.[46]

TRADITION BUILDING AND THE INTRODUCTION OF SHAMBHALA BUDDHISM

It seems that we now find ourselves at a crossroads. We are faced with a noticeable shift as the dharma is being passed on from one generation to another, and we need to look ahead. What will future generations call themselves? We have a unique culture ... We are not like other Buddhist or Zen sanghas. Much of what we assume to be Buddhist in our community is heavily influenced by the teachings of Shambhala. Ideally speaking we should all be trained to some degree in both sets of teachings. The Vidyadhara saw the need for Buddhism to adapt to this new world, and he also saw what this world needs. The Shambhala teachings came to him in these visions and he saw that this is the perfect time for them.

SAKYONG MIPHAM RINPOCHE, *Shambhala Buddhism*

Chögyam Trungpa believed that the Shambhala teachings were the appropriate vehicle for expressing ideas associated with Buddhism to Westerners. Since the mid-seventies, the Shambhala path and the Buddhist stream of teachings have run parallel, each offering a distinct set of teachings and practices. Originally, each tradition was held in separate centres, one housing the Shambhala Training program and another Buddhist instruction and practice. Over the years, under the Sakyong's leadership, the two branches have gradually been integrated combining the symbology and principles associated with the Shambhala teachings with those of the Tibetan Vajrayana tradition. Although at present the community still offers distinct Buddhist and Shambhalian teachings, it appears to be in the process of fully integrating the two paths: "In essence, the emphasis of the Buddhist path is to help us attain enlightenment, and the emphasis of the Shambhala path is to help us create and maintain a good society. When we put these two together, we have the Shambhalian Buddhist view of enlightened society. Thus the two paths work in tandem, not in competition" (Sakyong 2000).

In 2002 the community revamped the structure and presentation of its Buddhist program under the "Shambhala School of Buddhism," a series of "Four Cycles" beginning with an introduction to Shambhala Buddhism called "Fearless Buddha, Peaceful Warrior."[47] The program teaches basic Buddhist tenets, such as karma, emptiness, teachings on the Refuge and Bodhisattva Vows, as well as the Six Paramitas, Logong, and so forth. Incorporated throughout are Shambhala teachings and terminology, such as warriorship, as well as Maitri: Five Wisdom Energies, a set of teachings and practices based on the Five Buddha families presented in a psychological framework.[48]

Liturgy and iconography reflecting this integration have developed along with the merging of the two traditions. For instance, the Sakyong has recently introduced a program referred to as "Enlightened World: The Three Yānas of Shambhala Buddhadharma." New *sadhanas* (spiritual practice or teaching), such as "The Windhorse of Authentic Presence," have also been conceived by the Sakyong. This has involved the introduction of new devotional images. For example, the Primordial Rigden Thangka was created to visually represent the intersection of Shambhalian principles of "basic goodness" and the Buddhist teachings on "awakened mind." The Primordial Rigden is now the principal *thangka* exhibited in Shambhala Buddhist shrine rooms throughout the world.[49]

While the Shambhala and Buddhist curricula are still run as distinct paths, both now culminate in Shambhala Seminary. Previously, the Buddhist path followed the threeyana course of Hīnayāna,[50] Mahayana, and Vajrayana, concluding with Vajradhatu Seminary and Vajrayana *ngöndro* ("preliminary practice") before advancing on to the secret Tantric teachings. Presently, both Shambhalian and Vajrayana practitioners proceed to Shambhala Seminary and undertake Shambhala *ngöndro* which includes the recently conceived liturgy, The Primordial Rigden: The Magical Heart of Shambhala. These are followed by more advanced teachings, such as the Roar of the Werma *sadhana* and the Scorpion Seal of the Golden Sun practice, which are also regarded as *terma* and are taught during Rigden Abisheka. The heart of these senior practices is realizing enlightened society.

Senior students or *acharyas*, long-term practitioners upon whom Chögyam Trungpa and the Sakyong have conferred authority to transmit the teachings, lead most programs. Advanced post-seminary practices, such as Vajrayogini and Chakrasamvara Abhishekas, Madhyamaka and Dzogchen are taught by Sakyong Mipham Rinpoche. Further studies are held through what is called the "Mipham Academy," led by the Sakyong and Khenpo Gawang, a monastic from Namdroling Monastery in India who acts as the central teacher.

Considerable adjustments have been made to "streamline" the practices in order to accommodate contemporary Western lifestyles and to make them more accessible for practitioners restricted by obligations of work, family, and financial limitations; participants can enter at any point in the four-cycle program. For example, Seminary previously consisted of a three-month intensive study and practice. Currently, it is divided into two month-long sessions (Shambhala Sutrayana Seminary and Shambhala Vajrayana Seminary respectively). Further, the traditional sequence of four 100,000 practices[51] that constitute *ngöndro* has been adapted so that counting is not essential to the practice. The focus has shifted to an emphasis on group *ngöndro* practice. One may count the practices in the traditional manner, but this is no longer a requirement. The following is a description of the Shambhala *Ngöndro* Dathun. "Counting is not necessary, but if you choose, you are free to recite 100,000 mantras. This practice is meant to be accomplished at a gathering of Shambhala warriors over a period of one month. Its purpose is to galvanize those warriors and foster friendship, camaraderie, and celebration thus mixing practice and life. This will increase personal windhorse and invigorate the windhorse of the group, giving power and potency to the vision of Shambhala" (Sakyong 2004b).[52]

The merging of these two streams has met with some confusion and resistance among members of the community. Many have expressed concern that the Sakyong is putting the Shambhala teachings above and in place of the

Buddhist teachings. Some first generation Buddhists have complained that integrating the two traditions is a misinterpretation of Trungpa's original vision. Conversely, those in the Shambhala stream have balked at the blending of the Buddhist tradition with the secular Shambhala path, countering that they "do not want another religion," a view expressed in the following comment: "When I go to the local Shambhala Center, all I see is the Buddhist tradition, and very little in the Shambhala tradition. As a relatively new Shambhala student, this disturbs me. I am repeatedly told they are distinct paths, and I want them to be distinct paths, yet the shrine room is devoted to red and gold of Tibetan Buddhism and all the apparent Buddhist artefacts" (Horvath 1998, 11).

A further conundrum has been how to effectively blend the secular teachings with the more esoteric and culturally unique features of the Vajrayana tradition. Equally puzzling is the question of how the monastic branch of Shambhala International located at Gampo Abbey will fit into this restructuring. While much of the focus of the community's teachings is on lay practice, Trungpa established Gampo Abbey with the aim of transplanting and fostering the monastic tradition in the West. In fact, the director of Gampo Abbey, Ani Pema Chödrön, a fully ordained Bhikshuni nun, has garnered international recognition through her publications (*The Wisdom of No Escape* [1991], *Start Where You Are* [1994], *Awakening Compassion* [1997a], and *When Things Fall Apart* [1997b]) and lecture tours.[53] Although the expansion of monastic tradition has been slow, the monastery appears to be flourishing. While few elect to pursue full monastic ordination, the monastery functions as a remote location for intensive training in Tibetan Vajrayana Buddhism. The Abbot, the Venerable Khenchen Thrangu Rinpoche, oversees monastic training, including the three-year retreat.

Determining how to balance the Buddhist and Shambhala teachings – how to make available an established religious tradition alongside and in tandem with its secular teachings – continues to be an issue. A member of the Shambhala board of directors, highly conscious and deliberate about these modifications, expresses well some of the dilemmas involved in tradition building:

As directors, we consider one essential question to be how we can maintain the integrity of these teachings, or the message, while making the teachings user-friendly. The challenge of any spiritual tradition as it reincarnates into a new land, or when the founder dies, is to propagate the doctrine without editing, yet to reach the populace by speaking the language and culture at hand. An entity is dead if it doesn't move with the times, but it also dies if it moves too rapidly and crashes in messianic zeal ... (Holecek 1996, 8–16)

For the time being, the community remains in the throes of redefining the presentation of its unique blend of teachings. The challenge, as it is for all religious traditions, is preserving tradition while continually adjusting to make the teachings and practices resonate with contemporary issues and practitioners. Part of this accommodation has been the introduction of various contemplative arts and educational programs, and initiatives related to social action and diversity.

CONTEMPLATIVE ARTS, SOCIAL ACTION, AND DIVERSITY

Encompassed in the Shambhala mandala of teachings is a wide range of educational, cultural, and artistic programs. A brief listing gives some indication of the breadth and variety currently offered: Shamatha Yoga, Zen Golf, Deep Listening, Shambhala Art, workshops on contemplative gardening, wilderness and shaman retreats, leadership training, seminars for people of colour, diversity retreats, death and dying courses, and programs for gays and lesbians. A number of educational programs have been developed under the rubric of "Engaged Buddhism" which blend contemplative spirituality with issues related to social action, peacemaking, restorative justice, and environmental education. These initiatives include "The Peace Maker Institute," "The Institute for Transformative Justice" and "Ecopsychology."[1] Programs incorporate meditation and Shambhala Buddhist principles to find answers to contemporary social and environmental problems.

Such initiatives are designed to meet contemporary privatized spiritual interests and to appeal to prospective practitioners or, to borrow Tweed's expression, "sympathisers," – "those who have some sympathy for a religion but do not embrace it exclusively or fully" (Tweed 1999, 74). These are individuals who may not want another religion but who are searching for teachings and practices (in particular meditation) to enhance their lives. The programs serve as an entry point into the larger Shambhala mandala and locus for prospective membership, while at the same time providing an important source of revenue for the community.

Historically, Shambhala International has attracted predominantly white, middle- to upper-middle class adherents. Ineffective mobilization, particularly of younger practitioners, the second generation, and non-white or ethnically diverse members, has left this community demographically stagnant. To make the community more inclusive, Shambhala International is endeavouring to appeal to more varied populations through practices such as diversity training that infuses Shambhalian principles with goals of inclusiveness and by striving to make its teachings accessible, culturally, physically, and economically. The following statement expresses this integration:

> Diversity training in the context of the Shambhala Buddhist community is an integral part of the path of realizing egolessness, discovering compassion, and manifesting an enlightened society. It is related to the development of equanimity, the way of seeing all others as equal in basic goodness, although different in characteristics, styles and manifestations. Diversity training provides a skillful means for working with our tendency to pigeonhole ourselves and others ... Diversity training in the Kingdom of Shambhala is not a fad, or a crisis response to interpersonal problems arising in any given community, but an ongoing daily practice. It is a foundation both of our personal journey and the development of a good human society. (Rajney et al. 2006, 1)

Further initiatives have included translations of teachings into several languages, creating materials for visually and hearing impaired participants, and using on-line courses for distance study.

Such adaptations contribute a certain degree of "cultural continuity" (Stark 1996) that resonates with the trend among North Americans to integrate self-realization with social change (Melucci 1996, 338) and have the potential to enhance the vitality of the community. A concern with such alterations, however, is "excessive adaptation" whereby the teachings are altered to suit the individual tastes and demands of contemporary Westerners, "rather than individuals being transformed by the teachings" (Tanaka 1998, 294). Furthermore, such "eclectic tendencies," remarks Tanaka, run the risk of encouraging "diffused affiliations" whereby participants maintain affiliations with multiple groups with no explicit commitment to one group (1998, 296). Shambhala International is experiencing a free-rider problem. Individuals participate in various programs without committing to the community as a whole through regular financial contributions or voluntary efforts. Consequently, the introduction of numerous new programs has not, as anticipated, generated the commitment needed to sustain Shambhala International's extensive activities, and the community is experiencing a financial setback.[55]

On a positive note, over the years since his appointment as spiritual head of the community, the Sakyong has garnered a substantial amount of public attention and respect through his various publications and speaking tours. In contrast to his predecessors, the Sakyong does not manifest the crazy wisdom style of guru/discipleship, nor does he elicit controversy. Contrary to the lifestyle reported of Trungpa and the Regent, the Sakyong leads a very healthy lifestyle as a yoga enthusiast and long-distance runner. He has run several marathons raising money for the Konchok Foundation that supports the 12th Trungpa *tülku* in Tibet and the *shedra* school for monastic training in the Surmang region. His publications, *Turning the Mind into an Ally* (2004a) and *Ruling Your World: Ancient Strategies for Modern Life* (2005), have sold well[56] and the recent release of his CD, *What about Me?* (2007) has been viewed on YouTube and in entertainment media.[57] His teachings tend to emphasize compassion, "goodness, warmth and intelligence" that appeal to a broader audience.[58] Through his restructuring and presentation of the teachings, he has fostered a gentler approach to meditation and practice, emphasizing a gradual immersion and transformative process of routine over endurance, and commitment over conversion.

The Sakyong's message of peace and compassion led *Planet Magazine* to name him "one of the thirty global visionaries of our time"[59] and his recent marriage to Khandro Tseyang Palmo, daughter of His Eminence Tertön Namkha Drimed Rabjam Rinpoche of the Ripa lineage of Tibetan Buddhism, made international headlines. Dubbed, a "Royal Buddhist Wedding" (CTV 2006), the ceremony took place in Halifax in June of 2006 and was attended by approximately 1300 guests including visiting high Tibetan dignitaries and regional business and political figures. The Sakyong's personal popularity might be the drawing card that Shambhala International needs to help offset controversies that have plagued this community and to attract much needed new membership to their sangha.

CONCLUSION

"What are we? We are the lineage of Shambhala Buddhism.
This is what we are."

SAKYONG MIPHAM RINPOCHE, *Shambhala Buddhism*

One of the objectives of this volume is to analyse the many forms of Buddhism shaping and being shaped by North American culture. Speculation has abounded as to how Buddhism will be influenced by its confrontation with post-industrial Western society with its heightened individualism, capitalism, feminism, and religious pluralism. We are in a unique situation to track this development within Canada.

I have attempted to provide an overview of the history, teachings, and adaptations of one Buddhist community. Shambhala International has developed a rich and complex culture from existing religious and traditional forms and newly created elements assembled together in a unique and evolving pattern. Shambhala has devised an array of holidays, rituals, observances, songs, symbology, and liturgy that reflect its unique culture. A detailed analysis of this rich symbolic culture represents a promising field of future inquiry.

To remain vital, religious systems must change. Like old wine in new casks, Buddhism is being appropriated in innovative ways as it encounters Western culture. In the establishment of Shambhala Buddhism we witness the construction of a Western-influenced Shambhalian Vajrayana Buddhist tradition. These innovations illustrate a religiously based community attempting to avoid the perils of routinization while adapting to meet the demands of the contemporary secularized context. In situating itself amid the pantheon of religious competitors that make up the multicultural landscape of Canadian and North American society, Shambhala offers several avenues for engaging with its teachings and practices. It provides a serious religious path of practice and study rooted in the Tibetan Vajrayana tradition, and a path – Shambhala Buddhism – that bridges its religious cultural heritage with its new host culture. The community offers an advanced body of teachings and practices. Members can express their commitment through various initiation ceremonies, such as the Refuge ceremony, the Bodhisattva vow, and the Shambhala Naming ceremony. For those who do not want to convert to another religion, Shambhala offers a range of teachings and practices at the novice level through its arts and educational programs. This flexibility and non-exclusivity has been a factor that explains, in part, why Westerners have been drawn to Buddhism (Wuthnow and Cadge 2004, 366). Shambhala International does not require practitioners to self-identify as Buddhists or Shambhalians, or to give up other religious beliefs or traditions.

For these reasons, it is difficult to determine the growth of Shambhala International in Canada. Anecdotal information indicates that the core Canadian sangha has remained fairly small, and its contributing membership has not grown substantially since its appearance in the early 1980s. Given the "extremely tight 'religious' market" in Canada (Bibby 2002, 63–4), conversion to Buddhism and Shambhala Buddhism has been marginal. As Reginald Bibby's research shows, although participation in mainline religions has declined, Canadians are not in great numbers abandoning their religious origins for the new and transplanted religious traditions (2002, 16). Consequently, Canada remains "dominated by Catholic and Protestant 'companies'" (Bibby 2002, 63–4).

However, Canadians throughout the country are participating in Shambhala levels, as well as Buddhist and arts programs, in numbers that have helped sustain this community. And this may speak more accurately to the wider, more subtle cultural impact that Shambhala International is having, particularly in the eastern provinces where they are more concentrated. Thus we can ask whether Chögyam Trungpa's vision for Buddhism in the West is being achieved – "that dharma should not only be a religious affair of monastic people, but also carry a complete social vision. It needs to infiltrate society" (Dorje Loppon 2001).

At about four decades old, Shambhala International has maintained a foothold in the spiritual marketplace, despite challenges. Like all transplanted religions, Shambhala has grappled with the challenges of recruitment, retention, adaptation, and competition. Added to these have been events and controversies unique to this community. The premature death of its founding leader, Chögyam Trungpa, and the controversial leadership of the Regent have compelled the members of this community to step back and re-evaluate their interpretation of the teachings they had inherited and to reflect how best to make their unique blend of teachings and practices resonate with contemporary spiritual seekers.

How are we to classify the Shambhala Buddhists? They themselves seem to be caught in a quandary of self-definition. For individual members, the issue of whether to self-identify as "Buddhists," "Shambhalians," or "Shambhala Buddhists" remains contested terrain. As noted above, the majority of participants are "sympathizers" and "night-stand Buddhists" and make up a vital cohort of practitioners in this community. This raises the question, to what degree do these distinctions constitute sangha? Originally referring to the assembly of Buddhist monks and nuns, the term sangha now commonly encompasses lay practitioners. The issue of membership and affiliation has serious ramifications for establishing a committed support base that has yet to be solidified in this community. Related questions are, to what degree do the urban and land-based centres operate in isolation from one another, or as loosely connected extensions from the main centre in Halifax, and what effect does this have in terms of creating a sense of unity and allegiance? These questions are significant as they concern the kinds of bonds and divisions that sustain or hinder communities and are integral to the endurance of religious communities.

Nevertheless, the introduction of Shambhala Buddhism is a significant development in the transmission of Buddhism, potentially representing the entry of a distinct sect within Western Buddhism. The new forms of Buddhism constitute sites of social experimentation that reflect the changing shape of religion and religious participation in contemporary society. They are new formulations of old traditions for new purposes (Hobsbawm 1983, 5–8). Shambhala International is seeking to create an alternate community; to use its own terminology, to create an enclave of "enlightened society" within the boundaries of larger society. The unfolding of this endeavour has been a gradual process of adaptation and accommodation. For the present, the community is attempting to straddle the boundary between the secular and the religious, working to preserve ties with Tibetan Buddhism[60] while being attentive to changes in the wider cultural arena and the shifting spiritual appetites of Western practitioners.

NOTES

1 The phrase "Golden Sun of the Great East" is found in the Dedication of Merit chant and is the title of a central text for advanced Shambhala practitioners.

2 The name Chögyam is derived from the Tibetan *Chögyi Gyatso* which means "ocean of dharma." Trungpa is a Tibetan term meaning "attendant" or "he who is close to the teacher." Rinpoche is an honorific title accorded high-ranking Tibetan *tülku*s. Literally it translates as "precious jewel." Depending on the context, Trungpa is addressed variously by a number of titles such as Vidyadhara, "he who holds the scientific knowledge" or "he who has achieved complete crazy wisdom" (Trungpa 1991a, 41); Vajracara, a title accorded him by the 16th Karmapa for his efforts in bringing Buddhism to the West, denotes his mastery of the Vajrayana wisdom. Vajradhāra, a title accorded him in movement liturgy, poetry, and student recollections, places Trungpa among the "ever-present enlightened beings who continually dispense their blessings" (Kongtrul 1986, 2). Dorje Dradul is used within the Shambhala context and denotes his supremacy as a master

warrior. Lord Mukpo, emphasizes his historical "clan" connections to the legendary Tibetan folk hero, Gesar of Ling.

3 Trungpa Rinpoche has simultaneously been referred to as "the bad boy of Buddhism" and "one of the greatest spiritual teachers of the 20th century" (Demetrakas and Leeman 2008).

4 The Sakyong is recognized by the community to be the incarnation of the revered Tibetan scholar Mipham Jamyang Namgyal Rinpoche.

5 Interview conducted in Cape Breton, Nova Scotia, 1993.

6 See Swick's publication *Thunder and Ocean* (1996) about the integration of American Buddhists into the Halifax, Nova Scotia community.

7 Trungpa Rinpoche founded the Naropa Institute (now Naropa University) in 1974 with the vision of integrating contemplative studies with traditional Western scholastic and artistic disciplines. See http://www.naropa.edu/.

8 There are four predominant branches within Tibetan Buddhism: Nyingmapa, Kagyupa, Sakyapa, and the Gelugpa school whose leader, the Dalai Lama, represents the head of state now in exile. Each tradition is distinguished by specific interpretations of root doctrines and practices associated with particular deities.

9 The process is ongoing, though it seems to be the Sakyong's intention to fully integrate the two bodies of teachings. I sense that the administration is moving cautiously because of some resistance in the community (particularly among first generation students).

10 The Bön tradition refers to the indigenous shamanic religion which existed in Tibet prior to the introduction of Buddhism in the seventh century. Vajrayana Buddhism emerged out of a unique blending of Mahayana Buddhism with many esoteric beliefs and practices from the Bön tradition (Feuerstein 1992, 34).

11 The term Rimed (pronounced re-may) means "unbiased" and represents a nineteenth-century movement in Tibet which sought to overcome sectarian bias in the various schools of Tibetan Buddhism. The Rimed movement became known for discovering and reviving lost teachings, called *terma* ("treasures") (Schuhmacher and Woerner 1989, 290). While formally trained in both the Kagyu and Nyingma traditions, Trungpa was also an adherent of the Rimed movement. The Shambhala teachings are believed to be a *terma* discovery, rooted in these Tibetan traditions and blended with Western cultural practices.

12 Data for this article was collected primarily between 1998 and 2002. In 1998 I spent two months at Shambhala Mountain. This was followed by two weeks at Shambhala's largest European retreat centre, Dechen Chöling. Over the course of data collection, several extended visits were made to the main centre in Halifax, Nova Scotia. Interviews were

conducted primarily face-to-face; they were open-ended and unstructured in format lasting between one and three hours in length. One interview was conducted by telephone. Interview data includes comments, remarks, and exchanges made by members throughout field investigations.

13 *Tülku* is a Tibetan term meaning "transformation body" and reflects the Buddhist belief in the reincarnation of a previously deceased person (Schuhmacher and Woerner 1989, 385). In Tibet, the tradition of locating such incarnated *tülkus* began in the thirteenth century and continues to the present. Prior to the Chinese invasion, it was estimated that there were approximately three thousand reincarnated lamas. Today there are roughly five hundred, most of whom are living in exile (Fowler 1999, 134). Along with the relocation of Tibetan teachers to the West has come the recognition of important reincarnations, or "child *tülkus*," in Western persons (see Lavine 1998). While the system of tülkuhood may be said to have avoided many of the problems associated with succession, disputes over authenticity have led to incidences of infighting. The two Karmapas is a case in point.

14 Trungpa's marriage to Diana Pybus caused a media stir at the time largely because of the "exotic" nature of their marriage; a former Tibetan monk to an upper-class English woman, but also because of Diana's age. Their marriage was permitted under a recently passed Scottish law that sanctioned marriage at the age of sixteen. See Mukpo and Gimian (2006), which contains Diana Mukpo's memoirs recounting her life with Chögyam Trungpa.

15 Trungpa's first stop in North America was Montreal where he and his new bride spent three months waiting for their American visas. During his stay he gave three public talks – possibly his first in North American – facilitated by faculty from Dawson College (See Fordham, n.d.).

16 Trungpa had appointed seven female students as *sanyums*, consorts.

17 *Mahāsiddha* means "great adept" and is used to refer to Tantric gurus who used unconventional methods to bring about full awareness of reality, the goal of the Buddhist path. For a discussion of this tradition, see Dowman 1985 and Ray 2005.

18 Trungpa believed that the unorthodox style of the crazy wisdom tradition was the most appropriate method for reaching his Western disciples. The crazy wisdom approach, he reasoned, is effective only in "savage countries, where there is more opportunity to take advantage of chaos" (Trungpa 1991a, 174).

19 Member of the Shambhala sangha in conversation with the author, Colorado, 2001.

20 Member of the Shambhala sangha in an interview with the author, Halifax, 1999.

21 See Lopez 1998.

22 Lavine remarks on this "inverted" form of monastic practice evident among Western practitioners who undertake intensive tantric practices and rituals typically performed by monks and nuns in Tibet (1998, 107).

23 Member of the Shambhala sangha in an interview with the author, Halifax, 1999.

24 Many of these formalizing changes coincided with the first visit to the West of the spiritual head of the Kagyu school of Tibetan Buddhism, His Holiness the 16th Karmapa, in September 1974.

25 See Samuel (1993) for a discussion of this tradition within Tibetan Buddhism.

26 Evidently, the authenticity of the Shambhala teachings as "genuine *terma*" was corroborated by Dilgo Khyentse Rinpoche, the former head of the Nyingma school of Tibetan Buddhism (Hayward 1995, 38).

27 Telephone interview with a member of the Shambhala sangha, 2001.

28 Tom Clark (1980) and Ed Sander (1977) specifically address the Snowmass episode. Sander's publication contains the findings from a class of Naropa students who investigated the incident. Peter Marin's detailed critique of the event was reported in an article entitled "Spiritual Obedience," in *Harper's Magazine* (1979).

29 Trungpa first visited eastern Canada in 1977 and again in 1984, when he spent a yearlong retreat in Nova Scotia.

30 Gampo Abbey was established in 1984.

31 The Life of Chögyam Trungpa Rinpoche, slide presentation, 1999. Halifax, Nova Scotia: Shambhala Archives 1:16.

32 Member of the Shambhala sangha in conversation with the author, Halifax, 1999.

33 In the interest of tracking the development of sects within North American Buddhism, a group claiming the "true" lineage following from Trungpa Rinpoche, the Regent, and his successor, Patrick Sweeny, has formed in California under the name Satdharma. See http://www.satdharma.org.

34 Letter to the Board of Directors, 28 January 1989. Uncatalogued document, Naropa Institute, Boulder, Colorado.

35 "New Religious Movement" is used here to refer to new and imported religious traditions. The term arose in response to the resurgence of religious activity in the West following the Second World War, which sparked considerable scholarly inquiry and public misgivings about the new and alternative forms of religious movements appearing during this period (see Stark and Bainbridge [1985]). Jan Nattier (1998) has opted for the term "transplants" to refer to recently transplanted movements such as Buddhism.

36 Personal communication, September 2008.

37 The image of the cosmic mirror refers to the primordial state of being, beyond confu-

sion and preoccupation with the past and future. The objective is to cultivate a state of "nowness," or awareness in the present moment. This is fostered through the practice of meditation (Trungpa 1995, 29).

38 A description of these and other teachings related to this tradition can be found on the Shambhala International website: http://www.shambhala.org/shambhala-training.php.

39 See http://www.shambhala.org/arts.php for a detailed description of these programs.

40 Miksang is a Tibetan word meaning "good eye." The practice of Miksang brings meditation techniques of mindfulness and awareness to the practice of producing photographic images. See http://www.miksang.com.

41 However, drills, military strategy, and a rigid regard for hierarchy and command are strongly valued in this practice. See Trungpa (2005).

42 Interview with the author, Halifax, 1994 (Eldershaw 1994, 84).

43 Interview with the author, Halifax, 1999.

44 Interview with the author, Halifax, 1994 (Eldershaw 1994, 84).

45 See Shambhala School http://www.shambhalaschool.org/.

46 By way of example, see www.shambhalashop.com for illustrations of Shambhala culture that may be purchased.

47 See Shambhala School of Buddhist Studies, http://www.shambhala.org/ssbs.php.

48 See The Five Wisdom Energy Practice, http://www.maitripractice-international.org/vajra/index.htm.

49 For more information about this image see http://www.shambhala.org/about_rigden.php.

50 Mahayana Buddhists coined the polemical term "Hīnayāna" as a way to favourably distinguish Mahayana teachings. While it is a contested term, Shambhalians generally use it rather than the more acceptable "Theravada." In keeping with the use by Shambhala, I am retaining this term, but its pejorative meaning of "lesser," "lower," or "inferior" path/vehicle should be noted.

51 The core requirements of *ngöndro* include the execution of one hundred thousand full prostrations, one hundred thousand recitations of a hundred syllable (Vajrasattva) mantra, one hundred thousand symbolic offerings, and one million repetitions of a guru supplication. The *ngöndro* practices are regarded as the "supreme test" necessary before initiation into the secret Tantric teachings of Vajrayana Buddhism (Kornman 1988, 199).

52 This quote is from The Primordial Rigden: The Magical Heart of Shambhala cited in "The Shambhala *Ngöndro* Practice and Study for the Coming Year" (Sakyong 2004b). I have not seen the entire text because it is prohibited.

53 Pema Chödrön was nominated one of the "50 Canadians to Watch For" by *Maclean's Magazine* (20 January 2003). The article lauds Pema for having "struck a chord with the

spiritually malnourished around the world" and speculates that she "may be Canada's best-selling author" (2003, 28). According to Shambhala Publications, her book sales (in English) have exceeded 1.5 million copies (personal communication, January 2008).

54 See http://www.naropa.edu.

55 The community newsletter reported that "Severe measures are needed to avert an even greater crisis at the end of this year." Aggravating this situation, the recent increase in the value of the Canadian dollar has negatively impacted the exchange rate on American contributions which form the bulk of Shambhala's support base (*The Dot*, 2003, 13).

56 *Turning the Mind into an Ally* sold in excess of 20,000 in its first publication and has been reissued.

57 The title track can be heard at http://www.mipham.com/readnews.php?id=4.

58 See Shambhala International, "About Shambhala: Shambhala Vision."

59 "*PLANET Magazine* Names Sakyong Mipham Rinpoche One of Thirty Global Visionaries," (6 May 2005), http://www.mipham.com/newsitem.php?id=73.

60 To this end, the Sakyong has journeyed twice (2002 and 2004) to Tibet for the purpose of establishing relations with the Surmang region and the 12th Trungpa *tülku*, Chokyi Senge. Chokyi Senge was recognized to be the incarnation of Trungpa Rinpoche in 1989 by His Eminence Tai Situ Rinpoche. His living and educational expenses are being funded through the Konchok Foundation initiated by Sakyong Mipham Rinpoche and Trungpa's widow, Lady Diana Mukpo. See http://www.Konchok.org.

PART FOUR From Local to Global

Globalization and Modern Transformation of Chinese Buddhism in Three Chinese Temples in Eastern Canada[1]

TANNIE LIU

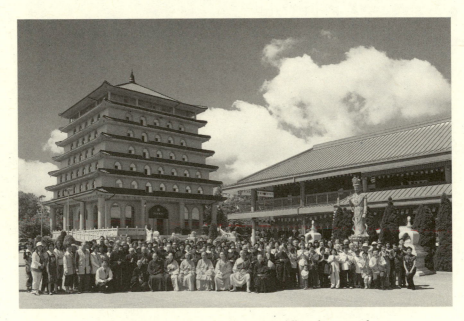

On 1 July 2008, monks, nuns, and Buddhist devotees of
Cham Shan Temple gathered to mark the 7th anniversary
of the opening of the Niagara Falls branch of Cham Shan,
the Ten Thousand Buddhas Sarira Stupa.
Photo courtesy of Cham Shan Temple, Toronto

Alexander Soucy, in this volume, points out that to identify Buddhist groups in the West as either American or Canadian has little relevance to their own self-understanding. Rather, many of these groups are global movements that originated in Asia and were transported to the West. His conclusion resonates with my research in several Chinese Buddhist communities in Canada. In the present analysis, I focus on three major Chinese Buddhist temples in eastern Canada, the Cham Shan[2] Temple in Toronto, the Fo Guang Shan Temple in Ottawa, and the True Buddha School in Montreal. I argue that the local presence of these Chinese temples cannot be understood simply as organizations established by immigrants to help them adapt to Canadian society and assert their ethnic identity. Rather, as Soucy observes, they belong to global movements within Chinese Buddhism which are intended for the global migration of the religion among competing ideologies in the world. The three temples reflect the modern transformation of Chinese Buddhism resulting from various historical and social developments in China in the last two centuries. The temples differ significantly from one another because of the different ideologies of the founders and their orientations to globalization.

Globalization often refers to a macro-sociological theory. For the purpose of this paper, globalization is defined as the process in which the world is rapidly compressing into a single global community (Robertson 1992, 8). Roland Robertson describes the current phase of globalization starting from the 1960s and ending in the twenty-first century as a crisis in which different cultures are juxtaposed in an unprecedented manner. This juxtaposition, which thrusts different cultures, once widely separated, into close contact with each other, is due to rapid advances in communication and transportation and the fluid movement of people around the world (Robertson 1992, 58–9).

Public attention and debate focused intensely on globalization beginning in the eighties as people became keenly aware of its impact on their daily lives and on the environment. One of the debates concerns the origin of globalization and whether it is something new or something old. Sociologists Manfred Steger (2003) and Peter Beyer (2006b) argue that if we consider globalization as a phenomenon which has its roots in the development of modern technology, then it is fair to conclude that it began in the West about five centuries ago. This development in the West eventually spread to the rest of the world by way of Western imperialism and capitalism, which influenced economic, social, cultural, and political relations around the world. However, if we consider globalization as awareness of increased communication around the globe, then this process has been evolving since the dawn of humanity (Steger 2003, 17–18; Beyer 2006b, 29). With respect to religion, I agree with Beyer that globalization has its roots in the Western world. Western imperialism, a result of Western technological advances, carried with it Christianity during the nineteenth and the early part of the twentieth centuries, eventually influencing religious traditions around the world (Beyer 2006b, 29).

Moreover, globalization is not merely Americanization, as frequently thought by the public, nor is it a homogeneous process. In other words, it is not a one-way spread of Western ideologies to the rest of the world; the West also has been enormously transformed in the process. Furthermore, Robertson points out that globalization is not a homogeneous process because certain aspects of particular cultures resist outside influences and prevent total assimilation into the group culture. Robertson identifies this phenomenon as the interpenetration of the local and the global, a dynamic interplay of give and take between the particular and the group culture (Robertson 1992, 113). In the present analysis, the study of globalization, therefore, is the study of a continuously emerging global culture which exerts its influence over all individual cultures throughout the world (Beyer 1994, 9). Beyer argues that, due to this process, religious traditions in the world cannot be understood on their own without situating them within the social, historical context from which they emerged (Beyer 1998).

GLOBALIZATION AND THE SOCIAL AND POLITICAL UPHEAVAL IN MODERN CHINA

Until the early part of the twentieth century, China was under the imperial rule of the Qing dynasty (1644–1911). Western capitalist expansion into China began around the end of the eighteenth century, and with it came a large number of Christian missionaries. Western imperialism accelerated in the nineteenth century culminating in the First Opium War (1839–1842). This war was the result of China's resistance to the British effort to import, and eventually smuggle, opium into China in exchange for Chinese silk and tea. China's defeat resulted in the signing of the Treaty of Nanjing (1842), yielding certain territorial and trading rights to Britain, including the ceding of Hong Kong as a colony. Even though the Chinese pride themselves as the inventors of firearms as early as the twelfth century, the modern technological advances in Europe and the Industrial Revolution in the late eighteenth and early nineteenth centuries had rendered Chinese weapons obsolete. This technological disadvantage, along with the weak Qing government, made China particularly attractive to Western imperialism. From 1838 to 1900 China experienced numerous defeats during foreign invasions including those by France, Germany, Japan, Austria, Italy, Russia, and the United States. With each defeat China was forced to sign a treaty that gave special territorial and trading rights to the winning nation. For a time it seemed that China was fast degrading into fragments of colonies under foreign domination (Li 1998, 17; Pittman 2001, 13–15).

As a result of this pattern, nationalism and revolutionary spirit increased in China. The first revolution was the Taiping Rebellion (1850–1864). The Taipings were an unorthodox Chinese Christian sect led by Hong Xiuquan (洪秀全, 1814–1864) who promised reform and better economic conditions to desolate peasants. They had suffered the loss of their livelihood due to the import of Western manufactured goods, local political turbulence, and exorbitant taxation. The revolution lasted for fourteen years and the Qing government was able to suppress it only with the help of the French and the British who were interested in keeping that government in place for further economic exploitation.

The Taiping Rebellion was followed by another uprising, the Boxer Rebellion (1900), against foreign domination and Christian influence. Finally, the Qing government was overthrown in 1911 by the Revolutionary Alliance of Sun Yat-sen (孫逸仙, 1866–1925), a Christian trained in Western medicine. But Sun did not succeed in unifying China; the country quickly fell into the control of local warlords. In 1912, the Nationalist Party was established with Sun as its leader and soon engaged in a series of uprisings against the warlords. The main warlords were finally defeated in the Northern Expedition of 1926–1927 although minor warlords remained active. However, the Nationalist Party was soon fighting an internal conflict with the growing number of Communists who were influenced by Russia in the 1920s. For a time the Communists and the Nationalists joined forces to fight against further Japanese invasions from 1937 to 1945. The Second Sino-Japanese War ended in 1945 when Japan was defeated by the Allies in World War II. Soon afterwards, the two parties resumed their conflict which quickly escalated into a civil war in 1946 with the Communist Party winning control over China in 1949 (Li 1998, 16–19, Pittman 2001, 16–21).

THE CHALLENGE OF CHRISTIANITY AND THE REFORM WITHIN THE SANGHA

By the nineteenth century, Chinese Buddhism was in a state of deterioration. In accordance with Buddhist customs regarding compassion, the sangha was open to all comers. Over the centuries it became an asylum for social misfits and even criminals, thus earning the disrespect of the Chinese. Moreover, with the turbulence in China, many parents were forced to present their children to the sangha for their survival. Of the estimated half million monks and two hundred thousand nuns (Welch 1967, 416; Chan 1978, 80; Pittman 2001, 47) in the early part of nineteenth century, few had sound knowledge of Buddhist doctrines. The majority of the sangha made a living by performing death rituals. Masses of the Chinese population, together with the leaders of the Nationalist Party, turned to Christianity upon the arrival of the missionaries who were highly educated, many equipped with Chinese language skills, and who actively engaged in charitable activities in society (Chen 1973, 449–54; Chan 1978, 80–2, Pittman 2001, 28–38).

Yang Wenhui (楊文會, 1837–1911) is esteemed as the father of modern Chinese Buddhism. His work on the revival of Buddhism in the latter part of the nineteenth century was a reaction to Buddhism's encounter with Christianity. For example, Yang's establishment of a Buddhist printing house was the direct result of the destruction of Daoist and Buddhist temples and scriptures by the Taiping rebels, who believed that the Christian God tolerated no rivals. Moreover, Yang developed the Jetavana hermitage to train the Chinese sangha for overseas missionary work, directly inspired by Christian methods. Yang stands out in modern Chinese Buddhism for being the first lay teacher to teach the sangha; among his students were the famous Taixu and the outstanding lay educator Ouyang Jingwu (歐陽竟無, 1871–1943). Yang also invited the famed Tiantai master Dixian (諦閑, 1858–1932) to serve as a faculty member (Welch 1968, 1–22; Pittman 2001, 40–5).

Taixu (太虛, 1890–1947) is famed as the "St. Paul of modern Chinese Buddhism" (Pittman 2001, 59). Throughout his life he used the traditional concepts of Buddhist thought to confront the crisis created by the coming of the West and seek a solution to it. Having witnessed the First and Second World Wars in the course of his lifetime, Taixu was convinced that modern positivistic science had brought about technological advance but had, at the same time, undermined religious claims because of its materialistic bias. This had dire consequences for humanity because it impoverished human consciousness and fuelled the incessant desires of the ego (Skt *tṛṣṇā*). The result was a consumerist culture in the West, the evil behind capitalism and imperialism which led to international conflicts that threatened to destroy humanity. Taixu was convinced that the Mahayana emphasis on the spiritual understanding of reality and the Bodhisattva ideal of selfless service to humanity would be a potent aid to countering the force of such destructive greed. The Bodhisattva, according to Taixu, understands the nature of ultimate reality (Skt *dharmakāya*); it appears as emptiness (Skt *śūnyatā*) but is in fact the force that creates the phenomenal world including each and every one of us. In this cosmological view, there is no separate independent ego, as all persons are interconnected at the deepest level. Taixu uses the analogy of waves connected to the sea. In consequence, there is no individual victory to be won; harming others is the same as harming oneself, since everybody else is an extension of our larger cosmic self. The Mahayana Bodhisattva ideal, Taixu argued, is translated into an ethic that extends beyond the boundaries of race and nationality, and this alone can ensure lasting peace in the world (Pittman 2001, 105–52; Taixu 1947/1989, 7–66).

Taixu's aspiration for a new sangha was very much a revival of the Buddhism of Yang Wenhui. Taixu envisioned a new sangha of highly educated monks and nuns who would be actively engaged in spreading the dharma globally. He thus pushed to reform the sangha from its traditional other-worldly emphasis and habitually reclusive nature. The new sangha that Taixu envisioned would consist of monks and nuns who had an education that reached beyond the traditional Buddhist study of scriptures. The new sangha would consist of men and women who were well acquainted with social and political affairs, understood the impact of modern science, and accepted cultural differences. They would also be equipped with language skills in order to adapt to a new global culture and provide valuable service to humanity.

Furthermore, Taixu advocated a kind of purified Buddhism free of religious Daoist practices such as divination, astrology, and spirit mediumship. Such practices had come to be viewed by the public as particularly superstitious due to the influence of Western positivistic science. The new Buddhism according to Taixu was to be scientific, humanistic, and socially engaged in order to catch up with modernity. Taixu was also the first person to realize the power of a centrally controlled organization in the global development of Buddhism. Until this time a national Buddhist church in China had never been formed, but he pushed for the development of such an organization based on the Christian model (Chen 1964/1973, 455–7: Chan 1978, 55–9, Pittman 2001, 59–152).

Holmes Welch is careful to point out that Taixu was often ridiculed as an idealist and did not win the support of the majority of the sangha (Welch 1968, 53–71). However, Taixu did win the support of some of his contemporaries in reviving Buddhist studies, notably Venerable Tanxu (倓虛, 1875–1963). Tanxu, a student of Dixian, was a well-known monk in modern China who was actively involved in restoring Buddhism, particularly the Tiantai sect in northern China. Tanxu revived several smaller monasteries destroyed by the Taipings and built several large monasteries including the famous Cham Shan Monastery in Qingdao (1931) which had about one hundred students enrolled in the study of Buddhist doctrines (Welch 1968, 96–7). Historians Kenneth Chen, Wing-tsit Chan, and Don Pittman all observe that Chinese Buddhism began to show signs of a revival under the vigorous efforts of Taixu and a number of his contemporaries, including Tanxu, Xuyun (虛雲, 1840–1959), Ouyang Jingwu, and Yinguang (印光, 1861–1940) among others. Many scriptural presses were established together with the building of Buddhist institutions. More importantly, the modern characteristics of Chinese Buddhism were established, namely, Buddhism freed of the traditional preoccupation with death rituals, a return to the study of Buddhist doctrines, and the involvement of the laity in the spreading of the dharma. Taixu stands out in modern Chinese Buddhism as a monastic who openly affirmed the attainments of the laity as equivalent to the sangha, given the same amount of effort and dedication, and actively encouraged the laity in the spreading of the dharma (Chen 1964, 455–7; Chan 1978, 55–92; Pittman 2001, 59–152; Taixu 1947/1989, 64–6).

The success of these Buddhist seminaries was reflected in the number of knowledgeable monks and laymen who emerged during this period. Although Taixu himself did not appear to accomplish much in his own lifetime, his ideas inspired many monks who went on to put them into practice. The entire movement known today as Humanistic Buddhism in Taiwan and Hong Kong started with Taixu. Taixu inspired directly or indirectly prominent monastics such as Yinshun (印順, 1906–2005) who, at the time of his death, was revered as one of the most prominent monks in the Chinese Buddhist world, Shengyan (聖嚴, 1930–2009), a scholar-monk and highly respected leader of the Dharma Drum organization, and Cheng Yen (證嚴, 1937–), the charismatic founder of the Tzu Chi Foundation (Pittman 2001, 255–98). Most importantly, Master Hsing Yun (Xingyun), a young contemporary of Taixu, adopted much of his ideology while he was in China; he later went to Taiwan and established the Fo Guang Shan following Taixu's vision.

With the victory of the Communist Party, many monks congregated in Hong Kong and Taiwan, and some eventually aspired to spread the dharma to the West. Three of Tanxu's students, Masters Sing Hung (性空, 1924–), Shing Cheung (誠祥, 1920–2006), and Lok To (樂渡, 1923–), came to Canada and established the Cham Shan Temple in Toronto in memory of the monastery in Qingdao. Thus, the Cham Shan Temple is in the second generation of the Buddhist reform movement begun by Taixu. Cham Shan appears to be a "traditional" Chinese Buddhist temple which, people assume, is adapting Chinese Buddhism to a Western environment. Little do people realize that Chinese Buddhism first encountered Western culture in China and underwent a major reform during the mid-twentieth century. The adaptations which Cham Shan is making in Canada are minor local adjustments in comparison.

THE FOUNDING OF CHAM SHAN (湛山精舍): THE FIRST CHINESE TEMPLE IN CANADA

Cham Shan Temple in Toronto is the earliest Chinese temple in Canada. It was established by Masters Sing Hung, Shing Cheung, and Lok To in the 1960s. The Chinese community credits these three monks with founding Chinese Buddhism in Canada.

Master Sing Hung was born in 1924 in Hebei Province in China. In 1937, when the Second Sino-Japanese War spread to Hebei, his studies were interrupted. The next year, on the advice of his father, he became a novice under Master Zhi Yuan. He was fully ordained at sixteen under Master Xianming and studied at Fayuan Temple Seminary. In 1943, he went to Cham Shan Temple Seminary in Qingdao and studied under Tanxu. He graduated in three years and worked afterwards as an administrator in the temple. In the winter of 1948, he went to visit Master Zhi Yuan in Nanjing. While he was returning to the temple via Shanghai, the Civil War was spreading to Qingdao. He was hesitant about whether to return when he met Lok To, another classmate. Lok To, along with other masters, was on an assignment to set up a Buddhist seminary in Hong Fa Temple in Hong Kong. Sing Hung went with them. As monks were unpopular under Marxist ideology, Tanxu had moved to Hong Kong after the victory of the Communists in 1949 and had begun teaching at the newly established Hua Nan Buddhist Seminary. This move gave Master Sing Hung another opportunity to further his studies under Tanxu (Yu 1996, 299–300).

Master Shing Cheung was born in 1920 in Ningjin County of Shandong Province. He was a trader in herbal medicine in Harbin when he was young. After the Second Sino-Japanese War ended in 1945, he went to a dharma discourse given by Tanxu in Tianjin. For Shing Cheung this was an awakening experience; he immediately took refuge with Tanxu and aspired to be a monk. In 1946 with Tanxu's recommendation he became a novice at Dabei Temple and received full ordination the next year. In 1949, he moved to Hong Kong and, in 1952, he enrolled in the Hua Nan Buddhist Seminary, where he graduated in three years. In 1957, he had an opportunity to further his study in Burma (Myanmar) for another year. Afterwards, Shing Cheung worked closely with the other masters to spread the dharma in Hong Kong before coming to Canada (Yu 1996, 300–1).

Master Lok To was born in 1923 in the Xiao County of Anhui Province. He became a novice at the age of ten. At nineteen he received full ordination and began his study at Cham Shan Buddhist Seminary. Lok To was influenced by the teachings of Taixu. He was also inspired by Professor Liang Jingxing about the potential of spreading the dharma in the West in the aftermath of the Second World War. He studied English in preparation and arrived in San Francisco in 1963, shortly after Masters Miao Feng and Hsuan Hua, to promote the dharma in North America.[3] After his arrival, he tried to purify the syncretic nature of Chinese religions as practised overseas where deities in the Daoist pantheon were placed together with Buddhist figures in the same temple. In 1964, Lok To established the Buddhist Association of the United States, where he acted as chairman, and the Dajue Temple, where he served as abbot for ten years. In 1974, he organized the North America Sutra Translation Society and dedicated himself to the translation of Chinese Mahayana texts (Yu 1996, 144–6).

In 1967, Lok To invited Masters Sing Hung and Shing Cheung to visit North America. Because Montreal was hosting the World Expo, they came to Canada. In Montreal, they met Mrs Yingjin Yutang, founder of the North American Buddhist Association. She was concerned that despite the increased number of Chinese in Toronto there was no proper temple. She urged the monks to stay in Canada and pledged to provide full support of their daily expenses. Initially, they rented various places for gatherings but soon the followers grew in number and they decided that it was time to purchase a permanent facility. They bought 100 Southill Drive in 1968, renamed it Nan Shan (Ch. South Hill) Temple, and applied for registration under the name Buddhist Association of Canada (Yu 1996, 301–3). Master Lok To, Master Sing Hung, and Master Shing Cheung were later honoured as co-founders of the temple.

Ho Nansang and Ho Nanji, two other students of Tanxu, donated a piece of property in 1973 and the monks soon fundraised to establish the current temple at 7254 Bayview Avenue in Thornhill. After many expansions the temple currently occupies three acres of land. The design models the traditional Chinese monastery of an ancient palace within a garden. As the number of followers rapidly grew, they decided to buy a property near the subway station for the convenience of people who did not own a car. In 1984 they bought a 20,000-square-foot restaurant (including basement) at 1330 Bloor St West and renamed it Hong Fa (Ch. Dharma Transmission) Temple. In the 1990s they established the 30,000-square-foot Cham Shan Buddhist Library at 1224 Lawrence Avenue West, under the leadership of lay supporters, to extend the dharma to the English-speaking world. By 2001 they had established the Ten Thousand Buddhas Temple of Peace with huge Buddhist statues at Niagara Falls. In recent years, they have also established the Cham Shan Buddhist Seminary in Toronto, the first Chinese Buddhist seminary to train clergy in Canada. There are now impressive temple structures in Toronto and neighbouring areas of Hamilton, Maple, and Bethany.[4]

The Role of the Cham Shan Temple

The Cham Shan Temple is a branch of the Tiantai Buddhist sect in China. It is a place to learn the Buddhist dharma, particularly the Tiantai doctrines, as well as a place to increase one's merit according to the Buddhist karmic law of cause and effect. When I did my fieldwork, Masters Sing Hung and Shing Cheung would give a discourse after every religious ceremony. They also regularly invited Lok To to give discourses on the dharma. The primary teaching of this temple is the Mahayana concept of emptiness. Emptiness, as mentioned previously, is not a mere absence, nothingness, but a fullness of creative principle that makes manifest the phenomenal world. *The Heart Sūtra,* which is frequently recited in the temple during all the ceremonies, reads: "form is emptiness and the very emptiness is form, emptiness does not differ from form, form does not differ from emptiness" (Conze 1958, 86). According to this belief, any dualistic separation of life from death is an illusion. The temple teaches that not only is our every prayer heard by our own Buddha consciousness, but our ancestors, too, can benefit from our good intentions to move to a better existence.

The monks begin their morning prayer rituals at 5:00 a.m. in the main temple hall, together with a special dedication to world peace. The temple organizes religious ceremonies during major Buddhist festivals and on the first and the fifteenth days of the month according to the traditional Chinese calendar. It also has a special Kṣitigarbha Hall for the installation of ancestral tablets for special prayer ceremonies and hosts rituals almost daily for the appreciative families who wish to honour their recently deceased beloved. For the general public who wish to seek some guidance from Guanyin[5] or petition for a specific goal, it offers a divination service at the Guanyin Hall and people can do promissory sacrifices at the Mahābrahmā shrine in the garden.[6] In addition, the temple has several comprehensive Buddhist libraries and publishes a quarterly journal, *Prajña*, on Buddhism. The temple also gives away free audio books, mantra machines, and booklets of Buddhist teachings. There are sutra books and exegeses by various masters of the sutras, including Taixu's commentaries, which were donated by the laity in Hong Kong and Taiwan.

The primary texts used in the temple are the traditional Mahayana Buddhist texts, namely, the *Lotus Sūtra*, the *Pure Land Sūtras*, the *Heart Sūtra*, the *Diamond Sūtra*, and the *Śūraṅgama Sūtra* among others. During my fieldwork, besides the three elderly masters who regularly gave discourses and exegesis on the sutras, there was also a lay teacher, Ms Liang Kai-miao, who gave Pure Land teachings to the laity and the younger nuns within the temple. However, the practice of the laity teaching to the sangha is a new development in modern Chinese Buddhism starting with Yang Wenhui, as mentioned above. In the Cham Shan Buddhist Library at Lawrence Avenue, the laity also assist in organizing classes on various aspects of Chinese culture and give video classes on the teachings of Thich Nhat Hanh. The temple also allows the Vipassana Foundation to use their premises for day-long meditative retreats.

The Monastic Order
The Cham Shan complex has about twenty monks and nuns. The elderly nuns mostly help in the kitchen since they have not received any formal Buddhist education. The younger clergy either have an education from a foreign uni-

versity or are sent to Taiwan to study in Buddhist colleges. Cham Shan follows the traditional Buddhist practice that anybody can join the sangha; there are no formal selection criteria for acceptance into the temple and all applicants are judged individually by the masters based on their capabilities and their suitability to adapt to temple life, which often involves a lot of hard work and frugal living.

The election of the abbot is also not based on seniority but individual capabilities. For example, in 2003 the elderly monks jointly elected a new abbot, Master Dayi (達義). Dayi was born in 1967 in Guangdong Province and received formal Buddhist education and taught Buddhist doctrines in China. In 1991 Master Lok To invited Dayi to New York, and under his mentorship Dayi enrolled in City University of New York in 1997. Dayi received his Bachelor degree in psychology and Asian studies in 2001 and a Masters degree in Asian history from the same university in 2003. In the summer of 2003, he received the transmission of the Tiantai lineage and in the winter of the same year he was invited to Toronto by the elderly monks and the title of abbot was conferred upon him.[7]

During my fieldwork, I found that many Chinese immigrants appreciate the Cham Shan Temple because it is familiar to them. The architecture, the rituals, the teachings are similar to other Tiantai temples which are predominant in Hong Kong, China, and Taiwan. It is also a source of pride in Markham, among other distinguished places of worship. Many respond to the teachings of emptiness and nonattachment as constantly explained by the masters. These precepts help them to let go of unpleasant situations in life and to be skeptical of any dogma. With his election as the new abbot, Master Dayi actively engages in spreading the dharma to the community and extends his teachings to Caucasians. His activities contribute to the modernization of Chinese Buddhism and have resulted in a marked increase in the English presence in the temple and on the Internet.

FO GUANG SHAN (佛光山)

The Fo Guang Shan (Ch. The Buddha Light Mountain) in Ottawa is part of a global network of temples named Fo Guang Shan, which was established by Venerable Hsing Yun (星雲) in Taiwan in the 1960s. The temple group is the most famous strand of Chinese Buddhism in the world. Master Hsing Yun was born in Jiangsu province in China in 1927. According to the biography translated by Amy Lui-Ma, Hsing Yun's mother had an auspicious dream during her labour; when the child was born, he had unusual birth marks. Hsing Yun's mother interpreted these signs as showing the child to be an incarnation of an extraordinary being with a mission in life (Lui-Ma 2000, 7). As a boy Hsing Yun was influenced by his grandmother who was a Buddhist and a meditator. Hsing Yun's father was a businessman. He disappeared during one of his trips when China was engulfed in war. Hsing Yun was only twelve years old when he went with his mother in search of his father, but when he came into contact with Buddhist monks he aspired to become a monk. He soon joined the sangha. Life was hard as a novice and food was scarce during the war. This did not change his mind. As a young monk he showed a proclivity for reading and devoured not only Buddhist texts but also Chinese literature and translated works of Western thought (Lui-Ma 2000, 19–32).

In 1945, while studying in Jiaoshan Buddhist College in Zhenjiang City, Hsing Yun came across the teachings of the Buddhist reformer Taixu. He was well aware of the decay of the sangha during this time and was particularly inspired by Taixu's call for reform (Lui-Ma 2000, 39–40). Later, when Hsing Yun became the principal of White Pagoda Primary School in 1947, he constantly contemplated ways to support Taixu's visions of a new sangha and the global migration of Chinese Buddhism. Hsing Yun wrote many articles to bring Taixu's ideals to the Buddhist community and started the journal *Raging Bellows*. He called for reforms and urged the sangha to return to the study of Buddhist doctrines (Lui-Ma 2000, 41). Taixu died in 1947 on the eve of the Communist victory. In 1949, after the Nationalist Party's defeat by the Communists, Hsing Yun left with seventy fellow monks and two million Nationalist Party loyalists and went to Taiwan. His intention was to preserve the dharma and to further propagate Taixu's ideal even though China was unreceptive. After an initial difficulty in settling in Taiwan, where monks were unpopular because of the influence of Western positivistic science and the fact that most of the leaders of the Nationalist Party were Christians, he began to attract a following in Illan, Taiwan (Lee 1990, xvii; Lui-Ma 2000, 42–3).

Hsing Yun relentlessly pushed for the modernization of Buddhism and the formation of a new sangha. He wrote many articles and appeared on the Central Broadcasting Station as well. After close to two decades of dedicated effort, he finally founded the Shou-shan Buddhist College in 1965 and established the Fo Guang Shan (FGS) complex in 1967 in Kaohsiung, southern Taiwan (Lui-Ma 2000, 95–106). The multi-functional Taiwanese complex of Fo Guang Shan time. Lu began having extraordinary religious experiences as an adult and changed his religious orientation. In 1975, he published his first book, *Encounters with the World of Spirits*, and instantly became famous. He is a prolific writer and has over 189 books in print[8] many of them dealing with his mystical experiences and his understanding of various religious traditions. Some of these texts are now available in English including *Encounters with the World of Spirits*, *Talks by a Living Buddha*, and *Detailed Exposition of the True Buddha Tantric Dharma* (Liu 2005, 195–6).

Lu attracted a large following soon after the publication of his first book; many readers were fascinated by his description of the spirit world. The group was originally known as Lien Shen (Ch. Spiritual Immortal) sect in 1975, but the name was changed to Lien Shen True Buddha School in 1984 and afterwards to True Buddha School.

Lu claimed as part of his spiritual quest that he had been learning from many teachers in both human and spirit forms. Initially a Christian, he turned to Daoism due to his mystical experiences as an adult; eventually he studied Mahayana Buddhism and finally settled in Tibetan Buddhism. He urged his students to honour all his teachers, even those who resided in the spirit realms including Sir Three Mountains Nine Realms and the Daoist Hermit of Purity. He declared that he had studied under and received empowerments from a host of Tibetan teachers and received initiation by Buddha Śakyamuni, Amitābha, Maitreya, and Padmasambhava in his visions. His attainments were recognized by some Tibetan lamas, including H.H. Ganden Tripa of the Shavagon Monastery and Rinpoche Amchor of the Amdo Monastery (Liu 2005, 196–7).

Master Lu is esteemed by his followers as possessing great psychic and healing powers. He explains that, out of his compassion, he cultivated these powers for alleviating suffering as a tool to help people to develop faith. He is reported to be able to cure people of diverse diseases including cancers, ulcers, tumours, psychoses, and other handicaps. Many of these miraculous cures were documented in the publications of the TBS (*Purple Lotus Journal*, May-June 1993, 48–50; Winter 1997, 27).

Master Lu is also famous for the Chinese art of feng shui, the art of the proper siting of cities, homes, and graves in harmony with their environment. Lu believes strongly that unseen forces in our environment, including energy and symbols (landscapes, architectural designs, belongings), have positive or

is designed like a traditional Chinese monastery and resembles an ancient palace. However, the temple is equipped with the latest technology. The complex provides a multitude of social, educational, and charitable facilities, including a museum, a secondary school, a Buddhist college, a nursery, and a cemetery. It is a popular place for Buddhist pilgrims and a vibrant tourist centre.

Fo Guang Shan is one of the most successful strands of Chinese Buddhism around the world. Since its establishment, it has founded and currently operates sixteen Buddhist colleges, three universities, one hundred temples, and 180 associated centres globally. Hsing Yun has received many honours for outstanding public service from the government of the Republic of China (Taiwan) and honorary doctorates from various universities globally. Fo Guang Shan currently has 1,300 monks and nuns and its structure resembles that of a papal hierarchy (Chandler 2004, 70–1). The central controlling unit, the Committee of Religious Affairs, with the abbot at its head, supervises the training and the placement of the monks and nuns overseas. The abbot and the committee members are elected once every six years under a democratic system (Lui-Ma 2000, 138–42). In 1985, Hsing Yun resigned from the post of abbot after serving three consecutive terms, and the group has had seven transfers in leadership since; the current abbot (since 2005) is Master Hsin Pei.

Soon after Hsing Yun resigned from the post of abbot, he started the Buddha Light International Association (BLIA) as the lay extension of the sangha. The idea was to transfer some of the responsibilities of spreading the dharma to the laity (Lui-Ma 2000, 258). From my observation, this move was strategic in the overseas development of the group, as in the case of Toronto and Ottawa. The laity can take the lead in setting up a centre and when they have enough support they invite Fo Guang Shan to establish a formal temple.

Fo Guang Shan in North America

As early as the 1970s Hsing Yun had already noticed the multicultural nature of California and the need for a Chinese temple. He sent some of his clergy to California in the eighties and soon established the Pei Ta (Ch. White Pagoda) Temple with monetary support from Taiwan. With the rapid increase of followers this soon led to a grander project. In 1988, with the global support of Fo Guang members, he organized the Hsi Lai Temple in Hacienda Heights, southern California. This temple, which is the largest Chinese temple in North America, cost more than $30million (Lui-Ma 2000, 239–44; Lin 1996).

The Hsi Lai Temple became a stepping stone for the development of the Fo

Guang group in North America. In 1991, there was a huge influx of Chinese immigrants into Canada, particularly from Hong Kong, in the face of the pending return of Hong Kong from a British colony to mainland China in 1997. Some members of the Fo Guang Shan in Toronto established the BLIA to better serve the community. By 1994 they were already strong enough to build a temple at 6525 Millcreek Drive in Mississauga (part of the Greater Toronto Area). The $7 million Fo Guang Shan Temple of Toronto is the most impressive Chinese temple in Canada. The group has now established temples in Vancouver, Ottawa, Montreal, and Edmonton (Liu 2005, 169–70).

The Toronto temple provided a foundation for missionary work into the neighbouring areas. Ottawa had a very small Chinese community until the 1990s. In 1971 there were only 3,060 members and by 2001 the number had increased to 30,240 (Statistics Canada 1976, 6; 2006). Moreover, many of these Chinese were Christians. Until the establishment of the BLIA there was no Chinese Buddhist temple in Ottawa. The only place available was a meditation centre organized by Master Yunfeng (雲峰) on Somerset Street shortly before the BLIA was established in 1996. Master Yunfeng had a small following of about twenty people; however, within a few months he moved to Halifax due to insufficient funding to organize a proper temple.

Many of my informants told me that before the establishment of BLIA they did not have any spiritual guidance. Some mechanically followed the Chinese traditions of having shrines for an Earth Deity and Guanyin in the house and of venerating ancestors. They did this without knowing the meaning of these practices. Many also tried Christianity but found that its philosophy conflicted with their beliefs. The public lectures given by the Fo Guang masters in various community centres were an eye-opening experience. To many it was like tasting the nectar in life and they definitely wanted more. Shortly afterwards, in 1996 they established a centre at 886 Somerset Street West under a lay director, Victor Leung, a civil servant. He constantly invited masters and lay teachers to give dharma talks and to host religious ceremonies (Liu 2005, 170–4).

Eventually some followers expressed the desire for masters to host the ceremonies regularly as the laity were not trained to do so. Soon afterwards, Fo Guang Shan sent two nuns, Masters I-yu and Yong Do, to Ottawa. Shortly after the two nuns arrived, they began to urge the local community to purchase a permanent place for a centre rather than pay rent every month. There was some concern as they were a relatively small group, but the masters intensified their missionary activities and started fundraising. Eventually, they had sup-

port from the local community and also from members of branches in Toronto, Montreal, Taiwan, and Hong Kong. By 2000, they had established a temple at 1950 Scott Street. The temple was housed inside a modern two-storey office building of about 4,000 square feet. The total cost of the building was $400,000 (including structure and renovation), modest compared to other Fo Guang Shan temples but already a source of pride among the local Chinese. It was also a source of amazement among the local Buddhist community as the group was relatively new. For the opening ceremony in May 2000, the temple invited the head abbot of Fo Guang Shan, Hsin Ting, Mr Richard Patten, an MPP in Ottawa, and Mr S.T. Shen, a senior executive of the Taipei Economic and Cultural Office. The practice of inviting politicians on major temple occasions is a special characteristic of Fo Guang Shan; it reflects Master Hsing Yun's philosophy that a warm relationship with politicians will aid in the spreading of the dharma (Liu 2005, 175–83). Shortly after the opening ceremony, Masters I-yu and Yong Do were transferred to other temples of the Fo Guang Group and the temple has been under the guidance of Master Miao Tsun (妙遵) since 2001.

The temple is a place of Buddhist learning and cultural activities. The organization of Chinese festivals and cultural shows along with traditional Buddhist ceremonies is also a special feature of FGS. It reflects Master Hsing Yun's ideal of humanistic Buddhism and the affirmation of the joy and sacredness of life. The group also pays particular respect to the elderly on every occasion in accordance with Chinese custom. Most of the teachings of the group are centred on the Buddhist concept of cause and effect, the doctrine of impermanence, nonattachment, and the Bodhisattva path. Fo Guang Shan practises a socially engaged form of Buddhism which is radically different from the traditional Buddhist practice of focusing on the suffering of life, manifested in seclusion from society and looking forward to a reward in an afterlife in the Pure Land.

THE TRUE BUDDHA SCHOOL (真佛宗)

The True Buddha School in Montreal is part of the global True Buddha School (TBS) network. The True Buddha School was found by Master Lu who is honoured as the Living Buddha Lian Shan (蓮生) among his followers. Born in 1945, he is a native of Taiwan Chiayi County. He was a Christian as a boy. He later graduated in land surveying and worked for the civil service for some

negative effects on human lives. He develops ways to increase the positive while eliminating the negative.

In 1982, Lu declared that he had received instructions from the spirit realm to go to Seattle. After this oracle, eight families of close disciples moved with Lu and his wife and two children to Seattle. With the help of the close disciples and True Buddha School members globally, they soon established the Rey Tsang (Ch. Thunderstorm) Temple in Redmond, near Seattle. It is a half million dollar property situated at 17012 NE Fortieth Court, Redmond, Washington. The temple houses a host of Daoist, Mahayana Buddhist, and Tantric deities. In 1986, Lu ordained himself to become a monk[9] and started his world travels to spread the True Buddha School Dharma (Liu 2005, 197–8).

The True Buddha School is a controversial group among the Chinese sangha due to Lu's innumerable claims in his writings and lectures to extraordinary religious experiences and spiritual attainments. Lu admits that in the course of his career he has received massive criticism particularly from the dominant Chinese Buddhist sangha. However, he claims that his mystical experience when he was twenty-six years old – of a visit to the Double Lotus Ponds in Pure Land where he encountered his celestial body Padmakumāra (Skt for Lotus Boy) – sustains him in his work (*Purple Lotus Journal* July–September 1993, 7). Moreover, Master Lu and his disciples also believe that rather than treating these experiences in the traditional Buddhist way, as illusion and therefore unimportant,[10] they should be treasured and shared among the followers and with the public. This communication would counteract the influence of positivistic science, reinforce each other's faith in the practice, and lead to a more complete and better understanding of human religious phenomena.

According to Lu, the ultimate goal of practice is to return to our Buddha nature and attain the Pure Land which is a realm within our consciousness; this means that there is no need for an outside quest. He also believes that the endless disputes among religious traditions are due to the exclusive nature of sectarian bias. This exclusiveness results in an improper understanding of other religious traditions and eventually causes prejudice. He argues that the Four Persecutions of Buddhism[11] in Chinese history were due to the arrogance of the majority of the Buddhist sangha. The sangha believed that they had the highest wisdom and scorned the seemingly lowly practices of the Daoists. This intensified the hostility between the two traditions resulting in the persecutions of Buddhism. Lu sees the many shamanic practices of folk and Daoist origin such as divination, geomancy, astrology, spirit mediumship, and others as ways to lure people onto the path and attract a larger following in the world (Liu 2005, 202–3).

Master Lu also holds that there is no conflict between science and religion because both are children of human imagination. He argues that the public is spiritually confused when it regards some of the practices of the TBS as normal, for example, meditation and prayer, and others, such as divination and burning of paper money[12] as abnormal religious activities. Spiritual insight, he concludes, is gained through an interdisciplinary approach combining philosophy, psychology, sociology, anthropology, and mystical experiences, together with a focus on meditation and direct religious experiences. He also urges practitioners and scientists alike to be radical, to use themselves as subjects to verify the data (Lu 1978, 144–50).

In spite of the worldwide presence of the True Buddha School which currently has 282 chapters (*True Buddha School Net*), Lu advocates group practice but not necessarily the building of temples. He believes that the collective mind present during group practice is optimum in securing one's goal.

The earliest organizations of TBS had no formal structure and some were housed in an apartment or a house or commercial buildings. But the diamond masters (meaning the lineage holders) were handpicked by Master Lu based on a system of astrology and intuition. The masters can be married. Because they are deemed to be incarnated masters, their status is much higher than the monks and nuns in the order. There is no requirement for formal education either. The early masters were mostly converts from other traditions, especially Christianity, since Taiwan is very much influenced by Christianity (*Zilian Yuekan*, January–April 1996, 34). True Buddha School also has a lay extension, the Lotus Light Charitable Association, which does charity work. The laity do not host any religious ceremonies because they are not trained to do so.

True Buddha School Comes to Canada

The earliest temple of the TBS in Canada is the PTT Buddhist Society (formerly Pu Te Town) at 514 Keefer Street, Vancouver, British Columbia. With 6,000 square feet including the basement, it was converted from a Christian church and modelled after the Potala Palace in Lhasa. The second temple in Canada was the Ling Shen Ching Tze Temple (Jim Sim Branch) at 18 Trojan Gate, Unit A&B, Scarborough, Ontario inside a commercial building. The TBS currently has eleven chapters in Canada.[13]

The Montreal Chan Hai Lei Zang Temple, where I have done most of my fieldwork, was singlehandedly established by Diamond Master Lien Shih, a middle-aged housewife. It was originally inside an apartment building at Queen Mary and Snowdon Streets and when the number of followers increased they moved to the present address at 125 rue Charlotte in 1993. The temple hosts the same kind of deities as the Rey Tsang temple. Moreover, in accordance with the practice of TBS, in the middle of the shrine is a statue of Master Lu adorned with a white scarf symbolizing the group's belief that it is through Master Lu's spiritual guidance and intervention that attainments are made easily available because he has already walked the path (Liu 2005, 208–10).[14]

One of the principal practices of the group is the Guru Yoga based on the visualization of Padmakumāra, the *saṃbhogakāya* (Skt celestial body) of Master Lu. According to Lu the practice may evoke many religious experiences but ultimately it will lead to the realization of nirvana[15] and the understanding that as all the deities and realms are within the consciousness of the practitioner, there is no need for an outside quest. Therefore, the Guru Yoga is the beginning and the culmination of all the practices.[16]

Another important practice of the group is the recitation of the *High King Avalokiteśvara Sūtra*. The sutra describes a mandala of deities in all the cardinal points and the open space. Master Lu and many of his disciples attest to the efficacy of the sutra because of the numerous spiritual beings invoked. This sutra apparently has a Daoist origin and is used by Daoist groups like Fung Loy Kok in Toronto, but not by other Buddhist groups. Other practices of the group include the use of geomancy and various visualization practices to attract prosperity in one's life.

The temple offers a range of services to improve one's merit and ward off negativity. Besides the traditional Buddhist Bright Light Offerings and tablets for the ancestors in the temple, it has offerings for the Guardian of the Chinese Zodiac and the Year as practised by the Daoists.

GLOBALIZATION AND MODERN CHINESE BUDDHISM

Globalization in the nineteenth and early part of the twentieth centuries led to severe social and political upheaval in China, together with a significant influx of foreign ideologies and religious practices into China – Marxism, positivistic science, and Christianity, for example. This juxtaposition of different ideologies in modern China imposed severe challenges on Chinese Buddhism and inspired religious leaders, notably Yang Wenhui and Taixu, to initiate reforms. Moreover, the reformer Taixu vigorously promoted the global development of Chinese Buddhism as a Chinese effort to promote world peace in the face of global crisis (Pittman 2001, 105–52). Due to these changes within the tradition, according to some historians, a modern Chinese Buddhism was formed. It is a Buddhism that is freer than the traditional Buddhism, which was seen as engaging in mechanical rituals. Modern Chinese Buddhism encourages the increased involvement of laity in the spreading of the dharma. It is an engaged Buddhism that is similar to the Christian model (Chen 1964, 455–60; Chan 1978, 55–92; Pittman 2001, 59–152). My research confirms that these features are an expression of modern Chinese Buddhism, most notable in the development of Fo Guang Shan by Master Hsing Yun, a movement which accounts for Chinese Buddhism's global success. One obvious local example is the success of FGS in Ottawa, where it has succeeded in establishing a temple within a short time where other Chinese groups have failed.

But as Robertson has pointed out, there are always aspects of a particular culture that are resistant to outside pressure for change. During Taixu's time there were already many monks who opposed his forward-looking reforms. The monks also ridiculed Taixu's dabbling in politics as a way to gain international recognition for Chinese Buddhism; this was not suitable for a monk (Welch 1968, 71; Pittman 2001, 152). I found in conducting the present study that Master Hsing Yun has often been criticized by some Buddhists under the same charge. There still are conservative members of the clergy and the laity who admire monks like Masters Xuyun, Dixian, Tanxu, and Yinguang. These monks wanted to reform Chinese Buddhism, not by Westernizing, but by going back to Buddhist scriptural studies and the spreading of the dharma. They also adhered to the ancient tradition and remained otherworldly and aloof from political affairs. This conservative tradition is very much alive and remains the guiding principle of the present Cham Shan Temple in Toronto where the masters are students of Tanxu.

Confucianism and Daoism: Other Cultural Constraints

Throughout Buddhism's long history of assimilation into Chinese culture, there were two important aspects of Chinese culture, Confucianism and Daoism, which were constantly in conflict with Buddhism, resulting in frequent disputes and even massive persecutions of Buddhism. Throughout the centuries there were various efforts within China to harmonize the three traditions. According to scholars such as Arthur Wright, starting from 900 CE to the present there have been significant borrowings of Buddhist ideas by Daoist practitioners, particularly the idea of the karmic law of cause and effect. Likewise, Buddhist clergy with little education and organization often served the role of a popular shaman (Wright 1990, 29–32). On the surface, one could conclude that the sangha had degenerated into monks dabbling in healing and astrology. However, there was and still is within Chinese culture the belief in the paranormal as represented by the esoteric arts such as divination, astrology, and geomancy, etc., which are practised by popular religious Daoism.

The consensus belief within the sangha is that our good and bad fortunes are tied to the karmic law of cause and effect. The popular practices of a shaman or a Daoist priest continue to be very much part of Chinese culture. These practices have great popular appeal and are thus tolerated. Prominent monks in the past, such as Master Xuyun, and in the present study Masters Sing Hung and Shing Cheung of the Cham Shan Temple, practised geomancy and included divination halls in the temple, but, following Buddhist doctrines, Master Hsing Yun of Fo Guang Shan does not. Nevertheless, it is clear that none of the clergy in either Cham Shan Temple or Fo Guang Shan serve as psychics and spirit mediums, in accordance with Buddhist teachings.

In my research, Master Lu of the True Buddha School exemplifies the belief in the paranormal within the Chinese world view that is resistant to outside pressure for change. Master Lu is famed for his knowledge of geomancy and psychic abilities, and many of the school's masters are psychics and spirit mediums. Moreover, Daoist practices such as astrology, geomancy, and spirit mediumship are freely practised. The result of the development of the True Buddha School is a new religious movement[17] which has combined Chinese Mahayana Buddhism, Daoism, Tibetan Buddhism, and even some elements of Christianity into its repertoire of belief, and has returned to the global arena as a distinctive form of Chinese syncretism.

CONCLUDING REMARKS

Modern Chinese Buddhism is not, in reality, a homogeneous religion. There are unity and diversity among the three Chinese temples examined in the present study. The unity includes a strong belief in the Pure Land, faithfulness to various Pure Land practices, veneration of Bodhisattva Guanyin, belief in the Buddhist law of cause and effect, and ancestor veneration. The diversity is apparent in the organization of the temples, the recruitment of the clergy, the monastic life, the use of particular texts, the daily rituals, the aspiration of the laity, food preferences, etc. The differences among the temples are so great that there are controversies within the sangha as to what is "authentic" Buddhist practice. On closer examination, these differences can be seen to be the result of the ideological beliefs of the founders responding differently to the global challenge.

In addition, my research shows that Chinese Buddhism is able to respond to issues relevant to the global culture, for example, the enhanced status of women. During my fieldwork, I observed that women spiritual teachers and nuns occupied an important place within the sangha and some temples were headed almost exclusively by nuns, notably, the Fo Guang Shan in Ottawa.

In summary, in this chapter I endeavour to show that Chinese Buddhism in Canada cannot be identified unquestioningly as organizations developed by immigrants to adjust to Canadian society and assert their ethnic identity. Rather, the temples are transnational movements aimed at the global migration of Chinese Buddhism among competing ideologies. The structure of the temples, the nature of their rituals and practices, and the roles of both ordained sangha and lay members can only be properly understood against a global context.

It is still too early to predict whether these groups will survive and prosper in the long term and realize Taixu's dream of the global migration of Chinese Buddhism. However, on reflecting on the social and political upheaval of China in the last two centuries and the resilience of Chinese Buddhism in face of these challenges, I am optimistic about the future development of these temples.

NOTES

1 The current chapter is an adaptation and elaboration of many ideas expressed in my doctoral thesis, "Globalization and Chinese Buddhism: The Canadian Experience" (University of Ottawa, 2005). For this reason, I want to thank my thesis advisers Drs Marie-Françoise Guédon, Peter Beyer, and Charles Laughlin for their guidance. I also want to thank Dr Mary Slade for reading an earlier version of this manuscript. The

research was done in two phases. In 1996–1998, I focused on the Fo Guang Shan group in Ottawa. In 1999–2000, the research focus was on the Cham Shan temple in Toronto and on the True Buddha School in Montreal. In the fall of 2004, while teaching at Concordia University in Montreal, I did some further follow-up research on the True Buddha School. I have taken this opportunity to update the research.

2 The use of Chinese phonetics for proper names follows those used by the individuals, the country, and the organizations themselves. Otherwise, the author uses the pinyin system.

3 Master Miao Feng (妙峰, 1927–) , student of Taixu and Xuyun, the founder of the China Buddhist Association of New York, is esteemed as the first monk to go the United States to spread the Dharma. The second monk went to San Francisco. This was Master Hsuan Hua (宣化, 1918–1995), a student of Xuyun, and the founder of The Sagely City of Ten Thousand Buddhas in Ukiah, California (Yu 1996, 145; Sagely City of Ten Thousand Buddhas).

4 For a complete listing of their addresses, please visit their website www.chamshantemple.org.

5 A Chinese Buddhist Bodhisattva in female form.

6 A shrine in the garden devoted to Mahābrahmā is a popular practice in South East Asia and is known to be particularly effective for the fulfillment of a specific goal. However, not every Buddhist temple has one, and it is absent from both Fo Guang Shan and True Buddha School.

7 See http://www.chamshantemple.org.

8 True Buddha School Net.

9 According to an official biography of Master Lu, "In 1986, the Living Buddha became a monk," but it does not mention who ordained him. Apparently, Lu ordained himself to be a monk (*Zilian Yuekan* 1993, 4).

10 According to the Mahayana viewpoint, only the Absolute is real and all other forms of existence, which include our everyday existence, dreams, and visions, are transient in nature, therefore, are illusory and have no real existence. Moreover, craving for extraordinary experiences in the course of practice is another form of craving that the Buddhist seeks to avoid in order not to promote dissatisfaction (Skt *duḥkha*) in life. In turn, except for the occasional Guanyin's rescue or precognition about death stories, many Buddhist masters do not talk about their religious experiences and if disciples talk about them they are sometimes rebutted. For a complete understanding of this philosophy, please refer to the *Diamond Sūtra* (Conze 1958).

11 The ideological differences between Buddhism, Confucianism, and Daoism resulted in

major conflicts known as "Four Persecutions of Buddhism." Chronologically they occurred in 446 CE, 574 CE, 845 CE, and 955 CE. For detailed description of the conflicts, see Chen (1964, 145–233); Wright (1990, 1–29).

12 A special currency for the unseen realms, available in most Chinese spiritualist and grocery stores in Canada.

13 For a complete listing of their locations please consult www.tbsn.org.

14 See the photograph of Master Lu in Casey's report on the True Buddha School (Casey, n.d.), found on the website of the Montreal Religious Sites Project at http://mrsp.mcgill.ca/reports/html/ChanHai/index.htm.

15 Nirvana, in this context, means realizing the empty nature of existence through the cognition during meditation that all deities are manifestations within one's consciousness and thus attaining the cessation of craving of the phenomenal world.

16 For more details concerning this practice, please consult Liu (2005, 211–13); Liu (1995).

17 For the last two centuries many new religious movements have emerged. According to Fisher (1999) the term "new" does not mean an entirely new religion; rather "new religions" are adaptations or reinterpretations of the established tradition due to modern circumstances. However, they do not constitute the mainstream religious tradition.

The Tzu Chi Merit Society from Taiwan to Canada[1]

ANDRÉ LALIBERTÉ AND MANUEL LITALIEN

Tzu Chi volunteers (in blue and white uniforms) visit
the elderly at the Montreal Chinese Hospital.
Photo courtesy of Tzu Chi Foundation, Montreal

This chapter introduces Tzu Chi Canada, the national branch of a charity organization known among Chinese communities around the world. Tzu Chi is the offshoot of one of the two major ethnic Chinese Buddhist organizations that have developed in Taiwan since the 1960s.[2] Because the chapters by Henry Shiu and Tannie Liu discuss Chinese Buddhism in Canada, we will not cover the ritual dimension of the branch of Mahayana Buddhism with which volunteers from Tzu Chi identify. Our goal is to discuss Tzu Chi specifically as an organization. We want, first, to present it as a case of contemporary lay Buddhist philanthropy. We also want to underline that despite the enormous goodwill and energy that its members are bringing to the functioning of Tzu Chi, considerable obstacles remain in the way of its further expansion in Canada. Finally, we want to emphasize its hybrid nature; it reconciles in its practice the local and the global, tradition and modernity

Tzu Chi is a remarkable expression of an East Asian form of Buddhist practice because it embraces globalization, yet it is far less known in the West than Tibetan Buddhism, the Soka Gakkai movement, or even Thich Nhat Hanh's Plum Village in France. Tzu Chi promotes a form of Mahayana Buddhism that emphasizes philanthropy as its main form of practice. The vicissitudes of Tzu Chi's growth worldwide have been shaped partly by the difficult position of the society where it has emerged, Taiwan – or the Republic of China (ROC), as this polity is known officially. Its giant neighbour, the People's Republic of China (PRC), constantly threatens this small polity with absorption through military means. Although important for understanding the growth of Tzu Chi on the international stage, this issue will not be addressed here. In Canada members of the organization face difficulties in expanding their presence because of demographic and cultural, not geopolitical, factors. The chapter will first describe the activities of Tzu Chi in Canada, provide some of its background in Taiwan, assess the opportunities for Tzu Chi's expansion in Canada, and finally reflect on the significance of the organization's achievements.

The Tzu Chi Foundation is a widely respected actor in Taiwanese civil society: it is the largest of its kind on the island. In 1993, 18 per cent of the population was recognized as a member (Wang 1999, 178). A nun named Cheng Yen established Tzu Chi in 1966, during the period of martial law imposed by the Nationalist Party (better known as *Kuomintang*, hereafter KMT) between 1947 and 1987. The small charity has become a major philanthropy running hospitals and educational institutions, engaging in television broadcasting and publishing, and providing international relief. Its branch in Canada is one of three major international branches, along with those in the United States and Malaysia.

THE TZU CHI FOUNDATION IN CANADA[3]

In 1992, Gary Ho, a Taiwanese immigrant to Vancouver, set up Tzu Chi Canada. After twenty years in Taiwan as a real estate developer, Ho had become a successful entrepreneur. Already a devoted Tzu Chi supporter in Taiwan, it took him only three years to raise $2 million from the community in Vancouver for a number of local projects in health care. In 1994, he became chief executive officer of Tzu Chi Canada and in a story published by the *Vancouver Business* magazine in 1995, he stated that he devotes seven months each year to running Tzu Chi. In 1996, Ho made the cover of the Chinese version of *Maclean's* magazine as one of the local heroes (*difang yingxiong*) in Canada.[4] Over the years, Ho set up branches in other major Canadian cities. In 2005, Tzu Chi had a chapter in Vancouver,[5] a branch in Markham, student associations at the University of Toronto and the University of Waterloo, and contact points in Calgary, Edmonton, Mississauga, Ottawa, and Montreal. The organization has established a number of volunteer stations throughout the country; thirty-seven serve as food banks, senior homes, centres for Meals on Wheels, care centres for the disabled, hospitals, and centres for street cleaning.

As of 2002[6] the organization had 13,000 members, of whom 9,000 were British Columbia residents and 910 were full-time volunteers. These numbers represent a significant proportion of the Taiwanese community in Canada. Although Statistics Canada does not have figures for immigrants from Taiwan, who are included among the 1,094,700 residents who claimed a Chinese identity,[7] we can rely on figures from the Canadian Council on Social Development (CCSD), which claims that in 2001, 53,755 immigrants considered Taiwan their country of birth.[8] Volunteers of the Canadian branch of Tzu Chi with whom we have met claim that as much as 90 per cent of their organization's membership is composed of Taiwanese recent immigrants, and another 5 per cent are from Mainland China, Hong Kong, and Vietnam. These numbers are confirmed by participant observations and a look at internal documents that name participants to Tzu Chi's activities. If we accept the figure quoted above for the membership of Tzu Chi Canada in 2002 and if we take into account the fact that most members of Tzu Chi are Taiwanese, then up to 17 per cent of that community could be involved with the Foundation in that year.

Therefore, despite this expansion in Canada, Tzu Chi remains an ethnic Chinese – or even Taiwanese – organization. In that respect, Tzu Chi is similar to Fo Guang Shan, the other major Buddhist organization from Taiwan that has established a strong presence outside the island (Chandler 2004, 120, 271). Members and volunteers often affirm their willingness to admit non-Taiwanese and even non-Chinese into their ranks, and we have no reason to doubt their sincerity and openness. Yet data about membership in the organization outside Taiwan reveals it is difficult to cross over ethnic boundaries. Caucasians represent less than one per cent of the membership. One could argue that language is the biggest obstacle to expansion, although the organization makes considerable efforts to overcome this barrier. The languages used in the website of Tzu Chi Canada, for example, are English, Chinese written with traditional characters, and French for the Montreal branch. Those who want more details about the specifics of Tzu Chi are redirected to the website in Taiwan, and even then they can receive information in English produced by the personnel of the cultural services. The same difficulty in reaching out into the broader host society can be seen in other national branches. The register of the Malaysian branch, for example, shows very few Malay or Indian names, and a preponderance of Chinese names.

Vancouver plays an important role in the global network of the organization. Of the thirty-one countries and territories[9] outside Taiwan where it has established a chapter (*fenhui*), an office (*zhihui*), or a liaison office (*lianluo-dian*), only three countries have established chapters and offices with their own websites: Canada, Malaysia, and the United States.[10] This partly reflects the concentration of Taiwan's expatriates in North America and the presence of overseas Chinese who also speak *Minnanhua* in Southeast Asia. In 2003, Tzu Chi had websites in Toronto and Montreal, and planned to open another one for its liaison office in Ottawa. However, it has recently shelved these plans, and in 2005 closed these sites. Although the Greater Toronto area seems an important centre of activities for Tzu Chi, the headquarters remain in Vancouver. The decision reflects the structure of Tzu Chi in Taiwan, which is highly centralized. The strategy is also consistent; the organization wants to limit costs and devote most of its resources to the accomplishment of its four missions (*zhiye*): charity, medical care, education, and culture. Because they are central to understanding the behaviour of the institution, we will now elaborate on the four missions, or what Tzu Chi members call the "eight footprints."[11]

Charity

In Taiwan, the first mission for which people know Tzu Chi is charity (*cishan*), which we translate as humanitarian relief. This mission corresponds to the foundational motto promoted by Cheng Yen:[12] "help the poor and educate the rich" (Wang 1999, 200). Tzu Chi Canada has offered an impressive number of services over the years to the community: emergency relief, financial and material assistance to low-income families, funeral assistance for the poor, donations to charitable organisations, distribution of New Year gift money and winter clothing to street kids. The mission of charity aims at helping people within the community where Tzu Chi volunteers live. It differs from the Tzu Chi mission of overseas humanitarian relief, where a few volunteers and professional doctors join international NGOs to provide emergency relief.

In Vancouver, Tzu Chi volunteers have delivered, on a daily basis, hot meals to the Salvation Army, distributed food to food banks, visited seniors' homes, cleaned streets, and provided comfort for the homeless. The organization has been involved with the provincial Emergency Response Team, a project aimed at getting volunteers first on the scene to help victims of local disasters such as forest fires or floods. Tzu Chi volunteers have provided 35,000 meals and have been involved for more than 700 weeks (fourteen years) in local organizations such as the Little Mountain Elderly's House. The Tzu Chi Toronto office has helped homeless people by visiting Toronto's Covenant House, Canada's largest shelter for young homeless adults, and has received an award from the Tendercare Senior Home for top volunteer organization. Tzu Chi

Canada has also sought to develop its charitable activities by working with the Salvation Army for the past ten years. In centres such as the Montreal Tzu Chi liaison bureau, volunteers focus on relief because they lack resources for other missions.

Medical Care

The second most important mission in Taiwan is medical care. Cheng Yen had witnessed the suffering among aboriginal people who could not receive health care in Taiwan. She found the experience heartbreaking and decided to establish a hospital for people who could not afford health care. For Cheng Yen, poverty is the result of sickness and sickness arises from poverty, and therefore health care is the best way to alleviate poverty. Tzu Chi has built five hospitals in Taiwan and plans to complete a sixth soon. It has also established clinics in Malaysia and the United States. In 1996 Tzu Chi founded an organization of professional physicians, the Tzu Chi International Medical Association (TIMA), to promote its medical mission. TIMA has established seventeen branches in nine countries but it has yet to gather medical professionals and volunteers to form a branch in Canada.

The absence of TIMA in Canada does not mean that Tzu Chi cannot perform this part of its mission, however. Although it does not run its own hospitals and clinics in Canada, as it does in Taiwan, Malaysia, and the United States, the organization has been able to contribute to the welfare of various hospitals and clinics.[13] In Toronto, the local Tzu Chi branch has given supplies to the Street Health Community Nursing Foundation that included cold medicine, first aid kits, various vitamins, anti-lice medicinal shampoo, and other non-prescription medication needed to treat the homeless. Tzu Chi Canada has been providing funding for medical research and equipment purchases since 1992; its medical donations amount to $4 million.[14] Its contribution, moreover, is not limited to gifts in cash or in kind: it has established the Tzu Chi Institute for Alternative Medicine to promote traditional Chinese medicine. After Tzu Chi's information campaign on acupuncture, the British Columbia Ministry of Health agreed to reimburse costs of alternative forms of health care.

Education

Cheng Yen believes that a solid education will bring hope, stability, and strength to a society. The emphasis on education has two dimensions, regardless of where the students live. First, Tzu Chi Canada agrees with the mainstream of the Canadian population and its government that universal access to education matters. To help achieve that goal the organization complements the services already offered by the local and provincial governments. Tzu Chi Canada has provided scholarships to Canadian students every year since 1994.[15] It also gives financial assistance to blind children and poor families. Since 1999, it has donated $100,000 annually in scholarships to more than 800 low-income Canadian students in over sixty-nine schools. This mission serves the local communities where volunteers are active.

Second, Cheng Yen and the educators in Tzu Chi's university and colleges in Taiwan also believe that Tzu Chi's education mission should not be limited to training in technical skills: moral formation and Cheng Yen's philosophy have to be combined with traditional aspects of the school curriculum. Tzu Chi Canada has established, to this end, various Tzu Chi Academies to promote educational methods that incorporate both knowledge and ethics. Teachers, parents, and volunteers are expected to focus on morality and encourage students to cultivate altruistic values of compassion, honesty, and integrity. Competitions held in these academies, such as the Still Thought Poster Competition and the Chinese School Speech competition, encourage the development of a positive attitude in daily life. Activities range from calligraphy, speech, drawing, and painting, to visits to seniors' homes. After establishing the first of these academies in Richmond in 1997, Tzu Chi Canada created branches in Coquitlam, Vancouver, Surrey, Burnaby, Mississauga, and Toronto. Approximately 1,700 students from these areas are enrolled.

Culture

The mission of education, with its moral dimension, intertwines with Tzu Chi's mission of culture. In Taiwan, the cultural mission is implemented through the broadcasting and publishing of Cheng Yen's views and of information about the international activities of Tzu Chi. Great Love TV (Da ai dianshitai) runs its own programs and news broadcasts, with the full panoply of professional actors, producers, and journalists. The Cultural Centre in Taipei's suburb of Guandu publishes and distributes a wide range of materials. These publications include Cheng Yen's speeches, commentaries on Buddhist teachings, commemorations of Tzu Chi's work in Taiwan and abroad, books presenting inspirational stories about Tzu Chi volunteers, and glossy magazines, such as Rhythm, which sees itself as the Chinese equivalent of National

Geographic. In addition, the team in the Cultural Centre translates most of the material published by Tzu Chi into English, Spanish, even Japanese.

Satellite TV and the Internet bring Tzu Chi's cultural mission to Canada. The much smaller staff of the Tzu Chi Canada chapter distributes some of these materials and informs the public about the activities of Canadian volunteers through such publications as the bi-monthly *Tzu Chi Canada*, distributed since 1996. The Canadian volunteers can also rely on a national Internet site developed in 1998 in Vancouver. At some point, as discussed before, two other sites, for Toronto and Montreal, were briefly developed but they were closed in 2005. Tzu Chi also reaches out to Canadians through cultural events such as the photography exhibition "Dust in the Wind," which describes the pilgrimage of the Chinese monk Xuanzang to India during the Tang dynasty.

Four Other "Footprints"

There are four other activities, called "footprints," that Tzu Chi promotes in its Chinese language website along with the four "missions" just discussed: service to the community (*shequ zhigong*), environmental protection (*huanbao*), bone marrow donation (*gusui juansheng*), and international relief (*guoji zhenzai*). Their impact on Canadian society varies.

Tzu Chi Canada has been successful in Vancouver with respect to community service. In 2004, the City of Vancouver awarded it the "Cultural Harmony Award." One year later, Mayor Larry Campbell and the City of Vancouver declared September 4 "Tzu Chi Day" during the opening ceremony of the Taiwanese Cultural Festival and later the mayor visited Cheng Yen in Taiwan, in order to thank Tzu Chi's headquarters for its support of the local Canadian branch.

In the area of environmental protection, on the other hand, the activity of Tzu Chi is unlikely to have much impact. First, several important pressure groups and NGOs, such as Greenpeace and Equiterre, have a long history in Canada and are better able to mobilize large groups of people. Second, Tzu Chi Canada takes a low profile approach to political action and is therefore unlikely to affect environmental protection on a significant scale. Cheng Yen disapproves of Tzu Chi volunteers being involved in politics.

The bone marrow data bank operated by Tzu Chi helps to identify compatible donors for people who require a bone marrow transplant. This activity is highly significant at the international level and indirectly affects Canada. The bone marrow data bank that Tzu Chi has developed in Taiwan is already the third largest of its kind in the world. Tzu Chi's data bank includes a considerable number of overseas Chinese, including many who live in Canada.

As already mentioned, Tzu Chi is involved in overseas humanitarian relief, not only in developing countries in Latin America, Africa, Asia, and the Middle East, but also among the poor of wealthy countries. Hence, local branches in the United States have been involved in the aftermath of Hurricane Katrina in Louisiana. As for Tzu Chi Canada, it sent volunteers to countries devastated by the tsunami in 2004. But it launched its first operations in 1992, when flood struck in Bangladesh and the PRC. That year, Taiwan and Mainland China were entering a thaw in their relations, and the Chinese government welcomed Tzu Chi's provision of relief in the interior. Tzu Chi Canada volunteers joined others from Taiwan. Even when tensions grew in the Taiwan Strait in 1995, 1996, and 1999, volunteers from Tzu Chi Canada still had access to China because of the good relations between Canada and the PRC. Furthermore, while many people in Taiwan criticized these relief activities, there was no opposition in Canada.

TZU CHI CANADA: AN INCREASINGLY SELF-SUPPORTING ORGANIZATION

The difference in involvement in Mainland China does not, however, demonstrate the independence of Tzu Chi Canada from the Taiwanese headquarters, but the opposite: Tzu Chi Canada continued to offer relief in the PRC because this was the wish of Cheng Yen and her close collaborators on the executive committee in Hualien. If the Taiwanese population was reluctant to support the relief activities in the PRC when the latter was threatening the safety of Taiwanese, Cheng Yen herself was determined to continue. She saw the Chinese as compatriots and deserving of the same love as Taiwanese, and moreover, she and many in Tzu Chi believe that the work they do now in China sows seeds of love that will yield improved relations between the two sides of the Taiwan Strait. However, if Tzu Chi Canada must follow directives from Hualien, it must at the same time rely on its own forces to survive and expand.

In order to fund their numerous activities, the Vancouver chapter, the offices, and the liaison bureaus in the other Canadian cities rely exclusively on the generosity and commitment of their regional members. Outside of receiving some literature from headquarters, the individual offices receive no funding from Hualien, even if they must ultimately follow the directives from Cheng Yen herself. Initiatives for the four missions undertaken in Canada must come from volunteers and members within the local Tzu Chi community. Volunteers of Tzu Chi Canada ultimately abide by the principles that apply in Taiwan. For example, intermediates are not allowed to handle donations: Tzu Chi members ensure that they are involved directly at all stages in the process of giving. When help is needed, they engage in fundraising, buy their own plane tickets, and go on-site to give directly to those in need. In sum, volunteers pride themselves on keeping operational costs to a minimum and on their philosophy of direct intervention and autonomy.

TZU CHI AS A MODERN BUDDHIST PHILANTHROPY

In the official taxonomy of religious organizations recognized by the ROC government, Tzu Chi (Compassion and Relief) is not a new religious movement or a congregation. According to the Himalaya Foundation, a research institute that studies philanthropy, it is ranked as the largest charity in Taiwan (HF 2002). It is registered as an International Non-Government Organization (INGO) in the *China Development Brief*, the reference for such organizations in the PRC (ZFJ 2007). In Canada, the federal Revenue Agency registers Tzu Chi as a charitable trust involved in welfare. In Taiwan its corporate identity is the Tzu Chi Merit Society (*Ciji Gongdehui*), an umbrella organization that includes the Tzu Chi Foundation (*Ciji Jijinhui*), TIMA, and Great Love TV (*Da ai dianshitai*). However, its Buddhist identity is not in doubt: the full legal name of the foundation is the Buddhist Compassion and Relief Foundation for Philanthropic Activities (*Fojiao Cibei Cishan Shiye Jijinhui*).

The Tzu Chi Foundation emerged during the period of martial law. Under that regime, all Buddhist temples and associations had to register as members of the Buddhist Association of the ROC (BAROC), an organization which, until 1987, exercised a monopoly of representation for all Buddhists in Taiwan (Jones 1999, 136). During the first two decades of its existence, Tzu Chi kept a low profile in Hualien County, the location on the impoverished East Coast where it was founded, but it started to attract the attention of the county government in the 1980s when Cheng Yen decided to build a hospital to help the local population. In 1992, after Tzu Chi responded to appeals from foreign governments for humanitarian relief outside Taiwan, the ROC authorities realized that the organization could contribute to improving the image of Taiwan internationally.[16] In 1999, the organization attracted the attention of foreign media when a deadly earthquake hit Taiwan on 21 September and Tzu Chi appeared at times more efficient and diligent than the government (Reitman 1999, 1).

At the time of writing, Cheng Yen is still the head of Tzu Chi. People within the organization often refer to her as *shangren*, literally, the "one above." She is venerated by some, respected by many, and criticized by very few. She is a quiet, almost self-effacing figure, but the adherents of the organization consider Cheng Yen a charismatic personality (Huang 2005, 203). She lectures in Hualien, where she also receives visitors, but she seldom travels outside her community. However, her lectures are broadcast on Great Love TV, disseminated by CD and tape, and printed in newspapers, weeklies, magazines, and books published by the Cultural Centre in Guandu. The target audience is not only Taiwanese: the printed material is translated into English and Spanish,[17] and printed in both traditional and simplified Chinese characters.[18] The spiritual authority of Cheng Yen inspires a devotional literature, and her leadership within the organization is uncontested. However, there is no mechanism to ensure continuation of the organization after her death. People outside the Buddhist milieu also respect her: throughout the island, she is known as the "Mother Teresa of Taiwan," and officials within the KMT have repeatedly nominated her for the Nobel Peace Prize.

Tzu Chi enjoys its status as the most prominent charity in Taiwan because of it's effectiveness and the support of influential politicians over the years (Ding 1999, 20). The foundation has established its record for good management by running four hospitals, as well as a college of medicine and nursing – incorporated recently as a university. In addition to its regular staff, the organization relies on more than 10,000 volunteers throughout the island and a few thousand more around the world. Successive governments in Taiwan have appreciated the contribution of Tzu Chi to local welfare and have assisted its activities in that domain. For example, the Ministry of Interior in the 1980s helped Tzu Chi secure ownership of land in Hualien County to ensure it could build its hospital on the East Coast. Despite this cosy relationship, however, Tzu Chi has managed to operate at arm's-length from the state. Officials in government need Tzu Chi more than the organization needs them.

Tzu Chi's status as a religious institution is more ambiguous. Its volunteers describe their organization as a charity or as a philanthropic society, and none of the members we have interviewed in Canada and Taiwan see it as a religious congregation.[19] Most would describe themselves as Buddhists but they would happily invite Christians and people of any faith to join their ranks.[20] Finally, volunteers and members of Tzu Chi keep a low profile about their religious belief and refrain from engaging in proselytizing. This is understandable in the PRC, where the Chinese Communist Party (CCP) forbids this activity. In other countries where Tzu Chi volunteers intervene, such as Indonesia, being overtly religious could have unfortunate consequences for the local ethnic Chinese population, which has often suffered from persecution. Even in Taiwan, however, Tzu Chi remains discreet about its religious dimension. Its headquarters, known as the Abode of Still Thought (*Jingsitang*), is a small, self-sufficient monastic community where visitors are welcome. Except for the modest sanctuary where its founder launched the organization, there is no large temple, in contrast to the many structures found in the monastic complex of Fo Guang Shan in southern Taiwan (Chandler 2004). Cheng Yen herself grants interviews or gives lectures to visitors in the Abode or in a large lecture hall, known as the Still Thoughts Hall (*Jingsi jingshe*), for special occasions such as conferences.

Tzu Chi's members adhere to a particular current within the Mahayana tradition, known in Taiwan since the 1960s as "Buddhism for the human realm" or "Humanistic Buddhism" (*renjian fojiao*) (Jones 1999, 134; Jiang 1992, 171). This trend is unique to Taiwan. It developed from the theological innovation of Yin Shun (a respected Chinese monk who emigrated from China to Hong Kong and then to Taiwan after the Communist Party took power), who promoted and then transformed an older trend within Chinese Buddhism (*rensheng fojiao*). His approach built on the innovations of Taixu, another famous monk during the first half of the twentieth century. While Taixu proposed that Buddhism should not be limited to the practice of meditation and should involve lay people in the promotion of the tradition, Yin Shun emphasized the importance of charity. While Taixu was a rather eccentric monk, Yin Shun was a more conservative figure who disdained politics (Jones 1999, 134).

Many conflate "Buddhism for the human realm" with another vaguely defined trend known as "Engaged Buddhism."[21] The latter does not describe a specific doctrinal movement or a school but a proactive way for Buddhist organizations, lay and monastic, to approach social work, and even politics (Queen 2000). Organizations such as the Japanese Soka Gakkai or the United Buddhist Church in Vietnam, far from restricting themselves to liturgical activities, have been involved in social work, if not in the politics of their respective countries. The social causes these leaders embrace vary. For example,

Ambedkar, who stood as the defender of India's untouchables, and the Dalai Lama represent historically marginalized communities. Others share serious reservations about capitalism. The leaders of the Sarvodaya movement in Sri Lanka and Thai monks like Buddhadasa, the proponent of dharmic socialism, claim to return to the original wholeness of the Buddhist tradition in their emphasis on social teachings. These organizations differ from Tzu Chi because they have been quite vocal about the politics of their respective countries. In contrast, Tzu Chi and the other organizations that belong to "Buddhism for the human realm" in Taiwan refuse entanglement in politics.[22]

Another important characteristic of "Engaged Buddhism" that is absent from "Buddhism for the human realm" is the remarkable audience the leaders of the former have garnered worldwide, outside the ethnic or cultural communities from which they hail. The Dalai Lama, Thich Nhat Hanh, and Dr Ambedkar have generated a broad audience for their teachings among people who barely knew about Buddhism beforehand. Some "Engaged Buddhist" organizations have nurtured wide-ranging links over the years that transcend boundaries. For example, the Soka Gakkai International has established an international presence in over twenty countries on all continents, and its membership includes a significant proportion of non-Japanese. The international audience of these charismatic leaders has further encouraged the politicization of Buddhist institutions, thanks to the globalization of ideas, particularly the transmission of values associated with human rights and environmentalism (Queen et al. 2003, 1–2) through organizations embracing a wide range of goals in response to the various aspects of modernity, from colonialism to totalitarianism (Harris 1999, 19). In this last respect, Tzu Chi differs from "Engaged Buddhism." Among non-ethnic Chinese it does not enjoy the same audience or name recognition as the Dalai Lama and other leaders.[23]

This is not to say that Tzu Chi is not present outside Taiwan. Quite the contrary. Tzu Chi is present in many countries over six continents. It has chapters and offices in more than 235 locations in twenty-four countries, including sixty-four in the United States alone. Also, these different locations, in coordination with the headquarters in Hualien, can send volunteers into other countries to provide emergency relief. Tzu Chi has managed to expand outside Taiwan thanks to this emphasis on charity and international relief. This expansion materialized when the process of democratization in Taiwan began to consolidate in 1992 with the first free election for the Legislative Yuan, Taiwan's parliament. Responding to calls for relief in Bangladesh and in Mainland

China following devastating floods, Tzu Chi's activities have extended since then to many societies in Asia that were not a priori hospitable to a Buddhist organization – predominantly Islamic Malaysia and Indonesia, as well as officially atheistic China. As we will see below, Tzu Chi Canada has played an important role in the latter case, albeit few Canadians know about it.[24]

Because of these international activities, Tzu Chi has recruited many adherents around the world. The documentation provided by the Tzu Chi headquarters claims ten million members worldwide, including four million who are residents of Taiwan. Independent and credible statistical information about the number of adherents, however, is difficult to obtain. In addition, individuals who are open about their Tzu Chi membership will vary in their level of involvement with the organization. People who have pledged to make donations to the organization are considered members. There is no obligation to attend dharma lectures or to perform any specific activities. People who are members of Tzu Chi as commissioners, workers, honorary members, or who belong to one of the five other constituent organizations in Taiwan, however, do have higher degrees of involvement.[25]

In addition, the total number of people who identified as Buddhists in Taiwan's census amounts to about four million (MOI 2008). However, not all of them agree with Tzu Chi's approach to charity. Many prefer the more traditional and individualist practice of meditation; others are simply not comfortable with the size of the organization, which they see as incompatible with the original vows of poverty of its founder. Moreover, some belittle Cheng Yen's approach to Buddhism as unsophisticated. Although she is the disciple of the late Yin Shun, who enjoyed a high standing on the island, she does not benefit from the respect for Buddhist intellectuals that is granted to Sheng Yen (Shengyan), the leader of the Dharma Drum Mountain (*Fagushan*). On the other hand, she is far less controversial than Hsing Yun (Xingyun), the head of Fo Guang Shan, who is seen as too close to the authoritarian regime that ruled Taiwan until 1987. In addition, many Buddhists prefer the more low-key and humble approach of Tzu Chi to the flamboyant style and wealth that Fo Guang Shan displays.

Outside Taiwan, Tzu Chi is not likely to attract overseas Chinese for a number of reasons. Many of them profess Christianity as a religion. Many others are attached to the impressive economic achievements of the PRC and look down on anything that evokes tradition or the ROC. In addition, the number of overseas Chinese who have kinship ties with Taiwan is smaller than the entire Taiwanese population. In other words, it is difficult to imagine that Tzu Chi's appeal would be strong outside the expatriate Taiwanese community. But even if we can dispute the numbers above, the fact remains that millions of people in Taiwan and among overseas Chinese donate to Tzu Chi and many thousands of them volunteer. Regardless of their national origins, millions of ethnic Chinese over the world respect the organization for its philanthropic work and look in admiration to its founder, Cheng Yen, for her dedication.

Moreover, Tzu Chi represents a formidable transnational actor (Huang 2005, 191; 2003, 145–6). Many of the members of Tzu Chi outside Taiwan and the PRC speak *Minnanhua*, the language of the majority of Taiwan residents and of Cheng Yen herself. In the complicated politics of nationalism and identity between China and Taiwan, Tzu Chi tries to act as a bridge between different communities and link together the *Minnanhua* speakers in Taiwan, Malaysia, Indonesia, and North America. Cheng Yen herself seeks to transcend narrow ethnic boundaries: she speaks Mandarin fluently, identifies Mainland Chinese as compatriots, and has always promoted relief work in the PRC, regardless of the tensions existing between the two sides of the Taiwan straits (Laliberté 2003, 244). She also often reiterates in her speeches that compassion ignores boundaries of race, ethnicity, and religion. The Taiwanese feel that this approach has found a receptive audience in Canada.[26]

THE FUTURE OF TZU CHI IN CANADA

Despite the generosity of wealthy sponsors and many donors in Taiwan and elsewhere, the existence of Tzu Chi Canada remains uncertain. Its growth is hampered by a series of formidable obstacles that no amount of goodwill can overcome. Most have nothing to do with the way in which Tzu Chi members live their religion and present it to outsiders. They have to do with the growth of the Taiwanese Canadian community and its ability to preserve its unique cultural traits; the future of the organization once the charisma of its founder is transferred to another leader; and, finally, how Taiwan can survive as an independent political entity – de facto if not de jure.

Taiwan has been, for a few years, one of the largest sources of immigrants to Canada, along with the PRC, India, and Iran. A mixture of political and social considerations motivated immigration until the 1980s. Many Taiwanese sought to escape persecution because of their political opinions critical of the KMT, but after the process of democratization on the island became more consoli-

Tzu Chi Organizational Structure

Source: Ciji 1992, p.34

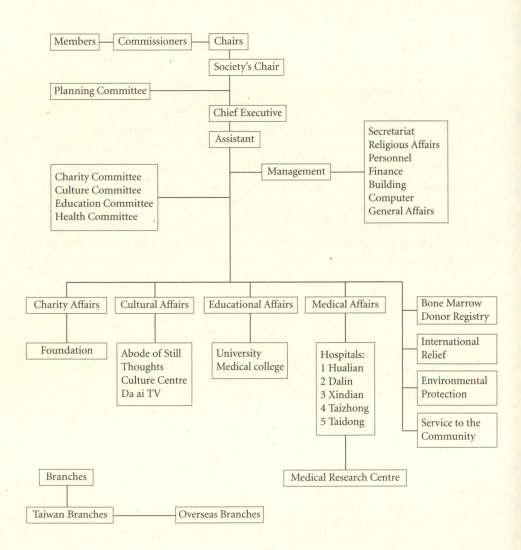

dated, others migrated for other reasons. Many chose Canada for its quality of life and the economic opportunities that they expected here. Naturally, the growth of the Taiwanese community has provided a pool out of which Tzu Chi could recruit volunteers. However, the democratization process and the improvement in the social and economic conditions in the ROC have resulted in a diminishing number of Taiwanese immigrants to Canada in the 1990s. It remains unclear whether Canadians whose parents were born in Taiwan are likely to show the same enthusiasm for Tzu Chi that their parents did. In addition, Taiwanese themselves, whether in the ROC or abroad, are not unanimous in their support of Tzu Chi.

Taiwanese Canadians are divided by competing political, regional, and religious allegiances. In June 2007, the ROC government granted tax-exempt status to 687 religious organizations belonging to two dozen categories (GIO 2008). Numbers for 2006 show that a good number of Taiwanese, in fact a majority, are not even Buddhist (MOI 2008). Furthermore, Taiwanese Buddhists do not follow the same masters. Some prefer the popular and media-savvy monk Hsing Yun and his embrace of prosperity embodied by the two organizations he has founded, the Buddha Light Mountain (Fo Guang Shan) monastic order and its lay affiliate, the Buddha Light International Association (BLIA). Others prefer the more austere and rigorous approach of the scholarly monk Sheng Yen of the Dharma Drum Mountain (*Fagushan*) organization. Finally, some judge Cheng Yen too "localized," while others criticize Tzu Chi's humanitarian relief in the PRC.

In addition, one can surmise from the history of Taiwanese immigration to Canada in the recent past that a greater proportion are not Buddhist but Christian, and particularly Presbyterians, in contrast to the relatively small number of adherents to that church found in Taiwan (GIO 2008). In the nineteenth century, Canadian missionaries established the Presbyterian Church in Taiwan (PCT). Many of the PCT leaders and followers suffered persecution from the authorities in the 1970s and 1980s because they advocated self-determination for Taiwan, and, as a result, many became refugees in Canada. The attitude of Presbyterians contrasted vividly with that of the Buddhist organizations during the period of martial law (1947–1987) in Taiwan and although there is no animosity between these two communities, we have observed over the years that Buddhist and Presbyterian networks among Taiwanese Canadians do not overlap. In other words, the potential for Buddhist converts among Taiwanese Canadians may be much smaller than we assume.

If Tzu Chi hopes to expand by converting – or including – people outside the Taiwanese Canadian communities, it still needs to overcome some formidable cultural barriers. Canadian branches have so far had limited success in recruiting outside the Taiwanese Canadian communities. They have attracted some support from Vietnamese and Chinese Canadians, but there are very few non-Chinese and virtually no Caucasians among their members. Tzu Chi volunteers have tried hard to overcome cultural barriers: they produce a bilingual (Chinese-English) website for their chapter in Vancouver and have attempted sites for other branches including a bilingual French-English site for the Montreal branch. Unfortunately, we have seen over the years that English- and French-speaking Canadians hesitate to get deeply involved once they realize that the dominant language among volunteers is Mandarin or *Minnanhua*.

The greatest obstacle for the expansion of Tzu Chi in Canada, however, resides in the organization's own structure, which is very centralized. Heads of chapters and branches must report to Cheng Yen on a regular basis to inform her of their projects, as well as the needs of their branches, and to request instructions for the overseas missions they would like to supervise. The reliance on Cheng Yen's authority ensures a great degree of conformity within the organization for its missions and its integrity. However, it also reveals one of the main problems that will face the organization in the future: ensuring that another person can transmit the charisma of Cheng Yen and inspire volunteers. It is hard to know whether Tzu Chi Canada will continue to depend on instructions or advice from Hualien, or whether it will seek to rely more on the local Taiwanese Canadian community.

The Cultural Affairs Bureau in Guandu produces much of the literature Tzu Chi volunteers and commissioners rely on to perform their missions in Canada. The production of books, monthly magazines, and newspapers that disseminate Tzu Chi's ideals, as well as the technical sophistication displayed in its four hospitals and *Da ai* TV, require an enormous amount of resources. The small Taiwanese Canadian community, should the latter decide to be self-reliant, could hardly muster them. In other words, Tzu Chi Canada will depend on the resilience of a wealthy headquarter in Taiwan to ensure its continued expansion. The endurance of Tzu Chi is likely, thanks to the enormous amount of expertise and experience accumulated over the years by its different organizations. We do not want to speculate about possible divisions between its constituent units. The point is that the future of Tzu Chi Canada rests in part in the hands of decision-makers in Hualien.

Finally, the most important challenge to the existence of Tzu Chi Canada relates to the future of Taiwanese society as a de facto independent polity. There exists much uncertainty about the future of Taiwan as a sovereign entity. If the PRC forcibly incorporates Taiwan, the future of Tzu Chi as an independent organization is likely to face some difficult tests. Tzu Chi is the kind of independent and articulate association that the PRC fears for its potential to gain influence. Interviews with local leaders in central and north China about Tzu Chi over the years have made clear that many of them feel embarrassed by its capacity to provide services (Laliberté 2008, 98–9). Moreover, assuming that the PRC develops into a more tolerant regime with respect to religion in general and organized religions in particular, Tzu Chi would risk becoming marginalized in the broader world of Chinese Buddhism. Fieldwork in the PRC has revealed that recently established Buddhist charity organizations in Hebei, Shanghai, and Guangdong are ready to emulate its approach to social services. In the end, much hinges upon the transnational network that Tzu Chi is nurturing in Southeast Asia, and on its ability to sustain branches in North America.

TZU CHI IN CANADA: AN INTERPRETATION

The Tzu Chi Foundation is a remarkable example of a religiously inspired philanthropic society that is expanding in the context of globalization and late capitalism. It reconciles in its practices the local and the global, the sacred and the profane, the traditional and the modern. Tzu Chi volunteers, and especially those who were born in Taiwan, carry with them the legacy of a local culture that is itself hybrid and a religious tradition that has adapted to these changes. Tzu Chi members continue to adapt, on the global stage as they move from Taiwan to the new societies where they live, and as they travel to deliver relief in other parts of the world. In addition, for professionals employed by its institutions, as well as for volunteers, the work routines are becoming intertwined with the religious practice, to a point where striving to attain salvation becomes blurred with meeting more mundane objectives. A result of this fusion between spiritual longings and mundane pursuits is that while Tzu Chi's volunteers are the carriers of a centuries-old Buddhist tradition, they also embody modernity in the ways in which they approach their practice.

Within Taiwan, people have seen Tzu Chi as the expression of the more austere local culture of Hualien, a rain-drenched area east of Taiwan long known as the most impoverished part of the country. The state-of-the art hospital that Tzu Chi has built in the region in the 1990s has changed these perceptions, however. Tzu Chi stands now as a symbol for a region that has reinvented itself as a peaceful and quiet location for tourism. Alongside these local influences, observers can also find in Tzu Chi the effect of Taiwan's relations with the outside word. Although Tzu Chi emerged two decades after the Japanese left Taiwan, its austere ritual and architecture evoke some aspects of the latter's more sober architectural style. Because Japan ruled Taiwan for over half a century and because the east coast is relatively isolated from Mainland China,[27] this part of the island bears the architectural style and aesthetic imprint of Japan more so than of China .

These characteristics aside, there is no doubt that the Tzu Chi Merit Society represents an example of Chinese Buddhism. Yet, this description does not capture the whole reality of the Chinese Buddhist tradition as it is lived today around the world. Most Chinese in the PRC have never heard about Tzu Chi. In addition, the variant of Chinese Buddhism practised in Taiwan and overseas differs in many respects from that which we have observed in the PRC.[28] Taiwanese Buddhists run their own media and get involved in public and even in political life. Lay Buddhist communities organize in very visible fashion; volunteers wear distinctive uniforms, and regularly hold major public rallies. These developments are exceptional in China.[29]

In addition, there is the issue of "Chinese-ness" itself in relation to "Chinese Buddhism." The written language of the organization is Chinese, the morality they promote makes reference to filial piety and other traditional Chinese moral values, and the identification of Tzu Chi with a Chinese version of Buddhism makes it a culturally ethnic Chinese movement. Yet, to describe Tzu Chi as Chinese does not tell the whole story. China encompasses a variety of local cultures. Moreover, the ways in which Tzu Chi volunteers experience their practice has little to do with the practices of traditional Chinese religiosity. Tzu Chi does not display the colourful exuberance typical of Chinese popular religions, which can be seen in other Buddhist associations, such as Zhongtaichan, in Central Taiwan. The sobriety of Tzu Chi is visible in its ritual, in its architecture – the grey buildings of its headquarters and the offices it operates – as well as the indigo uniforms of its volunteers. All these distinctive elements of Tzu Chi contrast with the colourful displays of the popular Chinese religions. Again, this may signal a Japanese influence.

In addition to the local, Japanese, and Chinese influences, the Christian missionaries' approach to philanthropy has also influenced Tzu Chi, although this influence is recognized somewhat reluctantly in the interviews with its volunteers. Many biographies of Cheng Yen mention that she felt ashamed when she realized that Christian nuns were doing philanthropic work while local religious persons did not do much. The literature in Guandu often cites this as one of her major motivations for launching Tzu Chi.[30] The influence of Christianity in philanthropy has certainly been significant in Taiwan: the Presbyterian Church in Taiwan has been active in health care with the Mackay Hospital, and the Roman Catholic Church has left its mark in education with Fu-jen University. This influence has even left a visible and surprising mark at the symbolic level in the Hualien hospital, where a representation of a healing Buddha looks like a mosaic in the Byzantine art style, in a curious counterpoint to Chinese representations of the Virgin Mary, who often look like Guanyin, the Chinese Buddhists' Goddess of Mercy.

In Canada, most non-Chinese people are struck by the obvious "Asian-ness" of Tzu Chi when they meet its volunteers, but most may not be aware of the culturally hybrid nature of the organization. The less subtle distinction between Asian/ethnic and Western/converts, criticized by Victor Hori at the beginning of this book, in this case may appear a more relevant one. Over the years, we have asked many Canadians without any Asian background who are nevertheless interested in Buddhism and who know a good deal about the Dalai Lama, Zen Buddhism, and even the Soka Gakkai, if they knew anything about Tzu Chi, only to find out they had never heard about the organization. Although the members of Tzu Chi themselves embody different heritages, and no doubt will add more to their repertoire as they strike new and deeper roots in Canada, the distance between most of them and the rest of Canadian society remains important. This is not because Tzu Chi volunteers seek to remove themselves from the mainstream of Canadian society; far from it. We have seen that they are trying to reach out to the rest of Canadian society.

The global nature of the organization certainly strikes Canadians who meet Tzu Chi volunteers. As we have seen, its members connect instantly with both their headquarters in Taiwan and the people they help in disaster areas. Inhabitants of Canadian cities who see the local building from which Tzu Chi's volunteers go out to do fundraising or offer relief to the poor may think they see a local ethnic Taiwanese benevolent association serving the community.

However, most do not see that such branches are part of a global network present in Malaysia, Indonesia, and the United States, with activities in regions as remote to the cradle of Chinese Buddhism as the Middle East or as difficult to access as the PRC. Tzu Chi Canada relates to overseas Taiwanese communities that have been established relatively recently (such as the communities in Canada and the United States), and to ethnic Chinese communities that have more distant kinship ties with Taiwan and the southern province of Fujian – from which many early immigrants to Taiwan hail.

In its philanthropic work worldwide, Tzu Chi is reconciling the sacred and the profane. Tzu Chi volunteers are an excellent example of a lived Buddhist practice that is secularized in two of the three dimensions of secularization identified by sociologists of religion (Dobbelaere 2002, 8), the dimension of religious organization and the dimension of individual involvement. With respect to religious organization, we have seen that Tzu Chi represents the institutional form of a continuing process of religious change within Mahayana Buddhism in China tending toward a greater involvement with the "this-worldly" sphere of existence. Its founder, Cheng Yen, is even reluctant to consider the Merit Society a religious institution and prefers to describe it as a charity. Tzu Chi does not figure in the state registry of religious associations in Taiwan. Civil servants interviewed on Tzu Chi were themselves unclear whether the government should consider the organization a religious institution or a philanthropic society.[31] In Canada, as we have seen before, the Revenue Agency registers it as a charity.

With respect to the individual level of religious practice, the religious practice of Tzu Chi's volunteers is largely devoid of a sense of sacredness and the type of rituals that we usually associate to the more traditional Buddhist temples in China and Taiwan. The performance of charity, the volunteer work performed by commissioners, the visits to homes for the elderly, and all the forms of philanthropy practised by people identifying with Tzu Chi represent steps toward the achievement of Buddhahood. We can analyse this practice as the secularization of the religious organization itself, to the extent that the charity performed by the volunteers of the organization serves needs related to this-worldly concerns: helping the poor, bringing comfort to the sick, and looking after the destitute. The ritual is minimal and lacks the elaborate form observed in the Fo Guang Shan monastery, in the newly refurbished Buddhist temples in the PRC such as the Bailin temple in Hebei, or even in other Buddhist temples in Canada.

Finally, the teachings of Cheng Yen and Tzu Chi's mode of operating reconcile the traditional and the modern. Cheng Yen's own views perpetuate a doctrinal innovation that dates from the end of the nineteenth century, as a response to the modern state's attacks against Buddhist tradition. As we have seen, Taixu proposed a modernization of Buddhism while Yin Shun – the mentor of Cheng Yen – wanted to ensure that "Buddhism for the human realm" would actualize the original Buddhist teachings. Cheng Yen's stewardship of a vast lay organization like Tzu Chi in a sense represents the culmination of Taixu's original vision. But her lack of interest in politics, in addition, reflects the more cautious approach of Yin Shun. The administrators, doctors, and other professionals who ensure the workings of the organizations are for the most part devoted Buddhists. Yet, they have also studied in some of the best institutions in their area of expertise, in the United States, Canada, Japan, or Taiwan. As such, they are the embodiment of that reconciliation between tradition and modernity. These types of individuals can thrive in Canada, as in Taiwan, where there is no fundamental chasm between individuals' religiosity and their social commitments.

CONCLUSION

The history of Tzu Chi represents a remarkable example of a modern Chinese form of Mahayana Buddhism that both embodies a localized Taiwanese identity and embraces globalization through a practice that emphasizes philanthropy. Its presence in Canada is not as visible as that of other religious organizations because it has always worked quietly, providing relief to the needy, nurturing identity within the Taiwanese Canadian community, and reaching out to categories of people usually marginalized. Yet, it has established itself solidly in some parts of Canada, most notably in Richmond, Markham, and Verdun, suburbs to Canada's three largest cities, close to where there are concentrated Taiwanese communities. It has even managed to become an important actor in the health care system of British Columbia and an important source of social capital among Canadians with a traditional Chinese cultural background who want to preserve their heritage. In those two particular aspects, the success of Tzu Chi illustrates some of the benefits that the promoters of the Canadian policy of multiculturalism have always envisaged.

The future of Tzu Chi in Canada, however, remains uncertain. Members face difficulty in expanding their presence in Canada because of demographic and cultural factors. Although they do not spare their efforts to reach out to non-Taiwanese via charity, community work, and their efforts to nurture and promote Chinese culture to the larger host society, the organization's growth remains hampered by the shift in immigration patterns to Canada. They also have to contend with the enormous cultural difference between a unique Taiwanese culture, shaped by Chinese heritage, Japanese influence, and Taiwan's aboriginal culture, and the mainstream of both English and French Canadian cultures. In addition, the organization's reputation and effectiveness depends so much on the exceptional charisma of its leader Cheng Yen that there is uncertainty about the future of the organization until an equally capable leader emerges to succeed her. Finally, its vicissitudes worldwide reflect the difficulty of Taiwan, the society in which it has emerged, constantly threatened with absorption by its giant neighbour.

The importance members of Tzu Chi attach to philanthropy and other mundane activities, the absence of a visible temple attached to it in Canada's large cities, and the small size of the monastic community in its home base of Hualien in Taiwan, may lead some to question the nature of the association as a genuinely Buddhist organization. Yet, as the reference to Buddhism by the volunteers and the founder reminds outsiders, the orientation of the association toward "helping the poor" and "educating the rich" represents for them the quintessential way to express the compassion that the Mahayana tradition embodies. For them, providing relief to the poor is actualizing one's Buddhahood. In that sense, members of Tzu Chi can claim to be "Buddhists" as authentically as Catholic nurses can claim to be Christians who fulfill their vows when they run hospitals and clinics.

IN LIEU OF AN EPILOGUE

As the book went to press, dramatic events in the Chinese province of Sichuan have attracted an unprecedented outpouring of sympathy to the victims of the devastating earthquake that struck southwest China in May 2008. Two months earlier, a more auspicious event occurred, in the eyes of the Chinese government: the Taiwanese electorate voted in March for the presidential candidate whom the authorities in Beijing preferred. This conjunction of circumstances had a major consequence for Tzu Chi, which has been duly registered in China and can operate on a more regular basis in that country. This means that the potential for the future development of Tzu Chi may take a turn for the better, a situation which, in turn, may affect its activities in Canada.

NOTES

1 This paper uses material provided by the Tzu Chi Merit Society itself, interviews with journalists and government officials, exchanges with Taiwanese scholars who have studied the organization, as well as several visits since 1995 to Tzu Chi's headquarters, university, and hospital in Hualien, and to other branches in Taipei, Yunlin, Vancouver, Toronto, Ottawa, and Montreal.

2 The other association is the Buddha Light International Association, whose headquarter in South Taiwan is located in the Buddha Light Mountain (Fo Guang Shan) monastery, in Kaohsiung county.

3 The information on Tzu Chi for this section is taken from www.tzuchi.ca/canbranch/ journal/others/10yearsreview.pdf and from interviews in Montreal, at Tzu Chi's bureau, on 20 January 2005, unless indicated otherwise.

4 The story was published in the English version of the magazine as well.

5 This office serves as the headquarters of the corporate entity "Tzu Chi Canada."

6 These numbers became available in 2007.

7 http://www40.statcan.ca/l02/cst01/demo26a_f.htm.

8 http://www.ccsd.ca/factsheets/demographics/.

9 Tzu Chi has a branch in Mainland China and in Hong Kong: the latter is not a country, but a Special Administrative Region within the PRC.

10 There are five websites for the United States: the central site (*zonghui*) serves as the home of the English-speaking website; the sites for San Jose, Chicago, Houston, New Jersey, and Washington DC are all in Chinese.

11 The four missions are grouped under the expression "One Step, Eight Footprints." The Eight Footprints are charity, medicine, education, culture, international disaster relief, bone marrow donation, environmental protection, and community volunteerism.

12 Or Zhengyan in the Hanyu Pinyin transliteration used in the PRC and adopted by most international organizations.

13 Some of the beneficiaries include the BC Multiethnic Marrow Transplant (Richmond), the BC Multiethnic Marrow Transplant (Vancouver), the BC Cancer Foundation, the BC Children's Hospital, the BC Women's Hospital, the Canada China Child Health Foundation, the Canadian Red Cross Society, Doctors Without Borders, the Eagle Ridge Hospital Foundation, Mount St Joseph Hospital, the Royal Columbia Hospital Foundation, Simon Fraser Healthcare, St Paul's Hospital, Sunny Hill Foundation for Children, the Tzu Chi Institute, and Vancouver Hospital and Health Science Centre.

14 The list goes as follows: Greater Vancouver Food Bank Society, Vancouver Native Health Society, Surrey Food Bank Society, Squamish Flood Victim Relief, North Thompson Relief Fund, Variety Club, the Canadian Red Cross Society, Association of First Nations' Women, Association of Neighbourhood Houses, Canada China Child Health Founda-

tion, Family Service of Greater Vancouver, Multiethnic Marrow Transplant Society, Quest Outreach Society, Sara Society, the Salvation Army.

15 The list of recipients for educational bursaries given by Tzu Chi Canada includes Douglas College Foundation, Dr Charles Best Secondary School, Earth Save Canada, International Children's Festival, North Surrey Secondary School, Point Grey Secondary School, School District #36 (Surrey), School District #37 (Delta), School District #39 (Vancouver), School District #41 (Burnaby), School District #42 (Maple Ridge), School District #43 (Coquitlam), School District #45 (West Vancouver), Surrey Library, University of British Columbia, Vancouver Library, Vancouver Public Schools Foundation, Vancouver Community College, West Vancouver Education Foundation.

16 It had deteriorated after the United States shifted diplomatic recognition to Beijing in 1981.

17 Many of the twenty-four states with which the ROC maintains diplomatic relations are in Latin America, and Tzu Chi has branches in Spain and five Spanish-speaking Latin American countries.

18 Readers in the PRC and in Singapore use the simplified characters.

19 Interview in Montreal, Tzu Chi's bureau, 20 January 2005.

20 Interview in Hualien, Tzu Chi headquarters, on 25 and 26 February 2004.

21 See the chapter by Henry Shiu in this volume for a discussion of Engaged Buddhism.

22 The official booklet given to volunteers mentions this principle as one of the ten precepts they must respect.

23 For example, Raphael Liogier (2004), in his book on global Buddhism, barely mentions the trend.

24 Interview in Montreal, at Tzu Chi's bureau, on 20 January 2005.

25 Sources in the headquarters indicated over 11,000 commissioners and honorary members in Taiwan.

26 Interview in Montreal, at Tzu Chi's bureau, on 20 January 2005.

27 The migrations from China in past centuries were to the west coast, where the majority of Taiwan's population is concentrated.

28 In temples located in all regions of China, such as Bailin (Hebei), Jing'an (Shanghai), Zhanghua (Hubei), Jiuhuashan (Anhui).

29 The state-choreographed First World Buddhist Forum convened in Hangzhou by the Buddhist Association of China in the winter of 2006 is an example.

30 Cheng Yen's encounter with a pregnant aboriginal Taiwanese woman, left uncared for in front of a local hospital because she was too poor, is also often mentioned as a determinant of her decision to develop a hospital.

31 Interview in Taipei, Ministry of Interior's Bureau for Religious Affairs, 23 February 2006.

A Relationship of Reciprocity
Globalization, Skilful Means, and Tibetan Buddhism in Canada

SARAH F. HAYNES

His Holiness the Dalai Lama on Parliament Hill with
an RCMP officer and Senator Consiglio Di Nino, Chair of
Parliamentary Friends of Tibet
Photo by Chris Kralik, Courtesy of Canada Tibet Committee

When the iron bird flies and horses run on wheels, the Tibetan people will be scattered like ants across the face of the earth, and the dharma will come to the land of the red men.

PADMASAMBHAVA, eighth century[1]

INTRODUCTION

The prophecy quoted above, often read as a prediction about the Tibetan diaspora and the arrival of Buddhism in North America, is ascribed to the eighth-century CE figure Padmasambhava, commonly referred to as Guru Rinpoche (Precious Master) by Tibetan Buddhists. Some 1200 years later, Tibetan Buddhists believe, his prediction was realized. In 1959, His Holiness the Dalai Lama fled Tibet and launched the first wave of Tibetans seeking refuge in India and later in Europe and North America. Padmasambhava's prediction came to fruition in the mid-twentieth century, ultimately taking Tibetan Buddhism through an experience of globalization and a process of preservation in exile communities while threats to religion and culture existed at home. While it is too early to draw conclusions about the fate of Buddhism in Tibet, the popularity of Tibetan Buddhism in Western countries such as Canada has contributed to the preservation of Tibetan religion and cultural traditions.

This chapter focuses on Tibetan Buddhism in Canada. Specifically, it examines the relationship between Tibetan Buddhist communities, both "ethnic" and "convert," and methods used in the process of the globalization of Tibetan Buddhism. The dynamics that exist within Tibetan Buddhist communities and the aspects that draw Canadians to Tibetan Buddhism on different levels, as practitioners and interested observers, are described. After giving a brief history of Tibetan Buddhism in Canada, this chapter examines the refugee-based Tibetan Buddhist communities and the larger, diffuse, Western practitioner-based communities.[2] Finally, the issue of a globalized Buddhism is addressed in connection with the multidimensional appeal of Tibetan Buddhism and an understanding of *upāya-kauśalya* (skilful means/appropriate action) as a force in the preservation of Tibetan religion and culture. Using examples based in Canada, this chapter will investigate how a key component in the Western attraction to Tibetan Buddhism has been cultivated in the arena of the global market and will argue that ultimately we need to rethink Tibetan Buddhism in light of globalization.

TIBETAN BUDDHISM IN CANADA

The history of Tibetan Buddhism in Canada has been relatively short, yet marked by significant growth in the last several years in terms of refugee communities and Canadian interest. For instance, in *Many Petals of the Lotus,* McLellan cites the Canadian Tibetan Association of Ontario (www.ctao.org) in 1997: "the Tibetan population in Toronto consists of 133 individuals in thirty family units, both single and extended" (1999, 74). Currently, the Tibetan community is thriving and numbers approximately 3,000 to 4,000 people (according to the Canadian Tibetan Association of Ontario) (Sandler 2007; Scrivener 2004). In the approximately thirty-five years that Tibetan Buddhism has had a physical presence in Canada there have been two very different yet important factors that have had a hand in exposing Canadians to Tibetan Buddhism. The first is the Canadian government's acceptance of Tibetan refugees in the 1970s. The second, also related to a community of immigrants but this time from the United States, is the Nova Scotia-based Shambhala International founded by Chögyam Trungpa Rinpoche. Although very divergent in their goals, both have been successful in bringing the religious and cultural traditions of Tibet to the attention of Canadians. This chapter will focus more on the Tibetan refugee communities and their relationship with Western-based Tibetan Buddhist communities in Canada since the chapters in this volume by Alexander Soucy and Lynn Eldershaw address the Shambhala community extensively.

Tibetan Buddhist Refugee Communities

The short history of Tibetan Buddhism in Canada began in 1968 when the government finally accepted the Dalai Lama's request to resettle Tibetan families, a total of 228 refugees who arrived in 1971 (McLellan 1999, 81–2). The Dalai Lama's resettlement proposal included the following stipulations: "the Tibetans should be resettled in groups of at least 20 persons under the spiritual guidance of a lama in order to preserve their culture. They should live in communities where they will become self-supporting through their own work and reach a standard of living equal to that of the local people. They should also be given the opportunity to receive training according to their will and abilities, and the children should be allowed to go to school and learn a profession" (Smith 1975, 1). These stipulations are significant as they clearly identify the importance the Dalai Lama placed on preserving cultural and religious identities. As a diaspora community, Tibetans in Canada struggle to maintain their cultural and religious identities through various means. These aspects of Tibetan identity are often considered inseparable for Tibetan Buddhists. Unfortunately, the stipulations laid out by the Dalai Lama were not fully implemented, resulting in the 228 Tibetans being scattered across several provinces and experiencing extreme culture shock (McLellan 1999, 82). Nevertheless, the Tibetan refugee communities in Canada have grown immensely, established thriving businesses, and maintained a strong and vibrant ethnic and religious identity.

The original refugees were placed in eleven communities throughout Quebec, Ontario, Manitoba, and Alberta, with the larger groups being accompanied by a monk to guide them in whatever way possible (McLellan 1999, 82). The Montreal community was accompanied by a scholastically trained monk from the *Geluk* tradition named Geshe Khenrab Gajam. He also guided the refugee communities in Ontario (Des Jardins n.d., 1). Tibetan Buddhism in Quebec continues to thrive. There are several centres throughout the province, and both McGill University and Concordia University support the academic study of Tibetan religious traditions.[3]

Those refugees who were resettled in Ontario, particularly in the Toronto area and northeast of the Greater Toronto Area, in Belleville and Lindsay, have also flourished. Many have a public presence within their larger communities, as successful business owners, professionals, or organizers of the various events open to the public in support of Tibetan religious and cultural heritage. The Toronto Tibetan Buddhist community, alongside the Vancouver groups, is among the most active and diverse in Canada.[4] Toronto is home to the largest Tibetan community in Canada and is second only to New York City in North America (Sandler 2007). Many of these refugees and their families have made a niche for themselves in the neighbourhoods of the Queen Street West area. A walk through the Parkdale neighbourhood will show a thriving Tibetan community that includes several Tibetan-owned restaurants, import shops, and the newly opened Tibetan Canadian Cultural Centre recently visited by the Dalai Lama. Further attempts to preserve Tibetan culture can be seen at Parkdale Public School; a large number of Tibetan children attend and have organized a Tibetan Book Club, which has resulted in the publication of *Tibet: Our Lives, Our Stories,* a collection of the Tibetan children's stories.[5] The Toronto community continues to grow and is an active force in fighting for the Tibetan cause and the preservation and promotion of Tibetan religious and cultural traditions.

The province of Alberta is home to sizable Tibetan communities of resettled refugees in both Calgary and Edmonton. The Alberta communities were originally settled by a group of refugees that included Jetsunma Chimey Luding, the sister of the current head of the Sakya school, Ngawang Kunga, the 41st Patriarch of the Sakya (Des Jardins n.d., 1-2). While Jetsunma has since left the province, she continues to teach in British Columbia at *Sakya Tsechen Thubten Ling* in Richmond. The Calgary community consists of a very active group of about 200 Tibetans who are instrumental in bringing important Tibetan Buddhist teachers to the city for public and private sessions. His Holiness the Dalai Lama visited Calgary in September 2009, a city he had not visited since 1980.

One of the last provinces to welcome Tibetans has been British Columbia. However, it quickly developed into one of the most vibrant and thriving Tibetan Buddhist locales not just in Canada, but North America. Des Jardins notes, "it wasn't until much later in the 1980s and the late 1990s that Tibetans settled in British Columbia. The present population does not exceed 100 families" (n.d., 1). While the current population of Tibetans in British Columbia is relatively small when compared with Ontario, the Tibetan Buddhist communities in that province are experiencing interesting changes that have not been noted elsewhere. Vancouver is home to centres and temples of all the Tibetan Buddhist traditions and, as Des Jardins writes, "a little over a third of all its Buddhist centres are of Tibetan persuasion with several Western Buddhist and non-Buddhist organisations (non-Tibetan and non-Asian based in lineage) which adopt Tibetan techniques of meditation within the curriculum of their regular practice" (n.d., 4–5). Another significant change within the Tibetan Buddhist community in British Columbia has been the arrival of Tibetan Buddhist teachers from contemporary China who are being supported by the Chinese community in Vancouver and overseas and who give instruction in Chinese or have attendants who translate the teachings into Chinese for the local Chinese-speaking community (Des Jardins n.d., 5). Further work is required on this development; however, it undoubtedly affects how the various Tibetan Buddhist communities in Vancouver intersect with one another.

Finally, the University of British Columbia has a long history of the academic study of Asian religions, and this factors into the place of Tibetan Buddhism in British Columbia as well. Between 18 and 20 April 2004, UBC awarded His Holiness the Dalai Lama an honorary doctorate and hosted a series of public lectures by the Tibetan leader. The Dalai Lama's visit coincided with an academic conference titled "Tibetans in the Contemporary World," for which he gave the keynote address. The conference was held to mark the launch of the Institute of Asian Research's Contemporary Tibetan Studies Program. The conference brought together leading scholars from around the world on issues dealing with Tibetan religion, culture, and politics. Finally in 2006, UBC appointed Tserying Shakya, a world expert in Tibet studies, to the Canada Research Chair in Religion and Contemporary Society in Asia.

These recent developments can be traced back to the early resettlement period, which saw both highly trained Tibetan Buddhist teachers and nobility making North America their new home. As these teachers settled into life in Canada and the United States, they established important connections with other Western communities. Specifically, during this period in the late 1970s and 1980s, many Tibetan teachers were affiliated with academic institutions. In line with the Dalai Lama's desire to preserve Tibetan Buddhism, university campuses became the place to find a qualified Tibetan teacher. As Seager notes, "A second, less noticed, but highly significant development was a concerted effort on the part of Asian and Western Buddhist scholars and publishers to preserve Tibetan religious texts and disseminate them in the West" (Seager 1999, 113). This effort by scholars and distinguished Tibetan Buddhist teachers has continued in American and Canadian universities, creating a place for Tibetan Buddhism in academia and, in many cases, adding these distinguished teachers to academic departments as faculty members.

Western Practitioner-Based Tibetan Buddhist Communities

These early Tibetan Buddhist teachers established further affiliations with Western communities. For the most part, Westerners were more interested in connecting with these teachers in their role as practitioners than their role as academics. Tibetan Buddhist groups composed of non-Asians quickly grew throughout North America; the most widespread and influential of these remains Chögyam Trungpa Rinpoche's Shambhala International. While the Western communities were experiencing rapid growth, the ethnic Tibetan communities were slower to establish themselves. However, significant growth has occurred in the last decade so that now in the larger cities of Canada the presence of these Tibetan communities is evident. Whether it is the Tibetan restaurants in the Queen Street West neighbourhood of Toronto or the three Tibetan shops in the 17th Avenue S.W. corridor of Calgary, Canadians are clearly being exposed to the religion and culture of Tibet. Canadians in Halifax and Cape Breton particularly have seen the impact that Tibetan Buddhism can have on their communities with the arrival of Chögyam Trungpa Rinpoche and his students in the 1980s.

The history of Tibetan Buddhism in Canada would not be complete without an examination of the influence of Chögyam Trungpa Rinpoche and Shambhala International.[6] Trungpa, his students, and scholars have written a great deal on the teachings of the Shambhala lineage. Moreover, the contributions by Eldershaw and Soucy in this volume describe and analyse Shambhala in the context of Buddhism in Canada and in relation to issues of identity, including the inadequacy and distortion of labels such as "American" or "Canadian" Buddhism. Therefore, what follows is only a brief discussion of the contributions of Trungpa and Shambhala to Canadian Tibetan Buddhism with particular focus on the relationship between this group and other Tibetan Buddhist communities.

Chögyam Trungpa was a Tibetan-born and trained monk who first visited Nova Scotia in 1977. Seven years later he established Gampo Abbey, a *Karma Kagyu* monastery that provides traditional monastic training to Western students on Cape Breton Island. Midal notes: "He conceived of the future in Nova Scotia as a marriage of the local culture with the culture of Shambhala. Each had something to give the other" (2004, 476). Following the death of Trungpa in 1987, many of the American citizens who followed him to Halifax remained. Today, the presence of the Tibetan Buddhist community is still felt. The Shambhala community provides an excellent example of what the typical relationship looks like between various Tibetan Buddhist communities in Canada. The Shambhala community, as noted by Eldershaw in this volume, presents an interesting synthesis of Tibetan Buddhist ideas and other nontraditional practices. Trungpa believed that meditation would be beneficial for Western practitioners; thus, lay practice in Shambhala differed from the devotional emphasis of Tibetan Buddhist lay practice. Furthermore, Shambhala has attracted primarily well-off Caucasian practitioners who recognize that Shambhala adapts practices to suit a Western lifestyle. The adaptations and accommodations provided by Shambhala result in a significantly different type of lay Tibetan Buddhist teaching and practice from that which ethnic Tibetans have been taught. Nevertheless, the Shambhala community maintains connections to very prominent Tibetan Buddhist teachers around the world, including Venerable Khenchen Thrangu Rinpoche, who serves as the abbot of Gampo Abbey.[7]

It is evident that Canada has distinct communities of Tibetan Buddhist practitioners. In many instances, it appears that the ethnic and convert communities rarely come together, as seen in the Shambhala community. In relation to the Toronto Tibetan Buddhist communities McLellan writes, "The nature and intensity of the Tibetan community's interaction with non-Asian and other Asian Buddhists remains limited" (McLellan 1999, 85). Typically, religious space is not shared, and when it is there are often different teachings given in Tibetan and English. But there are exceptions to this rule. When an important teacher, such as the Dalai Lama, comes to town to give teachings, all groups will gather together. And some communities do interact; at the Temple Bouddhiste Manjusri in Montreal space and teachings are shared by Tibetans, Vietnamese, and Québécois. Furthermore, the ethnic Tibetan Buddhist communities often open themselves up to Westerners during such events as *Losar* (Tibetan New Year), cultural bazaars, when a group of monks is in town to perform the sacred arts of Tibet, or when a relic tour is passing through the city. And a final exception to the division that exists is the Students for a Free Tibet group that is found on campuses across Canada. While typically focused on politics, many members also uphold and promote Tibetan Buddhism.

WHY ARE CANADIANS ATTRACTED TO TIBETAN BUDDHISM?

Tibetan Buddhism is a readily recognizable form of Buddhism in Canada. Whether it is through television shows, the shelves of your local bookstore, or the frequent trips His Holiness the Dalai Lama makes to Toronto, Ottawa, and Vancouver, Canadians are regularly exposed to the cultural and religious traditions of Tibet, often without knowing it. While exposure in the public arena can be measured, it is difficult to quantify how many Canadians define their religious practice as Tibetan Buddhist. Statistics will not be addressed in this chapter, both because of the difficulty of categorizing Canadians and their religious practice and also because the issue of Canadians identifying as

Buddhist has been dealt with perceptively by Beyer in this volume and by Angie Danyluk in her fieldwork among Tibetan Buddhist communities in Toronto (Danyluk 2003).[8] As Danyluk notes, "by exploring 'Buddhist' as an identity or self-representation, we can problematise the construction of 'Buddhist' as a category or label, seeing it instead as a multidimensional matrix of meaning" (2002, 134). Leaving the "multidimensional matrix" aside, the interest Canadians have in Tibetan Buddhism can be observed by looking at the website Buddhism in Canada.

Regularly updated by George Klima, this site provides information on all types of Buddhism found in Canada. Klima's site includes a link to the Statistics Canada website which notes that during the period from 1991 to 2001 those who identified themselves as Buddhist in Canada rose 84 per cent to over 300,000 (Statistics Canada 2001b).[9] The information provided on this site clearly indicates that of the different Buddhist traditions in Canada, the one with the largest number of centres is Tibetan Buddhism.[10] More specifically, the site lists seven centres or temples of the *Gelugpa* school, five major centres of the *Nyingmapa* school (with numerous smaller affiliated centres), two *Sakyapa* centres, and twenty-three temples and centres affiliated with the *Kagyupa* school. The vast majority of these centres are located in southern Ontario, Vancouver, Montreal, Calgary, and Edmonton. In addition to representing the four major schools of Tibetan Buddhism, the site lists at least nine Shambhala centres across Canada, as well as Bön and Rimed centres (Buddhism in Canada, n.d.) While Tibetan Buddhists may have the largest number of centres, there is no indication that the number of practitioners attending these centres is greater than those of other Buddhist traditions in Canada. In addition to these centres, there are Tibetan Buddhist teachers who travel across the country with no permanent centre or temple, performing rituals and giving teachings in exchange for housing. These listings illustrate some of the interest in Tibetan Buddhism that exists among Canadians.

A set of common themes can be identified in the narratives of Western convert Buddhists regarding their motivation to practice Buddhism. In her dissertation, "Caught between Worlds," Danyluk identifies two major themes, with several subthemes, that run throughout the narratives of her research participants – Torontonians, primarily from Judeo-Christian backgrounds, interested in and practising Tibetan Buddhism. These themes have been identified elsewhere in the literature on North American Buddhism,[11] but have been labelled by Danyluk as attraction and aversion – with the subthemes of secularization and personal religious practice, individual and social malaise, the rational and the scientific, universality, disillusionment and the Western experience, and the impact of gender (2002, 73–98). These themes point to why Canadians often turn to Buddhism. Issues of egalitarianism, self-reliance, universally applicable ideas and practices, and disappointment with Western monotheistic religions have been cited as reasons for interest in Buddhism and often for conversion. Moreover, converts often refrain from defining Buddhism as a religion, and instead frame their discussion in terms of philosophy or a lifestyle that can be applied in all aspects of daily life. The practical aspect of Buddhism is further noted in what many convert practitioners perceive as the individualistic nature of the teachings, i.e., if Siddhārtha Gautama attained enlightenment on his own, then anyone can!

The convert's individual pursuit of enlightenment is usually focused on meditation. The Western interest in Asian forms of meditation is over one hundred years old, since the swamis of India and gurus of various types of Buddhism introduced meditation and yoga techniques, often presented as scientific and practical, to the United States in the late nineteenth century. Meditation continues to be promoted not simply as a path that will lead to enlightenment, but as a useful technique that will help one alleviate the sufferings of daily life, such as stress and other medical conditions, again placing emphasis on the practical aspects of the religion. These characteristics apply to most meditation techniques; however, distinctions exist between traditions.

But why do so many of those interested in Buddhism in general turn to Tibetan Buddhism in particular? For well over one hundred years, Westerners have imagined Tibet as a mystical mountain paradise, or Shangri-La. Tibet's long isolation from Western influence resulted in the creation of a picture of Tibet in many Western minds that was largely unrealistic and based on relatively few firsthand accounts. The romantic ideals held by Westerners greatly affected the appeal of Tibetan Buddhism. "The religions of Tibet have long been objects of Western fascination and fantasy. From the time Venetian travelers and Catholic missionaries encountered Tibetan monks at the Mongol court, tales of the mysteries of their mountain homeland and the magic of their strange religions have held a peculiar hold over the European and American imagination" (Lopez 1997, 3).

Christian missionaries were the first Westerners to visit Tibet in the seventeenth century. For the next three centuries Tibet became the destination for missionaries and adventurers, who often presented an exaggerated and misleading picture of Tibetan Buddhism to Westerners. One of the most prolific and influential adventurers was Alexandra David-Neel who in the early twentieth century made her way to Tibet, which was at that time forbidden to outsiders. David-Neel is widely recognized for perpetuating the myth of Tibet as a Shangri-La. Her travels through Asia were well documented, most famously in *Magic and Mystery in Tibet* and *My Journey to Lhasa*, which helped to form the Western perspective on Tibetan Buddhism as a religion full of mystery and exoticism. In discussing the influence of the foreign characteristics of Buddhism during the nineteenth and early twentieth centuries, Tweed notes: "Christian critics, of course, also emphasized its divergence; and some, like the Reverend Clarence Edgar Rice, even reluctantly acknowledged the lure of Buddhism's exotic and alien world ... A handful of Buddhist apologists, like their Christian opponents, also used this exotic language of enchantment, and even the bracing idiom of negation, to describe the religion, to live the Buddhist life was to abide in a remote land –a 'fairyland' – where inhabitants celebrated the absence of all that was familiar and dear" (Tweed 2000, 80).

Tweed's discussion focuses on Buddhism in general during the nineteenth and early twentieth centuries. However, this perspective speaks to the exoticism applied to Tibetan Buddhism by Westerners since the seventeenth century, and for many Westerners, these notions are still retained in the twenty-first century. Tibetan Buddhism continues to be viewed by many Westerners as a pure, mysterious, exotic religion, a perspective that ultimately leads to gross misconceptions about the country and its religious traditions.[12] Nevertheless, these romantic notions continue to attract Westerners to the practice of Tibetan Buddhism. There are other misconceptions about Tibetan Buddhism held by Westerners that have successfully helped in presenting Tibetan Buddhism as an attractive religion. Specifically, in the West there has been a sensationalized understanding of tantric practice and a belief that Tibetan Buddhism is a religion rooted in compassion; therefore, all practitioners must be bodhisattvas who practise a religion of equality.

The Particular Appeal of Tibetan Buddhism in the West

Despite the misrepresentations that exist in the West regarding Tibetan Buddhism, there are legitimate differences between Tibetan Buddhism and other Buddhist traditions; these might ultimately lead Westerners to choose this particular form of Buddhism. While many of the larger themes noted by Danyluk are relevant to those choosing Buddhism, there are indeed distinctions within the Tibetan Buddhist tradition that set it apart. As Wallace notes, "Among all the schools of Buddhism presently being propagated in the West, Tibetan Buddhism is internally the most diverse, in terms of its views, meditative practice, and lifestyles" (2002, 44). Many Canadians who are interested in, or are serious practitioners of, Tibetan Buddhism, are coming to the tradition from a monotheistic background. Much of the rhetoric from those leaving monotheism behind revolves around turning to Tibetan Buddhism because it is understood to be a more universal, rational, practical, and less rigid tradition (Danyluk 2002, 31, 40, 79, 81).

A clear distinction between the majority of other Buddhist traditions and Tibetan Buddhism is the Vajrayana background that informs much of Tibetan Buddhist practice. For instance, the meditative practices of Tibetan Buddhism provide the practitioners with options that are not present in other popular traditions like Zen and Vipassana.

> To begin with, while meditation in the Zen and *vipassanā* traditions is mostly non-conceptual in nature, in Tibetan Buddhism, meditation includes not only the cultivation of non-conceptual concentration and mindfulness, but a wide range of conceptually discursive practices. Tibetan Buddhist meditative practice usually begins with reflecting on such topics as 'the four thoughts that turn the mind,' namely: 1) the significance of having a human life of leisure and spiritual opportunity, 2) death and impermanence, 3) the unsatisfactory nature of the cycle of existence, and 4) the laws of karma. In addition, this tradition is known for its strong emphasis on ritual chanting of prayers, mantras, and long liturgies, all of which are conceptually discursive in nature. (Wallace 2002, 45)

The conceptually discursive element of Tibetan Buddhism is present in the highly ritualized *sadhana* (means of achievement) practice where the practitioner considers such topics as those mentioned above while simultaneously engaging internally and externally in exercises that aim at recognizing one's own buddhanature. *Sadhana* serves as a means of achievement for the practitioner, as a way to uncover the true nature of the mind through meditation and visualizations often in conjunction with external objects and physical acts. The varied nature of *sadhana* practice allows the Tibetan Buddhist access to many avenues in realizing the true nature of reality.

For instance, Tibetan Buddhist practice integrates daily mind-training practice (*lojong*) where "one of the central features ... is the transformation of all the vicissitudes of life, including adversity and felicity, into spiritual maturation ... In marked contrast to the 'bare attention' emphasized in the *vipassanā* tradition, both the mind-training tradition and the practice of Vajrayāna powerfully employ one's intellectual and imaginative faculties in daily life" (Wallace 2002, 46).

Within Tibetan Buddhist practice the senses are engaged on various levels to make significant changes in one's understanding of reality, which in turn influences one's daily actions. Tibetan Buddhist meditation practice includes the use of internal and external exercises not found in other meditation traditions. Characteristic of these internal and external exercises are ritualized practices that include meditation, visualization, and physical actions that engage the senses and use sensory experience for the purpose of recognizing the true nature of reality. Ideally, the practitioner comes to use a *yidam*, "or a personal deity ... an embodiment of our own buddhanature. Practice of the yidam enables us to connect with that nature and identify more and more fully with it" (Ray 2002, 209). Employing a *yidam* in meditation allows practitioners to make significant changes in their lives, including how they experience the world on a daily basis. In discussing the importance of *yidam* practice Snellgrove notes: "In learning to produce mentally such higher forms of emanation and eventually identifying himself with them, the practitioner gradually transforms his evanescent personality into that higher state of being. Thus belief in them is essential; otherwise the means by which one would progress dissolve before the desired 'success' (*siddhi*) is achieved" (Snellgrove 1987, 131).

The sensory engagement and mental transformation cultivated during *sadhana* practice are aided by the use of external objects and physical actions not seen in other forms of Buddhism. Furthermore, while providing the practitioner an access point to tantric practice, and of course the benefits of meditation as with other Buddhist schools, Tibetan Buddhism offers a vibrant ritual tradition that is significant in drawing Westerners. Prayer flags, rosaries, prayer wheels, and in particular chanting, mandalas, and *thangkas* (scroll paintings) provide Westerners with something tangible and concrete on which they can ground their practice. The highly developed visualization techniques of Tibetan Buddhism are anchored to these meditation tools in a way that is specific to this branch of Buddhism. Furthermore, tantric practice allows for intense meditation practice within the framework of lay practice. The intense meditation practice often goes beyond standard sitting meditation to include tantric techniques. Many Westerners are initially drawn to Tibetan Buddhism because of the sensational element of these ritual meditative practices. In particular, the element of tantric sexual ritual draws the curious as well as the serious practitioner. Tibetan Buddhism has a highly developed tantric ritual tradition that has often been considered antinomian. The goal of tantric practice is to achieve enlightenment by using one's own body as a vehicle or tool to bring about the experience of awakening. For those practitioners who have progressed quite far in their practice, initiation into some of the highest tantras is possible. In the higher levels of tantra one may use sexual rituals to come to an experience of enlightenment. Rituals involving tantric sex are traditionally practised by only a very small portion of Tibetan Buddhist practitioners; more importantly, these rituals are understood by many to be just as successful if they are visualized or mentally enacted. Nevertheless, the fact that Tibetan Buddhist practice *can* include a sexual component has lured Westerners to the tradition and continues to lead some to hold misconceptions about the tantric practices of Tibetan Buddhism.

Egalitarianism is also related to the individualistic and self-reliant characteristic of Buddhism and is a key factor in the narratives of Canadians involved with Tibetan Buddhism. Egalitarianism is related to several factors: gender roles, structure and hierarchy, and social engagement. Often when people are drawn to Tibetan Buddhism they are leaving behind a highly structured, formal, and hierarchical monotheistic tradition. These converts may believe that Tibetan Buddhism provides options for involvement in religious practice and community that they were previously lacking. In theory, Mahayana Buddhism, to which Tibetan Buddhism adheres, provides a foundation of equality and opportunity for practice and enlightenment, both based on the ideas of sunyata (emptiness) and the bodhisattva ideal. However, Tibetan Buddhism is traditionally hierarchical and quite rigid in structure, based on a system of reincarnated beings. At present Tibetan Buddhist nuns are prevented from full ordination as a *bhikshuni* (nun) within their own precept tradition. In the last several years, His Holiness the Dalai Lama has spoken out in support of re-establishing full ordination for Tibetan Buddhist nuns, thus trying to remain true to the ideas presented in Mahayana philosophy.[13] Adaptations to this traditional system are apparent in Western Buddhist communities in that not only is there often unimpeded access to high-ranking teachers and even instances of Westerners being recognized as reincarnated beings, but there is also willingness to ordain women and allow female practitioners to assume positions of authority.[14]

There is an inherent egalitarianism in Tibetan Buddhist communities in Canada and the United States where gender is insignificant and access to teachings is open to all. Judith Simmer-Brown notes in her discussion of Buddhist women teachers the impact of Pema Chödrön, principal teacher at Gampo Abbey. Pema Chödrön is an American-born Tibetan Buddhist nun within the Shambhala community who has reached unprecedented "success" as a female monastic. Along with being the principal teacher at Gampo Abbey, she has published best-selling books on topics related to Tibetan Buddhism. The Shambhala tradition has provided Pema Chödrön the opportunity to not only succeed personally but to develop a style of teaching that has "attracted thousands of students, roughly three-fourths of them women, many of whom had no previous experience of Buddhist meditation" (Simmer-Brown 2002, 317).[15] Specifically, she focuses her teachings on the bodhisattva ideal, which at its core is a teaching of equality, with all beings having the potential to reach enlightenment.

Tibetan Buddhism also provides a greater number of female role models in the form of historical women and enlightened beings than other forms of Buddhism. In particular, the *chod* tradition, a complex system of tantric ritual practices credited to Machig Labdrön (eleventh–twelfth centuries), portrays her as a powerful *yogini* and the only female to found a lineage of teachings and practices in Tibetan Buddhism. Tibetan Buddhism, due to its tantric background, includes a large pantheon of female deities and bodhisattvas; none of these deities are more important than Tārā, an enlightened Buddha who manifests in twenty-one different forms and in all levels of tantric practice. These two examples, along with the other highly trained women and female bodhisattvas and goddesses, often act as role models for practitioners, both Western and convert, and are testaments to the equality that is inherent within the teachings of Tibetan Buddhism, particularly in Western communities.

One last point regarding egalitarianism worth noting is related to social engagement. The push for equality in North American Buddhist communities grew alongside the feminist movement of the late 1960s and 1970s and the push toward applying the universal aspects of Buddhism to social crises. An important and well-documented component in Western Buddhist communities is social concern and involvement in improving society.[16] Whether teaching meditation to prisoners, counselling AIDS patients, or examining the environmental crisis from the perspective of dependent origination, Buddhist communities in the West are drawn to alleviating the suffering of others based on compassionate ideals. In the Tibetan Buddhist communities in Canada – both ethnic and convert – social engagement most often manifests in the fight for a free Tibet: "[T]he Free Tibet Cause is not primarily an explicitly Buddhist movement, although many of its members have been Buddhists ... The Tibet cause has attracted an exceptionally diverse group of people, some of whom see their activities on behalf of the cause as connected with Buddhist belief and practice, while others are concerned with human rights, opposing communism, and a range of other motivations" (Powers 2000, 220–1).

Lhadon Tethong is a prominent Tibetan Canadian engaged with this cause. As a Tibetan activist she became involved with Students for a Free Tibet. She has received worldwide attention for her August 2007 trip to Beijing to highlight the Chinese government's human rights violations as the countdown began to the 2008 Summer Olympics in Beijing.[17] While in China, Lhadon was posting a blog about her experiences there; the Chinese government became aware of her activities, had her followed by security agents, questioned by police, and subsequently deported for sharing her Beijing experiences.[18]

Tibetan Buddhism, as a religion of an oppressed people, has as part of its recent history a call for social awareness. Thus, Westerners who are attracted to the social engagement that characterizes Buddhism in the West see Tibetan Buddhism as providing religious teachings and practices while fulfilling their desire to be socially involved, in this case in the Free Tibet cause. The appealing aspects of meditation, egalitarianism, and social engagement are by no means exclusive to Tibetan Buddhism in the West. It is, however, the variations on these aspects that are unique to the tradition and make it all the more attractive. The popularity of Tibetan Buddhism in North America is very much dependent on the politics that distinguish it from other forms of Buddhism and on the manifestation of its rich practices and traditions as presented by important teachers such as the Dalai Lama.

HOW ARE CANADIANS ATTRACTED TO TIBETAN BUDDHISM?

While all the above-mentioned themes indicate the reasons Westerners are motivated to practice Tibetan Buddhism, this section considers how people are initially drawn to Tibetan Buddhism before they decide to fully engage in the religion. That is, what is appealing about Tibetan Buddhism for Canadians, how is Tibetan Buddhism being disseminated to the public, and what is the relation between the two? The remainder of this paper will consider the attraction to Tibetan Buddhism and what exactly contributes to and fosters this attraction. Specifically, the following interrelated factors will be examined: the media's influence on the attraction to Tibetan Buddhism and its popularity; the impact of the Tibetan political situation and the Dalai Lama's role, particularly his influence on how Tibetan Buddhist religious practice manifests in the West; and the use of *upāya-kauśalya* (skilful means/appropriate action) in response to a globalized religion.

Western Fascination: Media, Popular Culture, and Tibetan Buddhism

Tibet and its religious practices have intrigued the West since the arrival of the first Westerners in the mountainous country in the seventeenth century. Since then, Westerners have portrayed Tibetan Buddhism as a mystical religion tucked away in the snow-capped Himalayas – a very romanticized perspective. On the one hand, it was depicted as vastly different from monotheistic traditions, yet on the other, it was somehow already known; or, as Lopez has noted "Lamaism" appeared as a "strange – yet strangely familiar – religion" (1998, 3). A concern related to this theme of Western curiosity is the role of the media and popular culture in the spread of Tibetan Buddhism in North America. This has been briefly explored by others, particularly in relationship to the role of influential celebrities. However, on a larger scale it is quite difficult to ignore the relationship between Tibetan Buddhism's status in the West, popular culture, and the media attention it receives.

A high-profile religion that attracts significant public attention experiences both positive and negative outcomes. Over the past ten years I have questioned non-Tibetan Canadians who self-identify as Tibetan Buddhist and others with varying levels of interest in the philosophy and practices of Tibetan Buddhism about their initial interest in the religion.[19] I specifically asked where they first learned about Tibetan Buddhism rather than why they converted or what they valued most about the religion. The majority of responses were linked in some way to the media or an aspect of North American popular culture. Answers ranged from Richard Gere, to Lisa Simpson, to an Apple Computer ad-campaign featuring the Dalai Lama, to the music of the Beastie Boys, to a group of monks performing sacred music and dance. These Tibetan Buddhists usually did not seek out the religion initially; the contact was accidental or initiated out of simple curiosity about a passing reference to the religion. The high-profile celebrity association and other aspects of popular culture have attracted people to the religion at varying levels in ways that other Buddhist traditions have not experienced. Furthermore, the media attention has brought awareness of the political situation in Tibet.

The Dalai Lama: Politics and Religion in Exile

His Holiness the Dalai Lama and the political situation of Tibet add to an already complicated relationship between Tibetan Buddhism and the media and popular culture. The Dalai Lama tirelessly travels to Western countries teaching compassion and peace, while simultaneously establishing connections with political leaders and influential North Americans. While on his speaking tours the Dalai Lama frequently visits Canada and meets with politicians on both the federal and provincial levels.[20]

The Chinese invasion has forced Tibet's religious and cultural traditions into the global market. When the Dalai Lama went into exile in 1959, his role as religious and political leader was forever changed. The Dalai Lama has become the face of Tibetan Buddhism and the Free Tibet cause in North America. His work has made him a kind of ambassador for the culture and religion of Tibet. The media has closely covered his presence in Canada, noting when Canadian politicians were willing to discuss political and religious issues, despite threats from the Chinese government (Blanchfield and Heyman 2004; Stanford 2004). The Dalai Lama continues his annual trips to Canada, including a September 2006 visit during which he was presented with honorary Canadian citizenship, one of only three people to ever be awarded this distinction.[21] Typically, these trips are promoted as religious talks; however, he often discusses political issues as well. Seager notes, "Because the Dalai Lama is also the political leader of his country and an astute statesman, his tours usually balance politics with religion" (1999, 116). The Free Tibet Movement has become a global cause, with the Dalai Lama serving as the guiding force through the political turmoil faced by Tibetans around the world. According to Given, "Tibetans see the person of the Dalai Lama as an emanation of Chenrasigs. He is, for many, a living deity" (n.d., 18). The influence of the Dalai Lama in both Tibetan and Western communities is seen on multiple levels, particularly the political and religious. The role undertaken by the Dalai Lama is ultimately linked with the Tibetan sense of identity. Through interviews with Tibetans in Canada, Given writes, "When we discuss issues of resistance people invariably link the Dalai

Lama and his teachings on society, politics and spiritual transcendence and especially compassion and non-violence, to their sense of what it means to be Tibetan" (n.d., 12). Therefore, the power and influence of the Dalai Lama for this community is based on the Tibetan Buddhist understanding of reincarnated beings, an inherent power that has been astutely harnessed in compassionate ways.

Upāya-kauśalya: *Skilful Means in the Global Market*

The Dalai Lama's role as an exiled religious-political leader allows him to be the primary influence behind how Canadians experience Tibetan Buddhism. Not only is the Dalai Lama the most recognizable Tibetan, but the role he has assumed in bringing awareness to the Tibetan cause, and the relationships he has established with influential Westerners, could be understood from within the tradition as exemplary of *upāya-kauśalya* (skilful means/appropriate action). *Upāya-kauśalya* is often discussed in the context of an enlightened being employing certain devices (*upāya*) to help sentient beings. Gethin discusses skilful means as "clear devices (*upāya*) employed by the Buddha in order to get beings to at least begin the practice of the path" (1998, 228). On a broader scale, *upāya-kauśalya* has been identified as a useful tool in the adaptation of Mahayana as it comes into contact with new cultures and religions. Pye writes, "This style of thinking, in which insight (*prajñā*) and means (*upāya*) are inextricably related, is the key to understanding the proliferation of new forms which the Mahayana has woven across half Asia" (1978, 4). Furthermore, in relation to the successful adaptation of Buddhism in China, Harvey notes, "Adaptations were facilitated by the notion of skilful means" (1990, 150). The Dalai Lama has skilfully used his position, based on compassionate ideals, to simultaneously draw attention to the political situation in Tibet and actively promote and preserve Tibetan religious and cultural traditions while also disseminating the foundational Buddhist ideas of compassion and peace to Western audiences.

Richardson notes that "until too late, the Tibetans showed no proper understanding of the power of publicity and expressed the ingenuous hope that the truth would surely make itself known. Partly from inexperience and partly from anxiety not to provoke the Chinese ... they relied on others to put their case for them, but there were few people to attempt that" (1991, 35). The Dalai Lama can no longer be characterized in this way; he has become proactive when it comes to the Tibetan political situation. The primary methods he uses in spreading his political and religious messages are the preservation of Tibetan culture and religion as well as the spread of the dharma to Westerners by means of his connections with influential celebrities and world leaders, both of which garner significant media coverage. Furthermore, there have been deliberate moves at preserving Tibetan religious and cultural traditions by tapping into the vibrancy of Tibetan Buddhist ritual and the aspects of these traditions that Westerners find appealing, perhaps even exotic.

A commercial frequently shown in 2008 appealed to viewers to support Tibetans living in harsh conditions in the Himalayas. This type of media attention has helped to bring Tibetan Buddhism and the Tibetan political situation into the homes of average Canadians and has turned Tibetan Buddhism into a global religion. In Tibet, religion and politics have always been bound together, so the Free Tibet Movement is often connected to the religious traditions. Therefore, the appeal to Westerners for help for exile communities and those under oppressive Chinese rule in the Tibetan Autonomous Region is also usually religiously and culturally grounded. One of the major concerns of the Dalai Lama and Tibetans throughout the world is not just the return of an independent Tibet, but the preservation of religious and cultural practices. Much of what the media portray of Tibetan Buddhism, whether in an episode of the *Simpsons* or a nightly news broadcast, is related to the urgency of the political and cultural situation.

Ritual Commodification or Preservation of Tradition?

This sense of urgency has influenced how Tibetan Buddhism is disseminated in the West. The ways in which the dharma and the cultural traditions of Tibet are made known to Westerners are many. Within the last five years, Canadians have had access to a significantly greater number of sacred events and rituals open to the public. While on a tour of Canada in 2004, the Dalai Lama performed the *Kālacakra* (Wheel of Time) Initiation at the National Trade Centre at Exhibition Place in Toronto over an eleven-day period. Traditionally, the *Kālacakra* is high-level tantric practice; however, the Dalai Lama has begun to perform mass initiations of this tantra in public. The ritual ceremonies last many days (usually eleven) and are filled with empowerment or initiation into the teachings and the more popular sand mandala (cosmic diagram used in meditation) creation and destruction, a combination of esoteric and exoteric ritual. In the last decade it has become increasingly popular to translate high-level tantric texts or perform tantric empowerments for those without qualification, thus making the esoteric practice of Tibetan Buddhism available to a larger audience.[22] Making available material that was once considered inappropriate for public audiences has become a method for preserving the traditions and disseminating the teachings to interested Western audiences, and often is viewed as entertainment by non-Buddhists and Buddhists alike.

The *Kālacakra* Initiation is not the only Tibetan Buddhist ritual practice available for viewing by both practitioners and nonpractitioners. As Lavine notes, "American Vajrayāna has thus far proven its ability to make the Buddha's teachings widely available through networks of personal connections with Tibetan teachers and their American successors, education enterprises, ritual environments, and, now, electronic media" (Lavine 1998, 101). Another example of Tibetan Buddhists using ritual in a way that aims to entertain and educate Westerners is the performance of "The Mystical Arts of Tibet" tour.[23] The tour consists of a group of monks from *Drepung Loseling* Monastery in India who are trained in the multiphonic singing of Tibet. Typically the performance includes chanting, traditional Tibetan instruments, as well as dances that one finds in both religious and secular aspects of Tibetan culture.

The methods by which the media disseminate Tibetan Buddhism to the West appeal directly to the fascinations of Westerners, i.e., popular culture and "exotic" entertainment. Religious ideas have always been spread through current media technology.[24] In the twenty-first century technological advances have resulted in the globalization of religion: "Globalization is the product of the growing interdependence of cultures through emerging global techno-economic and sociocultural networks. These networks transcend national boundaries and in the process tend to challenge previous forms of authority and identity ... Mass media have played an important role in bringing about this transition by generating profound alteration in human consciousness ... the interdependence of religions and the media suggest that globalization represents an important shift in human consciousness ..." (Esposito et al. 2008, 3).

Through mass media, Tibetans have simultaneously spread the dharma, brought awareness to the political situation of Tibet, and preserved their cultural and religious practices. As Lavine explains, "American Vajrayāna is able to reach countless numbers of interested people in such a way that it may capitalize on the premium placed on the swift retrieval of information and the constantly moving and relocating nature of American culture. The ability to download Tibetan icons, photos of beloved lamas, and the texts of chants creates a level of access and a vicarious experience of participation unheard of in traditional Tibet" (1998, 113).

Naturally questions arise for those within and outside the tradition. These range from questions of whether the use of traditional ritual and cultural practices to spread the dharma are a legitimate use of *upāya-kauśalya* to whether Tibetan Buddhism is in danger of becoming little more than a commodity that can be bought and sold for interested North Americans. Tibetan Buddhism needs to be examined in the context of globalization to address these questions.

In the 2,500-year history of Buddhism, the religion has adapted as it came into contact with different cultures. Globalization in the twenty-first century has influenced the shape of Tibetan Buddhism, particularly in Canada and the United States, in that Tibetan Buddhism has developed in a pluralistic environment. And as Peter Berger notes, "the key characteristics of all pluralistic situations, whatever the details of their historical background, is that the monopolies can no longer take for granted the allegiance of their client populations ... The pluralistic situation is, above all, a *market situation*" (1990, 138). The market situation of North America has pushed Buddhist communities to vie for the attention of demanding and fickle North American consumers. This becomes especially important when one considers that both Canada and the United States are exceptional religious environments where virtually all branches of Buddhism coexist in relative harmony (Tanaka 1998, 295). For Tibetan Buddhism to remain competitive, the interdependence of religion and the media is valuable in bringing unfamiliar religious ideas and practices to mainstream North America.

CONCLUSION

It can be argued that the skilful means of His Holiness the Dalai Lama have guaranteed the preservation of Tibetan Buddhism in the West for the foreseeable future, at least in an adapted form. And while adaptation has characterized the spread and development of Buddhism throughout its history, both ethnic and convert communities have to acknowledge that Tibetan Buddhism in the West will not mirror what existed in Tibet before the Chinese invasion.

Reflecting on the second question of religious commodification, it can also be argued that the methods used in the dissemination of Tibetan Buddhism and the two distinct communities that are present in Canada are based on a relationship of reciprocity. That is, while Westerners may be searching for what they perceive to be practical or rational religious techniques such as meditation, they often in turn support Tibetan Buddhist communities and aid in the preservation of the tradition through donations or by attending religious and cultural events. Essentially it is a relationship structured around dependence and exchange. For convert Buddhists, paying for a ritual empowerment or buying a *thangka* may aid in their path to enlightenment, while at the same time these two acts may be carrying on a ritual lineage and preserving an artistic and meditative tradition.

If Tibetan Buddhists fear that their religious ideas and practices, as they go through this process of adaptation in the West, will become watered down and stray from what existed in Tibet, the Dalai Lama and other influential Tibetan teachers have partially assuaged these fears by establishing clear connections with academic institutions that aim to keep the tradition intact through textual preservation, philosophical inquiry, and the documentation of life stories and practices. Furthermore, in attempting to demystify Tibetan Buddhism and provide accurate interpretations of the more esoteric teachings to Western audiences, the Dalai Lama has supported the translation of tantric texts into Western languages.

It is difficult to predict how future events will impact Canadian Tibetan Buddhist communities. As these communities continue to grow in many directions, bringing together individuals from various backgrounds, globalization will continue to have an impact on Tibetan Buddhism in the West. Consistent with Padmasambhava's eighth-century prophecy, Tibetan Buddhism has become an international religion that is susceptible to adaptations that may drastically alter the tradition from its state in Tibet before 1959. While change is inevitable and fundamental to Buddhist ideology, Canadian Tibetan Buddhist communities are faced with the challenge of preserving traditions, yet fostering growth in a pluralistic environment. Ultimately, in the next twenty years significant changes will take place within Tibetan Buddhism, particularly in relation to the Free Tibet Movement and the political relationship between the Dalai Lama, China, and North America. How these changes will play out in Canadian Tibetan Buddhist communities cannot be foreseen. However, in spite of the unpredictable future, there is no doubt these dynamic communities are thriving as they continue to establish new cultural centres and religious spaces, bring in new teachers, attract newcomers, and welcome those from other exile Tibetan communities around the world.

NOTES

1 Quoted in Powers (1995, 186). Padmasambhava is credited with overcoming demonic and human opposition in order for Buddhism to be successfully established in Tibet.

2 See Tanaka (1998, 296) for a discussion of the idea of diffuse communities.

3 For further information on the Tibetan community in Quebec see the work by Louis Cormier (n.d.)

4 For an in-depth examination of the Toronto Tibetan Buddhist communities see McLellan (1999) and Danyluk (2002).

5 One informant, who teaches at Parkdale Public School, has noted that the majority of her 2006–2007 class consisted of Tibetan children, and that this marks a significant change in numbers in the last few years.

6 For more information on the Shambhala community in Nova Scotia see Swick (2002).

7 In February 2005, I attended Ven. Thrangu Rinpoche's teachings at the Vajravidya Institute in Sarnath, India. Sarnath is a Buddhist pilgrimage site that has a large population of Tibetans, both lay practitioners and monastics; it is home to several Tibetan Buddhist temples and the Buddhist University, the Central Institute of Higher Tibetan Studies. However, at the teachings given by Ven. Thrangu Rinpoche the majority of the attendees were Westerners from North America and Europe; it is well known among the residents of Sarnath that every February a large number of Westerners will be in town to attend his teachings.

8 See also Danyluk (2002).

9 http://www12.statcan.ca/english/census01/Products/Analytic/companion/rel/canada. cfm#growth.

10 http://www.buddhismcanada.com 27 August 2007, provides information on organizations, centres, and temples of all four Tibetan Buddhist schools. The majority of the centres fall under the *bka'-brgyud* (*Kagyu*) school or Shambhala International; however, the total number of institutions is approximately fifty across all of Canada.

11 Several articles are devoted to these themes in Prebish and Baumann (2002), and Prebish and Tanaka (1998).

12 See Lopez (1998) for a detailed examination of the Western fascination with Tibet.

13 See http://www.sakyadhita.org and www.congress-on-buddhist-women.org for further information on the attempts to establish a full ordination lineage in Tibetan Buddhism.

14 See Tsomo et al. (1995, 121–48).

15 See also Pema Chödrön (2000).

16 See, for example, Queen (2000).

17 Lhadon Tethong was accompanied on the trip to Beijing by a British Free Tibet activist named Paul Golding.

18 For further information on Lhadon Tethong and her experiences in China see http://www.beijingwideopen.org.

19 Fieldwork was conducted in 1999 in Waterloo, Ontario, and in 2005–2006 in Calgary, Alberta, and Sarnath, India.

20 For instance, see "Dalai Lama to Meet Harper this Month" (CBC 2007), and "Honouring Dalai Lama Could Have Economic Cost, China Warns" (CBC 2006).

21 The other two people who have been awarded honorary Canadian citizenship are Nelson Mandela and Swedish diplomat Raoul Wallenberg. See Office of His Holiness the Dalai Lama (n.d.) and World Tibet Network News (2006).

22 In the foreword to *A Manual of Ritual Fire Offerings,* His Holiness the Dalai Lama writes: "With the growth of interest in Tibetan Buddhism in recent years, the practice of Tantra has attracted particular attention. Traditionally Tantra is supposed to be kept secret. However, this unique path is often subject to severe misunderstandings, which are more harmful than the partial lifting of secrecy. Therefore, it is important that books containing authentic explanations be made available. Moreover, there is an increasing number of people, who even though they do not understand the Tibetan language, have received complete initiation from qualified masters of the lineage and sincerely engage in the requisite practices. Such people are dependent on good translations of the necessary texts" (Gyatso 1987).

23 See http://www.mysticalartsoftibet.org.

24 See Esposito (2008) for a discussion of the influence of technology and media on religion.

PART FIVE Lives

Albert Low
A Quest for a Truthful Life

MAURO PERESSINI[1] IN COLLABORATION WITH ALBERT LOW

Albert Low
Photo by Marie-Louise Dervaz of the Canadian Museum of Civilization, Ottawa

INTRODUCTION

The text that follows is a brief portrait of Zen master Albert Low. Now eighty years old, Low began practising Zen over forty years ago. He has been director of the Montreal Zen Center (MZC)[2] for almost thirty years and its spiritual director since 1986, the year he received full transmission from his own master, Philip Kapleau. Despite his many years of practice, his mastery of Zen thought reflected in his numerous publications (see the bibliography), and the rigour of his teachings, Low remains relatively unknown. This article is a step toward bringing him out of the shadows.

I have reconstructed Albert Low's life story based on my reading of many of his works and his 213-page unpublished autobiography (Low, n.d.) In addition, I conducted a series of filmed interviews (approximately 4.5 hours) with Low in relation to a larger project presently in its research phase at the Canadian Museum of Civilization (CMC). In the CMC project, I am hoping to create a collection of life stories of non-Asian Canadian practitioners and teachers in several Buddhist traditions, which aside from their intrinsic interest, will constitute a database for other scholars. The project so far has resulted in some 175 hours of filmed interviews with thirty-six practitioners or teachers.

I was trained as an anthropologist at the Université de Montréal and my particular method in field research is to record personal narratives, in particular life stories. These recorded personal narratives consist of three parts: 1) the life story as freely told by the interviewee following the question "Please tell me the story of your life and how Buddhism came into your life." 2) answers to questions I ask in order to complete the life story, to fill in the gaps or clarify points, etc. 3) answers to questions I ask concerning the tradition followed by the interviewee, the centre or temple, issues on Buddhism in a Western context, etc. The life story – the story of a person's life told from his or her own perspective – allows us to learn that person's individual motivations and values. It highlights the uniqueness of a person's experience in the face of the tendency within sociological and anthropological research to seek generalizations. And where such research often muffles and silences the subject's voice, the life story maintains a record of the subject's voice as the principal document in the research.

In our interviews and in his autobiography, Albert Low narrated his life story in more or less chronological order but there were many omissions which were filled in later, events presented out of order, repetitions, revisions, etc. I have edited this content to form a single orderly narrative. As much as possible, I have tried to present Albert Low's life story as he himself tells it, without interjecting any of my own comments. Albert Low has read the manuscript and given his approval. During the course of the interviews, I also did what is called participant-observation in anthropological research by attending MZC's activities.

THE BEGINNING OF THE QUEST

Albert Low's spiritual journey began in adolescence, originating from an intense dissatisfaction with day-to-day life. Like others who embark on spiritual quests, the young Low felt that "that" could not be all there was to life, that there had to be "something else."

In Low's case, the dissatisfaction can no doubt be explained in part by socio-historical context. Born into a poor working-class family in 1928, just before the 1929 stock market crash that ushered in the Depression, he lived with his parents near the London docks, in a neighbourhood then called Canning Town. In those days, it was one of the most destitute in East London, home to soapworks, sugar refineries, lumber mills, and chemical plants. The Second World War also brought traumatic experiences: the evacuation of school children from London, gas mask drills, and especially the 1940 bombing of London by the Germans, which Low experienced from an underground shelter. Those were amplified by a documentary film on the horrors of Belsen, Buchenwald, and Auschwitz, which Low saw one day in 1945. It marked him deeply: "Coming out into the vast summer twilight, one could do little more than blink in a vacant way. Not blink back tears of shame, rage or regret: those would come later, some much later. No, just blink in a stupid way, wondering somewhere in the groggy depths: what do we do now, what is one supposed to do after that?" (Low n.d., 3)[3]

The young Low's dissatisfaction with reality can also be explained by positive early experiences that hinted at "something" to be found beyond apparent reality. There were experiences of premonitory dreams, for example, when he was but seven years old.[4] And the experience he had at the age of thirteen, during a walk in the village of Cornwall, England: "I was walking up a slope, and all of a sudden, I knew I was me! That is not quite right because, when I put it like that, it seems as though 'I' knew 'something' (me). It would be truer to say knowing was me. It was an intense and penetrating cognition" (Low n.d., 106). Finally, at the age of seventeen, Low had another important experience while lying on the grass in a park: "Quite suddenly, I was no longer simply a body. It was as though I were the space and that everything were made of space. The trees, the grass, the sky were all of one substance, and that substance was, in some way, me" (Low n.d., 106).

Though confusing and unclear, those experiences were undoubtedly fundamental to keeping Low on a spiritual quest, fragile and doubtful in its early years. We must bear in mind that Albert Low entered his twenties in a world that was radically different from the 1960s, the decade in which so many Westerners undertook spiritual journeys. In London, the late 1940s and the 1950s were not really conducive to fundamental questioning, or to spiritual experimentation of any sort. People devoted most of their energy to basic material issues (employment, housing, food, etc.). Moreover, Western culture was not open to the world. Publications on world philosophies or religions were scarce. Psychoanalysis and behaviourism were practically the only tools available to those who sought the slightest understanding of the human condition. But neither the fantastical sexual portrayals of the human being proposed by Freud nor the transformation of humans into machines satisfied the young Low.

He began to emerge from this spiritual "desert" somewhat by chance, in 1950, when he went for a medical check-up at a clinic run by a Dr Nothman. Also a philosopher, the latter led a reading and discussion group for young people interested in philosophy and psychology. To pass the time in the waiting room, Low had taken along A.N. Whitehead's *Adventures in Ideas*. That did not go unnoticed by Dr Nothman, who immediately invited him to join the group. Low suddenly found himself thrust into the world of a range of thinkers. He read and discussed works that questioned conventional thinking on the nature of reality. During those meetings the whole issue of "reality" – what is meant by it – began to force itself upon him with a certain degree of anxiety.

A False Start: Scientology

One of the authors discussed by the group was Lafayette Ronald Hubbard, founder of Dianetics, which would later become Scientology. To the young Low, who was grappling with unanswered questions and hungered for new approaches to reality, Hubbard "was like a fresh breeze blowing through a war weary and psychologically exhausted era" (Low n.d., 9). In 1950, Hubbard's theory had not yet drifted into fantasy and science fiction. As presented in *Dianetics: The Modern Science of Mental Health* (Hubbard 1950), it is a simple, resolutely practical theory that everyone can grasp. In its initial form, Dianetics proposed the reliving of traumatic moments to defuse the "engrams" that developed during those past events and continued to govern an individual's behaviour, even if they were no longer pertinent to the new situations experienced. Once all the engrams, sources of inappropriate or fixated behaviour, were "audited out" (cleaned out), the subject became a "clear," as opposed to a "preclear" (who had yet to do the cleaning out). Presented thus, there was nothing farfetched about Dianetics, in view of what was being done in other areas of psychology.

In London, a small informal group had come together to discuss Hubbard's ideas. Albert Low joined it and invited his girlfriend, Jean, along. Shortly thereafter, Hubbard went to London to found a permanent centre. In 1953, Albert and Jean married and, in lieu of a honeymoon, decided to take the nine-month evening course offered by Hubbard. At the end of the training, Hubbard invited Low to become a full-time lecturer at the centre. The work was demanding and kept Low busy from eight in the morning till late in the evening. But it was also gratifying. Eager students arrived from all parts of the world. Committed and sincere, Low really believed he had found "the key to unlock the secrets of the universe" (Low n.d., 21). One day, two students from South Africa expressed a desire to have a teacher in Johannesburg and pressed him to accept the position. Hubbard, eager to become known throughout the world, approved the project. Thus, Albert and Jean moved to Johannesburg in March 1954.

The couple quickly set up the South African Association of Scientology, whose numerous members kept them busy from morning till night. This success brought huge financial rewards. But Low soon began to question Scientology and what Hubbard was doing. He had the impression that the theory was drifting toward increasingly fantastical conclusions, with incessant developments coming from Hubbard: the existence of prenatal engrams going all the way back to the moment of conception; a new state to be attained beyond clear – the "thetan," without mass and exterior to the material world, capable of remaining outside one's body in a continuous and stable manner, etc. All these developments, and many others even more fantastical,[5] were sources of doubt for Low.

Hubbard's theorizing was also coupled with increasingly miraculous promises of self-realization for students dealing with suffering, despair, and depression. Low's doubts now became ethical problems. Around June 1955, about fifteen months after his arrival in South Africa, Low wrote to Hubbard and sent him a list of twelve points that he felt needed clarifying. Hubbard responded by saying that Low's questions simply proved that he had not progressed sufficiently in the therapy and that he should make an effort to apply the latest methods developed. Disappointed, because the latest developments were precisely the ones that posed the greatest problems for him, Low invited Hubbard to give a course in South Africa. Hubbard declined the invitation and instead sent his right-hand man, J.H., for a six-week course. It was during those sessions that Low broke away from Scientology:

> Right from the beginning of the course, I could see that things were not going to work. I did have real doubts, doubts that were backed by the anguish that had been daily presented to me by people seeking relief, not in fairy tales, but in some substance. But the instructor came on like the Delphic oracle. When I objected [with the twelve questions], he said, "But this is what Ron says is so!" Within three weeks from the commencement of the course I realized that the mountain was but a very little hill. Scientology was no longer for me. Halfway through a morning session, I got up from my seat, left the room, and left behind a whole way of life, most of my friends, and a livelihood that had had the potential to make me a very rich man. (Low n.d., 53)

CRISIS AND GROPING IN THE DARK

With this decision, Low says that he was right back where he started, asking the same questions he had asked since childhood regarding reality, himself, and the world: "I turned in on myself to what, in retrospect, was a dangerous degree. The vacuum of my mind was filled with the most strange ideas and thoughts, which expressed themselves in bizarre behaviour, and for about two months I was at sea in a storm without compass or stars" (Low n.d., 59).

That was the beginning of a confusing period during which Low, Jean, and two of their friends who had also broken away from Scientology embarked on a whole series of random readings and experiments: hatha yoga, raja yoga, "two-way communication" exercises based on techniques used in Scientology, experiments with a Ouija board with a glass that seemed to move on its own, "automatic" writing, hallucinations induced by prolonged sleep deprivation, exercises in which you spin around faster and faster while being "neither giddy nor tired out, but, on the contrary, quite exhilarated" (Low n.d., 59).

Gurdjieff

In all this confusion, Low says he had two lifelines that prevented him from being totally lost. The first was the thought of Georges Ivanovitch Gurdjieff. Low had been introduced to the Russian author in the days of Dr Nothman's group, where they had discussed *In Search of the Miraculous*,[6] by Piotr Demianovich Ouspensky, one of Gurdjieff's followers. It was while reading about Gurdjieff's ideas, in the early 1950s, that Low experienced what he now clearly sees as his first *kenshō* (awakening experience):

> I am lying on the grass in a London park, reading, and a phrase "man does not remember himself" comes shooting out of the page and then goes like an arrow to the heart of things and, for a brief moment, I remember myself, and the world makes simple sense … It was this book … that turned my world upside down and awoke me spiritually. For months, after reading this sentence, I just wanted to laugh whenever I thought of it. I walked through barriers which before had seemed so impenetrable as though walking through the mist. It was all so easy – all that we had to do was to remember our*selves*. It was this that opened in me the conviction that we could indeed wake up at a very profound level, that we could "see into our true nature" as Zen Buddhism, which I was yet to encounter, would say.[7]

Only later would Low in fact be able to reinterpret his experience in more "Zen" terms: to link Gurdjieff's "remembering oneself" to being aware "upstream," i.e., prior to the imposition in consciousness of all dualistic opposites – "me" and "the world," "me" and "others"; and to view the "self" that must be remembered as being this Unity that is upstream of everything one can say about oneself, this pure "seeing" or "knowing" that is the screen on which everything is projected, a screen we always forget.[8]

It is easy to understand why, following such an experience, Low naturally turned to Gurdjieff once again during the major crisis he faced when he severed his relationship with Hubbard. Gurdjieff, who helped him come to terms with suffering and gain some understanding of what was happening, remains to this day one of Low's principal spiritual companions.

The view proposed by Gurdjieff also echoes the Zen Low would later encounter. Central to Gurdjieff's thought is the idea that every human being has the natural capacity to attain Objective Reason and, therefore, to see things as they really are, beyond the veil of subjectivity. However, we all possess a type of organ (humorously called the *kundabuffer*) that hinders the actualization of this potential by compelling us to satisfy ourselves with the mere realization of our selfish desires. To free ourselves from this organ and its harmful consequences, Gurdjieff proposes conscious labour and intentional suffering, consisting in exposing ourselves to the hurtful actions of others. At his institute in Fontainebleau, for example, Gurdjieff himself systematically exposed those who attended – among them many scientists, philosophers, and artists – to humiliation, in order to free them from the illusory satisfaction offered by the *kundabuffer*.

As he read Gurdjieff, Low quickly became convinced of the absolute necessity of this conscious and intentional labour that consists in facing our own suffering. For him, it became a prerequisite to serious spiritual practice.

Hubert Benoit

Interestingly, Low's second lifeline during the confusing period that followed the break with Scientology was a work on Zen, *The Supreme Doctrine*, which he happened upon in 1955. Written by Hubert Benoit, a French surgeon and psychiatrist, the book was quickly added to those Low, Jean, and their friends read and discussed. It is a work that Low would read again and again, even today, considering it to be the best Western reference on Zen ever written (Benoit 1951).[9] Benoit essentially stresses the starting point of Zen and Mahayana Buddhism: each of us is perfect and complete, so nothing can be rendered more perfectible. He also clearly explains the meaning of the "non-doing" Zen proclaims, thus avoiding the apparent contradiction of a tradition that affirms that "there is nothing to be accomplished," but which itself implies effort and discipline when practised. This point is critical to understanding Low's approach to Zen and the disagreements that would later surface between him and his principal teacher, Philip Kapleau.

Benoit emphasizes the fact that, although complete and perfect, human beings nevertheless live their daily lives under the illusion that their reality is dual, composed of positive and negative aspects: me/non-me, subject/object, spirit/body, good/evil, knowledge/ignorance, having/lacking, power/power-lessness, etc. Furthermore, they conceive of these opposing poles as being separate, independent, and incompatible. They do not see that neither of these poles can exist without its opposite since they are in fact emanations of the Unity that is situated "upstream," prior to the occurrence of the formal realm of concepts and values. As a result of this ignorance, human beings think the way to happiness is to ensure that the positive aspect triumphs over its negative opposite: destroying what threatens us, eliminating our faults to become better or more intelligent, acquiring something that is missing, etc. By trying to acquire material possessions, power, fame, wisdom, kindness, health, youth, etc., human beings thus commit themselves to making a constant effort to restore *downstream* of the illusory division a unity that they believe is lost. This unity takes the form of an ego, i.e., a unique and distinct "me" that would elim-inate every "non-me" that denies it. But since the two poles are inseparable, the work inevitably fails. Because it can only offer partial and ephemeral rewards, the work is in fact a source of worry, inner agitation, frustration, ego-tistic clinging to oneself-as-distinct, -unique, -superior, etc.

Therefore, what Zen proposes, according to Benoit, is, to begin with, a "non-doing" on the dualistic formal plane on which we usually struggle. It is a matter of deeply realizing – through exhaustion, so to speak – the deceptive illusion of all the paths we can take on that plane. Zen shows us that only if we stop losing ourselves in vain attempts on this plane of our phenomenal life can we hope to remember the principal Unity situated upstream of that plane – a Unity that has always been there, that was never lost. The specific work Zen proposes we accomplish, therefore, simply consists in awakening our dormant faith to the fact that we have never been split or divided, that we lack nothing, that we are One.

Whereas Hubbard's Scientology sought self-transformation into a "clear" conceived as a sort of superman, the Zen expounded by Benoit proposed work made of patience and humility, an indirect and negative work that simply requires that we be present to our absurd efforts to transform ourselves and the outside world, and to the humiliations and suffering brought on by all that. The way is thus unconsciously paved for the awakening that itself constitutes a sudden leap to the real view that there is nothing to be done, nowhere to go, for we have always been at the unique and principal centre of everything.

In Benoit's book, therefore, Low found the theme of humiliation he had already encountered with Gurdjieff. But contrary to the work of exposing oneself consciously and voluntarily to humiliating situations, which Gurdjieff advocated, the Zen Benoit presented showed that, most of the time, life itself is sufficient for accomplishing this task, that "the 'nature of things' is our best and most affectionate teacher, and the one that humiliates us the most."[10]

A Second Fundamental Kenshō

The years spent in South Africa were also marked by one of the most fundamental events in Low's life: the attainment of a second *kenshō* outside the formal practice of Zen. It occurred in 1958, when Albert, Jean, and their first child were staying at a ranch in the Transvaal desert belonging to their friend Hilda so that Low could devote himself to his correspondence studies in philosophy and psychology at the University of South Africa. Immersed in Kant's *Critique of Pure Reason*, Low came across the notion of "noumenon" and wondered how one could talk about an unknowable noumenon: when one looks at an object, one cannot in any way say that it is what one sees or thinks one sees, and yet the only information one has about that object is what one sees or thinks one sees. For Low, this problem eventually simplified itself to: how one can know that one does not know or how not-knowing is possible. It was as he reflected on this that the event occurred, making him see what he would later call "the fundamental ambiguity of human existence," which he sums up as "me-as-centre / me-as-periphery" in several of his books:[11]

> Then one day, while out walking, an insight came which opened up in me a whole new way of "seeing," a way that ever since I have, in the course of writing half a dozen books, struggled, unsuccessfully, to communicate. I saw that each of us views the world totally with nothing left outside, so to speak; there is no unknowable on the other side of a screen of appearance. This view that is totality is not "my view," because it lies upstream of all duality of subject and object, of "I" and "it," but even so is not an abstraction. It is "me" that views, but what is viewed is not differentiated from me but coextensive with me, much as the clay of the jug is coextensive with its form, or the mirror is coextensive with its reflections … But a moment of

differentiation, even so fine a differentiation that arises from simply focusing the attention, causes a rift in the view, and this primordial unity "me" then appears to be divided against itself. In that the world and me are one, focusing the attention focuses on me, and yet it is me that focuses. Me becomes a viewpoint which is simultaneously at the centre and at the periphery of what is focused upon. It is both viewer and viewed simultaneously. It is centre as viewer, but periphery as viewed. Even so, the primordial unity is not lost, but marred, and this marring carries with it a tension that is interpreted as a need to realize once again the original purity of unity. It is out of this feeling of the need to rediscover unity that, after all, has never been lost that ignorance is born. From this "ego" eventually arises as well all we know as experience, culture and, in short, "our life." Although it has taken me some time to express it, this insight lasted but a flash. (Low n.d., 81)

Emigration to Canada

Low at first held a series of jobs before finding a position as a junior personnel supervisor in an important company. In five years he climbed the professional ladder to the most senior level. And so, nine years after his arrival in South Africa, Low found himself once again in a materially satisfactory situation. With a good income, he was able to provide well for his wife and three children. However, as members of the privileged white minority, Albert and Jean had never felt at ease with the discrimination to which the black population was subjected. The 21 March 1960 Sharpeville massacre, the imprisonment of Nelson Mandela in 1962, and the increasing repression and violence against Blacks intensified their problems of conscience, given their incapacity to take concrete action to change things.

Unable to find a solution, Low and Jean finally decided to leave the country, conscious of the fact that it was not the most courageous thing to do. In May 1963, they emigrated to Canada, where their friend Hilda, who had also left South Africa, was waiting for them and helped them get settled.

FORMAL ZEN PRACTICE

The family settled in quite quickly, taking up residence in Chatham, a small town in southwestern Ontario where, less than ten days after arriving, Low found a job as a manager in the personnel department of the Union Gas Company. In addition to administering the firm's wage scale system, and the employee and executive pay procedures, Low also conducted research on organizational analysis.

Concerning his questioning and deep dissatisfaction with regard to apparent reality, Low remained convinced that he had to arrive at a new way of understanding, a new path to find his way through the suffering and confusion caused by the endless pursuit of his immediate selfish desires. This conviction was evidently reinforced by his experiences of "awakenings." Low was certain that the *kenshō* of the Transvaal desert had taken him upstream of the rupture of being (me-as-centre / me-as-periphery) and, hence, upstream of all experience proper to the dualistic formal plane. He was already persuaded that it was no use searching for new experiences, adhering to new beliefs or theories, or even trying to transform his behaviour. Since the problem resided in an erroneous view of reality, what he needed to do was find a way to adjust it, to get a "right view."

In March 1964, Low began getting up at 4:30 a.m. to sit on a chair "in *hara*" (the area below the navel, a centre of focus during meditation) and meditate until 6:30, before the children got up. At the time, he had no formal training. Not knowing exactly what to do, he improvised his practice. His deep dissatisfaction made him feel that he was at a dead end, experiencing a "dark night of the soul," as he stated in an interview, quoting Saint John of the Cross.[12] Practising was not a choice; it seemed more like a matter of life or death.

One day in 1966, Low and Jean came across *The Three Pillars of Zen*, edited by Philip Kapleau (1965). As they read the transcriptions of talks given by Yasutani Hakuun Roshi, they immediately felt his teachings were based on a living tradition. Moreover, contrary to Benoit, Yasutani emphasized the practice of *zazen* (sitting meditation). Finally, while stressing that one must not do *zazen* merely as an instrument to attain awakening, Yasutani considered *kenshō* to be of primary importance. Low felt he understood what Yasutani meant, and he sensed that his teaching might finally confer meaning on his practice. By pure chance, their friend Hilda, who lived in Toronto, learned that Yasutani came regularly to North America to lead workshops and retreats and that one such retreat was coming up in New York. Since Low could not take seven days off at the time, Hilda was sent to the retreat in New York, on a mission to invite Yasutani to Canada.

A first workshop (*zazenkai*) was organized at a hunting and fishing camp north of Toronto, for receiving Yasutani's teachings. Looking back on that initial meeting, Low describes Yasutani as a small, thin man, both unfathomable and intensely dynamic, who, with the help of his assistant, a monk called Tai-san,[13] spoke sincerely and with conviction. Low, Jean, Hilda, and a dozen other participants learned, among other things, how to sit in the lotus and half-lotus positions, and how to count and monitor their breathing. The days were spent listening to Yasutani, and practising *zazen* and *kinhin* (walking meditation). That workshop had a huge impact on Low. Not only did he feel in contact with an authentic tradition that is more than a thousand years old, but Yasutani's teachings allowed him to place the work of meditation in a broader "religious" context.

At the end of the workshop, Yasutani announced that he was going to lead a four-day *sesshin* (intensive retreat) in Rochester, New York, and invited those interested to contact his student Philip Kapleau. That is what took Low and Jean to the Rochester Zen Center (RZC) in October 1966. During the *sesshin*, they had their first experience of *dokusan* (individual meeting with the rōshi) and received their first *kōan: Mu!*[14] At that time, Low was not yet able to link the resolution of that *kōan* to his own efforts to go back upstream of all experience and to the fundamental ambiguity of me-as-centre / me-as-periphery. That would come later. In the meantime, he and Jean strove to attend as many *sesshins* as possible offered by Yasutani or Kapleau in Rochester or elsewhere. More than ten years after his break with Scientology, Low finally found himself committed once again to a practice that imparted meaning and direction to his spiritual quest.

But Low's "existential" suffering was far from over. The possibility of real transformation awakened in him a terrible fear that would haunt him until his first awakening, a fear that he describes as "dread of nothing," meaning that it was impossible to say that it was dread of "this or that." Added to the dread was a constant fear of death, anxiety attacks, states of psychological numbness, countless nights of insomnia, and a mortal fear of being alone. His blood pressure rose to alarming levels, which did nothing to ease his mind. In spite of everything, Low remained confident that his practice would get him through the difficult time. Kapleau gave him encouragement, seeing those phenomena as *makyō*, the sometimes quite severe illusory states of mind that arise as one practises Zen. He exhorted Low not to give up, saying that his fears supplied energy that Low could bring to his *zazen* practice.

Once again, books offered Low great support. At the time, he read books on spirituality almost to the exclusion of all others. Gurdjieff, his old travelling companion, was, of course, ever present. But Low read other traditions as well: Zen, Buddhism, yoga, Sufism, Christian mystics, etc. In addition to certain haiku, he discovered a text in the *Acts of John*: "If you knew how to suffer, you would be able not to suffer."[15] He also found comfort in T.S. Eliot's words: "The only hope, or else despair / Lies in the choice of pyre or pyre / To be redeemed from fire by fire" (Eliot 1943). But the greatest consolation was to be found in Saint John of the Cross's *The Dark Night of the Soul* (1959). These readings were combined with manual work, such as rug weaving, in which Low also found great solace.

The Choice to Continue with Philip Kapleau

Shortly after beginning formal practice with Yasutani and Kapleau, Albert and Jean were faced with a difficult decision following a seven-day *sesshin* in Rochester led by Yasutani. During the *sesshin,* it became clear that the relationship between Yasutani and Kapleau had seriously deteriorated. Not long after, the two officially parted ways. Just when they believed they had finally found a teacher, Low and Jean had to choose between pursuing their practice with Kapleau, who became teacher at the RZC, or following Yasutani and practising under Tai-san, the Japanese monk, who by then was teaching in the Catskills under the name of Eido Tai Shimano Rōshi. Their friend Hilda's tragic experience drove them to follow Kapleau. Hilda had decided to continue with Yasutani. One evening, while attending a *sesshin* given by him and Tai-san in New York, she phoned Low. She was in a psychiatric hospital, in serious condition. She asked Low and Jean to take her in, but Low, who was in the depths of anguish and anxiety, felt unable to accept. Low and Jean doubted that Yasutani, being Asian, had grasped and understood the very serious problems Hilda faced, problems that are specific to Westerners who practise Zen. Thinking that they would be better off with a Westerner, they chose to follow Kapleau.

Awakening

At that time, Low and Jean already had an established routine of daily practice that began at 4:45 a.m. Low's four weeks of holidays were all spent at the four annual *sesshins* held at the RZC. He and Jean also attended weekend *sesshins* as often as possible, at the Toronto Zen Centre or in Ann Arbor, Michigan. Sometimes they organized their own weekend retreats at home, with a schedule similar to that of a centre. In addition to the aforementioned *makyō,* which were not always negative,[16] the practice of Zen had other repercussions on Low's lifestyle. Early on, he spontaneously stopped consuming alcohol. Shortly after commencing seated meditation on a regular basis, Jean developed an aversion for meat. Low had no difficulty joining her in a new vegetarian diet, but he did not do it for any moral reason.

In December 1974, during a *sesshin* at the RZC, Low attained his first awakening within the context of Zen practice. The description of that *sesshin* and the awakening itself was published, at Kapleau's request, in the RZC's *Zen Bow* magazine (Winter and Spring 1975). In the article, Low described the awakening as follows:

> At the time of awakening, I received no new knowledge, no secret of the universe, no fundamental wisdom, not even an insight. I knew nothing more than I had known before awakening. Awakening was a flash of pure knowing released from all sheaths of knowledge. But even that this was so took me years to realize ... Of course I felt a great deal of euphoria. For several nights after, I found it difficult to sleep, as I was continually washed over by joy and relief. When I tell people that awakening is not an experience but a new way of experiencing, they are often bemused and will sometimes ask: but was not your awakening an experience? They confuse the joy at coming to awakening with awakening itself, although, of course, they are quite different. (*Zen Bow* 1975)

Zen and Management

After his awakening, Low pursued his training with Kapleau for another twelve years. It consisted essentially in working on the forty-eight *kōans* compiled in the *Mumonkan* and on the one hundred of the *Hekigan-roku*.[17]

To Low, it stood to reason that the profound understanding of reality he derived through the practice of Zen should be applied to his work, in order to question the generally accepted ideas about management and gain a new understanding of this field of human activity. This was a period of intense creativity during which Low integrated various authors' ideas into his own works. Although not directly associated with Zen thought, all those authors promoted a systemic way of thinking that "resonated" with Zen because it approached reality in terms of systems of interrelation and interdependence, as opposed to analytic thinking that emphasized discrete elements. At the time, Ludwig von Bertalanffy had just published his general system theory, which was still largely unknown (Bertalanffy 1968). Low was particularly interested in John

Godolphin Bennett's work on systems (Bennett 1957–1966),[18] which he integrated into that of a Canadian, Elliott Jaques. Devoting himself to writing for a year, Low eventually produced an article, "The Systematics of a Business Organization," published in *Systematics,* a magazine edited by Bennett (1966). Later, the article became the book *Zen and Creative Management*, published in 1976 and republished in several languages since then, with over 70,000 copies in print.

A Radical Life Change

The publication of the book also marked the end of Low's research on management. Several members of the Union Gas Company's senior management were opposed to it, saying that Low was encroaching on their area of responsibility. In addition, the firm's new president, who had taken office in 1972 and was much less open to fundamental research on management, asked Low to abandon his research. Since it was no longer possible to integrate his spiritual practice into his work, Low essentially lost interest in his job. Together with Jean, he began planning his departure from the firm and preparing a new phase in his life.

The awakening attained in 1974 influenced his decision. It strengthened Low's desire to deepen his practice of Zen and made him feel that his life would best be spent giving to others what he himself had received by practising Zen. But first, he needed not only to deepen his practice, but also to receive authorization to teach.

In 1972, Low and Jean had begun setting money aside by drastically reducing their spending. Four years later, in 1976, when their three children had left home, they finally decided to sell their property and possessions. That same year, they left for the RZC, where they spent three years, living on their savings and the generous pension Low received from the Union Gas Company.

Upon his arrival at the RZC, Low pursued the work on the *kōans* he had begun after the 1974 awakening, and while doing so, he attained other *kenshō*.[19] He and Jean faced many difficulties on first arriving at RZC. They had given up an independent family life for life in a community, when Low was forty-eight and Jean forty-six. They were in the company of people who, for the most part, were fifteen to twenty years younger. Low and Jean were therefore often placed under the supervision of young people in their twenties who, in spite of that, were as pretentious as anyone "imbued with the samurai spirit of death or glory" (Low n.d., 186). After leaving behind a house, a career, friends, and possessions to move to the RZC, Low found himself assigned to kitchen duty. The work was so hard that he lost ten kilos in just a few months and then developed bronchitis. This situation was a source of humiliation but also a source of much learning.

The Disagreements with Philip Kapleau

Fortunately, Low became editor of the center's magazine, *Zen Bow*, a task that was more in keeping with his skills. But Low soon had to face an even greater ordeal: the rapid deterioration of his relationship with his master, Kapleau. That ordeal was rendered all the more painful by the fact that Low would always feel greatly indebted to the RZC and Kapleau, whose accomplishments he admires.

Setting aside the more personal aspects of the relationship between the two men, the disagreements between Low and Kapleau were related mainly to the practice of Zen in a Western context and, in particular, to the way in which Kapleau reproduced the extreme severity of the tradition he inherited from his own masters, Harada Sogaku Daiun, of the Hosshinji Monastery, and his disciple Yasutani. Low soon came to doubt the effectiveness of "external stimulation," either symbolic or physical, and of the harsh discipline used to intensify the practice.

Initially, the harshness of the discipline advocated by Harada and Yasutani could be explained by their desire to put an end to the state of decadence in which the Sōtō Zen tradition, to which Harada adhered, found itself. A literal interpretation of the Zen affirmation that "nothing needs to be done" had led several practitioners to reject all effort, under the pretext that attaining awakening was doing nothing other than sitting – *zazen* itself being considered awakening. For his part, Kapleau felt that the very lax climate of the 1960s in North America justified importing such discipline and applying it as rigorously as possible. The RZC soon acquired a reputation as the "boot camp of American Zen," dominated by a certain "macho" spirit.

Low was irritated by Kapleau's tendency to idealize Zen. For example, Kapleau encouraged his students to view Zen as a unique spiritual approach superior to all others, which inevitably made the practitioners feel superior, contrary to what Zen espouses. Low also felt uneasy about the importance Kapleau attached to the title and status of roshi. In Kapleau's view, Zen came from an all-wise and omnipotent roshi, and he sometimes used the expression "The Roshi" to refer to such a perfect being. But the greatest problem for Low was the fact that Kapleau resorted to a whole series of "external" means to whip the students into intensifying their practice. Low had the impression that Kapleau did not believe in his students or in the "natural" maturation of their practice over time. Low felt that the effects of basic discipline, regular meditation, regular attendance at *sesshins,* work on the *kōans,* and the suffering one experiences in life were not enough for Kapleau. It was as if Kapleau could not endure "the steady, quiet *zazen* that is necessary over long periods of time, years in fact, for the practice to mature. He had to make something happen" (Low n.d., 155).

Thus does Low explain the highly emotional encouragement talks Kapleau gave during *sesshins,* talks seemingly designed to bring the *zendō* to a state of emotional frenzy. The same went for the intensive and energetic use of the *kyōsaku* (the Zen warning stick) – up to six or seven times during a thirty-five-minute meditation session – which transformed a practice tool into a source of personal challenge for the practitioners, leading them to believe that they could rate their practice in terms of how stoically they bore the blows.[20] Practice at the RZC was also emotionally intensified by the competitiveness surrounding *dokusan* (individual meetings with the Roshi). Since the number of places was limited to twelve, as soon as the signal was given, the fifty or so participants rushed toward the stairs leading to the room where Kapleau awaited them. In a sometimes dangerous race where one risked injury,[21] some people climbed the steps two at a time and grabbed those who were ahead of them to push them out of the way. Low questioned the validity of such a spirit of competition and wondered how Zen practice could benefit by encouraging "winners" to feel triumphant and "losers" to feel discouraged.

Competition among practitioners was also promoted through the use of status symbols. Kapleau normally reserved the best places in the *zendō* for those who were, in his opinion, most advanced in their practice. This hierarchy among the students was also expressed in concrete terms by the granting of *rakusu.*[22] In the Rinzai tradition, *rakusu* is given to a monk or nun upon ordination. But Kapleau began granting his students *rakusu* in 1974 as a sign that they had attained awakening. Low is not convinced that Kapleau made a clear distinction between getting through one's first *kōan* and attaining a *kenshō.* Rather, he believes that, in many cases, Kapleau authenticated *kenshō* when in fact the practitioner had simply exhausted the possibilities of using a particular *kōan.* The result was that a large number of *rakusu* were granted, giving the impression that many students had in fact attained awakening. Those who had not been granted a *rakusu* felt frustration and jealousy. Those who did receive a *rakusu* feigned modesty but indulged in self-congratulation. Neither set of emotions furthered Zen practice.

The harsh training offered at the RZC led to the departure of many students. The most striking case is without question that of Toni Packer, one of Kapleau's senior students. She left the center in 1981, taking almost half the members with her, to practise a form of Zen that was the exact opposite of what Kapleau taught, and was considered gentler and more suitable for Westerners. But Low's discontent with respect to the way Zen was practised at the RZC was not limited to the adaptation of Zen to Western culture. It was more deeply grounded and was related to the very essence of Zen practice. Low had always agreed with Harada, Yasutani, and Kapleau on the central importance of awakening in the practice of Zen. Like them, he had always disagreed with those who took a literal interpretation of Zen's invitation to "do nothing." In terms of Hubert Benoit's concept of the dualistic formal plane in which people exhausted themselves in illusory attempts to become "better," for Low, the use of "external stimulants," whether symbolic or physical, to intensify the practice prevented practitioners from stepping out of the dualistic formal plane. Those "external stimulants," on the contrary, reinforced the tendency to make Zen practice one more instrument at the service of vanity, pride, personal ambition, and the feeling of superiority – in short, of an ego that claims to be unique and distinct. Practice, he felt, should take the opposite course and recognize that this egotistic aspiration is precisely the source of our suffering.

With sadness Low recalls the numerous fruitless discussions he had with Kapleau on these issues; their exchanges served only to confirm their differences of interpretation. In spite of himself, and the admiration and attachment he felt for his teacher, Low could not help noticing the rift between them.

THE MONTREAL ZEN CENTER

Low had never intended to stay at the RZC indefinitely. Rather, his plan was to acquire the skills he needed to become a teacher and transmit to others what he himself had received. In late 1977, Kapleau was to lead a weekend workshop at the Montreal Zen Center (MZC), which he had founded in 1975, and he invited Low to go along. The francophone and multicultural city appealed to Low. Two years after the workshop, the leader of the MZC, who was anglophone, decided to move away to Toronto, fearing the results of the referendum on Quebec's independence, to be held in 1980. Kapleau proposed that Low take the position of leader of the MZC. Given the difficult situation between him and Kapleau, and since he had no hope of becoming a teacher in Rochester, Low jumped at the chance.

The group Low had to lead upon his arrival in July 1979 consisted of about thirty people, fifteen of whom made up the core. But the group was not very active. Its practice was limited to sessions of seated meditation on some week nights. The early days were difficult for Low. At the time, the members of the MZC manifested a strong allegiance to Kapleau expressed in various ways; they took great pains to reproduce every detail of the physical environment of the RZC: the colour of the walls, the lights dimmed exactly as they were at the RZC, etc. For Low, the essence of the practice was lost in all those accessory details. Moreover, faced with the differences between Low and Kapleau, their personalities and styles, the members of the MZC felt torn. Some became anxious and irritated, and directed their anger at Low.

To complicate matters, the MZC was housed in half of a rented duplex on Marlowe Street in a noisy location and with barely enough room for the members. Under such conditions, an increase in membership was out of the question, as was the possibility of organizing long *sesshins*. As soon as they arrived in Montreal, therefore, Albert and Jean began looking for a house. They found one with the necessary potential in a very different neighbourhood, near the Henri-Bourassa subway station and the Rivière-des-Prairies. It was finally purchased in October 1979, after shrewd negotiations to reduce the initial cost. As the *zendō* building required extensive renovation, the group was forced to practise in the dining room. After months of repairs to which several members contributed energy and expertise, the new *zendō* was finally ready at the end of 1982.

Still under supervision, Low had to negotiate with Kapleau every change he wanted to make to the practice. Nevertheless, he was able to increase the number of sittings quite quickly; in 1979 the centre was already offering meditation sessions in the mornings and three evening sessions a week. Furthermore, initially authorized to lead only two two-day sittings a year, Low got the right to lead three-day sittings, which were then scheduled on two consecutive weekends, in order to intensify the practice. When Kapleau finally granted him full transmission in 1986, rendering the MZC fully independent from the RZC, Low had *carte blanche.* He immediately established an annual agenda of thirteen *sesshins,* each with six days of intensive meditation; in addition, he offered six workshops in Montreal, as well as workshops in Kingston, Quebec City, Ottawa, and Granby. This restructuring of the centre's activities produced positive results. Membership increased steadily, and in 1986 Low was finally able to pay himself a salary, $500 a month, while Jean continued to work on a volunteer basis. Moreover, with time, several members reached a certain level of maturity in their practice and became sufficiently convinced of the meaning of their spiritual journey to overcome their initial doubt.

Today, as in the past, the MZC remains a lay community. It has about 220 members, both francophone and anglophone (the centre is bilingual), 150 of whom regularly participate in the activities. Men account for about 60 per cent of the membership, and the great majority of members are of non-Asian origin. In general, the members are above-average level in education, and most are middle class. The health professions (doctors, psychologists, psychiatrists, etc.) are strongly represented, probably accounting for over 50 per cent of the membership. Most members are between the ages of 30 and 60, but over the past several years, the centre has been faced with an aging membership. It is becoming increasingly difficult to attract young people to the practice of Zen. Even though close to 200 of them attend the annual workshops for beginners, only a handful remain after a year. For Low, this is the direct result of a lifestyle that is increasingly antithetical to the practice of Zen. With its accelerated pace and constant invitation to "zap," contemporary audiovisual culture (movies, television, Internet, MP3's, etc.) features quickly changing images and continuous splicing, inducing a consciousness that is the extreme opposite of the sustained attention required for spiritual practice. In a world where one is easily bored and caught up in the frenzy of distraction and distracting oneself from the distractions themselves, Low believes it is difficult to invite people to adopt a practice that involves crossing the desert of one's own existence without hoping to gain anything in terms of special experiences or personality change.

Albert Low's Zen at the MZC

When one reads Low's texts and *teishō* lectures, one sees that he does not hesitate to draw parallels between Zen teachings and the ideas found not only in a multitude of Western literary and philosophical works (for example, one can find Rainer Maria Rilke quoted next to T.S. Eliot or Henri Bergson), but also in a variety of spiritual traditions: Nisargadatta's *jñāna* yoga, Sufism, Christianity and its mystics, etc. In this respect, therefore, Low innovates by borrowing from sources other than Zen. Moreover, when Low borrows from Western texts it is not simply for the purpose of helping Westerners gain a better understanding of Zen. It is above all because he views Zen not as a tradition that is superior to others, but rather as one path *among others* – all of which can, in their own way, lead to the truth of things. With regard to Low's interpretation of what is a spiritual quest, one could ultimately say that he openly invites his students not to define themselves as "Buddhists" or "Zen Buddhists."

Regarding the more concrete way Zen is practised at the MZC, Low explains that he paid much attention to importing from the Japanese tradition only the elements that are strictly required for practice. Without hesitation, he gave up the title of "roshi." To him, the notion of roshi tends to create, among Westerners more so than among the Japanese, a whole aura of adulation and idealization, which are utterly contrary to Zen. For Low, attaining awakening does not make a master a special, unique person and an object of special attention. The master's awakening merely opens up a new possibility, the possibility of speaking from a source that is common to all, so that when the master speaks, the student can immediately acknowledge it as being true, as it emanates from the source that is common to all. That is why the object of devotion must not be the teacher, but rather the truth itself.

The filtering out of irrelevant accessory elements also applies to most of the rituals and ceremonies of Japanese Zen, which were numerous at the RZC. Low is in no way opposed to the rituals themselves. Rather, he is convinced that, as in the Asian countries where Buddhism has penetrated, the West will develop its own Zen rituals and ceremonies. Until then, the West needs to avoid copying foreign rituals and retain only those that are of utmost use to practice. As examples, the Buddha's birthday is not celebrated at the MZC; there are no ordinations, marriage ceremonies, or taking refuge ceremonies. Conversely, the recitation of the Four Vows and Hakuin Zenji's "Chant in Praise of Zazen" are an integral part of every meditation session because they are related to practice.[23]

The fact that the MZC is strictly a lay community also reflects Low's convictions with regard to the direction Zen must take in the West. In his opinion, given the socio-economic conditions in the past, the existence of a community devoted exclusively to practice was necessary in Asia; however, that is no longer the case today, particularly in the West. Low's argument can be presented in three points. First, he does not consider the monastic life, which aims to eliminate the sense of self through an extremely regimented life, very effective in a Western context dominated by a very strong sense of individuality and "I."

Second, in his view, by living such a life, separate from daily life, one is deprived of the teachings Western lay life has to offer. Due to the difficulties it entails, the suffering it brings, and the humiliation to which it subjects us, Western lay life makes an invaluable contribution to the "fragilization" of the ego. The master's role then consists in waiting for that work to be done and accompanying the students as they face the ensuing suffering. By contrast, a master in a monastery must artificially strive to get the students to face their desire to be unique, separate, and superior. Third, and last, it can be said that Low firmly believes that lay practice is somewhat superior to monastic practice. In his view, monks who practise in a "protected" context have more difficulty attaining the intensity, sincerity, and authenticity of a lay person who, to pursue such a spiritual journey, must constantly face family responsibilities, work constraints, etc. This is why Low believes lay persons can attain higher standards of achievement than monks.

The filtering of accessory formal and cultural elements from Zen practice, of course, also applies to the "external stimulation" mentioned earlier. To Low, it is obviously not a matter of abolishing all discipline and adopting the relatively loose type of approach espoused by Toni Packer. He has taken care, however, to retain only the essential discipline that is justified by the simple fact that the practice of Zen, whose ultimate goal is awakening, is necessarily difficult. The discipline must support the internal effort of the practitioners who do the real work. Montreal Zen Center *sesshins* therefore lack the emotional intensity of those at the RZC. The *teishō* lectures and encouragement talks are delivered not with the intention of exploiting the practitioners' emotionalism but to sustain the spiritual ardour, the flame that fills the practitioners with courage. Furthermore, contrary to many Zen centres that have abandoned the use of the *kyōsaku* for Westerners, the MZC has maintained its use. However, it is employed only at the practitioners' request, and not as intensively as at the RZC. The *kyōsaku* is strictly a tool at the service of practice, used when the meditators deem it necessary, to help them refocus when their mind starts wandering or to relieve physical tension (neck, shoulders, etc.). Similarly, at the MZC everyone has regular access to *dokusan*, thus eliminating all anxiety and competition among practitioners. In the same spirit, the practice at the MZC is free of all symbols or markers that might distinguish advanced practitioners (a specific place in the *zendō, rakusu,* etc.). This reaffirms the fact that it is absolutely impossible to judge, evaluate, or qualify a person's practice, since it does not take place at the level of the formal dualistic conscience, but rather upstream, where it happens in silence.

CONCLUSION

Can we draw conclusions from Albert Low's life story, conclusions which will help us understand how Buddhism is taking root in Canada?

"Strictly Zen"
A Western-born teacher of Buddhism always faces the task of what elements of the Buddhist tradition to preserve unchanged and what to adapt to the Western cultural context. Each teacher, of course, makes his or her own individual decisions. Albert Low's teacher Philip Kapleau was well known for his attempts to adapt Zen to the West. He expended great effort to translate sutra chants into English, for example. Low, however, sees his task not so much as adapting Zen but as strictly preserving Zen.

In the lectures (*teishōs*), articles, and books where he explains Zen, Low draws multiple parallels between Zen teachings and the ideas found in other Western and non-Western traditions, and thus pays little heed to the boundaries between spiritual traditions. But where *practice* as such is concerned it is another matter altogether; his teachings are strictly Zen. First, as we already saw, Low's rigour on that level has nothing to do with any desire to import Japanese Zen practices strictly adhering to their cultural form. On the contrary, it refers to filtering out the "cultural" – and hence accessory – content of the Japanese practice in order to retain only the essential elements that form the basic discipline needed to attain awakening. Second, Low's teachings regarding Zen practice are also strictly Zen in the sense that they never include practices coming from other spiritual traditions (yoga, martial arts, etc.) Does this combination of openness to other traditions in explaining Zen combined with strictness and rigour in practising Zen say anything about the way Zen is evolving in the West?

Lay Practice
Where many Zen teachers in North America assume that monastic practice provides the ideal model for practice, Albert Low has specifically designed a Zen practice meant for lay people. He feels that the Western lay life is so full of

sufferance (different forms of humiliations of one's ego) that it constitutes the best master one can have. By comparison, living in a monastery prevents someone from receiving the teachings from this precious master. Will the emphasis on lay practice as opposed to monastic practice become the characteristic direction of Zen, of Buddhism, in the West?

Teacher-Student Relations

In Asian tradition, the old teacher names his successor before dying; this transmission grants the successor his authority to be teacher. All the Zen schools in the West repeat this rhetoric of transmission. They all claim that theirs is genuine, authentic Zen because their line of transmission is unbroken for many, many generations.

The Philip Kapleau lineage in America, however, presents us with a lineage in which the student breaks relations with the teacher and on the student's own authority declares himself or herself a teacher. Kapleau himself broke off relations with Yasutani Rōshi and set himself up as Rōshi of the Rochester Zen Center without the approval of Yasutani. In turn, Kapleau's own disciple, Toni Packer, broke off relations with him and started her own training centre in 1981, the Genesee Valley Zen Center, subsequently renamed the Springwater Center for Meditative Inquiry and Retreat. And then, Albert Low himself, after receiving transmission from Philip Kapleau in 1986, later broke off relations with him because of disagreements over the conduct of Zen practice. Is this Western individualism rejecting authority in contrast to the Asian veneration of hierarchical authority? It is still too early to draw any conclusions about the significance of this phenomenon.

Humiliation

Finally, Low's emphasis on humiliation as part of Zen practice is unique in North American Zen and quite unusual in Zen as practised in Japan. Gurdjieff taught that the humiliation one experienced in suffering was a valuable tool for countering our constant need to fulfill selfish desire. Low found a similar theme in Hubert Benoit and now deliberately focuses on times of humiliation as opportunities to deconstruct the hard shell of the ego. Zen in the West is much more associated with the countercultural rebel whose style verges on arrogance. No other Zen teacher in the West refers to humiliation in this way. In Japan, humiliation as a Buddhist practice is much closer in spirit to Pure

Land Buddhist practice where repentance is the key to salvation. Given that Low's focus on humiliation seems to be linked to specific influences he received from Gurdjieff's and Benoit's writings, this example shows the importance of paying attention to individual variations in the interpretation of Zen or other Buddhist traditions that a careful look at the life stories of Buddhist practitioners can reveal.

A Truthful Life

I would like to end this chapter with a personal anecdote, which illuminates Albert Low's character. When I met with him in September 2007 to discuss this article, I had not seen him in over a year. In 2005, I had practised for a while at the MZC ("participant observation"), but then I progressively stopped attending the evening meditation sessions, under the pretext that I had a very hectic schedule. As a result, I left the MZC, and I never spoke to Low again about my practice of Zen. Our only communication, via email, consisted of questions related to my research project on Buddhism in Canada.

When I arrived at the centre to work on the article, Low suggested we sit outside on the balcony, to take advantage of the fine weather and the beautiful garden. The week before, I had sent him the first version of the article, and I expected him to suggest a whole series of corrections and cuts. Instead, he informed me somewhat casually that he agreed with everything. I had gone there expecting to do at least an hour's work in his company, but our discussions of the article lasted but a few minutes. Then, as I considered what else I might ask him before going back to the office, he asked me, "Well, now, how is your practice coming along?" He had turned to me, and his eyes seemed to say "Let's move on to serious matters, shall we? How is your practice coming along?" I suddenly felt, as I had when I conducted the filmed interviews, that I was in the presence of a man who, though faced with doubts and difficulties of all sorts during the course of his life, had never lost sight of the meaning of his quest, one who still came back – and would always keep coming back – to what is essential for him. In answer to his question, I informed him that I had practically stopped practising altogether. Taking no notice of my evident uneasiness, or my discouragement, he gave me a bit of advice to help me pick up where I had left off. And then, perhaps guessing that I was dying to reply "What's the point?" he added, "It's important, you know, if one wants to live – live a life – a truthful life."

NOTES

1 I would like to thank Albert Low for taking the time to meet with me while I was doing research on Buddhism in Canada, for the autobiographical material he kindly placed at my disposal, and for his invaluable advice. I also thank Paula Sousa for her patience and meticulousness in translating the French version of this article into English. I take full responsibility for any errors or inaccuracies the article may contain.

2 See the MZC Website, http://www.zenmontreal.ca/.

3 In the life story he provided during the filmed interview of 12 December 2005, Low begins with this episode, which is also mentioned in some of his works, including *Creating Consciousness*.

4 Filmed interview, CMC project, 12 December 2005.

5 Low mentions, for example, the idea of a "Fifth Invader Force who had imprisoned, with the aid of an instrument that looked like a camera, the thetans at some remote time in the past and locked them into the body" (n.d., 29).

6 Piotr Demianovich Ouspensky, *In Search of the Miraculous: Fragments of an Unknown Teaching* (London: Routledge and Kegan Paul 1950).

7 Low, "The Autobiography," 3, 17 (emphasis in original). In the interview filmed on 12 December 2005 (CMC project), Low describes that *kenshō* as follows: "I was lying in a park ... reading Ouspensky's book *In Search of the Miraculous*, and in there, Gurdjieff says, 'man does not remember himself.' And at that moment, when I read that phrase, I remembered myself. And for the next several months, I went around telling everyone how easy it was, all you have to do is remember yourself! [Laugh] ... This great insight stayed with me a good six months, and it seems as though I was living in another medium. I was living in a space which wasn't a space, which wasn't a physical space. And I tried to start talking to people about what it was that I'd seen. And I'm still, right now, trying to tell people about what I've seen."

8 In the interview filmed on 30 January 2006 (CMC project), Low interprets what happened at the time of that first *kenshō* in more "Buddhist" or "Zen" terms: "It is a change of awareness. You see, when you look around, you just see the room. You don't see the seeing. The seeing is yourself. You say, 'The room is there.' But really, in order to state the full truth, you should say, 'I know the room is there.' But you ignore the knowing. It's a constant, what you might say, background to life. It doesn't change ever, and it's always constant, immutable, unchanging. And so, you ignore it. And yet, that is reality. You give reality to the room. You don't find the room to be real. Most people think, 'The room is there and I see it.' But it's the other way around. I am seeing, and it happened to be now the room I am seeing. There's a very famous dialogue, in the *Śūrangama Sūtra*

between Buddha and Ananda, in which Buddha rings the bell and asks Ananda, 'When this bell stops ringing, do you stop hearing?' And Ananda says, 'Yes.' And Buddha does it three times. And each time Ananda says, 'Yes.' And Buddha says, 'Why are you so obtuse?' And he goes on to say – that's a paraphrase – 'If you can see into this, you'll have no fear of death.' But this is true. If you can remember yourself, there is no fear of death because it's all a projection onto that screen of yourself."

9 The first English translation was published in 1955. A better translation can be found in Benoit (2004). In 1963, when he was en route to Canada, Low met Benoit in Paris: "My impression is that he must have had some very deep awakening, although he did not say this himself … His simplicity and complete lack of any airs or graces, his obvious strength and openness affected me very much, and I am still of the opinion that he was the most deeply developed man I have yet met" (Low n.d., 68, 91).

10 The original reads: "Rappelons-nous que la 'nature des choses' est pour nous le meilleur, le plus affectueux, et le plus humiliant des maîtres; elle nous entoure de son aide vigilante" (Benoit 1951, 2: 233).

11 See the bibliography, and in particular *The Iron Cow of Zen*, *The Butterfly's Dream*, and *Creating Consciousness*, where Low elaborates on the problem of this fundamental ambiguity.

12 Filmed interview (CMC project), 12 December 2005.

13 Tai-san would later become Eido Tai Shimano Roshi, leader of the New York Zendo in Manhattan and the Dai Bosatsu Zendo in the Catskill Mountains of New York.

14 A *kōan* is a paradoxical question, such as "What is your original face before your father and mother were born?" used as focus of meditation. The *Mu! kōan* is, "A monk asked Jōshū, 'Does a dog have Buddha-nature?' Jōshū answered, 'Mu!' (No!)."

15 *Acts of John*, excerpt from Sections 94–6, known as the "Hymn of Jesus." The *Acts of John* is a second-century Christian collection of narratives inspired by the Gospel of John. See Gnostic Society Library (n.d.)

16 Low also experienced positive *makyō* in the form of periods of serenity, profound joy, gratitude, and ecstasy (Low n.d., 133).

17 Both the *Mumonkan* (The Gateless Barrier) and the *Hekigan-roku* (Blue Cliff Record) are standard Zen *kōan* collections. There are several English translations of the *Mumonkan*; Zenkei Shibayama, *The Gateless Barrier: Zen Comments on the Mumonkan* (Shibayama 2000) is a popular edition. There is only one complete English translation of the *Hekigan-roku* translated by Thomas Cleary and J.C. Cleary as *The Blue Cliff Record* (1977).

18 Low had met Bennett in London when he was on his way from South Africa to Canada.

19 Low mentions two. One was attained when he was working on the *kōan* "What is the highest teaching of Zen?" (Low n.d., 189). The other, more profound, occurred when he was working on *kōan* 26 of the *Mumonkan* collection (Low n.d., 190).

20 It should be noted that many Zen centres have abandoned the use of the *kyōsaku*. Such is the case at the Toronto Zen Centre (which was affiliated with the RZC), where it was discovered one day that several members did not dare say that they were filled with terror at the approach of the moment when the *kyōsaku* would be used (filmed interview with Sensei Taigen Henderson, abbot of the Toronto Zen Centre, [CMC project] 26 February 2007).

21 Low sustained two injuries: a fractured toe and a dislocated pelvis (Low n.d., 154).

22 A *rakusu* is an abbreviated Buddhist robe, a rectangle of cloth hung from the neck by a band. It has the same patchwork pattern as the larger Buddhist robe and is the specifically Buddhist element in a Zen monk's clothing. Every Zen monk or nun receives a *rakusu* at ordination.

23 For a careful, line-by-line commentary of Hakuin's text by Low, see *Hakuin Zenji's Chant in Praise of Zazen* (2004).

Suwanda H.J. Sugunasiri
Buddhist

VICTOR SŌGEN HORI AND JANET McLELLAN[1]

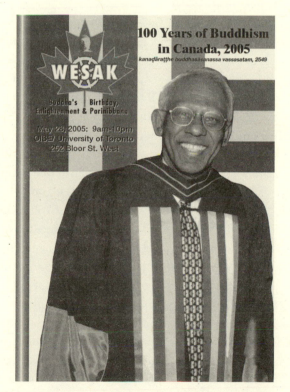

Suwanda Sugunasiri in dharma academic robe
Photo courtesy of Nalanda College of Buddhist Studies

On 24 May 2005, the five-coloured Buddhist flag unfurled on the flagpole on the south lawn of Queen's Park, the Legislative Assembly of the Province of Ontario. The flag-raising took place within a week-long conference entitled "100 Years of Buddhism in Canada."[2] The man who put the Buddhist flag atop the Ontario government's flagpole and the man who organized the conference was Suwanda Sugunasiri. This is his story.

Suwanda Hennedi Jayasumana Sugunasiri was born in Sri Lanka in 1936 and immigrated to Canada in 1973. As a committed Canadian, he has devoted his life to establishing a recognized place for Buddhism in the Canadian public square. In 1981, seeing the need for coordination among the Buddhist groups in the city of Toronto, he helped organize Toronto's first Wesak celebration and its first representative organization, the Buddhist Federation of Toronto. In the late 1980s, when the media invited different ethnic and religious groups to create their own television programs, Sugunasiri was there to propose programming on Buddhism. During the 1980s and 90s, he became the voice for Buddhism on numerous provincial and federal government bodies dealing with interfaith and multicultural issues. In 2000, he established the Nalanda College of Buddhist Studies in Toronto, of which he was the founder and first president. Sugunasiri's life story is doubly interesting for students of Buddhism in the West. It is first of all an example of how one man has dedicated his life to Buddhism. But second, Sugunasiri helped shape the development of Buddhism in this country. His life story is a prism through which the history of Buddhism in Canada comes into focus.

In his early life in Sri Lanka, Sugunasiri was not an active Buddhist. He thought of himself more as an artist; he wrote short story fiction, acted in theatre, and danced with a company. A Fulbright Scholarship brought him to the University of Pennsylvania in 1964–1966, where he completed an MA in linguistics.[3] He and his wife, Swarna, stayed in Toronto between 1967 and 1971, during which time Sugunasiri completed a second Masters degree, an MED at the Ontario Institute for Studies in Education (OISE).[4] After his return to Sri Lanka in 1971, he found that Sri Lanka did not seem to be interested in using him despite the training he had received in the United States and Canada. He calls himself "a re-entry casualty."[5] He and his wife thus returned to Canada in 1973, this time to stay.

ACQUIRING BUDDHISM

Although Sugunasiri was born into a Buddhist culture, as a youth he did not have much investment in a Buddhist identity. To acquire this, he had to learn about Buddhism, both its scholarly and cultural aspects, and to decide in what areas to involve himself. His interest in Buddhism started with home practice, then expanded to include Buddhist activity in the Sri Lankan community, then further expanded to include Buddhism in Toronto, and finally grew to encompass Buddhism in Canada.

When Sugunasiri was a child, his parents lit a lamp every evening and paid homage to the Buddha. When he and Swarna became parents, they did the same to teach their own children. During his first stay in the United States, Sugunasiri was in touch with the Buddhist Vihara in Washington, DC. In Sri Lankan custom, when a child learns to read, the first words should be read to the child by a monk. Teaching and learning are deeply associated with the Buddhist temple. As the Sri Lankan Theravada monk Piydassi was at the Washington Vihara at the time, the Sugunasiris asked Piydassi to read the first words to their son. Later when Sugunasiri came to Canada in 1967, he became a supporter of the Sri Lankan scholar-monk, Dr Hammalawa Saddhatissa, who was then a professor at the University of Toronto (1966–1969). Dr Saddhatissa lived in a not very good neighbourhood south of the University. One winter day, Sugunasiri went to visit him and found him in very bad shape – high fever, no food, and no medical coverage.[6] Incidents like this triggered his sense of social responsibility and soon got him involved in the Buddhist community beyond his own home.

From the mid to late 70s, Sugunasiri was co-vice president of the Sri Lankan Sinhalese Buddhist Temple, the Toronto Mahavihara, one of the oldest

Buddhist temples in Toronto. The temple started out, in typical fashion, as a group of Buddhists who met weekly in each other's homes and from time to time rented space for larger ceremonial occasions. By 1973, they had organized themselves into a temple and in 1978 purchased a small property at 3595 Kingston Road in Scarborough, which they renovated to create housing space for a resident monk and ceremonial space for the community. The community continued to grow and in 1998 the Mahavihara bought a much larger property at 4698 Kingston Road to house four resident monks.[7] Today it is recognized as a significant member of the many established Buddhist temples in the Greater Toronto area.

Sugunasiri became co-vice president of the temple at a time when it was still unsure of how to adapt to the Canadian environment. An early example of this uncertainty concerned the appropriate place to hold the temple's annual celebration of Wesak, one of the most important events in the Theravada Buddhist calendar. Wesak, the full moon day of the fifth lunar month, commemorates the birth, enlightenment, and death of the Buddha. Questions arose whether Wesak should be held within the small temple space or in a larger rented venue. There was sure to be a large crowd since Sugunasiri had invited a popular Buddhist scholar, Dr Gunaratna from the Washington Vihara, to give the Dharma discourse. To accommodate the large crowd, he booked a large hall at the Ontario Institute for Studies in Education (Sugunasiri was a doctoral student at OISE during the 1970s). The OISE hall provided an adequately spacious, but culturally alien, venue to host the Sinhalese-specific Wesak ceremony.[8] Another contentious issue concerned language. Sugunasiri wanted to use Sinhalese at the Wesak so that the children could learn their culture and heritage. But, in an interesting reversal of expectations, many in the Sri Lankan community wanted to use English. Most of the Sinhalese immigrants were well-educated professionals familiar with English, and their language of preference was English. For this Wesak, a conflict arose within the Mahavihara community between those who did and who did not want to come to OISE, and those who did and did not want to use Sinhalese language. Such contentions were common among the Asian Buddhist groups in Canada, who constantly wondered how to adapt to Canadian culture, how to transmit religious and cultural tradition to their children, and how to manage new kinds of conflict within their own group.

First-hand experience in grappling with such issues helped prepare Sugunasiri for working in the larger Buddhist community in Toronto. In one of his first steps out, he helped create the first ecumenical organization of Buddhists in Toronto. The catalyst for the first organization of Buddhists was an inter-faith service organized by the World Conference on Religion for Peace (WCRP), held in Toronto in October 1979 at Bloor Street United Church. Reverend Orai Fujikawa, then head minister at the Toronto Buddhist Church, and Sugunasiri were members of the WCRP Toronto branch. When the organizers of the inter-faith service asked for more Buddhist participation, Sugunasiri and Fujikawa called a meeting to which fifteen representatives from different Toronto Bud-dhist groups came. They included Sugunasiri; Reverend Fujikawa and Bishop Tsunoda (Buddhist Churches of Canada); Bhante Dhammika (Toronto Mahav-ihara); Fa Shih Sing Hung and Fa Shih Shing Cheung (Cham Shan Temple); Darshan Chaudhary (Ambedkar Group); Khan Lekim, Vietnamese, with no temple affiliation; and Samu Sunim with his students from the Zen Buddhist Temple. These leaders provided the necessary representative delegation for the interfaith service, and enabled approximately seventy-five Buddhists to participate from their different communities.[9] This was the first time that the Buddhist groups in Toronto had come together and engaged in any kind of united activity.

Following up on the interfaith service, Sugunasiri and Fujikawa organized a second meeting of the same group representatives in November 1979 at the Toronto Buddhist Church to explore the possibility of creating an ongoing for-mal organization of Buddhists in Toronto. By April 1980, the Toronto Buddhist Federation had emerged, with a constitution and government registration. Sugunasiri was asked to be the group's first coordinator. He thinks he was chosen because he spoke English and had a PHD (he had completed his PHD at OISE in 1978). Immediately he organized the first all-Toronto Wesak at Nathan Phillips Square (City Hall) in May 1981. The Toronto Buddhist Federation was probably the first representative organization of Buddhist temples and medi-tation centres in a local area in North America and the 1981 Wesak in Nathan Phillips Square was probably the first public celebration of Wesak in North America.[10]

In that first Wesak, in addition to the original members who had participated in the interfaith service, other participating Buddhist communities included the Burmese Association, Gaden Choling and Dharmadhatu (Tibetan), On-tario Zen Centre, and the Vietnamese Hoa Nghiem Temple. The youth group of the Hoa Nghiem Temple was especially active in putting decorations around the square and in creating and installing a 30-foot picture of the sitting Buddha. A picture of this Buddha painting appeared in the *Toronto Sun* newspaper, the only Toronto-based news media to feature, let alone mark, the first intra-Buddhist Wesak ceremony held in North America.[11]

Five members of the ordained sangha and 1,000 lay people attended the Wesak ceremony despite intermittent showers (perceived as a symbolic "rain of blessings"). The *puja* religious ceremony included a series of chanting and recitations, reflecting both Mahayana (Bodhisattva aspiration) and Theravada (transfer of merit) ritual, and an introduction to the *kambutsu* (Japanese for "bathing of the baby Buddha") ceremony, popular in East Asia. Two large *kambutsu* statues, images of the baby Buddha with one hand pointing up and one hand pointing down, were placed in large basins of sweet tea and people lined up to ladle the tea over the baby Buddha. At the makeshift altar, lay people placed flowers, burned incense, and made food offerings. Following the religious ceremony, a cultural program included the Tibetan Potala Dance Group from Lindsay, Vietnamese children from Hoa Nghiem Temple offering flowers, Sinhalese dancers from the Toronto Mahavihara, Ambedkar spiritual music, and Brent Titcomb giving the first performance of the song "Roll the Dharma Wheel," written by Bhante Punnaji (Mahavihara) and set to music by Titcomb.[12] This song became known as the "Unity Song," and was sung thereafter at every coreligious Buddhist activity to strengthen Buddhist ecumenism. Participants from each Buddhist community brought different types of food to contribute to the huge communal feast. The overall format of this first public Wesak set the tone for the next thirteen years.

During those thirteen years, the number of Buddhist groups in Toronto increased. Several had sizable membership, were incorporated as religious bodies, owned their own property, and had members able to speak English. Reflecting this growth and development, in 1989 the early Buddhist Federation of Toronto was replaced by the Buddhist Communities of Greater Toronto and it in turn was replaced by the Ontario Sangha Council in 1994 (McLellan 1999, 31–3). The Ontario Sangha Council altered the religious and cultural format of Wesak and changed the name of the event to a peace day commemoration. These changes ended the thirteen-year tradition of an all-Toronto Wesak. A public Wesak celebration, however, continued for several years thereafter within the much smaller University of Toronto Buddhist Students Association.

During those early years, although he was emerging as a leader in the Buddhist community, Sugunasiri still considered himself a student of Buddhism, always learning the Buddhadharma. As mentioned earlier, although he had been born into a Buddhist culture, he also had to study it and then decide to carry on a Buddhist practice. Most of his learning was self-study, triggered by whatever questions arose in the midst of meeting with the different Buddhist groups in Toronto. He says of this period, "I was able to one by one check out the basic Buddhism beliefs. For example, what does karma mean? Whatever was a question at the time, I was able to investigate that topic more fully."[13] During this early period, Sugunasiri was a PHD candidate at OISE. He found he could apply Buddhism to his intellectual work. "When I wrote my doctoral thesis, I patterned it after the Four Noble Truths. Here is a problem; here is the reason why; here is the fact that it can be done; here is my solution."[14] The Four Noble Truths are 1) the Truth of Suffering, 2) the Cause of Suffering, 3) the Cessation of Suffering, and 4) the Path to Cessation. This example shows how Buddhist concepts were starting to structure Sugunasiri's daily life and work. Sugunasiri was quite aware that although he was emerging as a spokesman for Buddhism, he himself had no formal credentials in Buddhism. He thus enrolled for a third master's degree, this time an MA in Buddhist Studies which he received from the University of Toronto in 1992.

IN THE PUBLIC SQUARE

During the 1980s, a variety of developments pushed Sugunasiri beyond the Buddhist community in Toronto to a much wider world. The first of these was involvement in the media. Rogers Cable Television as part of its Community Programming channel allowed religious and ethnic community representatives to make on-air presentations. Sugunasiri was pivotal in initiating media exposure of Buddhism through the local channel. Asian (new immigrant) and non-Asian (Caucasian, Canadian-born) Buddhist men and women were profiled to reveal the diversity of Buddhism in Canada and to show what it means to be Buddhist in the Canadian context. The television programming was not without its problems. The English language format, for example, was a barrier for many recent immigrants and refugees. This was one example of many where inability to work in English hindered immigrants and refugees in articulating their point of view in the public square.

Along with representatives from other faith groups, Sugunasiri participated in an interfaith meeting that officially requested the CRTC (Canadian Radio and Television Commission) to establish a Canadian Interfaith Network (CIN). Several members of this initial multifaith group later developed the Canadian Interfaith Coalition (CIC), which included Sikhs, Zoroastrians, and Unitarians. Through the joint efforts of the CIN and CIC, Vision TV emerged in 1988. Vision TV featured two programming divisions, Cornerstone and Mosaic. Mosaic programming enabled different faith communities to buy air time for their specific programs, whereas Cornerstone was funded by the station. Due to a lack of financial resources to buy air time, and possibly lack of interest, there were no Buddhist programs on Mosaic. Cornerstone, however, featured programs such as "The Long March," and films on Sri Lanka and on the Dalai Lama, thus increasing public exposure to Buddhism.[15]

The effort to create a Buddhist voice in the media led directly to the creation of a national Buddhist representative organization. Vision TV required that the religious groups applying for air time have some sort of national organization. For Buddhism, there was no such organization. Sugunasiri met with members of the Buddhist Federation of Toronto and, as a consequence, the BFT launched a new organization, the Buddhist Council of Canada (BCC), to act as the representative for Canadian Buddhists in dealings with Vision TV and other media. Sugunasiri became the first president of BCC. The Buddhist Federation of Toronto changed its name to the Toronto Chapter of the Buddhist Council of Canada. This provided a model for other local chapters to emerge across Canada.[16] In 1981, Louis Cormier had formed the Montreal Buddhist Council (Conseil Bouddhique de Montréal) with twelve Buddhist groups participating, and in 1986, Cormier brought his organization into the Buddhist Council of Canada. By the end of the 1980s, what appeared to be a national representative organization for all Buddhists groups in Canada was starting to form.

The year 1989 was particularly memorable in the history of Buddhism and the media in Canada. The Canadian Broadcasting Corporation (CBC) broadcast the Toronto celebration of Wesak for national television. The live Sunday broadcast of the Wesak celebration on "Meeting Place" from 12 noon to 1 p.m. was the first Buddhist celebration CBC had featured. Indeed, it was the first time a non-Christian theme or institution had appeared on "Meeting Place." The event itself was held at the Hong Fa Temple, a downtown branch of the now extensive Cham Shan temple complex in Toronto. Four languages (English, French, Vietnamese, and Chinese) were used in the event's opening remarks, the religious program, and the cultural presentations, highlighting the growing diversity within Toronto's Buddhist communities. The religious program featured Tibetan horns and traditional chanting by several local Tibetan teachers; Vietnamese chanting and flower offerings; traditional Chinese and Pali chanting by representative Sangha members; and a silent meditation led by Pema Chödrön, the Abbess of Gampo Abbey in Nova Scotia.

The Buddhist Council of Canada, however, did not succeed in becoming the official representative for all Buddhist groups in Canada, for several reasons. First, there were significant organizational problems. In promoting the idea of a Buddhist Council for Canada, Sugunasiri travelled the country from coast to coast trying to set up chapters. In 1989, coinciding with the Toronto Wesak celebration, the First Buddhist National Congress was held at the Hong Fa Temple in Toronto. Delegates from local chapters across Canada from British Columbia to Newfoundland participated.[17] A constitution was adopted and regional vice-presidents were elected. This formal structure meant little, however, without the support of local Buddhist temples and meditation centres. Getting their attention and consent proved to be too large a task for the BCC leadership. In addition, in Toronto in the initial stages, the leadership in the BCC advocated the Canadianization of Buddhism and the elimination of "cultural baggage" (McLellan 1999, 32). Most of the Buddhists from Asian countries immediately disagreed with this stance; in fact, they expected their Buddhist temples to preserve culture and tradition. In the face of such opposition, the Buddhist Council of Canada could hardly claim to represent all Buddhist temples and meditation centres in Canada. Very little further was done in the name of the Buddhist Council of Canada. The organization still exists but in name only.

In the 1980s, another local Buddhist leader emerged in Toronto, the Korean Buddhist monk Samu Sunim. He had been part of the WCRP Interfaith Service and his temple was a member of the original Buddhist Federation of Toronto. An extremely energetic monk, Samu Sunim built temples in Toronto, Ann Arbor, Michigan, and Chicago, Illinois. In July 1987, he hosted the Conference on World Buddhism in North America at his temple in Ann Arbor. The first of its kind, the conference brought together prominent scholars in Buddhist studies with the religious leaders of many Buddhist organizations. Then in 1990, at his Zen Buddhist Temple on Vaughan Road in Toronto, he hosted a similar week-long Conference on Buddhism in Canada, 8–14 July 1990, which brought together Buddhist Sangha and lay leaders from temples, monasteries, and centres across Canada and academics from Canadian universities. Although the event was held at his temple in Toronto, it was jointly sponsored by Hoa Nghiệm Pagoda, Tai Bay Temple, Tam Bảo Pagoda (in Montreal), Manshu Yuen, Buddhist Council of Toronto, and the Toronto Buddhist Church. For a while, Suwanda Sugunasiri as coordinator of the Buddhist Federation of Toronto and later president of the Buddhist Council of Canada, could claim to be the voice of the Buddhists in Toronto. But the Buddhist community in Toronto was growing quickly in size and complexity. By the mid 1980s, the community had many different interests and needed more than one spokesperson.

During the 80s and early 90s, Sugunasiri was active on many fronts. In addition to his involvement in the media and the Buddhist Council of Canada, from 1983 to 1988 Sugunasiri was appointed to the Ontario Advisory Council on Multiculturalism and Citizenship (OACMC).[18] For the Ontario Provincial Interfaith Committee on Chaplaincy, whose jurisdiction included prisons, Sugunasiri wrote an interfaith training curriculum for chaplains on dealing with Buddhist or other inmates.[19] He participated in numerous interfaith bodies, such as the North American Interfaith Network (NAIN), the Toronto chapter of the World Interfaith Education Association (WIFEA), and the Interfaith Ad Hoc Committee on the Constitution of Canada. He also provided leadership in Buddhist-Christian Dialogue and initiated Buddhist-Jewish Dialogue. From the late 1980s, Sugunasiri wrote columns on Buddhism for the *Toronto Star* newspaper, and was a guest speaker on several radio stations (CBC Radio, Ryerson, and CJRT), presenting facets of Buddhism in Toronto. He contributed to several multicultural and multifaith calendars, providing Theravada and Mahayana Buddhist dates and information. He even tried to create special dates for Canadian Buddhists, such as Founder's Day in October to commemorate the founding of the Buddhist Church of Canada which had established the first Buddhist temple in Canada.[20]

BUDDHISM IN THE WEST

Discussions about the growth of Buddhism in the West almost invariably evoke the classification of "Two Buddhisms," Asian ethnic Buddhism and Western convert Buddhists. Sugunasiri has his own comments on this distinction. In his paper, "Inherited Buddhists and Acquired Buddhists" (Sugunasiri 2006a), he says, is "an attempt to provide an alternative to the troublesome terms 'ethnic Buddhist' and 'white / Euro-Buddhist,' each lacking in precision and comprehensiveness and sometimes offensive."[21] In this article, he asks what the criteria are for deciding who is an "Ethnic-Buddhist" and who is a "Euro-Buddhist." He finds that people use three kinds of critera: geographical heritage, spiritual heritage, and cultural heritage. These can be combined together in so many different ways producing so many different kinds of Ethnic Buddhists and Euro-Buddhists that the terms become meaningless. He suggests the distinction "Inherited" and "Acquired" but by this terminology, he does not mean to imply that there are two types of Buddhist. There is only one type of Buddhist, although different people encounter Buddhism in different ways. "A Buddhist is a Buddhist is a Buddhist," he says.

What makes a Buddhist? Sugunasiri is quite clear on this: "There is a core of Buddhist teachings that every Buddhist is guided by – concepts such as the primacy of mind, *anattā* , rebirth, samsara, karma, Four Noble Truths, Noble Eightfold Path, Middle Path, conditioned co-origination, wisdom and compassion, centrality of ethics, etc."[22] Of course, a person's understanding of these concepts will be influenced to some degree by one's parents, cultural context, education, Buddhist teacher, meditative experience, etc. But these individual differences should not constitute the basis for dividing Buddhists into types. The important distinction between individuals is how strongly they are immersed in Buddhism. "The difference therefore is not in the type of Buddhist but the extent to which one follows the Buddhist teachings in one's daily living. How seriously are the precepts taken, to what extent is the Buddha's own maxim and model, 'I do as I say, I say as I do,' taken seriously or followed closely."[23]

Sugunasiri's list of core teachings of Buddhism includes karma and rebirth. For many Westerners, these two concepts in particular seem inconsistent with a modern scientific world view. For this reason, an author like Stephen Batchelor has argued that the Buddha's core teachings do not include karma and rebirth, that karma and rebirth are part of the Indian cultural context of 2600 years ago and do not need to be imported into present-day Western society (Batchelor 1999). Sugunasiri, however, vigorously defends the ideas of karma and rebirth. First, he points out that in the original Pali texts the Buddha's awakening experience is described in terms of karma and rebirth. When the Buddha sat beneath the bodhi tree in deep meditation, he gained three knowledges. Two were "knowledge regarding exit and rebirth" (*cutu.papatti nana*) and "knowledge of memory of formerly lived lives" (*pubbeniva.sananussati nana*). These are two of the three knowledges that constitute the Buddha's awakening experience.[24] If the concepts of karma and rebirth are dropped, how then does one explain the content of the Buddha's awakening? Second, Sugunasiri argues that there is scientific evidence for rebirth and is willing to provide a list of recent publications on rebirth. He also cites studies of paradoxical phenomena which by themselves cannot be explained, but which are explicable if the concept of rebirth is accepted. And although one may argue that rebirth is not a scientifically provable phenomenon, he points out that the theory of rebirth has not been disproved either.[25]

The concept of karma is not properly understood in the West, says Sugunasiri. Unfortunately most people think karma implies a rigid predeterminism under which humans can exercise no freedom. This may apply to karma in the Hindu sense but not to karma in the Buddhist sense. "In Buddhism, karma has both nature (karma acts on you) and nurture (you can act on karma)." The original meaning of karma in Buddhism is simply intentional action. "The Buddha said, 'Intent, I say, *bhikkus*, is karma.' Every time you make an intention, there is a psychological reaction in you. And that can have other reactions which have other reactions." But the origin is your intention.[26]

Sugunasiri feels strongly that Westerners are indulging in "cultural arrogance" when they recommend dropping ideas which do not fit their culture paradigm. Why should "my" cultural outlook be the criterion for judging which of the teachings of Buddhism are acceptable? In addition, he points out that what is culturally acceptable at any given time is constantly changing. Fifty years ago, talk about "the mind" was not considered scientific, but today quite respected researchers do mind-body medicine. Sugunasiri is willing to be patient. It takes time for a practitioner to see the applicability of the full range of the Buddha's core ideas.[27]

THE BUDDHIST SPOKESMAN

Since the early 1990s, Sugunasiri has written a weekly column for the *Toronto Star* newspaper. He has collected several of these and published them under the title *Embryo as Person* (Sugunasiri 2005). In many of these columns, he explains basic Buddhist concepts, for example, the ten perfections or *pāramitās* (2005: 68–70), the teaching on suffering (2005: 45–7), the teaching that hatred begets hatred (2005: 56–8), homelessness (2005: 34–6), and so on. He also explains how Buddhist principles apply to current events. Buddhism is against abortion, for example, since the precept against taking life expressly includes the foetus as a living human being (2005: 7–8, 24–7). On the other hand, there are Buddhist arguments both for and against euthanasia. If the moral intent of the person initiating euthanasia is to relieve suffering, then the karmic effect is positive. But there is also the side of the person dying. If that person is working out the negative karma of previous misdeeds, perhaps euthanasia is counterproductive (2005: 74–6, 77–9). In these columns, he advocates organ donation (2005: 12–14), urges us to repay kindness, especially to people accused of misdeeds (2005: 56–8), opposes a judge's decision that acquitted a woman who went bare-breasted on the street (2005: 65–7), and takes no position on homosexual marriage (2005: 15–17). He explains how meditation erases the fear of death (2005: 71–3) and shows how to do *mettā-bhāvanā*, Friendliness Meditation (2005: 85–7). And when we have allowed our minds to fill up with dirt, he recommends we vacuum our minds to get them clean (2005: 28–9).

In another publication, *You're What You Sense* (Sugunasiri 2001b), Sugunasiri sets himself a much more ambitious task. He proposes to explain one of the most difficult concepts in Buddhist thought, *anattā*, usually translated "no-self." *Anattā* does not deny the existence of the self in the ordinary sense. Sugunasiri goes to great lengths to point out that what it denies is the idea of a soul which is immortal and unchanging, as conceived in Hinduism or Christianity (2001b, 138). For this reason, he translates the term *anattā* (*na* "not" + *atta* "soul") as "asoulity" (2001b, 122–3). He sets out the Buddhist psychology of the six consciousnesses (seeing, hearing, smelling, taste, bodily sense, and mind sense) and shows how mind is a system which is just the sum total of these consciousnesses. There is no further entity called a soul which exists independently of the six consciousnesses. This is the point expressed in the title of the book, *You're What You Sense*. He mentions with approval the title of another recent book, Mark Epstein's *Thoughts without a Thinker* (Epstein 1995). To show how it is possible for there to be complex consciousness without a permanent soul, Sugunasiri likens the mind to the Internet. The five usual sense consciousnesses are like five users and the sixth consciousness or mind sense is like the Internet service provider. Just as there is no centre to the Internet and no master controller, so also there is no central controller to the mind, no immortal soul (Sugunasiri 2001b, 143–7).

Sugunasiri attempts to explain the relationship of scientific knowledge to the ultimate goal of awakening in Buddhism. First, the Buddhist practitioner is not asked to accept any of the Buddha's teachings on blind faith. Sugunasiri quotes from the *Kālāma Sutta*, the well-known passage that enjoins followers to "know for yourself": "Kālāmas, do not be led by reports, or tradition, or hearsay. Be not led by the authority of religious texts, nor by mere logic or inference, nor by considering appearances, nor by the delight in speculative opinions, nor by seeming possibilities, nor by the idea 'this is our teacher.' But,

O Kālāmas, when you know for yourself ..." (2001b, iii). How does one come to know for oneself? Through meditation (2001b, 163). Mindfulness meditation focuses in detail on each part of body, each part of mind, until its impermanence is seen, "bringing you the experiential realization of impermanence (*anicca̅*)" (2001b, 166). Thus are scientific knowledge and spiritual realization linked together.

INTERFAITH AND MULTICULTURAL ISSUES

"I was a Sri Lankan nationalist and now I am a Canadian nationalist. I believe that you need to give back to the country that nurtures you."[28] Sugunasiri's social activism is expressed in two theatres – his ceaseless support of Buddhism and his concern for citizenship in Canada's multicultural society. For Sugunasiri, the two overlap. He has strong ideals about citizenship in a multicultural society but his work on so many interfaith and multicultural bodies has removed any trace of romanticism from his thinking.

From his perspective, before multiculturalism, there was racism. In his book, *Towards Multicultural Growth,* Sugunasiri asks, prior to the revision of Canada's immigration laws in 1967, "Who was a Canadian?" Answer: "A Canadian was one who was white. Period" (Sugunasiri 2001a, 13). The only change in this assumption was that some white groups who were considered "out," like Irish Catholics, francophones, and Jews, succeeded in crossing the line and got "in." Who is still left "out"? Visible minorities – people not white (2001a, 6).

Even today, non-whites are not "in." This, of course, is the situation in many places around the world. But Canada now has multiculturalism. Canada reached a milestone when in 1971 Prime Minister Pierre Elliot Trudeau rose in the House of Commons and enunciated Canada's new policy of multiculturalism. He affirmed that while the first to arrive on Canadian shores to meet the First Nations peoples were the French and the English, nevertheless modern Canadian society rests on the contributions of many ethnic groups who have worked, lived, and died to build a better Canada. Trudeau's vision of Canada – one country, two languages, many cultures – affirmed the right of every person of whatever ethnic or cultural origin to be treated as an authentic Canadian.

Sugunasiri's first reaction to Canada's multiculturalism is not to rejoice in the new rights granted to minority groups. His first reaction, as is proper for a Buddhist, is to show gratitude. He feels that members of the ethnic minority communities need to remember that it was the White man who introduced multiculturalism. "To the White folks of Canada, then, we need to bow, with deep respect" (Sugunasiri 2001a, 29). Sugunasiri is serious about saying thank you to the White man. He lists the names of the White men who deserve respect: Pierre Trudeau, the Secretaries of State for Multiculturalism Jack Murta, Walter McLean, David Collenette, David Crombie, Gerry Weiner, provincial leaders like Ontario Premier William Davis, Attorney General Roy McMurtry, and so on. Aside from individuals, if asked to pick one ethnocultural community deserving praise for supporting multiculturalism, he would pick the British (2001a, 29). And if asked to pick a specific religious community for promoting multiculturalism, he would choose the United Church of Canada (2001a, 30). Sugunasiri encourages members of minority communities "to look at the next White woman or man you meet, and offer a smile, for offering us an olive branch, and ushering in the multicultural spring we are enjoying today" (2001a, 30).

While recognizing the high ideals embodied in Trudeau's vision of multicultural Canada, Sugunasiri also acknowledges that a noble policy may be less than perfect in practice. In practice, multiculturalism has been "chaotic" (Sugunasiri 2001a, 32). Both sides of the in/out divide contribute to the chaos. On the side of the visible minorities, new and belligerent leadership in ethnic communities, new immigrant "multicultural boomers," and fake political refugees exploit Canada's triplecare system – welfare, health care, and legal care. On the side of the Canadians trying to implement multiculturalism, no system of checks and balances prevents exploitation of the triplecare system; front line social workers are afraid to take action for fear of immediately being labelled racist; and the mainstream population meanwhile maintains silence (2001a, 43–9).

Of course, lurking beneath the surface, in the white mainstream there are still pockets of residual discrimination against other races and other religions. An example was the way the 1990 Interfaith Ad Hoc Committee on the Canadian Constitution, of which Sugunasiri was a member, was treated. This committee met with the Hon. Joe Clark, then Minister of Constitutional Affairs, to make two points: "(a) that the Constitution needed a spiritual dimension, and (b) that the way spirituality is expressed must embrace everyone" (Sugunasiri 2001a, 52). The phrase "the way spirituality is expressed must embrace everyone" was meant to include those Canadians whose professed spirituality is nontheistic, that is, those Canadians who do not believe in God and who, according to StatsCan 1991, account for fully 18 per cent of the population or approximately five million Canadians. This proposal was passed on to the House of Commons Beaudoin-Dobbie Committee appointed to deal with constitutional amendments. One of the members of the Beaudoin-Dobbie Committee, however, was a fundamentalist Christian member of parliament, who unbeknownst to Sugunasiri and the other members of the Interfaith Ad Hoc Committee, contacted other evangelical Christians. This private group together wrote an exclusively Christian text for the Preamble to the Constitution: "We affirm that our country is founded upon principles that acknowledge the supremacy of God, the dignity of each person, the importance of family, the value of community." Nothing in the text tried to represent the beliefs of the 18 per cent of the Canadian population who did not believe in God. Sugunasiri had composed other text for the preamble which represented both believers and non-believers in God, but the pre-emptive move by the evangelical Christians meant his version never got a hearing. Sugunasiri laments that even after three decades of multiculturalism, such residual discrimination remains a fact of Canadian life (2001a, 53).

In Sugunasiri's view, our present chaotic multiculturalism contains muted White racism against minorities but instead of the old policy of encouraging assimilation into the White Christian mainstream, the present policy encourages ethnic minority groups to remain enclosed within their own groups, a practice which perpetuates mutual stereotyping, miscommunication, and prejudice. And for Sugunasiri, "ethnocentrism is racism." "While in ethnocentrism … one is consciously *included*, in racism, one is consciously excluded. So ethnocentrism's inclusion can be seen as the other side of the coin of racism's exclusion" (2001a, 109). Sugunasiri's principled activism sometimes puts him, a member of an ethnic minority, in the position of defending the rights of the white Christian majority. When Christmas lights were banned from the Ontario Legislature several years ago, Sugunasiri took a stand in his *Toronto Star* column and on Vision TV opposing the ban (2001a, 96–7). "It is wrong for multiculturalism to deny the historical contribution of the majority community, the Christian community."[29]

BUDDHISM AND THE ACADEMY

When Sugunasiri completed an MA in Buddhist Studies at the University of Toronto in 1992, he realized that although many students at the university were interested in Buddhism, there were few courses; at times 500 students enrolled in a single class on Buddhism. In addition, the courses were "hit and miss" and did not present Buddhism systematically. This was true not only at the University of Toronto but at all universities in Canada. He concluded: "I thought it was necessary to provide a systematic study. Also, it was necessary to present not merely Buddhism in the books but Buddhism the living religion – and in depth."[30]

In 1992, Sugunasiri was appointed a Research Associate in the Faculty of Divinity at Trinity College, University of Toronto, and in 1993 began the first on-campus "Seminars on Buddhism." Guest speakers included academics from several Buddhist disciplines. They addressed a range of themes: North American Perceptions of Buddhism, Cambodian Refugees in Canada, Poverty in the Pali Canon, *Kōan* and *Kenshō* in the Rinzai Zen Curriculum, Women in Tang Dynasty Buddhism, Tibetan Medicine, *Pudgalavāda*: The Buddhist Doctrine of Indeterminate Self, Engaged Buddhism, Buddhist Skilful Means (*Upāya*), and Journeys to Sacred Buddhist Landscapes. In April 1995, with co-sponsorship from the Department for the Study of Religion and financial assistance from the Numata Program in Buddhist Studies and the University's Status of Women Office, Sugunasiri organized a three-day conference entitled "Buddhism after Patriarchy," based on the work of Rita Gross whose recently published book *Buddhism after Patriarchy* was then being eagerly read across North America. Dr Gross was guest of honour at the conference which brought scholars from all across North America together with non-academic Buddhist practitioners.[31]

The success of the Buddhist seminar series and the conference encouraged Sugunasiri to take concrete steps toward realizing his long-held vision of a college of Buddhist studies. He approached the Divinity Faculty of Trinity College within the University of Toronto in 1997 with a proposal to establish a certificate program in Buddhist Studies. As Sugunasiri was to discover, the decision to approve or disapprove his proposal turned out to be not strictly an academic one. With the support of the Dean, the proposal was accepted by the Committee of Teaching Staff, and forwarded to the Divinity Council. At this stage, although members of the council expressed discomfort with the idea of a Buddhist studies program in a faculty whose mandate was to train Christians for the ministry, still the council ratified the proposal on the basis of its potential to contribute to education in a multicultural setting and forwarded it to the Trinity Senate for approval. There the provost of the college introduced a "friendly amendment" – that the proposal be brought back after getting the approval of all the Anglican Bishops in Canada! (Sugunasiri 2008a). Sugunasiri did not pursue this avenue, in the belief that it was highly unlikely that his proposal would obtain such approval.[32]

Next, Sugunasiri approached the Department for the Study of Religion and proposed a program of Buddhism courses to complement the department's list of courses in religious studies. This proposal too was turned down, on the ground that there was insufficient teaching faculty to sustain the program.

Following those two disappointments at the University of Toronto, Sugunasiri went off-campus. He proposed an independent "College of Buddhist Education," which later became a "College of Buddhist Studies," to the Chinese Buddhist Temple Cham Shan Library Board and its affiliated Buddhist Association of Canada. The Cham Shan Temple Library, located on Lawrence Avenue in Toronto, agreed to provide a home for the college. A draft constitution was established providing for a board of directors that was representative of Buddhist diversity in Toronto and including a member from the Cham Shan Temple Library Board. Sugunasiri obtained Government of Ontario approval for the use of the label "College," registered the college name with the Ontario Ministry of Consumer Affairs, incorporated the college as a legal body, and received legal status as a charity. Commitments were secured from several Toronto area academics to teach courses, and the Toronto College of Buddhist Studies opened its doors to the first entering class on 8 September 2000. The Buddhist Association of Canada associated with the Cham Shan Temple contributed seed money to get the college started with the expectation that student fees would then support the college. The college planned to offer a one-year Certificate in Buddhist Studies and a two-year Diploma in Buddhist Studies. The courses on offer were Introduction to Buddhism; Systematic Buddhist Thought; History of Buddhism I: Asia; History of Buddhism II: West; Meditation: Theory and Practice and Application; Buddhist Ethics in Society; Buddhist Psychology; Buddhism and Science; courses in Pali and Sanskrit; and Buddhism: Profession and Practice. An innovative course called English as a Second Language for Dharma was directed at ordained monks or nuns who had already received Buddhist training but required instruction in how to teach Buddhism in English. Enrolment, however, was disappointing. Of the twenty-five students enrolled in the first year, only two were full-time. Eight of the twenty-five students registered in the English as a Second Language for Dharma course, showing that there was a need for such a course. The enrolment was small, but nevertheless in the year 2000 the first step had been taken (Sugunasiri 2008a).

The college immediately underwent further restructuring. First, it was re-named the Nalanda College of Buddhist Studies, taking its name from Nalanda University, the great centre of Buddhist learning which flourished in India between the fifth and twelfth centuries. Then the newly named Nalanda College was relocated to Queen's Park Crescent, within the University of Toronto campus and near the Ontario government buildings. In 2002, the college received an injection of solid funding. And the college added extra features. It began publishing the *Canadian Journal of Buddhist Studies* and established two research centres, one on Buddhism and Education and one on Buddhism, Bioethics, and Socioethics. In 2005, it organized a week-long celebration of One Hundred Years of Buddhism in Canada. As part of the celebration, the Buddhist and Wesak flags were raised on the grounds of the Ontario legislature, presumably the first time anywhere in Canada the Buddhist flag was raised on official public soil.

In 2006, Nalanda College applied to the Government of Ontario to offer a BA Honours degree in Buddhadharma Studies. Approval by the provincial government would constitute academic accreditation. Sugunasiri compiled two sets of documents, with help in particular from Professor Leonard Priestley of the University of Toronto and Professor Donald Wiebe, former Dean of Divinity at Trinity College. One document set out the entire curriculum in minute detail (138 pages), and the other set out the administrative procedures and funding structure of Nalanda College (108 pages). The application documents were reviewed by two panels appointed by the Post Secondary Education Quality Assessment Board (PEQAB), an independent advisory agency of the Government of Ontario set up to make recommendations to the Minister of Training, Colleges, and Universities of Ontario. The review by both panels was positive. On this basis, PEQAB recommended to the minister that Nalanda be given approval to offer an Honours BA program in Buddhist Studies. Despite this recommendation, on 22 December 2006, Christopher Bentley, the Minister for Training, Colleges, and Universities wrote to Sugunasiri rejecting his application and denying Nalanda permission to offer the Honours BA. He gave no reason for his decision.[33]

Now, in 2009, nine years after its founding, Nalanda College of Buddhist Studies has closed. Without accreditation from the provincial government, it was not able to attract students who were looking for a recognized academic course which would be accepted for exchange credit at universities. Without significant student enrolment, Nalanda faced difficulties fundraising since donors naturally wanted to fund a successful enterprise. Furthermore, Sugunasiri, the founder and first president, had reached the age of retirement. In North America today, there are several accredited Buddhist colleges: Naropa University in Boulder Colorado founded in 1974 by Chögyam Trungpa; University of the West in Los Angeles established in 1990 by Fo Guang Shan of Taiwan; and the Soka Universities in California with two campuses, Calabasas established in 1987 and Aliso Viejo established in 2001, run by Soka Gakkai International. There are other Buddhist universities, such as the Won Institute of Graduate Studies in Glenside, Pennsylvania, still in the process of applying for accreditation. All these Buddhist schools have managed to survive their early days, earn a reputation, and finally receive accreditation because they were supported by a major religious organization who could continue to fund them during the first few years of low enrolment and no accreditation. This is where the Nalanda College of Buddhist Studies was different. It was not the academic arm of a major religious organization; it was just a school standing on its own. And without some major outside support, it has closed on its own.

REFLECTIONS

Time passes and people grow older. With the closing of Nalanda College of Buddhist Studies, Sugunasiri is effectively in retirement, as befits his age. He is no longer a member of any particular temple, but he maintains his usual individual practice. He and his wife do home practice and every morning he sits in meditation. Still active, he devotes his energy to new projects. One of them is the recording of the history of Buddhism in Toronto, a research project he first began several decades ago with the Multicultural History Society of Canada. In 1984–1985, Sugunasiri conducted a long series of interviews with Buddhist leaders, both ordained and lay, in Toronto using a questionnaire. Some of the results of that research were published in an early article "Buddhism in Metropolitan Toronto, A Preliminary Overview" (Sugunasiri 1989). But thereafter the data lay untouched while Sugunasiri became involved in his many other projects. He has recently revived that research project and published *Thus Spake the Sangha: Early Buddhist Leadership in Toronto* (Sugunasiri 2008b), an account of the lives and activities of five Buddhist monks and nuns active in the 1980s. He tells their stories using copious quotations taken from the interviews. A follow-up volume is planned focusing on lay leadership in the Buddhist groups of Toronto during the 1980s. Aside from this history project, Sugunasiri continues to write explaining Buddhism for a popular audience. A new emphasis is books on Buddhism for children.

One theme runs throughout most of the events and projects in Suwanda Sugunasiri's life – preserving the true dharma. His emphasis is primarily on continuity and preservation of the Buddhist tradition, not on change and adaptation to the new cultural environment of the West. Buddhism has adapted to local culture wherever it has spread but, Sugunasiri believes, Theravāda Buddhism, especially as found in Sri Lanka, best preserves the original Buddhism of the Buddha. Its Pali texts come closest to the language of the Buddha himself, and by extension, the thought contained therein comes closest to the thought of the Buddha himself.[34] He acknowledges that the texts of other countries and cultures are authentically Buddhist; nevertheless they are based on layers of translations and interpreted through layers of cultural assumptions. This stance of preservation of the Dharma, which informs most of his career as a Buddhist leader, is strikingly different from the stance of a Western-born Buddhist leader, who is constantly trying, first, to distinguish what is authentic Buddhism from what is cultural context, and then second, to reinterpret that authentic Buddhism in a way that makes sense to a Westerner. In the study of "Buddhist Lives," every life is unique of course, but the life stories of different Buddhist leaders can still be compared along particular dimensions. The spectrum of "preservation of the Dharma vs adaptation of the Dharma" provides one of those dimensions of comparison.

Back in 1938 in New York City, the Zen monk Sōkei-an Sasaki, the resident teacher of the First Zen Institute of America, was asked how long it would take for Buddhism to take root in the West. He answered that since it had taken three hundred years for Buddhism from India to take root in China, it would take a comparable amount of time for Buddhism to do so in the West. Great patience and great dedication would be required. He likened the process to "holding the lotus to the rock."[35] So long as someone continues to hold the lotus of the Buddha's awakening to the rock, eventually the Buddha's awakening would send forth roots, penetrate the rock, and take firm hold to stand on its own. Not everything that Suwanda Sugunasiri did in his attempts to help establish Buddhism in the West had a lasting impact, but he was one of the very first beyond his own community to hold the lotus to the rock in Canada. The value of his effort can be measured by the number of younger people now extending their hands to take his place.

NOTES

1 The authors had two series of interviews with Dr Suwanda Sugunasiri. We cite these interviews as follows.

Interview 7 August 2008. Interview of Suwanda Sugunasiri conducted by Victor Hori, 7 August 2008, at Nalanda College of Buddhist Studies, 47 Queen's Park Crescent E., Toronto, Ontario, M5S 2C3.

Interview 15 August 2008. Interview of Suwanda Sugunasiri conducted by Janet McLellan and Victor Hori, 15 August 2008, at Nalanda College of Buddhist Studies.

Interviews 2000. Interviews of Suwanda Sugunasiri conducted by Janet McLellan, between September 9 and November 22, 2000.

The interviews were conducted in the offices of Nalanda College of Buddhist Studies, 47 Queen's Park Crescent E., Toronto. The authors would like to thank Dr Sugunasiri for his co-operation.

2 A photograph of this event can be seen at http://www.nalandacollege.ca/PDF/souvenir_proof.pdf.

3 Interview 7 August 2008; email 12 September 2008.

4 Interview 7 August 2008.

5 Ibid.

6 Ibid.

7 http://lankanstyle.com/mahavihara/history1.htm.

8 Interviews 2000.

9 Ibid.

10 On the history of Wesak celebrations in North America and pan-Buddhist organizations, see Turpie 2001.

11 This photo can be seen on page 54 of Turpie 2001 (http://mrsp.mcgill.ca/reports/pdfs/Wesak.pdf).

12 Reproduced in Sugunasiri 2008, 244–5.

13 Interview 15 August 2008.

14 Ibid.

15 Interviews 2000.

16 Ibid.

17 Ibid.

18 Interview 15 August 2008.

19 Ibid.

20 Interviews 2000.

21 email 29 August 2008.

22 Ibid.

23 Ibid.

24 Ibid.

25 Ibid.

26 Interview 15 Aug. 08.

27 Ibid.

28 Ibid.

29 Ibid.

30 Ibid.

31 Interviews 2000.

32 Ibid.

33 For the actual documents, see the PEQAB website, "Expired/Denied/Withdrawn Appli-
    cation" at http://192.139.188.172/PEQAB/index.asp?id1=27).

34 Interview 7 August 2008.

35 *Wind Bell* (Publication of the Zen Center of San Francisco) 8, no. 1-2 (Fall 1969): 19.

Conclusion

This book provides a high vantage point in space and time from which to survey the many kinds of Buddhism which Canadians have practised in the last century and which they practise today from sea to sea. Here one can discern clearly that Buddhism in Canada is strongly shaped by global currents and connections impacting local Canadian communities uniquely defined in society and history. From this same vantage point, is it possible also to discern the changing shape of the academic study of Buddhism in Canada? In the introduction, we stated that this book is intended to help bring order to an unorganized field. It is therefore fitting to present our conclusions and suggestions about where the study of Buddhism in Canada should go from here. Our five main conclusions are spread across three areas. The first three deal with the assumptions we bring to the study of Buddhism in Canada regarding 1) what is modern and what is traditional, 2) the division of Buddhism into Asian/ethnic and Western/convert, and 3) global and local influences. The last two deal with 4) the need to collect more factual data about Buddhism in the Canadian context and 5) the need to encourage universities in Canada to create programs that are better equipped to train researchers. We will deal with each in turn.

ASSUMPTIONS

What's Modern?
Both scholars of Buddhism and practitioners of Buddhism are wont to say that throughout its long history, as Buddhism has spread to many different countries, it has always adapted to the local culture. The historical result is the

situation we have today: many different forms of Buddhism – Chinese Buddhism, Sri Lankan Buddhism, Tibetan Buddhism, Thai Buddhism, Japanese Buddhism, and so on – and all are recognized as legitimate forms of Buddhism. But despite the surface agreement that the many cultural forms of Buddhism are equally legitimate, there is jockeying for privileged position. Some in Theravada Buddhism claim that their form of Buddhism, being directly descended from that practised by Śākyamuni Buddha himself, is the form of Buddhism with the least cultural interpretation. Others in the later, developed forms of Buddhism in East Asia think of Buddhism as starting from a seed in India and growing through history, finally coming to full flower in their own country and culture. And some writers in America today give the impression that the "American Buddhism" which they are busily creating will correct the hierarchy, sexism, and elite monasticism of Asian Buddhism, thus allowing Buddhism to finally be understood without cultural distortion. Research on how Buddhism adapts to a new culture is thus not done in a neutral field.

As the papers in this volume have shown, the process by which Buddhism is being transplanted into Canadian culture is quite complex. Soucy has demonstrated that the changes in Buddhism that have been used to characterize "American Buddhism" are in fact changes that were started in Asia by Asian Buddhists. Both the Shambhala organization created by Chögyam Trungpa and the Order of Interbeing founded by Thich Nhat Hanh display features that are identified with "modern" Buddhism: they focus on meditation as the central Buddhist practice, target lay people rather than ordained monks and nuns, and empower women. The Tzu Chi organization studied by Laliberté and Litalien and the Fo Guang Shan organization studied by Verchery are both "modern" in a similar sense: they actively promote modern secular education, forsake divination ritual, deploy relief teams in times of emergency, and place women in positions of leadership. If one stands back and takes a broader historical perspective, one can see that the modernization process began in the late nineteenth and early twentieth centuries when the Buddhist traditions in Asian countries faced the incursions of the colonial Western powers. The case of Chinese Buddhism, documented by Liu, is typical. In the new Buddhism, monks were to be literate and educated; death rituals and divination rituals were discouraged; Buddhist doctrine was reinterpreted to be compatible with science; and so on.

The "American Buddhism" which some practitioners are touting is just the latest in a series of modernized Buddhisms that began to appear more than a hundred years ago. Perhaps a more apt title for this movement would be "Post-Colonial Buddhism" rather than "American Buddhism" or "Canadian Buddhism." The forms of Buddhism that exhibit these characteristics – regardless of location – have more similarities with each other, globally, than any of them have with traditional practices. This is our first conclusion: that the adaptation of Buddhism in Canadian culture is not to be studied as a unique event in history but as the latest development in a global transformation of Buddhism which began more than a century ago when Buddhism in Asian countries encountered the colonial powers of the West.

Two Buddhisms

In almost all discussions of Buddhism in the West, people divide the field of study into "Two Buddhisms" under a variety of labels (ethnic Asian and white convert; cradle Buddhist and convert Buddhist; inherited and acquired; ethnic Buddhist and Euro-Buddhist; traditionalist and modernist; and more). This distinction, which is vigorously proposed by the Western/convert side, is meant to contrast the old traditional Buddhism of Asia and the new modern Buddhism being created in the West. But as we have seen in this book, the contrast between Asian and Western is not precisely the same as the contrast between traditional and modern. Asian Buddhism began to modernize in the 1800s in Asia long before Buddhism took firm root in the West. In fact, if Sharf is right, both the *vipassana* and Zen meditation movements as now known in the West were basically invented in the late 1800s and early 1900s and do not have roots going back in history for thousands of years (Sharf 1993, 1995). Many of the Asian temples in the West are products of that modernization movement although most Westerners are unaware of this fact. Thus, although there are individual temples where the priest performs shamanism under the name of Buddhism, it is far more likely that the local Asian temple is a branch of some form of modernized Asian Buddhism. The terms "Asian Buddhism" and "Western Buddhism" do not make a contrast between traditional and modern; in general, they are both modern.

The terms "Asian/ethnic" and "Western/convert" apply only to the first generation of Asian immigrants to the West and to the first generation of Western converts to Buddhism. In the second generation, the children of immigrants are no longer culturally Asian; they are culturally Western even though they may practise their parents' Asian form of Buddhism. In the second generation, the children of Western converts to Buddhism are no longer converts to Buddhism themselves if they practise their parents' Western form of Buddhism. In fact, no Buddhists in the second and later generations fit exclusively under one or the other label. Without exception, they all fit under some hybrid combination of the two forms "Asian/ethnic" and "Western/convert."

Because of the lack of clarity of who counts as "Asian/ethnic" and "Western/convert," it is impossible to arrive at a statistical count of their numbers, as Beyer's analysis in this volume shows. The utility of the categories "Asian/ethnic" and "Western/convert" does not, then, lie in their analytical ability to categorize Buddhist practitioners. As indicated by Hori, the true utility of this distinction lies somewhere else. Western scholars and practitioners who write on Buddhism in the West continue to use this distinction because Asian/ethnic Buddhism is the "other" against which the self of Western/convert Buddhism is defined. It is part of the self-identity of Western/convert Buddhism that "we" are not "them," that the new Buddhism being created in the West is not "ethnic." Thus the new Buddhism, it is believed, will correct the distortions imposed upon Buddhism by Asian culture. In this view, the new Buddhism is going to be egalitarian, not hierarchical; it will be gender neutral, not sexist; it will be democratic, favouring laypeople, and not elitist, privileging monastics; and so on. This is the *méconnaissance*, misrecognition, at the base of much writing about Buddhism in America. Instead of seeing egalitarianism, gender neutrality, democracy, etc., as characteristics of American ethnicity, the writers on Buddhism in America treat these as the defining characteristics of a Buddhism without ethnicity. And this brings us to our second conclusion: that the "Two Buddhisms" be redefined not to imply that only Asian Buddhism is ethnic while Buddhism in the West has transcended ethnicity. Buddhism in the West is also an ethnic Buddhism.

Local Studies and Global Interactions

It is tempting to think of this process of adaptation as a simple one-way process in which the surrounding local culture functions as the active agent reshaping the passive, newly arrived religion.[1] But as Patricia Campbell points out in her study of Zen students in chapter 8, adaptations take place on both sides: the students to Buddhism and Buddhism to the students. Every feature of a Buddhist community in Canada – its language, its social organization, its buildings, its teachings, its practices, its food – is a product of a complex negotiation between that community's Buddhism and the surrounding culture. Each side impacts the other; it is a mistake to think that one side is active and the other passive.

Furthermore, this transplanting is not simply a local process of adaptation following a one-time transfer; there is always an ongoing global dimension. The studies of the Japanese Pure Land community by Harding and Watada show that there were multiple processes, both local interests as well as global currents, at work throughout the history of this long-term community. In its continuing struggle to maintain itself as a legitimate Pure Land community, it sent its trainees across the Pacific to Japan for the final stages of ministerial training and regularly received visits from His Eminence (*monshu*) Ōtani Kōshin, the leader of the Nishi Hongwanji branch of Shin Buddhism. Meanwhile early in its history, it adopted a Christian camouflage in order to survive in the local hostile and racist majority community: "priest" became "minister"; "temple" became "church"; the parents sat in pews singing Buddhist "hymns" and the children attended Dharma School. Similarly White's work on the Lao Buddhist community in Ontario clearly reveals the global element intersected by the local. In this volume, she explains in detail how the reconstruction of the That Luang stupa on Canadian soil helps legitimate the Ontario Buddhist temple and connect the community to the Buddhist tradition in Laos. In her earlier study (White 2006), she described the united and prolonged opposition by the local homeowners surrounding the temple property, who tried every means at their disposal to prevent construction of the temple. The eventual construction of the That Luang stupa has even greater significance precisely because of the local opposition.

The interaction between global influences and local communities is similarly apparent in Eldershaw's chapter on the Shambhala community and Haynes's study of the process of globalization in shaping Tibetan Buddhism in North America more generally. Shiu's history of Buddhism since the 1970s surveys the proliferation of these Tibetan, Lao, Vietnamese, Chinese, Sri Lankan, and other communities – even scholars of Buddhism – while analysing how Canadian culture and society were changing in tandem with this increasing diversity of Buddhist groups. Canada's more liberal immigration laws and official policy of multiculturalism from the 1960s and 70s both responded to global influences and shaped the changing landscape of Buddhism in Canada. In short, our third conclusion is that the transplantation of Buddhism to Canadian culture cannot be adequately understood as a one-time transfer followed by one-sided local adaptation; in every case, it is shaped by both global and local forces in a continuing dynamic interchange. Though not immediately visible, every adaptation of Buddhism to Canadian culture is also an adaptation of Canadian culture to global currents in Buddhism.

FURTHER STUDIES

Our fourth conclusion reflects the need for more data and information. We call for further studies, which should be informed by these theoretical reflections and will in turn provide additional data and analysis to better establish this nascent field of Buddhism in North America. We need more basic field-work studies of the many Buddhist communities and Buddhist personalities across Canada. And, because Buddhism is not some disembodied religion that exists separate from actual living people, we need to collect the life stories of teachers and practitioners of Buddhism. Peressini's chapter on Albert Low and the life story of Suwanda Sugunasiri by Hori and McLellan contribute to this effort. Low and Sugunasiri are formative figures who exemplify in markedly different ways the diversity of backgrounds, motivations, influences, and expressions of Buddhism in Canada. There is an urgent need to document many more lives in order to understand the nature of being Buddhist in Canada. The Jodo Shinshu community, now entering its second century in Canada, has already said goodbye to its early leaders. The many different Buddhist teachers who began their practice in the 1960s and 70s are now passing on. We need to record their stories as soon as possible.

ACADEMIC TRAINING

Despite the growing interest in Buddhism in Canada, few Canadian university graduate programs are organized to train students to conduct advanced ground level research on Buddhism in Canada. Most doctoral programs in Buddhist studies presuppose that the student will study some topic in Buddhism through texts, usually written in one of the Buddhist primary languages such as Sanskrit, Pali, classical Tibetan, classical Chinese, and so on. This philological approach is excellent for those students interested in a historical or philosophical topic, but the study of Buddhism in Canada today requires different tools. Students who propose to study a Buddhist community in Canada will need training in both traditional Buddhist studies and also contemporary social science fieldwork. At present, no university in Canada offers such a program. In general, it would resemble the following. First, research students would still need to know Buddhist history and philosophy. Second, they would still need training in languages – not necessarily primary text languages but the languages of the communities they wish to research. Third, they would need training in how to do social science field research: how to conduct interviews, work with statistics, do competent participant-observation, and observe research ethic guidelines. In addition, social science comes with its own body of theories about social behaviour, ritual, institutional organization, etc., which the students would need to learn. Because Buddhism is another religion in Canada, research students need to learn the history of religion both in Canada and, more broadly, in North America. All these elements are taught in today's universities; they have not hitherto been combined into a single graduate program. The study of Buddhism in Canada as a nascent field has largely, to date, been conducted by scholars who were trained in other disciplines. Therefore, this is our last conclusion: Canadian universities which have programs of Buddhist studies should provide a program option that trains students to do advanced fieldwork research. More than anything else, the new field of Buddhism in Canada needs properly trained scholars.

Wild Geese presents a collection of critical theoretical reflections, statistical analysis, histories, diverse case studies, and complementary life stories which together make up the content of the study of Buddhism in Canada. It reflects both the unorganized nature of this new field and the promise of much new interesting and significant research. Our conclusions are tentative. We hope our readers take away not final conclusions but further questions. The study of Buddhism in Canada is just beginning.

NOTE

1 Precisely to challenge this assumption, Erik Zürcher wrote *The Buddhist Conquest of China: The Spread and Adaptation of Buddhism in Early Medieval China*, 2 vols (Leiden: Brill, 1959) to show that Chinese culture was as much changed by Buddhism as Buddhism was changed by Chinese culture.

Bibliography

Adachi, Ken. 1976. *The Enemy That Never Was: A History of the Japanese Canadians.* Toronto: McClelland and Stewart

Ambedkar Mission Canada. http://www.ambedkarmission.com/

Amstutz, Galen. 2002. "Limited Engagements: Revisiting the Non-encounter between American Buddhism and the Shin Tradition." *Journal of Global Buddhism* 3: 1–35

Armstrong, John. 1991. "Japanese Canadians in Toronto: Assimilation in the History of a Community, 1940–1965." MA thesis, University of California at Los Angeles

Arslanian, Varant. 2005. "Leaving Home, Staying Home: A Case Study of an American Zen Monastery." MA thesis, McGill University

Azuma, Eiichiro. 2002. "The Impact of Globalization on Nikkei Identities: Introduction." In Hirabayashi, Hirabayashi, and Kikumura-Yano, *New Worlds: New Lives*, 1–4.

Barker, Michelle. 2007. "Investments in Religious Capital: An Explorative Case Study of Australian Buddhists." *Journal of Global Buddhism* 8: 65–80. http://www.globalbuddhism.org

Batchelor, Stephen. 1998. *Buddhism without Beliefs: A Contemporary Guide to Awakening.* New York: Riverhead Books

Baumann, Martin. 2002a. "Buddhism in Europe: Past, Present, Prospects." In *Westward Dharma: Buddhism beyond Asia*, edited by Charles S. Prebish and Martin Baumann, 85–105. Berkeley: University of California Press

– 2002b. "Protective Amulets and Awareness Techniques: How to Make Sense of Buddhism in the West," in Prebish and Baumann, *Westward Dharma*, 51–65

BBC News. 2007. "Burma Leaders Double Fuel Prices." 15 August. http://news.bbc.co.uk/2/hi/asia-pacific/6947251.stm

Befu, Harumi. 2002. "Globalization as Human Dispersal: Nikkei in the World." In Hirabayashi, Hirabayashi, and Kikumura-Yano, *New Worlds: New Lives*, 5–18

Beijing Wide Open. http://www.beijingwideopen.org

Beit-Hallahmi, Benjamin. 2001. "'O Truant Muse': Collaborationism and Research Integrity." In *Misunderstanding Cults: Searching for Objectivity in a Controversial Field*, edited by Benjamin Zablocki and Thomas Robbins, 35–70. Toronto: University of Toronto Press

Bell, Sandra. 2000. "Being Creative with Tradition: Rooting Theravada Buddhism in Britain." *Journal of Global Buddhism* 1: 1–23. http://www.globalbuddhism.org

Bellah, Robert N., Richard Madsen, William M. Sullivan, Ann Swidler, and Steven M. Tipton. 1985. *Habits of the Heart*. Berkeley: University of California Press

Benoit, Hubert. 1951. *La doctrine suprême: réflexions sur le bouddhisme zen*, 2 vols. Paris: Le Cercle du Livre

– 1955. *The Supreme Doctrine: Psychological Studies in Zen Thought*. London: Routledge and Kegan Paul

– 2004. *The Light of Zen in the West, Incorporating the Supreme Doctrine and the Realization of the Self*. Translated by Graham Rooth. Brighton: Sussex Academic Press

Bercholz, Samuel. 1998. "The Meeting of Minds: Student-Teacher Relationship in Buddhism." In *Buddhism in America: Proceedings of the First Buddhism in America Conference*, edited by Al Rapaport and Brian D. Hotchkiss, 286–98. Boston: Tuttle Publishing

Berger, Peter L. 1990. *Sacred Canopy: Elements of a Sociological Theory of Religion*. New York: Anchor

Bernbaum, Edwin. 1980. *The Way to Shambhala*. New York: Anchor Books

Bertalanffy, Ludwig von. 1968. *General System Theory: Foundations, Development, Applications*. London: Allen Lane

Berthrong, John H. 1994. *All under Heaven: Transforming Paradigms in Confucian-Christian Dialogue*. Albany: State University of New York Press

Beyer, Peter. 1994. *Religion and Globalization*. London: Sage Publications

– 1998. "The Modern Emergence of Religions and a Global Social System for Religion." *International Sociology* 13, no. 2: 151–72

– 2005a. "Appendix: Demographics of Religious Identification in Canada." In *Religion and Ethnicity in Canada*, edited by Paul Bramadat and David Seljak, 235–40. Toronto: Pearson Longman

– 2005b. "Religious Identity and Educational Attainment among Recent Immigrants to Canada: Gender, Age, and 2nd Generation." *Journal of International Migration and Integration* 6: 171–99

– 2006a. "Buddhism in Canada: A Statistical Overview from Canadian Censuses, 1981–2001." *Canadian Journal of Buddhist Studies* 2: 83–102

– 2006b. *Religions in Global Society*. New York: Routledge

– 2007. "Religion and Globalization." In *The Blackwell Companion to Globalization*, edited by George Ritzer, 444–60. Malden, MA: Blackwell Publishing

– 2008. "'A Little Bit Buddhist': Incidental Religious Participation and the Repro-duction of Religions." Paper delivered to the Association for the Sociology of Religion, Boston, August

Bibby, Reginald W. 1987. *Fragmented Gods: The Poverty and Potential of Religion in Canada*. Toronto: Irwin Publishing

– 2002. *Restless Gods: The Renaissance of Religion in Canada*. Toronto: Stoddart

Blanchfield, Mike and David Heyman. 2004. "PM, Dalai Lama May Talk Politics," *Calgary Herald*, 23 April, A12

Bluck, Robert. 2004. "Buddhism and Ethnicity in Britain: The 2001 Census Data." *Journal of Global Buddhism* 5: 90–6. At http://www.globalbuddhism.org

– 2006. *British Buddhism: Teachings, Practice and Development*. London and New York: RoutledgeCurzon

Bodhi, Bhikkhu. 1988. "A Look at the Kālāma Sutta." *Buddhist Publication Society Newsletter* 9 (Spring). http://www.accesstoinsight.org/lib/authors/bodhi/bps-essay_09.html

Boisvert, Mathieu. 2005. "Buddhists in Canada: Impermanence in a Land of Change." In Bramadat and Seljak, *Religion and Ethnicity in Canada*, 69–88

Boord, Martin. 1994. "Buddhism." In *Sacred Place*, edited by Jean Holm and John Bowler, 8–31. London: Pinter

Borup, Jørn. 2004. "Zen and Art of Inverting Orientalism." In *New Approaches to the Study of Religion*, edited by Peter Antes, Armin W. Geertz, and Randi Ruth Warne, 451–88. Berlin and New York: Walter de Gruyter

Bramadat, Paul. 2005. "Beyond Christian Canada: Religion and Ethnicity in a Multicultural Society." In Bramadat and Seljak, *Religion and Ethnicity in Canada*, 1–29

Bramadat, Paul, and David Seljak, eds. 2005. *Religion and Ethnicity in Canada*. Toronto: Pearson Longman

Braun, Kelly. 2004. "The Tzu Chi Foundation and the Buddha's Light International Association: The Impact of Ethnicity in the Transmission of Chinese Buddhism to Canada." MA thesis, University of Alberta

Bubna-Litic, David and Winton Higgins. 2007. "The Emergence of Secular Insight Practice in Australia." *Journal of Global Buddhism* 8: 157–73. http://www.globalbuddhism.org

Buddha Light International Association (BLIA), World Headquarters. http://www.blia.org

Buddhism in Canada. http://www.buddhismcanada.com

Buddhism in Quebec. http://bouddhisme.buddhismcanada.com/quebec.html

Buddhist Council of the Midwest. http://buddhistcouncilmidwest.org/members.htm

Buddhist Education Foundation of Canada (BEFC). http://www.buddhistedufoun-dation.com

Buddhist Federation of Alberta. *Hikari – The Light*

Buddhist Hospice Care in the Greater Toronto Area. http://chass.utoronto.ca/~fgarrett/hospice/index.html

Caldarola, Carlo. 2007. "Japanese Cultural Traditions in Southern Alberta." In *Sakura in the Land of the Maple Leaf: Japanese Cultural Traditions in Canada*, edited by Carlo Caldarola, Mitsuru Shimpo, K. Victor Ujimoto, and Ban Seng Hoe, 5–72. Gatineau, Quebec: Canadian Museum of Civilization Corp.

Calgary Myanmar Buddhist Temple. http://www.members.shaw.ca/mbtcalgary/index.htm

Campbell, Patricia. 2004. "Buddhist Values and Ordinary Life among Members of the Toronto Zen Buddhist Temple." MA thesis, Wilfrid Laurier University

Canada. Dominion Bureau of Statistics. n.d. *Census of Canada, 1961 – General Review - Religious Denominations in Canada*. DBS Catalogue 99–521. Ottawa: Dominion Bureau of Statistics

– n.d. *Census of Canada, 1951 – Population - General Characteristics*. Ottawa: Dominion Bureau of Statistics

Canada Tibet Committee. "About CTC." http://www.tibet.ca/en/about_ctc/ Accessed 19 September 2009.

Canadian Council on Social Development n.d. "Demographics of the Canadian Population." http://www.ccsd.ca/factsheets/demographics/

Canadian Tibetan Association of Ontario. http://www.ctao.org

Canda, Edward and Thitiya Phaobtong. 1992. "Buddhism as a Support System for Southeast Asian Refugees." *Social Work* 37, no. 1: 61–6

Carman, John, Diana Eck, Robert Gimello, and Helen Hardacre. 2005. "Masatoshi Nagatomi," *Harvard University Gazette*. http://www.news.harvard.edu/gazette/2005/02.24/16-mm.html

Casey, Noah. n.d. "The True Buddha School: A Field Research Report on the Chan Hai Lei Zang Temple." *Montreal Religious Sites Project*. http://mrsp.mcgill.ca/reports/html/ChanHai/index.htm Accessed 19 September 2009.

CBC. 2006. "Honouring Dalai Lama could have Economic Cost, China Warns." http://www.cbc.ca/canada/story/2006/07/27/dalai-lama-china.html

– 2007. "Dalai Lama to Meet Harper this Month." http://www.cbc.ca/canada/story/2007/10/09/dalai-tour.html?ref=rss

Cham Shan Temple. "The Buddhist Association of Canada: Cham Shan Temple." http://www.chamshantemple.org Accessed 19 September 2009.

Chan, Wing Tsit. 1978. *Religious Trends in Modern China*. New York: Columbia University Press

Chandler, Stuart. 2004. *Establishing a Pure Land on Earth: The Foguang Buddhist Perspective on Modernization and Globalization*. Honolulu: University of Hawai'i Press

– 2005. "Spreading Buddha's Light: The Internationalization of Foguang Shan." In Learman, *Buddhist Missionaries*, 162–84.

Chapman, John. 2007. "The 2005 Pilgrimage and Return to Vietnam of Exiled Zen Master Thích Nhất Hạnh." In Taylor, *Modernity and Re-enchantment*, 297–341.

Chen, Kenneth K.S. 1964 [1973]. *Buddhism in China: A Historical Survey*. Princeton: Princeton University Press

Chidester, David and Edward Linenthal. 1995. *Sacred Space in America*. Bloomington: Indiana University Press

Cho, Kyuhoon. 2004. "Religion in Diaspora: The Transformation of Korean Immigrant Churches in Global Society." MA thesis, University of Ottawa

Chödrön, Pema. 1991. *The Wisdom of No Escape: And the Path of Loving-Kindness*. Boston: Shambhala Publications

– 1994. *Start Where You Are: A Guide to Compassionate Living*. Boston: Shambhala Dragon Edition

– 1997a. *Awakening Compassion: Meditation Practice for Difficult Times*. Boulder: Sounds True (audiocassettes)

– 1997b. *When Things Fall Apart: Heart Advice for Difficult Times*. Boston: Shambhala Publications

– 2000. *When Things Fall Apart: Heart Advice for Difficult Times*. Boston: Shambhala Publications

Clark, Tom. 1980. *The Great Naropa Poetry Wars*. Santa Barbara: Cadmus Editions

Clasquin, Michel. 2002. "Buddhism in South Africa." In Prebish and Baumann, *Westward Dharma*, 152–62

Cleary, Thomas and J.C. Cleary, trans. 1977. *The Blue Cliff Record*. Boulder: Shambhala

Coleman, James William. 1999. "The New Buddhism: Some Empirical Findings." In Williams and Queen, *American Buddhism*, 91–9

– 2001. *The New Buddhism: The Western Transformation of an Ancient Tradition*. New York: Oxford University Press

Condominas, George. 1975. "Phiban Cults in Rural Laos." In *Change and Persistence in Thai Society*, edited by G. William Skinner and A. Thomas Kirsh, 252–73. Ithaca: Cornell University Press

Conze, Edward, trans. 1958 [2001]. *Buddhist Wisdom: The Diamond Sutra and the Heart Sutra*. New York: Random House

Cormier, Louis. 2001. "Tibetans in Quebec: Profile of a Buddhist Community." MA thesis, Université du Québec à Montréal

– n.d. "Tibetans in Quebec: Profile of a Buddhist Community." *Montreal Religious Sites Project*. http://mrsp.mcgill.ca/reports/html/Cormier/ Accessed 19 September 2009.

Coward, Harold and Leslie Kawamura, ed. 1978. *Religion and Ethnicity*. Waterloo: Wilfrid Laurier University Press

CTV. 2006. "Royal Buddhist Wedding Draws Faithful to Halifax." 8 June, 10:30 PM ET. http://www.ctv.ca/servlet/ArticleNews/print/CTVNews/20060608/buddhist_wedding_060608/20060608/?hub=CTVNewsAt11&subhub=Print Story

Danyluk, Angie. 2002. "Caught between Worlds: An Ethnography of Western Tibetan Buddhists in Toronto." PHD dissertation, McMaster University

– 2003. "To Be or Not to Be: Buddhist Selves in Toronto." *Contemporary Buddhism*. 4, no. 2: 128–41

Demetrakas, Johanna (Director) and Lisa Leeman (Producer). 2009. Documentary *Crazy Wisdom: The Life & Times of Chogyam Trungpa Rinpoche*. http://www.crazywisdomthemovie.com/about

Des Jardins, Marc. Forthcoming. "Tibetan Religions in British Columbia." In *Asian Religions in British Columbia*, edited by Don Baker, Larry DeVries, and Dan Overmyer. Vancouver: University of British Columbia Press

DeVido, Elise Anne. 2007. "'Buddhism for This World': The Buddhist Revival in Vietnam, 1920 to 1951, and Its Legacy." In Taylor, *Modernity and Re-enchantment*, 250–96

Dharma Drum. *Maps and Directions*. http://www.dharmadrum.org/map-directions/maps-directions.aspx

Dickson, Alnis. 2002. "The Montreal Buddhist Chinese Society." *Montreal Religious Sites Project*. http://mrsp.mcgill.ca/reports/pdfs/BuddhistSociety.pdf Accessed 19 September 2009.

Ding Renjie. 1999. *Shehui Mailuozhong De Zhuren Xingwei: Taiwan Fojiao Ciji Gongdehui Ge'an Yanjiu* [Helping Behaviour in Social Context: The Case of the Taiwanese Buddhist Ciji Gongdehui]. Taipei: Lianjing

Dobbelaere, Karel. 2002. *Secularization: An Analysis at Three Levels*. Brussels: P.I.E.-Peter Lang

Dorais, Louis-Jacques. 2000. *The Cambodians, Laotians and Vietnamese in Canada*. Translated by Eileen Reardon. Ottawa: The Canadian Historical Association

– 2006. "Buddhism in Québec." In Matthews, *Buddhism in Canada*, 120–41

Dorje Löppön Lodrö Dorje. 2001. "Thunder over Ocean: Introductory Talk." 9 August. http://halifax.shambhala.org/thunder_dlld.html

Dot, The. 2003. "Shambhala Finances on Range Alert." 1, no. 3: 13

Dowman, Keith. 1985. *Masters of Mahamudra: Songs and Histories of the Eighty-Four Buddhist Siddhas*. New York: State University of New York Press

Duraisingh, Christopher. 1979. "A New Expression of Identity." *Religion and Society* 26, no. 4: 95–101

Economist, The. 2007. 384, no. 8548 (29 September): 29–30

Eldershaw, Lynn. 1994. "Refugees in the Dharma: A Study of Revitalization in the Buddhist Church of Halifax." MA thesis, Acadia University

– 2007. "Collective Identity and the Postcharismatic Fate of Shambhala International." *Nova Religio* 10, no. 4: 72–102

Eliot, Thomas Stearns. 1943. *Four Quartets*. New York: Harcourt, Brace and Co.

Epstein, Mark. *Thoughts without a Thinker: Psychotherapy from a Buddhist Perspective*. New York: Basic Books, 1995

Esposito, John L., Darrell J. Fasching, and Todd Lewis. 2008. *Religion and Globalization: World Religions in Historical Perspective*. New York: Oxford University Press

Evans, Grant. 1998. *The Politics of Ritual and Remembrance: Laos since 1975*. Honolulu: University of Hawai'i Press

Feuerstein, George. 1992. *Holy Madness: The Shock Tactics and Radical Teachings of Crazy-Wise Adepts, Holy Fools, and Rascal Gurus*. New York: Arkana Books

Fields, Rick. 1981 [1992]. *How the Swans Came to the Lake: A Narrative History of Buddhism in America*. Boston: Shambhala Publications

– 1998. "Divided Dharmas: White Buddhists, Ethnic Buddhists, and Racism." In Prebish and Tanaka, *The Faces of Buddhism in America*, 196–206

Fisher, Mary Pat. 1999. *Religion in the Twenty-first Century*. Upper Saddle River: Prentice Hall Inc.

Fishman, Joshua A. 1972. *Language in Sociocultural Change*. Stanford: Stanford University Press

Fo Guang Shan Temple of Toronto. http://www.fgs.ca/english/index.html

Fordham, Walter, "Montreal: Where It All Started." *The Chronicle Project*. http://www.chronicleproject.com/montreal_roadtrip.html

Fowler, Merv. 1999. *Buddhism: Beliefs and Practices*. Brighton: Sussex Academic Press

Freiberger, Oliver. 2001. "The Meeting of Traditions: Inter-Buddhist and Inter-religious Relations in the West." *Journal of Global Buddhism* 2: 59–71. http://www.globalbuddhism.org/toc.html

Fronsdal, Gil. 2002. "Virtues without Rules: Ethics in the Insight Meditation Movement." In Prebish and Baumann, *Westward Dharma*, 285–306

Gaden Relief Projects. http://www.gadenrelief.org

Gall, Susan, ed. 1995. *The Asian American Almanac: A Reference Work on Asians in the United States*. Detroit: Gale Research, Inc.

Gehlek Rimpoche. 2005. "Chögyam Trungpa: Father of Tibetan Buddhism in the United States." In *Recalling Chögyam Trungpa*, edited by Fabrice Midal, 413–16. Boston: Shambhala Publications

Gethin, Rupert. 1998. *The Foundations of Buddhism*. New York: Oxford University Press

Given, Brian J. n.d. "Transpersonal Symbols, the Tibetan Diaspora and Cultural Survival." Unpublished paper

Gnostic Society Library, The. n.d. "Gnostic Scriptures and Fragments: The Acts of John." http://www.gnosis.org/library/actjohn.htm

Godolphin Bennett, John. 1957–1966. *The Dramatic Universe*, 4 vols. London: Hodder and Stoughton

Gombrich, Richard. 1988. *Theravada Buddhism: A Social History from Ancient Benares to Modern Colombo*. London: Routledge

Gonnami, Tsuneharu. 2005. *The Perception Gap: A Case Study of Japanese-Canadians*. http://pacific.commerce.ubc.ca/kbe/japan/gonnami_t.pdf

Goss, Robert E. 1999. "Buddhist Studies at Naropa: Sectarian or Academic?" In Williams and Queen, *American Buddhism*, 215–37.

Government Information Office (GIO). 2008. *Taiwan Yearbook 2007*. http://www.gio.gov.tw/taiwan-website/5-gp/yearbook/22religion.html#02

Graham, Ron. 1990. *God's Dominion: A Sceptic's Quest*. Toronto: McClelland & Stewart

Gregory, Peter N. 2001. "Describing the Elephant: Buddhism in America." *Religion and American Culture* 11, no. 2: 233–63

Gross, Rita. 1998. "Helping the Iron Bird Fly: Western Buddhist Women and Issues of Authority in the Late 1990s." In Prebish and Tanaka, *The Faces of Buddhism in America*, 238–52

Grumbach, Lisa. 2005. "Nenbutsu and Meditation: Problems with the Categories of Contemplation, Devotion, Meditation, and Faith." *Pacific World: Journal of the Institute of Buddhist Studies*, Third Series 7 (Fall): 91–105

Gunn, Geoffrey. 1982. "Theravadins and Commissars: The State and National Identity in Laos." In *Contemporary Laos*, edited by Martin Stuart-Fox, 76–100. London: University of Queensland

Gyatso, Tenzin. 1987. "The 14th Dalai Lama, Foreword." In Sharpa Tulku and Michael Perrott, *A Manual of Ritual Fire Offerings*. Dharamsala: Library of Tibetan Works and Archives

Harding, John. 2007. "Jōdo Shin-shū Buddhism in Southern Alberta." *Our Diverse Cities* 3: 140–4

Harris, Ian, ed. 1999. *Buddhism and Politics in Twentieth-Century Asia*. London and New York: Pinter

Harvey, Peter. 1984. "The Symbolism of the Early Stupa." *Journal of the International Association of Buddhist Studies* 7, no. 2: 67–93

– 1990. *An Introduction to Buddhism: Teachings, History and Practices*. New York: Cambridge University Press

Hayes, Richard P. 1998. *Land of No Buddha: Reflections of a Sceptical Buddhist*. Birmingham: Windhorse Publications

– 2000. *A Buddhist's Reflections on Religious Conversion*. Montreal: Elijah School Lectures for the fourth summer program. http://www.unm.edu/~rhayes/conversion.pdf

Hayward, Jeremy. 1995. *Sacred World: A Guide to Shambhala Warriorship in Daily Life*. New York: Bantam Books

Himalaya Foundation (HF). 2002. *Directory of 300 Major Foundations in Taiwan.*
http://www.foundations.org.tw/English/list/index.asp?orderno=4

Hirabayashi, Gordon. 1978. "Japanese Heritage, Canadian Experience." In Coward
and Kawamura, *Religion and Ethnicity,* 57–70

Hirabayashi, Lane R., James A. Hirabayashi, and Akemi Kikumura-Yano, eds.
2002. *New Worlds, New Lives: Globalization and People of Japanese Descent in the
Americas and from Latin America in Japan.* Stanford: Stanford University Press.

Hironaka, Robert. 2009. "Now Is the Moment." Published privately

Hobsbawm, Eric. 1983. "Introduction: Inventing Traditions." In Hobsbawm and
Ranger, *The Invention of Tradition,* 1–14

Hobsbawm, Eric and Terence Ranger, eds. 1983. *The Invention of Tradition.* Cambridge: Cambridge University Press

Holecek, Andrew. 1996. "Director's Ask: What's My Motivation?" *Shambhala
News* (January): 8–16

Hori, G. Victor Sōgen. 1994. "Teaching and Learning in the Rinzai Zen
Monastery." *Journal of Japanese Studies* 20, no. 1: 5–35

– 1998. "Japanese Zen in America: Americanizing the Face in the Mirror." In
Prebish and Tanaka, *The Faces of Buddhism in America,* 196–206.

Horvath, Cindy. 1998. "Wow, Do I Feel Left Out." *Shambhala News* (March): 11–16

Hsi Lai Temple. http://www.hsilai.org

Huang, Julia. 2003. "The Buddhist Tzu-Chi Foundation of Taiwan." In Queen,
Prebish, and Keown, *Action Dharma,* 132–53

– 2005. "The Compassion Relief Diaspora." In Learman, *Buddhist Missionaries,*
185–209

Hubbard, L. Ron. 1950. *Dianetics: The Modern Science of Mental Health.* New
York: Hermitage House

Hunt-Perry, Patricia and Lyn Fine. 2000. "All Buddhism is Engaged: Thich Nhat
Hanh and the Order of Interbeing." In Queen, *Engaged Buddhism in the West,*
35–66

Hurst, Jane D. 1992. *Nichiren Shoshu Buddhism and the Soka Gakkai in America:
The Ethos of a New Religious Movement.* New York: Weatherhill

Ichikawa, Akira. 1993. *Canadian Treatment of Jodo Shinshu Ministers during World
War II.* Department of Political Science, University of Lethbridge, Lethbridge, AB

– 1994. "A Test of Religious Tolerance: Canadian Government and Jodo Shinshu
Buddhism during the Pacific War, 1941–1945." *Canadian Ethnic Studies* 26, no.
2: 46–69

International Buddhist Friends Association. http://www.aung.com/ibfa.asp

International Congress on Buddhist Women's Role in the Sangha: Bhikshuni
Vinaya and Ordination Lineages. n.d. "Information about Developments after
the Congress." http://www.congress-on-buddhist-women.org/ Accessed 19
September 2009.

Iwaasa, David. 1972. "Canadian Japanese in Southern Alberta, 1905–1945." MA thesis, University of Lethbridge

Jiang Canteng. 1992. *Taiwan Fojiao yu Dangdai Shehui* [Taiwanese Buddhism and Contemporary Society]. Taipei: Dongda Chubanshe

Jodo Shinshu Hongwanji-Ha. http://www2.hongwanji.or.jp/english/

Jones, Charles B. 1999. *Buddhism in Taiwan: Religion and the State, 1660–1990.* Honolulu: University of Hawai'i Press

Kanter, Rosabeth Moss. 2005. *Commitment and Community: Communes and Utopias in Sociological Perspective.* Cambridge: Harvard University Press

Kapleau, Philip, ed. 1965. *The Three Pillars of Zen: Teaching, Practice, and Enlightenment.* Boston: Beacon Press

Karunadasa, Y. 2001. "The Early Buddhist Teaching on the Practice of the Moral Life." The Numata Yehan Lecture in Buddhism, University of Calgary (Fall). http://www.dhammaweb.net/books/Karunadasa_2001.pdf

Kawamura, Leslie. 1978. "Changes in the Japanese True Pure Land Buddhism in Alberta – A Case Study: Honpa Buddhist Church in Alberta." In Coward and Kawamura, *Religion and Ethnicity*, 37–55

– 2006. "Buddhism in Alberta." In Matthews, *Buddhism in Canada*, 30–42

Kawamura, Yutetsu. 1997. *The Dharma Survives with the People: Memoirs of Yutetsu Kawamura.* Translated by Leslie Kawamura. Published privately

Kay, David N. 2004. *Tibetan and Zen Buddhism in Britain: Transplantation, Development and Adaptation.* London and New York: RoutledgeCurzon

Kemp, Hugh. 2007. "How the Dharma Landed: Interpreting the Arrival of Buddhism in New Zealand." *Journal of Global Buddhism* 8: 107–31. http://www.globalbuddhism.org

Ketelaar, James Edward. 1990. *Of Heretics and Martyrs in Meiji Japan.* Princeton: Princeton University Press

King, Sallie B. 1996a. "Thich Nhat Hanh and the Unified Buddhist Church: Nondualism in Action." In Queen and King, *Engaged Buddhism*, 321–64

– 1996b. "Conclusion: Buddhist Social Activism." In Queen and King, *Engaged Buddhism*, 401–36

Klima, George. 2006. "buddhismcanada.com: A Decade in Cyberspace." In Matthews, *Buddhism in Canada*, 162–6

– "Buddhism in Québec." Buddhism in Canada. http://bouddhisme.buddhism canada.com/quebec.html Accessed 19 September 2009

Kobayashi, Audrey. 2002. "Migration as a Negotiation of Gender: Recent Japanese Immigrant Women in Canada." In Hirabayashi, Hirabayashi, and Kikumura-Yano, *New Worlds, New Lives*, 205–20

Koné, Alioune. 2001. "Zen in Europe: A Survey of the Territory." *Journal of Global Buddhism* 2: 139–61. http://www.globalbuddhism.org

Kongtrul, Jamgon. 1986. *The Torch of Certainty.* Boston: Shambhala Publications

Koppedrayer, Kat and Mavis Fenn. 2006. "Buddhist Diversity in Ontario." In Matthews, *Buddhism in Canada*, 59–84

Kornfield, Jack. 1988. "Is Buddhism Changing in North America?" In Morreale, *Buddhist America*, xi–xxviii

Kornman, Robin. 1988. "Vajrayana: The Path of Devotion." In Morreale, *Buddhist America*, 191–202

Laliberté, André. 2003. "'Love Transcends Border' or 'Blood is Thicker than Water': The Charity Work of the Buddhist Tzu Chi Foundation in the People's Republic of China." *European Journal of East Asian Studies* 2, no. 2: 243–62

– 2008. "'Harmonious Society,' 'Peaceful Re-unification,' and the Dilemmas Raised by Taiwanese Philanthropy." In *The Chinese Party-State in the 21st Century: Legitimacy and Adaptation*, edited by André Laliberté and Marc Lanteigne, 78–105. London: Routledge

Laurendeau, André and Davidson Dunton. 1971. *Report of the Royal Commission on Bilingualism and Biculturalism*. October 8

Lavine, Amy. 1998. "Tibetan Buddhism in America: The Development of American Vajrayāna." In Prebish and Tanaka, *The Faces of Buddhism in America*, 99–115

Layman, Emma McCloy. 1976. *Buddhism in America*. Chicago: Nelson-Hall

LDJCA History Book Committee. 2001. *Nishiki: Nikkei Tapestry: A History of Southern Alberta Japanese Canadians*. Lethbridge: Lethbridge and District Japanese Canadian Association

Learman, Linda. 2005. "Introduction." In Learman, *Buddhist Missionaries*, 1–21

Learman, Linda, ed. 2005. *Buddhist Missionaries in the Era of Globalization*. Honolulu: University of Hawai'i Press

Lee, Wei-chin. Comp. 1990. *Taiwan*. World Bibliographical Series 113. Oxford: Clio Press Ltd.

Leontov, Tania. 1991. "Blessing or Curse. The Crazy Wisdom Teacher." *Karma Dzong Newsletter* (Boulder)

Lewis, James R. 1998. *Cults in American: A Reference Handbook*. Santa Barbara: ABC:CLIO

Li, Peter. 1998. *The Chinese in Canada*. Toronto: Oxford University Press

Lin, Irene. 1996. "Journey to the Far West: Chinese Buddhism in America." *Amerasia Journal* 22, no. 1: 107–32

– 1999. "Journey to the Far West: Chinese Buddhism in America." In *New Spiritual Homes: Religion and Asian Americans*, edited by David K. Yoo, 134–68. Honolulu: University of Hawai'i Press

Liogier, Raphaël. 2004. *Le bouddhisme mondialisé: Une perspective sociologique sur la globalisation du religieux*. Paris: Ellipses

Liu, Tannie. 1995. "Ritual and the Symbolic Function: A Biogenetic Structural Comparison of Techniques Used in Tibetan Buddhism and the Sun Dance Religion." MA thesis, Carleton University

– 2004. "Globalization and Chinese Buddhism: The Canadian Experience." PHD dissertation, University of Ottawa

Lopez, Donald S., Jr. 1997. "Introduction." In *Religions of Tibet in Practice*, edited by Donald S. Lopez, Jr., 3–36. Princeton: Princeton University Press

– 1998. *Prisoners of Shangri-la: Tibetan Buddhism and the West.* Chicago: University of Chicago Press

Low, Albert. 1966. "The Systematics of a Business Organization." *Systematics* 4, no. 3: 248–80

– 1976. *Zen and Creative Management.* Garden City: Anchor Press (reprinted by Playboy Paperbacks, Rockville Center, 1976 and 1982, and Charles E. Tuttle, Rutland, 1992)

– 1985. *The Iron Cow of Zen.* Wheaton: Theosophical Publishing House (reprinted by Charles E. Tuttle, Rutland, 1991 and 1992)

– 1989. *Invitation to Practice Zen.* Rutland: Charles E. Tuttle

– 1993. *The Butterfly's Dream: In Search of the Roots of Zen.* Boston: Charles E. Tuttle (reprinted by Charles E. Tuttle, Tokyo, 2003, and Airlift, Enfield, 2003)

– 1995. *The World a Gateway: Commentaries on the Mumonkan.* Boston: Charles E. Tuttle

– 1997. *To Know Yourself: Talks, Stories, and Articles on Zen.* Boston: Charles E. Tuttle

– 2000. *Zen and the Sutras.* Boston: Charles E. Tuttle

– 2001. *Creating Consciousness: A Study of Consciousness, Creativity, Evolution, and Violence.* Ashland: White Cloud Press

– 2004. *Hakuin Zenji's Chant in Praise of Zazen.* Columbia: Zen Books

– 2006. *Hakuin on Kensho: The Four Ways of Knowing.* Boston: Shambhala

– 2008. *The Origin of Human Nature: A Zen Buddhist Looks at Evolution.* Brighton and Portland: Sussex Academic Press

– 2008. *Conflict and Creativity at Work: The Human Roots of Corporate Life.* Brighton and Portland: Sussex Academic Press

– n.d. "The Autobiography of a Question." Unpublished manuscript

Lu, Sheng-yen. 1978. *Lunhui Di MiMi.* Hong Kong: Qingshan Chuban She

Lui-Ma, Amy, trans. 2000. *Handing Down the Light: The Biography of Venerable Master Hsing Yun.* Hacienda Heights: Hsi Lai University Press

Maclean's. 2003. "50 Canadians to Watch For." 20 January, 28

Madsen, Douglas and Peter G. Snow. 1991. *The Charismatic Bond: Political Behavior in Time of Crisis.* Cambridge: Harvard University Press

Makabe, Tomoko. 1998. *The Canadian Sansei.* Toronto: University of Toronto Press

Marin, Peter. 1979. "Spiritual Obedience." *Harper's Magazine* 258, no. 1545: 43–58

Matrix Mandala Garden. http://www.matrixmandala.org/matrixmandala garden.htm

Matthews, Bruce. 2002. "Buddhism in Canada." In Prebish and Baumann, *Westward Dharma*, 120–38

– ed. 2006. *Buddhism in Canada.* New York: Routledge

– 2000. "Buddhist Studies in Canada." In *The State of Buddhist Studies in the World 1972–1997*, edited by Donald K. Swearer and Somparn Promta, 144–70. Bangkok: Centre for Buddhist Studies, Chulalongkorn University

McAra, Sally. 2007a. *Land of Beautiful Vision: Making a Buddhist Sacred Place in New Zealand.* Honolulu: University of Hawai'i Press

– 2007b. "Indigenizing or Adapting? Importing Buddhism into a Settler-Colonial Society." *Journal of Global Buddhism* 8: 132–56. http://www.globalbuddhism. org

McHale, Shawn Frederick. 2004. *Print and Power: Confucianism, Communism and Buddhism in the Making of Modern Vietnam.* Honolulu: Kuroda Institute, University of Hawai'i Press

McKeever, William. 1980. "The Tradition of Shambhala." *The Vajradhatu Sun.* February/March 2, no. 3: 9–10

McLellan, Janet. 1993. "Many Petals of the Lotus: Redefinitions of Buddhist Identity in Toronto." PHD dissertation, York University

– 1999. *Many Petals of the Lotus: Five Asian Buddhist Communities in Toronto.* Toronto: University of Toronto Press

McLellan, Janet and Marybeth White. 2005. "Social Capital and Identity Politics among Asian Buddhists in Toronto." *Journal of International Migration and Integration* 6, no. 2: 235–53

McMahan, David L. 2002. "Repackaging Zen for the West." In Prebish and Baumann, *Westward Dharma*, 218–29

Melton, Gordon, J. 1991. "When Prophets Die: The Succession Crisis in New Religions." In Miller, *When Prophets Die*, 1–12

Melucci, Albert. 1996. *Challenging Codes: Collective Action in the Information Age.* Cambridge: Cambridge University Press

Metraux, Daniel A. 2003. "The Soka Gakkai in Australia: Globalization of a New Japanese Religion." *Journal of Global Buddhism* 4: 108–43. http://www.global buddhism.org

– 2004. "The Soka Gakkai in Australia and Quebec: An Example of Globalization of a New Japanese Religion." *Asia Pacific: Perspectives* 4, no. 1 (May): 19–30

Midal, Fabrice. 2004. *Chögyam Trungpa: His Life and Vision.* Translated by Ian Monk. Boston: Shambhala Publications

Miki, Roy. 2004. *Redress: Inside the Japanese Canadian Call for Justice.* Vancouver: Raincoast Books

Miller, Timothy, ed. 1991. *When Prophets Die: The Postcharismatic Fate of New Religious Movements.* New York: State University of New York Press

Ministry of Interior (MOI). 2008. *Department of Statistics: General Conditions of Religion.* http://www.moi.gov.tw/stat/english/index.asp

Montero, Darrel. 1980. *Japanese Americans: Changing Patterns of Ethnic Affiliation over Three Generations.* Boulder: Westview Press

Montreal Zen Center. http://www.zenmontreal.ca/

Morreale, Don, ed. 1988. *Buddhist America: Centers, Retreats, Practices*. Santa Fe: John Muir Publications

Muecke, Marjorie A. 1987. "Resettled Refugees' Reconstruction of Identity: Lao in Seattle." *Urban Anthropology* 16, nos 3–4: 273–89

Mukpo, Diana J. and Carolyn Rose Gimian. 2006. *Dragon Thunder: My Life with Chögyam Trungpa*. Boston: Shambhala Publications

Mullins, Mark. 1987. "The Life-Cycle of Ethnic Churches in Sociological Perspective." *Japanese Journal of Religious Studies* 14, no. 4: 321–34

– 1988. "The Organisational Dilemmas of Ethnic Churches: A Case Study of Japanese Buddhism in Canada." *Sociological Analysis: A Journal in the Sociology of Religion* 49, no. 3: 217–33

– 1989. *Religious Minorities in Canada: A Sociological Study of the Japanese Experience*. Queenston: Edwin Mellen Press

Mystical Arts of Tibet, The. http://www.mysticalartsoftibet.org

Nalanda College of Buddhist Studies. 2005. "100 Years of Buddhism in Canada." http://www.nalandacollege.ca/PDF/souvenir_proof.pdf Accessed 30 December 2008.

Namgyal Rinpoche Stories Project. http://namgyal.wikidot.com/ Accessed 17 September 2009.

Naropa Institute, Uncatalogued document. *Letter to the Board of Directors*, 28 January 1989. Boulder, Colorado

Naropa University. http://www.naropa.edu/

Nattier, Jan. 1998. "Who Is a Buddhist? Charting the Landscape of Buddhist America." In Prebish and Tanaka, *The Faces of Buddhism in America*, 183–95

Nguyen, Cuong Tu. 1995. "Rethinking Vietnamese Buddhist History: Is the Thiền Uyên Tập Anh a 'Transmission of the Lamp' Text?" In *Essays into Vietnamese Pasts*, edited by K.W. Taylor and John K. Whitmore, 81–115. Ithaca: Southeast Asia Program, Cornell University

– 1997. *Zen in Medieval Vietnam: A Study and Translation of the Thiền Uyên Tập Anh*. Honolulu: Kuroda Institute, University of Hawai'i Press

Nichols, Trevor. 1999. *Socially Engaged Buddhism for the New Millennium: Essays in Honour of the Ven. Phra Dhammapitaka (Bhikkhu P.A. Payutto) on His 60th Birthday Anniversary*. Bangkok: Sathirakoses-Nagapradipa Foundation

Nishiyama, Reyko. 2006. "Our Beloved Otera: Memories of Raymond Buddhist Temple." (DVD)

Numata Buddhist Studies Program. http://www.chass.utoronto.ca/buddhist studies/numata/index.html

Numrich, Paul David. 1996. *Old Wisdom in the New World: Americanization in Two Immigrant Theravada Buddhist Temples*. Knoxville: University of Tennessee Press

– 2006. "Two Buddhisms Further Reconsidered." In *Buddhist Studies from India to America*, edited by Damien Keown, 207–33. London and New York: Routledge

Obadia, Lionel. 2001. "Tibetan Buddhism in France: A Missionary Religion?" *Journal of Global Buddhism* 2: 92–122. http://www.globalbuddhism.org

– 2002. "Buddhism in the Promised Land: Outlines of the Buddhist Settlement in Israel." In Prebish and Baumann, *Westward Dharma*, 163–76

Obeyesekere, Gananath. 1972. "Religious Symbolism and Political Change in Ceylon." In *The Two Wheels of Dhamma: Essays in Theravada Tradition in India and Ceylon*, edited by Bardwell L. Smith, 58–78. Chambersburg: American Academy of Religion

– 1975. "Sinhalese-Buddhist Identity in Ceylon." In *Ethnic Identity: Cultural Communities and Change*, edited by George De Vos and Lola Romanucci-Ross, 231–58. Palo Alto: Mayfield Publishing Company

– 2003. "Buddhism." In *Global Religions: An Introduction*, edited by Mark Juergensmeyer, 63–77. New York: Oxford University Press

Offermanns, Jürgen. 2005. "Debates on Atheism, Quietism, and Sodomy: The Initial Reception of Buddhism in Europe." *Journal of Global Buddhism* 6: 16–35. http://www.globalbuddhism.org

Office of His Holiness the Dalai Lama, The. n.d. "Dalai Lama Presented with Honorary Canadian Citizenship." http://www.dalailama.com/news.67.htm

Ostrovskaya, Elena A. 2004. "Buddhism in Saint Petersburg." *Journal of Global Buddhism* 5: 19–65. http://www.globalbuddhism.org

Pas, Julian, ed. 1989. *The Turning of the Tide: Religion in China*. Oxford: Oxford University Press

Payne, Richard K. 2005a. "Hiding in Plain Sight: The Invisibility of the Shingon Mission to the United States." In Learman, *Buddhist Missionaries*, 101–22

– ed. 2005b. "Meditation in American Shin Buddhism," special issue of *Pacific World: Journal of the Institute of Buddhist Studies,* Third Series 7 (Fall)

PEQAB. "Expired/Denied/Withdrawn Applications." http://192.139.188.172/PEQAB/index.asp?id1=27

Pittman, Don A. 2001. *Toward a Modern Chinese Buddhism: Taixu's Reforms.* Honolulu: University of Hawai'i Press

Placzek, James, and Larry Devries. 2006. "Buddhism in British Columbia." In Matthews, *Buddhism in Canada*, 1–29

Poceski, Mario. 2006. "The Expanding Presence of Buddhist Studies on the Internet." *Religious Studies Review* 32, no. 4: 223–6

Portes, Alejandro and Ruben Rumbaut. 2001. *Legacies: The Story of the Immigrant Second Generation*. New York: Russell Sage Foundation

Powers, John. 1995. *Introduction to Tibetan Buddhism*. Boston: Snow Lion Publications

– 2000. "The Free Tibet Movement: A Selective Narrative." In Queen, *Engaged Buddhism in the West*, 218–44

Prebish, Charles S. 1979. *American Buddhism*. North Scituate: Duxbury Press

– 1998. "Introduction." In Prebish and Tanaka, *The Faces of Buddhism in America*, 1–12

– 1999. *Luminous Passage: The Practice and Study of Buddhism in America*. Berkeley: University of California Press

Prebish, Charles S. and Martin Baumann, eds. 2002. *Westward Dharma: Buddhism beyond Asia*. Berkeley: University of California Press

Prebish, Charles S. and Kenneth K.Tanaka, eds. 1998. *The Faces of Buddhism in America*. Berkeley: University of California Press

Pye, Michael. 1978. *Skilful Means: A Concept in Mahayana Buddhism*. Dallas: Gerald Duckworth & Co. Ltd

Queen, Christopher S. 1996. "Introduction: The Shapes and Sources of Engaged Buddhism." In Queen and King, *Engaged Buddhism*, 1–44

– 1999. "Introduction." In Williams and Queen, *American Buddhism*, xiv–xxxvii

– ed. 2000. *Engaged Buddhism in the West*. Boston: Wisdom Publications

– 2002. "Engaged Buddhism: Agnosticism, Interdependence, Globalization." In Williams and Queen, *American Buddhism*, 324–47

Queen, Christopher S. and Sallie B. King, eds. 1996. *Engaged Buddhism: Buddhist Liberation Movements in Asia*. Albany: State University of New York Press

Queen, Christopher, Charles Prebish, and Damien Keown, eds. 2003. *Action Dharma: New Studies in Engaged Buddhism*. London: RoutledgeCurzon

Rahula, Walpola. 1962. *What the Buddha Taught*. New York: Grove Press

Rainey, Cortez, Agness Au, Mary Whetsell, Hamish Maclaren, and Chuck Whetsel. 2006. *Going beyond Bias. Diversity Training in Shambhala Buddhism. Guiding Principles*. http://www.shambhala.org/congress/diversity/GuidingPrinciples GBBiasGuidelines.pdf

Ram, Bali. 1990. "Intermarriage among Ethnic Groups." In *Ethnic Demography: Canadian Immigrants Racial and Cultural Variations*, edited by Shiva Halli, Frank Trovato, and Leo Driedger, 213–27. Ottawa: Carleton University Press

Rambo, Lewis R. 1993. *Understanding Religious Conversion*. New Haven: Yale University Press

Rapaport, Al and Brian D. Hotchkiss, eds. 1998. *Buddhism in America: Proceedings of the First Buddhism in America Conference*. Boston: Tuttle Publishing

Ray, Reginald. 2002. *Secret of the Vajra World: The Tantric Buddhism of Tibet*, vol. 2. Boston: Shambhala Publications

– 2005. "Chögyam Trungpa as a Siddha." In Midal, *Recalling Chögyam Trungpa*, 197–220. Boston: Shambhala Publications

RCMP Report RG 36/27/30/F 1613. 1946. Royal Canadian Mounted Police, Alberta, Division K, Lethbridge Sub-Division. Filed 21 June 1946

Reader, Ian. 1991. *Religion in Contemporary Japan*. Honolulu: University of Hawai'i Press

Reitman, Valerie. 1999. "Buddhist Nun Is Taiwan's Master of Inspiration." *Los Angeles Times*, 5 October

Republic of China Yearbook, The. 2002. Taipei: Government Information Office

Richardson, Hugh. 1991. "The Independence of Tibet." In *The Anguish of Tibet*, edited by Petra Kelly, Gert Bastian, Pat Aiello, 33–6. Berkeley: Parallax Press

Robertson, Roland. 1992. *Globalization: Social Theory and Global Culture*. London: Sage Publications

Rocha, Cristina. 2000. "Zen Buddhism in Brazil: Japanese or Brazilian?" *Journal of Global Buddhism* 1: 31–55. http://www.globalbuddhism.org

– 2006. *Zen in Brazil: The Quest for Cosmopolitan Modernity*. Honolulu: University of Hawai'i Press

Rockwell, John. 2001. "Why Shambhala Buddhism?" *Shambhala News* (March): 7, 13

Sagely City of Ten Thousand Buddhas. http://www.cttbusa.org

Sagely City of Ten Thousand Buddhas, The. Related Links and Branches. http://www.cttbusa.org/cttb/relatedlinks&branches.asp

Saint John of the Cross. 1959. *The Dark Night of the Soul*. Garden City: Doubleday

Sakyong Mipham Rinpoche. 2000. *Shambhala Buddhism*. http://www.Shambhala. org/centers/Halifax/Shambhala_Buddhism.htm

– 2004a. *Turning the Mind into an Ally*. New York: Riverhead Books

– 2004b. "The Shambhala Ngöndro Practice and Study for the Coming Year (04/05)" Shambhala International, Office of Practice and Education. http://www. atlantashambhalacenter.org/resources/teachings/shambhala_ngondro.pdf

– 2005. *Ruling Your World: Ancient Strategies for Modern Life*. New York: Broadway Publishers

– 2007. *What about Me?* (CD) Sound and Silence Recordings

Samuel, Geoffrey. 1993. *Civilized Shamans: Buddhism in Tibetan Societies*. Washington: Smithsonian Institution Press

Sander, Ed. 1977. *The Party: A Chronological Perspective on a Confrontation at a Buddhist Seminary*. Woodstock: Poetry, Crime & Culture Press

Sandler, Jeremy. 2007. "Making Room for History." *National Post*, 2 July. http://www.phayul.com/news/article.aspx?id=17045&t=1&c=1

Sarvodaya USA. http://www.sarvodayausa.org/

Schuhmacher, Stephan and Gert Woerner, eds. 1989. *Encyclopedia of Eastern Philosophy and Religion*. Boston: Shambhala Publications

Scrivener, Leslie. 2004. "Tibetans Find a Haven in Parkdale." *Toronto Star*, 23 February

Seager, Richard Hughes. 1999. *Buddhism in America*. New York: Columbia University Press

– 2002. "American Buddhism in the Making." In Prebish and Baumann, *Westward Dharma*, 106–19

Seonaidh, Ven. (John A. Perks). 1998. "Buddha Born among the Celts." In Rapaport and Hotchkiss, *Buddhism in America*, 299–305

Shambhala Archives, 1999. *The Life of Chogyam Trungpa Rinpoche: A Slide Presentation from the Shambhala Archives.* Halifax

Sharf, Robert H. 1993. "The Zen of Japanese Nationalism." *History of Religions* 33, no. 1: 1–43

– 1995. "Buddhist Modernism and the Rhetoric of Meditative Experience." *Numen* 42, no. 3: 228–83

Shibayama, Zenkai. 2000. *The Gateless Barrier: Zen Comments on the Mumonkan.* Boston: Shambhala

Shimizu, Yon. 1993. *The Exiles: An Archival History of the World War II Japanese Road Camps in British Columbia and Ontario.* Wallaceburg: Shimizu Consulting and Pub.

Shiu, Henry C.H. 2005. "Buddhist Studies in Ontario." *Canadian Journal of Buddhist Studies* 1: 73–86

Shoji, Rafael. 2003. "Buddhism in Syncretic Shape: Lessons of Shingon in Brazil." *Journal of Global Buddhism* 4: 70–107. http://www.globalbuddhism.org

Simmer-Brown, Judith. 1994. "No Picnic at Spirit Rock: Power, Sex and Pain in American Buddhism." *Shambhala Sun*, 2 January (3): 40–2

– 2002. "The Roar of the Lioness: Women's Dharma in the West." In Prebish and Baumann, *Westward Dharma*, 309–23

Smith. Jonathan Z. 1978. *Map Is Not Territory: Studies in the History of Religions.* Leiden: E.J. Brill

Smith, W. 1975. *Tibetan Refugees: A Second Life in a New Land.* Ottawa: Canada Research Projects Group, Department of Manpower and Immigration

Snellgrove, David. 1987. *Indo-Tibetan Buddhism: Indian Buddhists and their Tibetan Successors.* Boston: Shambhala Publications

Soucy, Alexander. 1994. "Gender and Division of Labour in a Vietnamese-Canadian Buddhist Pagoda." MA thesis, Concordia University

– 2007. "Nationalism, Globalism and the Re-establishment of the Trúc Lâm Thiền Buddhist Sect in Northern Vietnam." In Taylor, *Modernity and Re-enchantment*, 342–70

Spuler, Michelle. 2002. "The Development of Buddhism in Australia and New Zealand." In Prebish and Baumann, *Westward Dharma*, 139–51

– 2003. *Developments in Australian Buddhism: Facets of the Diamond.* London and New York: RoutledgeCurzon

Stanford, Jim. 2004. "Plea to China: Punish Us, Punish Us – Please." *Globe andMail.com*. 26 April

Stark, Rodney. 1996. "Why Religious Movements Succeed or Fail: A Revised General Model." *Journal of Contemporary Religion* 11, no. 2: 133–46

Stark, Rodney, and William Sims Bainbridge. 1985. "Secularization, Revival, and Cult Formation." In *The Future of Religion*, edited by Rodney Stark and William Sims Bainbridge, 429–56. Berkeley: University of California Press

Stark, Rodney and Roger Finke. 2002. "Beyond Church and Sect: Dynamics and Stability in Religious Economics." In *Sacred Markets, Sacred Canopies; Essays on Religious Markets and Religious Pluralism*, edited by T.G. Jelen, 31–62. Lanham, MD: Rowman & Littlefield Publishers

Statistics Canada. 1976. *1971 Census of Canada Population 2, part 3*. Ottawa: Statistics Canada

– 1980. *Canada Year Book 1978–79*. Ottawa: Statistics Canada.

– 2001. Census Long Form. http://www.statcan.ca/english/sdds/instrument/3901_Q2_V2_E.pdf

– 2001. "Overview: Canada Still Predominantly Roman Catholic and Protestant." http://www12.statcan.ca/english/census01/Products/Analytic/companion/rel/canada. cfm#growth

– 2003a. *1971, 1981, 1991 & 2001 Census Custom Tabulations. DO0324*. CD-ROM. Ottawa: Statistics Canada, Advisory Services Division

– 2003b. *Religion (95) and Visible Minority Status (15) for Population, Canada, Provinces, Territories, Census Metropolitan Areas and Census Agglomerations 2001 – 20% Sample Data*. Catalogue No. 97F00022XCB01005. Ottawa: Statistics Canada.

– 2006. Census 2001. *Ethnocultural Portrait of Canada*. Cat. No. 97F0024XIE 2001006. http://www.statcan.ca

Statistique Canada. 2001. "Population selon certaines origines ethniques, par province et territoire." http://www40.statcan.gc.ca/l02/cst01/demo26a-fra.htm

Steger, Manfred B. 2003. *Globalization: A Very Short Introduction*. London: Oxford University Press

Sugunasiri, Suwanda. 1989. "Buddhism in Metropolitan Toronto: A Preliminary Overview." *Canadian Ethnic Studies* 21, no. 2: 83–103

– 2001a. *Towards Multicultural Growth: A Look at Canada from Classical Racism to Neomulticulturalism*. Toronto: Village Publishing House

– 2001b. *You're What You Sense: A Buddhian-Scientific Dialogue on Mindbody*. Dehiwela, Sri Lanka: Buddhist Cultural Centre

– 2005. *Embryo as Person: Buddhism, Bioethics and Society*. Toronto: Nalanda College of Buddhist Studies

– 2006a. "Inherited Buddhists and Acquired Buddhists." *Canadian Journal of Buddhist Studies* 2: 103–42

– 2008a. "Experiment in Buddhist Education." http://www.nalandacollege.ca/PDF/ExperimentInBuddhistEducation.pdf, date accessed 30 December 2008

– ed. 2008b. *Thus Spake the Sangha: Early Buddhist Leadership in Toronto*. Toronto: Nalanda Publishing Canada

Swearer, Donald. 1995. *The Buddhist World of Southeast Asia*. Albany: State University of New York

Swick, David. 1995. "They Came from Away; Now They're Part of Us." *The Daily News*, 19 May: 2

– 2002 [1996]. *Thunder and Ocean: Shambhala and Buddhism in Nova Scotia*. Lawrencetown Beach: Pottersfield Press

Swift, S. 1993. *The Regulation and Public Funding of Private Schools in Canada*. Toronto: Ontario Legislative Library, Legislative Research Service

Taixu 1947 [1989]. *Pusa Xuechu*. Comp. Meiyan. Toronto: Cham Shan Temple

Takata, Toyo. 1983. *Nikkei Legacy: The Story of Japanese Canadians from Settlement to Today*. Toronto: NC Press Limited

Tanaka, Kenneth K. 1998. "Epilogue: The Colors and Contours of American Buddhism." In Prebish and Tanaka, *The Faces of Buddhism in America*, 287–98

– 1999. "Issues of Ethnicity in the Buddhist Churches of America." In Williams and Queen, *American Buddhism*, 3–19

Taylor, Charles. 1989. *Sources of the Self*. Massachusetts: Harvard University Press

Taylor, Philip, ed. 2007. *Modernity and Re-enchantment: Religion in Post-Revolutionary Vietnam*. Singapore: Institute of Southeast Asian Studies

TBS *Purple Lotus Journal*, Purple Lotus Society, True Buddha School, San Bruno, California. http://www.purplelotus.org/temple/en/plpub/publisher.html

– 1993. *Purple Lotus Journal*, Purple Lotus Society, True Buddha School, San Bruno, California. (July–October): 4

TBS *Zilian Yuekan*, Purple Lotus Society, True Buddha School, San Bruno, California. http://www.purplelotus.org/temple/en/plpub/publisher.html

Thibeault, François. 2005. "Les enjeux actuels de l'étude de bouddhisme en Occident et la tradition Vipassan de S.N. Goenka." Unpublished paper presented at the Eastern International Regional Meeting of the American Academy of Religion, McGill University

– 2006. "Constructing Ethnoreligious Identities: Inheritance and Choice in Two Theravada Buddhist Organisations around Montréal." Unpublished paper

Thich Nhat Hanh. 1968. *Vietnam: Lotus in a Sea of Fire*. New York: Hill and Wang

Thurman, Robert. A.F. 1995. *Inside Tibetan Buddhism: Rituals and Symbols Revealed*. San Francisco: Collins Publishers

Topmiller, Robert J. 2002. *The Lotus Unleashed: The Buddhist Peace Movement in South Vietnam, 1964–1966*. Lexington: University of Kentucky Press

Toronto Mahavira n.d. "History of Toronto Maha Vira." http://lankanstyle.com/mahavihara/history1.htm Accessed 17 September 2009.

True Buddha School Net. http://www.tbsn.org

Trungpa, Chögyam. 1969. *Meditation in Action*. Boston: Shambhala Publications

– 1973. *Cutting through Spiritual Materialism*. Boston: Shambhala Publications

– 1984. *Shambhala: The Sacred Path of the Warrior*. New York: Bantam Books

– 1985 [1967, 1977]. *Born in Tibet*. Boston: Shambhala Publications
– 1988. *The Myth of Freedom and the Way of Meditation*. Boston: Shambhala Publications
– 1991a. *Crazy Wisdom*. Boston: Shambhala Publications
– 1991b. *The Heart of the Buddha*. Boston: Shambhala Publications
– 1995. "Reflections on the Cosmic Mirror." *Shambhala Sun* (July): 26–9
– 1999. *Great Eastern Sun: The Wisdom of Shambhala*. Boston: Shambhala Publications
– 2005. *True Command: The Teachings of the Dorje Kasung Volume One – The Town Talks*. Halifax: Trident Publications
Tsomo, Karma Lekshe, Eko Susan Noble, Furya Schroeder, Nora Kunli Shih, and Jacqueline Mandell. 1995. "The Monastic Experience." In *Buddhism through American Women's Eyes*, edited by Karma Lekshe Tsomo, 121–48. Ithaca: Snow Lion Publications
Turpie, David. 2001. "Wesak and the Re-creation of Buddhist Tradition." MA thesis, McGill University. http://mrsp.mcgill.ca/reports/pdfs/Wesak.pdf
Tweed, Thomas A. 1997. *Our Lady of the Exile: Diasporic Religion at a Cuban Catholic Shrine in Miami*. Oxford: Oxford University Press
– 1999. "Night-Stand Buddhists and Other Creatures: Sympathizers, Adherents, and the Study of Religion." In Williams and Queen, *American Buddhism*, 71–90
– 2000. *The American Encounter with Buddhism, 1844–1912: Victorian Culture and the Limits of Dissent*. Chapel Hill: University of North Carolina Press
– 2002. "Who Is a Buddhist? Night-Stand Buddhists and Other Creatures." In Prebish and Baumann, *Westward Dharma*, 17–33
– 2006. *Crossing and Dwelling: A Theory of Religion*. Cambridge: Harvard University Press
Tworkov, Helen. 1991. "Editorial: Many is More." *Tricycle: The Buddhist Review* 1, no. 2: 4
Tzu Chi. *Fact Sheet: Donation Distribution*. http://en.tzuchi.ca/canada/files/other/tcc-Smile-20060405-StatsSheet.pdf
University of Toronto/McMaster Numata Buddhist Studies Program (2006). http://www.chass.utoronto.ca/buddhiststudies/numata/
Usarski, Frank. 2002. "Buddhism in Brazil and Its Impact on the Larger Brazilian Society." In Prebish and Baumann, *Westward Dharma*, 163–76
Vajrayana Buddhism Association. http://www.vbatoronto.org/en/default.aspx
– "Cancer Care Meditation." http://www.vbatoronto.org/en/lesson/CCpamphlet.pdf Accessed 17 September 2009.
– http://www.vbatoronto.org/en/lesson/cancercaring.aspx
Van Esterik, Penny. 1992. *Taking Refuge: Lao Buddhists in North America*. Toronto: York Lanes Press
Verhoeven, Martin J. 1998. "Americanizing the Buddha: Paul Carus and the

Transformation of Asian Thought." In Prebish and Tanaka, *Faces of Buddhism in America*, 207–27

Vlastos, Stephen. 1998. "Tradition: Past/Present Culture and Modern Japanese History." In *Mirror of Modernity: Invented Traditions of Modern Japan*, edited by Stephen Vlastos, 1–18. Berkeley: University of California Press

Wallace, B. Alan. 2002. "The Spectrum of Buddhist Practice in the West." In Prebish and Baumann, *Westward Dharma*, 34–50

Wang Shunmin. 1999. *Zongjiao Fuli* [Religious Welfare]. Taipei: Yatai Tushu

Watada, Terry. 1996. *Bukkyo Tozen: A History of Jodo Shin-shu Buddhism in Canada, 1905–1995*. Toronto: HpF Press and the Toronto Buddhist Church

Wat Lao Booklet. 2006. *History of the Construction of Dhamma Hall of Watlao-Veluwanaram of Ontario, Canada*. n.p.: n.pub.

Welch, Holmes. 1967. *The Practice of Chinese Buddhism 1900–1950*. Cambridge: Harvard University Press

– 1968. *The Buddhist Revival in China*. Cambridge: Harvard University Press

Wetzel, Sylvia. 2002. "Neither Monk nor Nun: Western Buddhists as Full-Time Practitioners." In Prebish and Baumann, *Westward Dharma*, 275–84

White, Marybeth. 2006. "Lao Buddhism in Toronto: A Case Study of Community Relations." In Matthews, *Buddhism in Canada*, 105–19

Williams, Duncan Ryūken and Christopher S. Queen, eds. 1999. *American Buddhism: Methods and Findings in Recent Scholarship*. Surrey: Curzon

Williams, Paul. 1989. *Mahāyāna Buddhism: The Doctrinal Foundations*. London: Routledge

Wind Bell. 1969. (Publication of the Zen Center of San Francisco) 8, nos 1–2

Womack, James P., Daniel T. Jones, and Daniel Roos. 1990. *The Machine that Changed the World: The Story of Lean Production*. New York: Rawson/Macmillan

Womack, James P. and Daniel T. Jones. 1996. *Lean Thinking: Banish Waste and Create Wealth in Your Corporation*. New York: Simon and Schuster

Woodside, Alexander B. 1976. *Community and Revolution in Modern Vietnam*. Boston: Houghton Mifflin Company

World Tibet Network News. 2006. "Honorary Citizenship for Dalai Lama." http://www.tibet.ca/en/newsroom/wtn/archive/old?y=2006&m=6&p=23_1

Wright, Arthur F. 1990. *Studies in Chinese Buddhism*, edited by Robert M. Somers. New Haven: Yale University Press

Wuthnow, Robert and Wendy Cadge. 2004. "Buddhists and Buddhism in the United States: The Scope of Influence." *Journal for the Scientific Study of Religion* 43, no. 3: 363–80

Yamagishi, Rochelle. 2005. *Nikkei Journey: Japanese Canadians in Southern Alberta*. Victoria: Trafford Publishing

Yu Ningpo. 1996. *Meijia Huaren Shehui Fojiao Fazhan Shi*. Taipei: Xinwenfeng Chuban She

Zaslowsky, Dyan. 1989. "Buddhists in U.S. Agonize on AIDS Issue." *New York Times*, 21 February

Zen Bow. (Winter and Spring) 1975

Zen Centre of Vancouver. http://www.zen.ca/

Zhongguo fazhan jianbao (ZFJ) [China Development Brief]. 2007. *Guoji NGO* [International NGOs]. http://www.chinadevelopmentbrief.org.cn/

Zürcher, Erik. 1959. *The Buddhist Conquest of China: The Spread and Adaptation of Buddhism in Early Medieval China*. 2 vols. Leiden: Brill

Contributors

PETER BEYER is professor of Religious Studies (sociology of religion) at the University of Ottawa. His major area of expertise is religion and globalization, and in this context, he has maintained a strong research focus on the current state of religion in Canada, especially the religious diversity that has resulted from post-1970 immigration. Major publications include *Religion and Globalization* (Sage, 1994), *Religion in the Process of Globalization* (ed., Ergon, 2001), *Religions in Global Society* (Routledge, 2006), *Religion, Globalization, and Culture* (ed. with Lori Beaman, Brill, 2007), and *Religion and Diversity in Canada* (ed. with Lori Beaman, Brill, 2008). At present, he is completing two research projects on the religious expression of second generation immigrants of all religious backgrounds, including Buddhist, in Canada.

PATRICIA Q. CAMPBELL recently completed her PHD at Wilfrid Laurier University in its joint program, with the University of Waterloo, in Religious Diversity in North America. Her research interests are Buddhism in Canada and ritual studies. Her dissertation, "Knowing Body, Moving Mind: Ritualizing and Learning at Two Buddhist Centres in Toronto," explores learning through meditation and other ritual practices taught to newcomers at Friends of the Heart and Chandrakirti Buddhist centres.

LYNN P. ELDERSHAW is assistant professor in the Department of Psychology, Social Work, and Criminal Justice at the University of Maine at Presque Isle. Her primary research areas are new religious movements, health, illness and society, and qualitative methodology. This chapter stems from her dissertation "Collective Identity and the Postcharismatic Fate of Shambhala International" (University of Waterloo, 2004). Lynn has presented results from this work at several conferences and recently published an article with the same title in *Nova Religio* (2007). Her current research explores the integration of Buddhist principles and practices in the Western hospice movement.

JOHN S. HARDING received his PHD in 2003 from the University of Pennsylvania and is currently associate professor in the Religious Studies Department at the University of Lethbridge, Canada. Research interests include Japanese Buddhism and the cross-cultural exchange between Asia and the West that has shaped the development of modern Buddhism. He is the author of *Mahayana Phoenix: Japan's Buddhists at the 1893 World's Parliament of Religions* (2008), the co-author with Hillary Rodrigues of *Introduction to the Study of Religion* (2008) and *The Study of Religion: A Reader* (forthcoming 2010), and the editor of the volume *Studying Buddhism in Practice* in a forthcoming Routledge series, *Studying Religions in Practice*.

SARAH F. HAYNES is assistant professor in the Department of Philosophy and Religion, Western Illinois University. Her main research interests are Tibetan Buddhist ritual and ritual adaptation in Buddhism in North America. Her doctoral dissertation is entitled "In Praise of Sarasvati: An Examination of Tibetan Buddhist Ritual Practice" (University of Calgary, 2006) and she has published "An Exploration of Jack Kerouac's Buddhism: Text and Life," *Journal of Contemporary Buddhism* (2005).

VICTOR SŌGEN HORI received his PHD in Western philosophy in 1976 from Stanford University. The same year, he was ordained and thereafter spent thirteen years as a monk in the Rinzai Zen monastery system. He returned to North America in 1990 and joined the Faculty of Religious Studies of McGill University in 1993. He is presently associate professor in Japanese Religions. Research interests include Zen Buddhism, Buddhism in the West, Kyoto School of Philosophy, Japanese religion, comparative ethics. Publications include *Neglected Themes and Hidden Variations (Frontiers of Japanese Philosophy 2)*, co-edited with Melissa Curley (Nanzan, 2008); *Zen Sand: The Book of Capping Phrases for Zen Kōan Practice* (University of Hawai'i Press, 2003); *The Wheel and the Web: Collected Papers of the Teaching Buddhism Conference*, co-edited with Richard P. Hayes and Mark Shields (Curzon Press, 2002); *The Ten Oxherding Pictures: Lectures by Yamada Mumon Roshi* (University of Hawai'i Press, 2004).

ANDRÉ LALIBERTÉ is associate professor at the School of Political Studies, University of Ottawa. His research currently focuses on how governments manufacture religious identities to support their welfare regimes and articulate their cultural nationalist discourses. His publications include book chapters and journal articles on Buddhist philanthropy and on state policy toward religion in China and Taiwan, *The Chinese Party-State at the Turn of the Millennium: Legitimacy and Adaptation* (ed., RoutledgeCurzon, 2007) and *The Politics of Buddhist Organizations in Taiwan, 1989–2003* (Routledge, 2004).

MANUEL LITALIEN received his PHD in political science at Université du Québec à Montréal in 2009 and began a post-doctoral fellowship at McGill University. His research focuses on welfare regimes and religion in Southeast Asia and transnational theologico-political movements. His interests include the democratization process, social policy issues, identity politics, ethnicity and governance, as well as religion and the state in Southeast Asia. His dissertation is entitled "Social Development and Welfare Regime in Thailand: New Democratic Capital in an Increasingly Philanthropic Society." He has co-written an article, "Blurred Boundaries, Buddhist Communities in the Greater Montréal Region," in Matthews, ed., *Buddhism in Canada* (Routledge, 2006). His MA thesis explores the status and rights of women in Thai Buddhism.

TANNIE LIU teaches anthropology in the Social Science Department at Heritage College, Gatineau, Quebec. She has also taught as a lecturer in East Asian Religions at Concordia University, Montreal, Quebec. She received her doctoral degree in religious studies from the University of Ottawa (2005). Her current research interests include globalization and modern transformation of Asian religions, anthropology of religion, ritual and consciousness studies, new religious movements and research methodology.

JANET MCLELLAN is a professor in the Religion and Culture department at Wilfrid Laurier University. Her major research focus has been on Asian Buddhist immigrants and refugees as they migrate to and resettle in Ontario, reflected in the book *Many Petals of the Lotus: Five Asian Buddhist Communities in Toronto* (University of Toronto Press, 1999). A recent book, *Cambodian Refugees in Ontario: Resettlement, Religion, and Identity* (University of Toronto Press, 2009), provides a detailed analysis of this group's long-term adaptive and integrative challenges, particularly in recreating and redefining religious identities, practices, and institutions. Current research involves religious retreat centres in rural North America.

MAURO PERESSINI received his PHD in anthropology (ethnology) in 1992 from Université de Montréal. Since then, he has been a curator at the Canadian Museum of Civilization (Gatineau, Quebec). His major area of expertise is the construction of identities (ethnic, gender, class, religion) in multicultural societies. His main methodology is the life story approach used as a tool for social history research as well as for the understanding of the symbolic systems of identities and values of the subjects. He is presently conducting research on non-Asian Canadian Buddhist practitioners and teachers. Publications include *The Mediterranean Reconsidered: Representations, Emergences, Recompositions*, co-edited with Rathiba Hadj-Moussa (Canadian Museum of Civilization, 2005);

Migration, famille et communauté. Les Italiens du Frioul à Montréal, 1945–1980 (Université de Montréal, 1990); "L'inestimable lien qui nous unit aux autres. Le religieux dans les récits de vie d'immigrants italiens," in R. Klymasz and J. Willis, eds, *Revelation: Bimillennial Papers from the Canadian Museum of Civilization* (Canadian Museum of Civilization, 2001).

HENRY C.H. SHIU is assistant professor in the Department of Humanities at the University of Toronto, Scarborough. Shiu's research has focused on the doctrinal and historical studies of Mahayana Buddhism in India, China, and Tibet, particularly on the *tathāgatagarbha* theory. He also does research in the history of Buddhism in Canada and various forms of Socially Engaged Buddhism in the contemporary world. Shiu is the co-editor-in-chief of the *Monograph Series in Sino-Tibetan Buddhist Studies*, published jointly by Renmin University of China, China Tibetology Publishing House, and the Sino-Tibetan Buddhist Studies Association in North America. He is the author of "The Polarity in the Two Trends of Practicing Tibetan Buddhism in Hong Kong" in *The Image of Tibet in the 19th and 20th Centuries* (Paris, 2008), "The Non-Substantialism of the *Awakening of Faith*" (*Journal of Chinese Philosophy* 2010), and the co-author of "IOL Tib. 52: Another Version of the Tibetan Translation of the *Avikalpapraveśa-dhāraṇī*," *Journal of Buddhist Studies* (2007)" and "Buddhist Animal Release Practices: Historic, Environmental, Public Health and Economic Concerns," *Journal of Contemporary Buddhism* (2008).

ALEXANDER SOUCY received his PHD from the Australian National University in 2000 and is currently associate professor of Religious Studies at Saint Mary's University, Halifax. He has done research on Buddhism in Vietnam as well as Vietnamese Buddhism in Canada. He wrote "The Dynamics of Change in an Exiled Pagoda: Vietnamese Buddhism in Montréal" in *Canberra Anthropology* (1996) based on his research in Canada. Other publications include "Pilgrims and Pleasure Seekers" in *Consuming Urban Culture in Contemporary Vietnam* (Routledge 2003); "Consuming *Loc*, Creating *On*: Women, Offerings and Symbolic Capital in Vietnam" in *Studies in Religion / Sciences Religieuses* (2006); "Nationalism, Globalism and the Re-establishment of the Trúc Lâm Thiền Buddhist sect in Northern Vietnam," in *Modernity and Re-enchantment: Religion in Post-revolutionary Vietnam,* (Institute of Southeast Asian Studies, 2007): and "Language, Orthodoxy, and Performances of Authority in Vietnamese Buddhism" in *The Journal of the American Academy of Religion* (2009). Current research focuses on global Vietnamese Buddhist connections and the changes that these are bringing about.

LINA VERCHERY, who completed an undergraduate degree in religious studies at McGill University, is a graduate student in Buddhist studies and Frank Knox Fellow at Harvard University. As a Woodenfish participant in 2005 and a staff member in 2006, she has lived and worked in Fo Guang Shan monasteries throughout Taiwan and Japan. In addition to her academic focus on Chinese Buddhism, Verchery has a strong interest in Buddhism in the West. She recently wrote and directed a documentary film for the National Film Board of Canada on Gampo Abbey entitled *La Trappe*, which won Best French Documentary Short at the 2008 FICFA film festival. Verchery is also a fellow at the Harvard Film Studies Center where she is currently doing research for a new film that explores the development of Buddhist rituals for North American families adopting Chinese babies in southern China, as well as starting production on a documentary short that explores understandings of God and religion through the eyes of the homeless population of Cambridge, Massachusetts.

TERRY WATADA is a Toronto writer with many publications and theatre productions to his credit. His latest publications include a collection of poetry, *Obon: The Festival of the Dead* (Thistledown Press, 2006), and a novel, *Kuroshio: The Blood of Foxes* (Arsenal Pulp Press, 2007). His exploration of Buddhism includes his book *Bukkyo Tozen: A History of Jodo Shinshu Buddhism in Canada, 1905–1995* (HpF Press and the Toronto Buddhist Church, 1996).

MARYBETH WHITE is a doctoral candidate in the Religion and Culture Department of Wilfrid Laurier University. She completed her Master of Arts at Wilfrid Laurier. Her MA thesis explores Thich Nhat Hanh's and Rita Gross's views on family, community, and Buddhist practice and the validity of parenting as a path toward the Buddhist goal of enlightenment. Publications include a book review, "Buddha Mom: The Path of Mindful Mothering," *Journal of the Association for Research on Mothering* (2005); "Lao Buddhism in Toronto: A Case Study of Community Relations," *Buddhism in Canada*, ed. Bruce Matthews, (Routledge, 2006); and a co-authored article with Dr Janet McLellan, "Social Capital and Identity Politics among Asian Buddhists in Toronto," *Journal of International Migration and Integration* (2005). Her dissertation, "Awakening the Buddha: Laying the Foundations for the Re-creation of Lao Buddhism in Canada," focuses on the settlement and sacralization of space by a Lao community in Caledon, Ontario.

Index